JOURNAL FOR THE STUDY OF THE OLD TESTAMENT SUPPLEMENT SERIES
41

Editors
David J A Clines
Philip R Davies

JSOT Press
Sheffield

ZION
THE CITY OF THE
GREAT KING

A Theological Symbol of
the Jerusalem Cult

Ben C. Ollenburger

Journal for the Study of the Old Testament
Supplement Series 41

For
Edwin Charles Ollenburger
Esther Elizabeth Wiens Ollenburger
—*Wenn auch die Lippen schweigen*

Published by JSOT Press
JSOT Press is an imprint of
Sheffield Academic Press
The University of Sheffield
343 Fulwood Road
Sheffield S10 3BP
England

Typeset by Sheffield Academic Press
and
printed in Great Britain
by Billing & Sons Ltd
Worcester

British Library Cataloguing in Publication Data

Ollenburger, Ben C.
  Zion, city of the great king : a theological symbol of the Jerusalem cult.—
  (Journal for the study of the Old Testament
  supplement series, ISSN 0309-0787; 41).
  1. Symbolism in the Bible   2. Bible. O.T.—
  Criticism, interpretation, etc.
  I. Title   II. Series
  221.6'4   BS1191

ISBN 1-85075-015-7
ISBN 1-85075-014-9 Pbk

CONTENTS

PREFACE

This book began as a dissertation at Princeton Theological Seminary directed by Professor Bernhard W. Anderson. To him I am indebted for many things, including the suggestion to treat Zion as a symbol in a manner that is explained in the first chapter. My investigation of Zion was intended originally to serve as the introductory chapter to a more extensive treatment of the use of Zion symbolism in the later chapters of Isaiah. As sometimes happens, particularly with graduate students, the preliminary investigation became the center of attention. In this case I reached the conclusion that there were significant features of the Old Testament's Zion symbolism which had not received sufficient scholarly attention. This book is intended to fill a part of that gap. If that intention is fulfilled it will be due in large measure to what I have learned from my teachers and then colleagues, Professors Anderson, J.J.M. Roberts, and Katharine Doob Sakenfeld. Professor Sakenfeld made suggestions that strengthened the argument in several places. J. Christiaan Beker has helped me to learn what kinds of argument matter.

The body of this monograph is concerned with specific Old Testament texts and their interpretation. In the final chapter, however, I have attempted both to summarize systematically the textual study and to expand on these conclusions in a somewhat theological or perhaps even homiletical manner. While some may regard this expansion as out of place in a historical-critical treatment of biblical texts, I do not. I am concerned only that the claims made there follow legitimately from the exegesis which precedes.

I have tried throughout the book to use inclusive language, but have failed to do so in reference to deity. It proved to be beyond my literary ability to avoid masculine pronouns when treating texts that describe God primarily as king. In two instances of translation from Hebrew I used the term 'man'. This was done intentionally, although I thought it unnecessary there to spell out my intentions. All translations are my own, unless otherwise noted.

This study would not have been published apart from the encouragement of Patrick D. Miller, Jr, Leong Seow, and Tryggve Mettinger. While I want here to acknowledge my gratitude, none of those named in this preface should be held responsible for what I have written or blamed for my mistakes. I particularly regret that I was not able to make use of Professor Mettinger's work, *The Dethronement of Sabaoth* (CWK Gleerup, 1982), or Moshe Weinfeld's essay, 'Zion and Jerusalem as Religious and Political Capital: Ideology and Utopia' (in Richard Elliott Friedman, ed., *The Poet and the Historian* [Scholars Press, 1983]).

The context from which a book emerges has other than just academic dimensions, of course, and these too should be acknowledged. I am grateful to Wally and Millie Kroeker for their friendship and for the warm and creative atmosphere of their basement. The Princeton House Church provided over the course of several years a community in which biblical studies could make practical sense, and ancient texts could address real problems and be illuminated by them. Above all, Janice, Mary, and Katie have been a family. Nothing could be more important and no one more cherished.

Finally, this book is dedicated to my parents, Edwin and Esther Ollenburger. To say why, adequately, would require another book.

Princeton, New Jersey
July 18, 1986

ABBREVIATIONS

AB	Anchor Bible
AJBI	*Annual of the Japanese Biblical Institute*
AnBib	Analecta Biblica
ANET	J.B. Pritchard, ed., *Ancient Near Eastern Texts*
AOAT	Alter Orient und Altes Testament
AOS	American Oriental Series
ASTI	*Annual of the Swedish Theological Institute*
ATANT	Abhandlungen zur Theologie des Alten und Neuen Testaments
ATD	Das Alte Testament Deutsch
BA	*Biblical Archeologist*
BASOR	*Bulletin of the American Schools of Oriental Research*
BBB	Bonner biblische Beiträge
BBET	Beiträge zur biblischen Exegese und Theologie
BDB	F. Brown, S.R. Driver and C.A. Briggs, *Hebrew and English Lexicon of the Old Testament*
BEvt	Beiträge zur evangelischen Theologie
*BH*³	R. Kittel, ed., *Biblia Hebraica*, 3rd edn
BHS	*Biblia hebraica stuttgartensia*
BHS#	C. Brockelmann, *Hebräische Syntax*
BHT	Beiträge zur historischen Theologie
Bib0r	Biblica et Orientalia
BibS(N)	Biblische Studien (Neukirchen, 1951—
BK	*Bibel und Kirche*
BKAT	Biblischer Kommentar: Altes Testament
BO	*Bibliotheca Orientalis*
BR	*Biblical Research*
BRGA	Beiträge zur Religionsgeschichte des Altertums
BWANT	Beiträge zur Wissenschaft vom Alten und Neuen Testament
BZ	*Biblische Zeitschrift*
BZAW	Beihefte zur *ZAW*
CBQ	*Catholic Biblical Quarterly*
ConBOT	Coniectanea Biblica, Old Testament

CRAIBL	*Comptes rendus de l'Académie des inscriptions et belles-lettres*
CBA	A. Herdner, *Corpus des tablettes en cunéiformes alphabétiques*
CTM	*Concordia Theological Monthly*
ETL	*Ephemerides theologicae lovanienses*
EvT	*Evangelische Theologie*
ExpTim	*Expository Times*
FRLANT	Forschungen zur Religion und Literatur des Alten und Neuen Testaments
GK	*Gesenius' Hebrew Grammar*, ed. E. Kautzsch, tr. A.E. Cowley
HAT	Handbuch zum Alten Testament
HBT	*Horizons in Biblical Theology*
HDR	Harvard Dissertations in Religion
HeyJ	*Heythrop Journal*
HKAT	Handkommentar zum Alten Testament
HR	*History of Religions*
HSM	Harvard Semitic Monographs
HTR	*Harvard Theological Review*
HUCA	*Hebrew Union College Annual*
IDB	G.A. Buttrick, ed., *Interpreter's Dictionary of the Bible*
IDBS	Supplementary volume to *IDB*
IEJ	*Israel Exploration Journal*
JAAR	*Journal of the American Academy of Religion*
JAOS	*Journal of the American Oriental Society*
JBL	*Journal of Biblical Literature*
JCS	*Journal of Cuneiform Studies*
JETS	*Journal of the Evangelical Theological Society*
JNES	*Journal of Near Eastern Studies*
JNWSL	*Journal of Northwest Semitic Languages*
JQR	*Jewish Quarterly Review*
JSOT	*Journal for the Study of the Old Testament*
JSS	*Journal of Semitic Studies*
JTS	*Journal of Theological Studies*
KAI	H. Donner and W. Röllig, *Kanaanäische und Aramäische Inschriften*
KAT	Kommentar zum Alten Testament
KuD	*Kerygma und Dogma*

MT	Massoretic Text
NCB	New Century Bible
NICOT	New International Commentary on the Old Testament
Numen	*Numen: International Review for the History of Religions*
OECT	Oxford Editions of Cuneiform Texts
OTL	Old Testament Library
OTS	*Oudtestamentische Studien*
PEQ	*Palestine Exploration Quarterly*
PTMS	Pittsburgh Theological Monograph Series
RANE	Records of the Ancient Near East
RHPR	*Revue d'Histoire et de Philosophie Religieuses*
RSV	*Revised Standard Version*
SAHG	A. Falkenstein and W. von Soden, *Sumerische und akkadische Hymnen und Gebete*
SANT	Studien zum Alten und Neuen Testament
SBB	Stuttgarter biblische Beiträge
SBLDS	Society of Biblical Literature Dissertation Series
SBLMS	Society of Biblical Literature Monograph Series
SBM	Stuttgarter biblische Monographien
SBS	Stuttgarter Bibelstudien
SBT	Studies in Biblical Theology
SBTh	*Studia Biblica et Theologica*
SEÅ	*Svensk exegetisk årsbok*
SOR	Studies in Oriental Religions
SOTSMS	Society for Old Testament Study Monograph Series
ST	*Studia theologica*
STL	Studia Theologica Ludensia
STZ	*Schweizerische theologische Zeitschrift*
TBü	Theologische Bücherei
TDOT	G.J. Botterweick and H. Ringgren, eds., *Theological Dictionary of the Old Testament*
THAT	E. Jenni and C. Westermann, eds., *Theologisches Handwörterbuch zum Alten Testament*
ThEv	*Theologia Evangelica*
TLZ	*Theologische Literaturzeitung*
TQ	*Theologische Quartalschrift*
TS	Theologische Studien

TTS	Trierer theologische Studien
TUMSR	Trinity University Monograph Series in Religion
TZ	*Theologische Zeitschrift*
UF	*Ugarit-Forschungen*
UT	C.H. Gordon, *Ugaritic Textbook*
VT	*Vetus Testamentum*
VTS	Vetus Testamentum, Supplements
WMANT	Wissenschaftliche Monographien zum Alten und Neuen Testament
WHS	R.J. Williams, *Hebrew Syntax*
WO	*Die Welt des Orients*
ZAW	*Zeitschrift für die alttestamentliche Wissenschaft*
ZDPV	*Zeitschrift des deutschen Palästina-Vereins*
ZNW	*Zeitschrift für die neutestamentliche Wissenschaft*
ZRGG	*Zeitschrift für Religions- und Geistesgeschichte*
ZTK	*Zeitschrift für Theologie und Kirche*

Chapter 1

INTRODUCTION

Scholarly study of the Old Testament has been enriched in recent generations by the development of the traditio-historical method. This method and the constellation of procedures and approaches embodied within it[1] have served to highlight the historical character of the Old Testament texts as well as the dynamic processes that have gone into the transmission and shaping of those texts.[2] The method has been applied successfully and with epoch-making results to individual units, as in Hermann Gunkel's commentary on Genesis,[3] and to larger collections of material, as in the work of Gerhard von Rad and then Martin Noth on the formation of the Pentateuch.[4] More recently it has formed the basis of von Rad's *Old Testament Theology* and has influenced all methodological considerations of Old Testament Theology since von Rad.[5]

Among the important, specific contributions of traditio-historical study of the Old Testament has been its usefulness in the identification of various discrete themes having not only an identifiable literary and formal character, but also a discernible origin, development and history of transmission—that is, specific themes having the character of a tradition.[6] Among the most comprehensive and theologically significant of these traditions in the Old Testament is the Exodus tradition, to which an extensive amount of Old Testament scholarship has been devoted.[7] The identification of this tradition and the history of its transmission has contributed to a more adequate understanding of the theology not only of early Israel, as reflected in various strata of the Pentateuch, but also of later literature, including the prophets.[8]

Among the further gains of recent historical research into Old Testament traditions has been an appreciation of the diversity of those traditions. One way in which this diversity has become clear is through the identification of a Zion tradition which not only represents a tradition historically distinct from that of the Exodus, but also possesses a very different theological character. Our intention in this investigation is to examine the central elements of the Zion tradition's theological character. However, it is necessary to make certain distinctions at this point in order to clarify the approach of this monograph. In the first place, there is a certain ambiguity in the term 'traditio-historical' itself. Within German scholarship traditio-historical method refers primarily to *Überlieferungs-geschichte*, the study of the oral transmission of a unit prior to its written formulation.[9] That is, traditio-historical research concentrates primarily on those properties of a text that are antecedent to its written form. This raises at least two problems. First of all, some texts, in the prophets for example, betray no evidence of being the culmination of an earlier stage of oral transmission—there are no earlier oral texts, in other words, which are their antecedents. In the second place, the *überlieferungsgeschichtlich* approach is unable to uncover those antecedents of a text which are neither an earlier form of the text itself nor *'topoi* which appear simply because of the chosen genre'.[10] For this reason European scholars have broadened traditio-historical research to include *Traditionsgeschichte*, which investigates not the oral transmission of a text, but the conceptions or notions that lie behind a text, and the 'stream of tradition' in which a text is rooted.[11] In our investigation we are interested primarily in this aspect of traditio-historical research. That is, we are interested in examining the 'entire stock of notional elements' used in a complex of texts that speak of Zion and relating them 'to the larger intellectual spheres to which they belong and from which they derive'.[12]

As will be pointed out in the rest of this initial chapter, our interest is not principally in the Zion *tradition*, but in Zion as a *symbol* used within a specific theological tradition or 'stock of notional elements'. For that reason we will not be concerned primarily with the question of origin that has occupied past scholarship on the Zion tradition. Rather, our central concern is with Zion as a theological symbol. Thus, in the remainder of this chapter we will summarize briefly the results of past research on the Zion tradition, clarify the meaning of 'symbol' as it is employed in this monograph, and indicate our own procedure for investigating Zion symbolism in the Jerusalem cult.

A. THE ZION TRADITION

It is appropriate that discussion of the Zion tradition within Old Testament scholarship is based on the preliminary work of two giants in the field from the past generation, Martin Noth and Gerhard von Rad. In 1949, von Rad wrote a short article devoted to the exaltation of the city of Jerusalem in three prophetic texts, Isaiah 2, 60, and Haggai 2.[13] In the following year Martin Noth examined the significant relationship between Jerusalem and the earlier Israelite traditions, noting especially the growing importance of Jerusalem in the theology of the Old Testament.[14] But it is especially to the student of Gerhard von Rad, Edzard Rohland, that we owe the specific identification of a 'Zion tradition' among the traditions of the Old Testament.[15]

Rohland identified a cluster of motifs that are typically attached to Zion in the Psalms, and it is these motifs that are usually equated with the Zion tradition itself. As enumerated originally by Rohland these motifs are:

1. Zion is the peak of Zaphon, the highest mountain (Ps 48.3-4);
2. The river of paradise flows from it (Ps 46.5);
3. There Yahweh triumphed over the flood of chaos waters (Ps 46.3);
4. And there Yahweh triumphed over the kings and their nations (Pss 46.7; 48.5-7; 76.4, 6-7).[16]

Rohland regards the last of these motifs as central to the tradition and goes on to describe Yahweh's triumph over the nations who storm Zion's gates as

a. occurring through terror caused by Yahweh, either through theophany (Ps 48.6) or by the reproach of God (Pss 46.7; 76.7);
b. and occurring before morning (Ps 46.6).
c. In his triumph Yahweh destroys the weapons of war and makes a definitive end to war itself (Ps 76.4).[17]

Hans Wildberger, while generally following Rohland in the enumeration of motifs associated with Zion, has proposed that 'the pilgrimage of the nations' should be a fifth motif of this tradition.[18] A similar position was adopted by H. Junker.[19] It would seem much more likely, however, that the 'Völkerwallfahrt' motif was a later combination of the pre-exilic motifs of pilgrimage to a shrine and the 'pilgrimage' of kings and/or nations to the king in Jerusalem (Ps 72. 8-11). The post-exilic combination of these motifs is seen in Ps 102,[20] and is clearly evident in Isa 60-62, also post-exilic texts. Both Wildberger and Junker base their proposals on Isa 2.2-4, whose date is widely disputed. Even if this text is pre-exilic it seems insufficient to establish the presence of a pilgrimage of the nations as a constituent motif of the Zion tradition.[21]

If we limit ourselves to the motifs identified by Rohland and most other scholars, the Zion tradition consists of four principal motifs that express Yahweh's choice of Zion as his city, and the consequent security of the city against the threat of natural and super-natural forces.

The contours of this Zion tradition drawn by Rohland are taken, as the above references make clear, from those Psalms that have come to be designated as Songs of Zion. Hermann Gunkel first isolated a group of Psalms (46, 48, 76, 84, 87 and 122)[22] which he considered to be modifications of the 'hymn' form and which he called 'Songs of Zion', a designation he derived from Ps 137.3.[23] While these Psalms do differ somewhat in form from the broader hymnic genre,[24] Gunkel classed these five Psalms together primarily on the basis of their distinct subject matter and their presumed *Sitz im Leben* in the cultic celebration of Jerusalem's glory.[25] He further specified Pss 46, 48 and 76 as instances of Zion songs that had come under the influence of the prophets and presupposed the sort of prophetic hope attached to Zion in Isa 26.1; 27.2-5; Jer 31.23 and also Isa 61.10-11.[26] Perhaps the most controversial of Gunkel's claims was that the Songs of Zion were indebted to the prophets and especially to prophetic eschatology.

While later research has shown Gunkel's eschatological interpretation of the Zion Songs to be unlikely,[27] his isolation of 46, 48 and 76 as a separate category has continued to influence Psalms scholarship. However, it is important to note that these Psalms may not represent a distinct formal category or *Gattung*,[28] and clearly they do not represent a 'general doctrine of Zion's inviolability',[29] nor a systematic statement of the meaning of Zion or the tradition of its special status. Rather, they are individual, hymnic expressions of a coherent 'theological conception' which underlies most of the Psalms and is articulated above all in these Songs of Zion as well as in the creation Psalms, the Psalms of Yahweh's kingship and the royal Psalms.[30] This theological conception, along with the mythical themes and motifs and the cultic forms of speech by which it was expressed, were developed, nurtured and transmitted in Jerusalem as a tradition unique to the cult of that city.

It is this tradition that forms the horizon for our understanding of Zion as a symbol occurring in a wide variety of texts. This symbol is perhaps most prominent in the three Psalms designated Songs of Zion, but these are not the only texts in which Zion functions as a symbol, and these Psalms are not, as has already been pointed out, systematic expositions of a theological doctrine but hymns originally intended for use in cultic ritual. Nor can investigation of the meaning of Zion as a symbol be restricted to, or simply identified with, a cluster of motifs identified as constitutive of the Zion tradition. Rather, we must consider how this symbol 'Zion' focuses, within a broader theological tradition, those theological concerns that are evident in the Songs of Zion and elsewhere.

For that reason our principal concern will not be with questions regarding the date and origin of the Zion tradition. Thus it is sufficient here to summarize briefly the scholarly debate on these issues.

There is no scholarly consensus regarding the date and origin of the Zion tradition, but we are now able to say with some certainty that the efforts of Fohrer and Wanke, for example, to date the origin of this tradition to a period later than Isaiah of Jerusalem have failed. J.J.M. Roberts in particular has shown that the Zion tradition is most plausibly located in the early period of the monarchy in Jerusalem, and that the motifs associated with this tradition, in particular the defeat of the nations by Yahweh, were in existence before the eighth century.[31] Even recent authors such as Friedrich Huber and Ronald Clements, who wish to deny that there was a Zion tradition that could function in a central way for Isaiah, are forced to concede that the core elements of this tradition pre-dated Isaiah and were available to him.[32]

There are currently three general positions with respect to the question of the origin of the Zion tradition. First, there are those who believe that it is primarily a continuation of traditions already at hand in the Jebusite city which David conquered. This was the position of Rohland and is also adopted by H. Schmid, John Hayes, Josef Schreiner, Gerhard von Rad, Fritz Stolz, Hans-Martin Lutz, W.H. Schmidt and others.[33] Secondly, there are those who believe that the Zion tradition was a creation of the Davidic court, not a continuation of the Jebusite tradition. J.J.M. Roberts has championed this view.[34] Clements too, while disagreeing with Roberts on a number of other points, tends to see that material in the Psalms and Isaiah which is often associated with the Zion tradition as part of the Davidic royal ideology.[35] Finally, a third group of scholars believes that the Zion tradition is fundamentally the result of the transfer of older Israelite theology, already richly infused with Canaanite imagery, to a new geographical and political context in Jerusalem. This position, which sees the ark and the traditions associated with it at Shiloh as of fundamental importance to the creation of the Zion tradition, is represented most comprehensively by David Eiler.[36] He draws heavily, however, on the earlier work of Otto Eissfeldt and Martin Noth.[37] Eckart Otto also argues for the importance of the Shiloh sanctuary and the ark tradition in the formation of the Zion tradition, however he assigns a more creative role to the pre-Israelite Jerusalem traditions than does Eiler.[38]

In the past, much of the attention given to Pss 46, 48 and 76, as well as to the Zion tradition itself, has been provoked by a historical interest in the possible connection of the 'Völkerkampf' motif in these Psalms to the Old Testament's understanding of the events of 701, involving Sennacherib and Hezekiah. Generally speaking there have been two contrasting ways in which this connection has been reconstructed. Either the events of 701, and the miraculous deliverance of Jerusalem in particular (2 Kgs 19.32-37 = Isa 36.33-38), were the inspiration behind the Zion Songs and the tradition of Zion's inviolability, or the cultic celebration of Zion's inviolability was the inspiration behind the interpretation of the events of 701, particularly by Isaiah. These positions are roughly those of A.F. Kirkpatrick in his *Psalms* commentary of 1902, and Sigmund Mowinckel in his *Psalmenstudien* II of 1921, respectively.[39]

It is not our purpose, nor is it within our capacity, to settle this complicated issue. For our purposes we need only acknowledge that whatever the date of the Songs of Zion the notions expressed in them are ancient, dating probably to the United Monarchy. The significant point for us is that it is inappropriate in a consideration of the meaning of Zion as a symbol to restrict ourselves to one motif associated with it (e.g. 'Völkerkampf') and one theological theme derived from it (e.g. inviolability). Like any other central symbol Zion was capable of being placed in designs of more than one configuration, and was capable of evoking more than one response.

Our purpose in what follows is to examine the configuration of the Jerusalem cult tradition in which Zion functioned as a central symbol.[40]

B. ZION AS A CENTRAL SYMBOL

Before we begin our investigation of Zion in the Jerusalem cult tradition it is necessary to say a few words about the focus of this monograph on Zion as a *symbol*. It is not my intention here to give a review of recent scholarship on the nature of a symbol,[41] nor do I wish to create the impression that this study is in some methodical way concerned with the application of methods from the human sciences to the study of Old Testament traditions. Rather, I want merely to clarify the understanding of 'symbol' which underlies the following study of Zion as a symbol.

1. First of all, it is important to recognize that when we speak of symbols we are actually referring to a symbolic relationship.[42] This symbolic relationship consists of what are sometimes called vehicle and tenor, that is, the object and what it symbolizes. The relationship between the symbol and its meaning(s), vehicle and tenor, is not possible to determine merely on the basis of the symbolic object itself. That is because symbolic relationships are conventional; they are cultural conventions which, while not merely arbitrary, are not merely 'natural' either.[43] For that reason symbols have meaning within the cultural context, or symbolic processes, of which they are a part.[44]

2. Second, symbols are multivalent, or multivocal.[45] This means that a symbol may never be reduced to simply one meaning. According to Victor Turner a symbol actually comprises (a) an 'iconic' vehicle—iconic in the sense that 'at least one of its sensorily perceptible chracteristics can be readily associated with at least one of its denotations'; (b) 'a set of denotations, or primary meanings— not usually a single denotation'; and (c) 'a set of designations or connotations implied in addition to the primary meaning(s) of the symbol'.[46] We will try to demonstrate in this monograph that Zion as an iconic vehicle has among its denotations the kingship of Yahweh, and among its connotations Yahweh's exclusive prerogative to be the defender of and to provide security for his people.

3. Third, and related to the first point, symbols have meaning within a set of symbolic relations, or within a symbol system. This

means that symbols have to be interpreted within the 'symbolic design' in which they are located.[47] Within such a symbolic design symbols function as part of a 'network of relationships', and this network is structured around a 'central symbol'.[48] Because of this the central symbol, with its denotations and connotations, bears in itself the meanings available within the design of which it is a part. It makes this meaning available through a process of what Dan Sperber refers to as 'focalization' and 'evocation'.[49] Focalization displaces attention from what is immediately available through conceptualization to what is in some sense hidden in memory. Evocation is a search in memory, an 'evocational field', which seeks to provide orientation in light of present experience. In our investigation we will try to show how Zion 'focalizes' an 'evocational field' in order to orient the life of Israel and Judah in light of their experience. The field that is evoked by the symbol Zion is simply the Jerusalem cult tradition, which is the 'memory' particularly of Judah upon which it draws for orientation in the several periods of its history. For this reason interpretation of the Zion symbol cannot be restricted only to those texts that display the principal motifs of what has been identified as the 'Zion tradition', nor can it be restricted only to those texts which explicitly mention Zion or Jerusalem. It must rather be expanded to a range of texts which form the network of relationships within which Zion functions as the central symbol.

4. This also means that we will need to devote some attention to the tradition out of which Zion symbolism developed, and to the ritual setting in which this symbolism played a primary role. For that reason we will spend some time trying to establish the relationship of Zion symbolism to the celebration of Yahweh as king in Jerusalem. As Turner has shown, ritual is the necessary context within which a symbol's 'polarization of reference' is held together in a functional relation. By polarization of reference he means the relation between the physiological pole—in our case, Zion as a mountain—and the 'cognitive-normative' focus of a symbol. Our investigation will concentrate on this latter focus by emphasizing the theology evoked by Zion symbolism. While we cannot be either elaborate or specific in our description of the ritual context, in part because we do not have sufficient data to reconstruct it, we will attempt to delineate its essential contours.

5. Finally, as we just noted, one of the poles of symbolic reference is 'cognitive-normative'. Symbols not only evoke memory within a

traditional context, they impose obligations on those for whom they function as central symbols. This is especially true of religious symbols. They have the power to impose such obligations because they convey most concretely and with the most force the true nature of reality, the way the world really is. No one has said this better than Clifford Geertz:

> Religion is never merely metaphysics. For all peoples the forms, vehicles, and objects of worship are suffused with an aura of deep moral seriousness. The holy bears within it everywhere a sense of intrinsic obligation: it not only encourages devotion, it demands it; it not only induces intellectual assent, it enforces emotional commitment . . . Never merely metaphysics, religion is never merely ethics either. The source of its moral vitality is conceived to lie in the fidelity with which it expresses the fundamental nature of reality. The powerfully coercive 'ought' is felt to grow out of a comprehensive factual 'is', and in such a way religion grounds the most specific requirements of human action in the most general contexts of human existence.[51]

Our investigation of Zion symbolism will be pursued with this function of religious symbolism in mind. We will save for the concluding chapter a consideration of the obligation that the symbol Zion may be conceived to place on its contemporary heirs.

In the following chapters we will not find it necessary to indicate at each point how the understanding of symbols here outlined bears on the interpretation of the various texts. However, it is important to point out that the decision to treat Zion as a symbol, and the understanding of symbols outlined in the preceding paragraphs, bear significantly on the structure of the study itself. In the following chapters (2 and 3) we will be concerned with two aspects of Zion symbolism. First of all, we will place the symbol Zion within the Jerusalem cult tradition which functions as the evocational field, to use the language of Dan Sperber, or as the symbolic design for which Zion is the central symbol. Since symbols have meaning only within a network of symbolic relations our goal in Chapters 2 and 3 is first of all to set out the contours of this network, which provides what Steck has called the 'stock of notional elements' (see above) that are antecedent to the texts we will consider.

Second, following the analysis of Turner outlined above, we will attempt to show under what conditions Zion was empowered to function as an iconic vehicle. We will argue that the Ark's transfer to

Jerusalem provided such conditions and also supplied the 'set of denotations' or primary meanings for which Zion is an iconic vehicle. This set of denotations, we will further argue, centered on the kingship of Yahweh and the substance of Chapters 2 and 3 will treat this notion in relation to Zion.

Chapter 4, in which the 'exclusive prerogative of Yahweh' is described, is a continuation of our exposition of Zion symbolism. As Turner has pointed out, a symbol comprises not only a symbolic vehicle and a set of primary denotations, but a set of designations or connotations as well. We will argue in Chapter 4 that Yahweh's exclusive prerogative is a connotation of Zion symbolism and constitutes an essential component of the 'cognitive-normative' focus of Zion as a symbol. Past research has dealt very little with this aspect of Zion symbolism, so we will devote considerable space to the argument that the notion of Yahweh's exclusive prerogative must be understood as an important theological trajectory of Zion, the symbol of Yahweh's royal presence in the city of God.

As indicated above, the cognitive focus of a symbol is also normative: since symbols reveal the real world, or the world as it really is, they impose obligations on those for whom they function as symbols. In Chapter 4 the normative focus of Zion for Judah is adumbrated. In the concluding chapter suggestions are made, based on the body of the study, regarding some possible implications of Zion's cognitive-normative focus for those communities in which biblical symbols are still revelatory. The conclusion is thus a continuation of our study of Zion as a symbol.

It is not our intention in this monograph to investigate or even list every theme or notion that is associated with Zion, or is a part of the Zion tradition.[52] Rather, it is our goal to elaborate in as much depth as possible the scope and character of this symbol and its primary denotation, the kingship of Yahweh. We have before us, thus, a task with a fairly narrow focus: to see in what sense Zion is the city of the Great King.

Chapter 2

YAHWEH AS KING ON ZION

Introduction

The central feature of the Jerusalem cult tradition, and that which bestowed upon Zion its sacral character, is the belief that Yahweh dwells among his people in Jerusalem. That Yahweh's presence should be associated with Jerusalem, and with Mt Zion in particular, is certainly not unexpected, given the prominence of 'sacred mountains' in the ancient Near East and in Canaan particularly.[1] Nor is it unexpected that the notion of Yahweh's dwelling on Zion should be explicated with the help of a variety of motifs also common among the religions of Israel's neighbors. But it is essential to keep in view that everything else that can be said about Zion, and everything that took place within the Jerusalem cult, depended upon the prior notion of Yahweh's presence there.[2] As Clements says,

> The entire ideology of the Jerusalem temple centered in the belief that, as his chosen dwelling-place, Yahweh's presence was to be found in it, and that from there he revealed his will and poured out his blessing upon his people.[3]

Among the variety of ways in which Yahweh is represented as present upon Mount Zion the most prominent is as king. Already in the early 'entrance liturgy' of Psalm 24 Yahweh is described as the 'king of glory' (vv. 8-10) who enters his sanctuary on Zion, which is described as 'the mountain of Yahweh, the place of his glory'. Similarly, in Ps 68 Yahweh is depicted as king in connection with a procession of the tribes into the sanctuary (vv. 25-28). The imagery applied to Yahweh throughout this Psalm is royal in nature, particularly the image of kings bearing gifts to honor him in his temple in Jerusalem (vv. 29-30; cf. Ps 72.8-11).

A third processional hymn, Psalm 132, does not explicitly call Yahweh king, but the imagery here is also royal. In this Psalm, whose theme is David's bringing of the Ark to Jerusalem, the dual election of David and Zion is celebrated. In v. 13 Yahweh announces that his covenant with David and his sons is grounded in his choice of Zion as his dwelling place (מושב) and his resting place (מנוחה; v. 14. Cf. also v.8). Furthermore, it is likely that מנוחה here should be taken in the sense of 'place of rule', connected with the footstool in v. 7.[4] The references here are clearly to the Ark conceived as, or in association with, the throne of God. The placement of the Ark in the temple on Zion thus signified the dwelling of God as king in Jerusalem. The term has explicitly royal connections in Isa 11.10 and 1 Chr 22.9, as well as in other Northwest Semitic texts (cf. *KAI* #25, A.1.11-12),[5] and serves here to identify Zion as the site of Yahweh's sovereign rule.

A. PSALMS OF YAHWEH'S ENTHRONEMENT

As one should expect, the so-called Enthronement Psalms, 47, 93-99, present clear examples of the dominant conception of Yahweh as king of Zion in the Jerusalem cult tradition. The characteristic expression of these Psalms is יהוה מלך, which occurs in Pss. 93.1; 96.10; 97.1; 99.1. In all but 96.10 it occurs as the opening words of he Psalm. Virtually the same phrase occurs in 47.9, where אלהים may stand in the place of an original יהוה. It is thus obvious that Yahweh is here conceived as king, but the precise translation and meaning of this expression, יהוה מלך, is uncertain, as is the date and original setting of these Psalms.

Because these Enthronement Psalms emphasize so explicitly the kingship of Yahweh, and because they are so important for understanding the traditions of the Jerusalem cult in which Yahweh was venerated as king, we will pay a disproportionate amount of attention to their place within the cult and to the central traditions on which they draw.

1. *The problem of an enthronement festival*

The issue of the translation of יהוה מלך was raised in an acute way by Mowinckel in *Psalmenstudien II*.[6] Mowinckel argued that יהוה מלך was a cultic shout uttered as part of he festival of Yahweh's enthronement and should be translated 'Yahweh has become king'.[7]

On the basis of the Psalms and certain other biblical and post-biblical literature, and on the basis of Babylonian and anthropological evidence, Mowinckel reconstructed an enthronement festival in Judah which took place during the New Year celebration at the Autumn festival. This festival consisted of a sacred procession of the Ark, a drama celebrating Yahweh's victory over chaos, and the proclamation of Yahweh as king. Mowinckel was followed generally by Gunkel,[8] although the latter wished to emphasize to a greater degree than had Mowinckel the eschatological character of these Psalms.[9] Gunkel cited such passages as 2 Sam 15.10 and 2 Kgs 9.13, which announce the kingship of Absalom and Jehu repectively (מלך אבשלום; מלך יהוא) as evidence for an enthronement festival of the earthly king.[10] Mowinckel, however, correctly challenges Gunkel's assumption that Yahweh's enthronement is patterned in these Psalms after the enthronement of the earthly king, although he does acknowledge the influence of 'the poetical picture of the enthronement of the earthly king' on the Yahweh-enthronement Psalms.[11]

2. *The scholarly discussion*

In the period since Mowinckel there have been four basic responses to the theory which he propounded so comprehensively.

a. First of all, there have been those such as Hans Schmidt, who, in his 1927 publication, *Die Thronfahrt Jahves am Fest der Jahreswende im Alten Israel*,[12] followed Mowinckel in his reconstruction of a celebration of Yahweh's accession to the throne in the New Year festival.

b. Secondly, there have been those, such as Hans-Joachim Kraus, who have rejected the translation of יהוה מלך proposed by Mowinkel, as well as the existence of a festival of Yahweh's enthronement. Kraus and others have argued that syntactical considerations require that 'Yahweh' be understood emphatically and that 'Yahweh is king' is the appropriate translation of the phrase.[13] Kraus, in his *Die Königsherrschaft Gottes im Alten Testament* of 1951,[14] maintained that in the monarchic period there existed a 'royal Zion festival' in which the dual election of Zion and David was celebrated (2 Sam 6, 7; 1 Kgs 8; Ps 132) and the Ark was followed into the temple by a procession to celebrate Yahweh's royal presence there. After the exile this festival was altered drastically and the election of the Davidic house was eclipsed by the celebration of Yahweh's kingship, now to be understood eschatologically. Psalms 93-99 are from the post-exilic celebration of Yahweh's universal kingship, as this is reflected in Isa 52.7-10.[15]

Kraus and others have mounted several objections to the theory of a 'Yahweh-enthronement festival'. As presented in summary fashion by G.N.M. Habets these objections are:[16]

(i) No text explicitly mentions such a festival.

(ii) The existence of such a festival cannot be proved by reference to the Mesopotamian material, since it is relevant only if such a festival is assumed.

(iii) The theories supporting such a festival are based ultimately on the translation of יהוה מלך as 'Yahweh has become king', which is syntactically improbable. The verb is durative, not ingressive.

(iv) The examples cited to show that Yahweh's enthronement can be understood analogously to that of the earthly king (e.g. 2 Sam 15.10 and 2 Kgs 9.13) are not probative. They are not declarations of accession, and the order of subject-verb is reversed.

(v) In Israel Yahweh was understood to reign eternally.

(vi) Finally, to quote Habets, 'who should undertake the enthronement of Yahweh, who has all power within himself? Who should transfer to Yahweh, who alone is all-powerful, the power of royal authority?'[17]

c. A third position is represented by Oswald Loretz.[18] Loretz believes that Mowinckel was correct in translating the cry יהוה מלך as 'Yahweh has become king'.[19] He associates this cry very closely with יגדל יהוה in Ps 35.27 and 40.17 and places them both in the context of Yahweh's enthronement.[20] Loretz claims that those who translate the phrase as 'Yahweh is king' ignore the Ugaritic evidence collected particularly by W.H. Schmidt and J.C. de Moor.[21] De Moor associates the Baal myth with the Autumn New Year celebration which is connected with the enthronement or 'reinstallation' of Baal.[22] The Baal myth, according to de Moor, had its *Sitz im Leben* in the seven-day 'New Year and Wine Festival' which inaugurated the New Year at Ugarit.[23] Hence, the Enthronement Psalms should be seen against this cultic background, Loretz claims, in which the deity, Baal or Yahweh, assumes his throne.

Loretz also refers to the similarity between יהוה מלך and the formulaic *Mardukma sarru*, 'Marduk has become king!'.[24] This cry was presumably uttered in connection with the Akitu rites in which Marduk was congratulated for his victory over Tiamat, a battle which took place annually.[25] However Loretz does not believe that the Enthronement Psalms are part of a festival in which Yahweh's enthronement is annually celebrated. While there may have been such a festival in the monarchic period,[26] the Enthronement Psalms speak of Yahweh's accession as exhibiting Yahweh's rule over the gods (95.2; 96.4; 97.9) and the population of the earth (96.7; 97.9; 98.2-4) who will be subjected to his judgment (96.13; 98.6). Loretz believes that these Psalms leave behind the mythic framework of creation for a proclamation of Yahweh's sovereignty over foreign gods and their peoples. In other words, the Psalms look not to the past, but to the future, to Yahweh's ultimate 'Königsherrschaft'. According to Loretz this perspective could only arise in the Persian era.[27] So Loretz agrees with Mowinckel regarding translation, but with Kraus on the setting of these Psalms in post-exile.

d. Finally, a fourth position is represented by, among others, A.R. Johnson and A.A. Anderson.[28] Both of these men believe that syntactic and contextual consideration favor the translation 'Yahweh *is* king' for יהוה מלך. Both of them believe, however, that there was a festival in which Yahweh's kingship was celebrated, and that this festival took place at the Autumn New Year festival, during the feast of Tabernacles. Johnson is far more willing than is Anderson to speculate about the details of this festival, such as the king's participation in it,[29] but both are agreed that Yahweh's kingship was annually celebrated in conjunction with the New Year festival. According to Johnson, the enthronement festival comprised three principal movements: the celebration of Yahweh's cosmogonic victory, symbolized by the triumph of light over darkness; the subjection of 'sea' and Yahweh's enthronement in the assembly of gods; and the creation of the habitable world. Included in the festival were an assurance of ultimate victory over 'death', a summons to renewal of faith in Yahweh, and a challenge to faithfulness which would lead to peace.[30] Johnson further conceives the earthly drama played out in the temple as corresponding to the subjection of divine powers in heaven.[31]

In the interpretation of the Enthronement Psalms we are then confronted with four alternatives. These are:

1. These Psalms celebrate the enthronement of Yahweh in the context of a New Year enthronement festival.

2. These Psalms do not celebrate Yahweh's enthronement and there was no such festival.

3. The Psalms do celebrate Yahweh's enthronement, but they are post-exilic and do not reflect an enthronement festival.

4. The Psalms celebrate Yahweh's kingship, not his enthronement, in the context of the Autumn festival of the New Year.

3. *Evaluation of the discussion*

It is not possible here to evaluate in detail these four positions, nor to present comprehensive arguments for the function and setting of these Psalms within the Jerusalem cult. However, it may be useful to evaluate briefly the arguments offered against a festival of Yahweh's enthronement since this will lead us into a discussion directly relevant to the Zion symbol and its traditio-historical background.

a. While the majority of scholars have followed Diethelm Michel in suggesting that יהוה מלך be translated in a durative sense,[32] there are those who continue to see in this locution a reference to an act of enthronement, e.g. Niek Poulssen and Erhard Gerstenberger.[33] Even though the problem is impossible to solve on grammatical terms alone, the consistency with which the subject precedes the verb (but cf. Ps 47.9) may favor a durative sense with emphasis on the subject. In any case the significance of the distinction between ingressive and durative senses is probably over-emphasized.[34] That is, an annual festival which celebrated Yahweh's primordial victory over chaos (e.g. Ps 93.3-4) would not necessarily contradict the notion of Yahweh's eternally enduring kingship. In any event, the translation issue is something of a red herring since it has little to do with the probability of a liturgical setting for the Enthronement Psalms in which the kingship of Yahweh was celebrated, or with the probability that this celebration took place at the Autumn festival. The translation of יהוה מלך is not relevant to the question of whether there was a festival of Yahweh's enthronement, but only to the question of the nature of this festival, supposing that its existence can be assumed on the basis of other evidence.

b. The fact that no texts mention a New Year festival of Yahweh's enthronement is not in itself surprising. In the first place, what was celebrated in the Enthronement Psalms was not the New Year by itself, but Yahweh's kingship. Since in the Israelite conception, as it was developed within the Jerusalem cult, Yahweh's kingship was not secured through an annual battle against the forces of nature or of chaos, one could not expect that the New Year itself would receive special or independent prominence as a sacred season. Yahweh's conquest of chaos was conceived in the Jerusalem cult tradition as primordial, a creation event, and the absence of the kind of cosmic struggle that seems to have dominated other ancient Near Eastern New Year celebrations would naturally serve to depreciate the significance of the New Year itself in Israel.[35]

Second, the absence of references to a New Year festival in the ancient cultic calendars[36] should not be surprising. In the first place these calendars are all retrojections to a period prior to the celebration of Yahweh's kingship in Jerusalem. We simply do not have a rich supply of data for the festivals of the monarchic period.[37] On the other hand the Autumn festival, which was an agricultural festival and probably encompassed the celebration of the New Year, achieved a particularly prominent place during the monarchy.[38] This pilgrimage festival probably included among its central features a procession of the Ark into the temple and some form of covenant renewal.[39] It is important to note that while the Autumn festival in Jerusalem had very clear connections with the pre-monarchic pilgrimages to individual shrines,[40] the cultic calendars, which still assume a setting prior to the development of the Jerusalem cult, would have had no cause to describe a festival of kingship in Jerusalem. The fact is that the cultic legislation in the Old Testament, preserved primarily by Priestly tradents, is simply inadequate to the reconstruction of the Jerusalem cult. As Kraus himself says,

> The information that can be gained from the legal and historical traditions in the Old Testament is really very little, and we certainly cannot build up from these sources a picture of the actual course of worship at Jerusalem that is in any way adequate.[41]

We may conclude then that while it is true that no text explicitly mentions a specific festival celebrating Yahweh's kingship, this does not weigh heavily against the probability that there was a festival celebration of this central theologoumenon, even if its details cannot be reconstructed with certainty. The issue, rather, is how best to account for the form and content of these Enthronement Psalms.[42] In positing a historical and social situation that best accounts for the features of these Psalms it is hard to avoid the conclusion that a cultic event in Jerusalem that celebrated Yahweh's kingship in connection with the Autumn festival makes the best sense of the data.[43]

c. It is also true that the Mesopotamian material cannot *prove* the existence of an enthronement festival in Israel. But that is not the issue. The issue is whether the Mesopotamian and other ancient Near Eastern material cited by Mowinckel and his successors can shed light on the meaning and situation of the Enthronement Psalms. The conferral of scepter, throne and vestment upon Marduk by the gods in conjunction with the cry, 'Marduk is king!' (Enuma Elish 4.28) does not prove an enthronement ritual behind Psalms 93–99, nor does the cry, 'Aliyan Baal is our king' in the Ugaritic texts (cf. *CTA* 3.D.40). These texts merely illuminate the possible background of similar locutions in the Psalms, which is all that comparative material can be expected to do. When care is taken to observe the particularity of the Enthronement Psalms in the Israelite context these comparative data can provide a context for understanding the celebration of Yahweh's kingship in Jerusalem, even though they cannot prove the existence of a festival of enthronement. Proof is not the goal of historical research.

d. Habets and others are correct in noting the limited value of the material often cited to show an analogous relationship between the enthronement of the earthly king and the supposed enthronement of Yahweh. But beyond the difficulty of drawing conclusions from the announcement that, for example, Jehu or Absalom has become king to an enthronement festival of Yahweh introduced by the pronouncement יהוה מלך, there is the more complex problem of texts such as Psalms 2 and 110, and the presumed royal ritual of which they are a part.

There are actually two problems involved here. The first is the setting of the royal Psalms[45] in a royal ritual of enthronement. The second problem is the relation of this royal ritual to the celebration of Yahweh's kingship in the Enthronement Psalms.[46] These problems are strictly extraneous to our discussion. Here we need only make two cursory observations. First of all, it is likely that the liturgical material utilized in the celebration of the enthronement of the earthly king shares a common background with the Enthronement Psalms in the Jerusalem cult. One need only compare Psalms 2 and 110 with 47; 93–99, and the Zion Psalms, 46; 48; 76, to confirm this observation. In addition, it is likely that all of these Psalms draw on 'neighboring oriental court etiquette'.[47] One may thus safely conclude that the way in which the Jerusalem court celebrated the enthronement of the earthly king had some relation to the way in which Yahweh's kingship was conceived, and vice-versa, and that both are related to Near Eastern prototypes. This is not to argue, however, that the *notion* of Yahweh as king was a development from the earthly kingdom, since Yahweh was certainly conceived as king in the pre-monarchic period.[48]

Second, it is important to note that neither in the Enthronement Psalms nor in the Zion Songs is there any mention of the earthly king.[49] Because of this, and because of the formal dissimilarity between the Royal Psalms and the Enthronement Psalms, it is dubious to assign a common *Sitz im Leben* in a single festival.[50] It is likely that the Judean kings did date their accession to the Autumn, and that a new king's enthronement was celebrated in conjunction with the Autumn festival, but the connection between the king's enthronement and Yahweh's kingship was probably never such that the latter was simply modeled on the former.[51]

Thus, while we might agree that one cannot simply argue from the enthronement of earthly kings to an enthronement festival of Yahweh, the absence of a clear connection between the two merely leaves open the question of a festival of Yahweh's kingship.

e. The objection that Yahweh's reign is in perpetuity, and that a festival of enthronement would be on that basis contradictory, is not compelling. In the first place, some have argued that an annual celebration and dramatic portrayal of Yahweh's enthronement would not impose any constraints on the view that Yahweh reigned from eternity.[52] Kraus is here probably correct in his view that the celebration consisted not of an enthronement *per se*, but of a procession of the Ark into the temple, commemorating the choice of this site as Yahweh's dwelling.[53] This view is suggested by Ps 24.7-10 and 132. But just as this pilgrimage of the Ark in connection with the Autumn festival does not entail the theological conclusion that Yahweh has temporarily abandoned Zion as his dwelling, in the manner of a 'dying and rising' fertility god, so a celebration of Yahweh's enthronement would not imply periodic interruptions in the exercise of his sovereignty or in the duration of his rule.[54]

Second, we have already suggested that what the Enthronement Psalms celebrate is probably more accurately described as Yahweh's kingship, rather than his enthronement. This suggestion is based not merely on the syntax of יהוה מלך, but on the content of the Psalms themselves. If the Enthronement Psalms are regarded as belonging to the same liturgical setting as Psalms 24 and 132,[55] then they probably reflect not a simple enthronement, but the processional return of the Ark to the temple and the resumption of Yahweh's residence there. In that case the claim that Yahweh's rule is in perpetuity would have no bearing on the possibility of an Autumn festival of his kingship.

f. Finally, the last objections, that since there is no one who could enthrone Yahweh a festival of his enthronement is impossible, cannot be taken seriously. In the first place, as we have repeatedly stated, the celebration of Yahweh's kingship most likely occurred in association with the procession of the Ark into the Jerusalem temple and implied no actual act of enthronement. Secondly, many Old Testament texts partake of the notion that Yahweh reigns with a 'divine council' of heavenly beings.[56] Perhaps the clearest example of this is in Psalm 29, where the בני אלים are urged to offer praise to Yahweh (הבו ליהוה) upon his theophanic appearance with the accompanying convulsions of land and sea. This theophany is concluded by the enthronement of Yahweh over the flood (למבול ישב) and the proclamation that Yahweh will rule as king forever. This text stands very close to similar Ugaritic texts in which, for example, Baal's kingship is won in a struggle with other gods and is accompanied by convulsions in the natural realm. Baal's conquest is concluded by his procession, presumably in the company of his hosts,[57] to his abode on Ṣaphon, where he reigned in his temple as king of the gods (cf. *CTA*, 4.7.1-44).[58]

Similarly in Deuteronomy 32 and Psalm 82 Yahweh is portrayed as exercising authority over lesser divine beings in a way that is reminiscent of Canaanite notions of El as the high god in a pantheon of lesser deities. In just the same way that the 'pagan' notions of Psalm 29 and Deuteronomy 32 and Psalm 82 have been adapted to serve the veneration of Yahweh, so the notion of the deity's enthronement as king has been adapted in Psalms 47, 93, 95-99, to the veneration of Yahweh as king. Of course there can be within the Jerusalem cult tradition no notion of Yahweh's enthronement *by* his host, or the divine council, or of his appointment by a superior or older deity (cf. *CTA* 3.E.43-44).[59] Nonetheless the function of the 'sons of God' in acclaiming Yahweh as king in Psalm 29 does suggest some association between Canaanite notions regarding the Council of El and the celebration of Yahweh's kingship in an appropriately Yahwistic setting.

In sum, we find most of the arguments raised against the existence of a festival of Yahweh's enthronement or kingship to be not strictly relevant to the question. On the basis of the evidence available it would seem best to conclude that Yahweh's kingship, which was seen to endure from his primordial victory over chaos, and to be exercised on Zion from the time of the Ark's transfer there, was celebrated as part of the Autumn festival which incorporated many Canaanite and traditionally Israelite notions. There is insufficient evidence, it seems to me, to reconstruct this festival in detail, to ascribe a dominant role within it to the earthly king,[60] or to assign a whole range of Psalms to specific movements within the festival. We would thus concur with those who locate the Enthronement Psalms in the celebration of Yahweh's kingship at the Autumn festival.[61]

B. THE KINGSHIP OF YAHWEH IN THE ENTHRONEMENT PSALMS

We have been considering the arguments for and against the celebration of Yahweh's kingship in an Autumn festival based largely on the phrase יהוה מלך in the Enthronement Psalms. But in addition to this phrase there are other terms within these Psalms that describe Yahweh as king on Zion. For example, Ps 93.1 describes Yahweh as 'clothed in majesty, Yahweh is clothed, he is girded with strength'. The language here is reminiscent of Ps 68.35, where Yahweh's majesty (גאוה) over Israel is in parallelism with his power in the skies עזו בשחקים. In Psalm 93 the majesty of Yahweh is associated with his founding of the world and the establishment of his throne. Here again Yahweh's kingship is clearly in view and is exercised in the subduing of the chaos which threatens the established world order (vv. 3-4).

The final verse of this Psalm may contain a further explicit reference to Yahweh's kingship. Mitchell Dahood, following in part an earlier essay by James D. Shenkel,[62] renders the final verse

> Your enthronement was confirmed of old;
> in your temple the holy ones will laud you,
> Yahweh, for days without end.[63]

While Shenkel takes the initial עדתיך of the MT as a variant of Ugaritic '*d* ('seat, throne'), from the root '*dd*,[64] Dahood prefers to derive it from the verb יעד, to designate or appoint, indicating a royal function and justifying the translation 'throne' or 'enthronement'.[65]

Dahood thus interprets this verse as referring to the praise offered Yahweh by his heavenly host in his 'celestial temple'.[66]

However, this drastic revision of the text seems neither firmly grounded nor necessary. There is no other instance of the verb אמן used in connection with Yahweh's throne in the Old Testament. On the other hand אמן (niphal) is used frequently with respect to Yahweh's covenant (Ps 89.29), statutes (Ps 111.7; cf. 119.152) and the like. Furthermore, in Ps 19.8 אמן is used with respect to Yahweh's עדות, obviously from the same root as עדה. Thus עדהיך meaning 'your testimonies' seems very appropriate with נאמנו, while the latter would be a singular instance in connection with 'your throne'.[67] On the other hand the reference to Yahweh's testimonies or decrees should occasion no suprise in this context, especially if this Psalm does have its setting in the Autumn festival. As Kraus points out, the proclamation of Yahweh's decrees had a special place in this festival (cf. Ps 81)[68] and is elsewhere associated with Yahweh's kingship (Ps 99.4, 6ff.).[69] Among the enthronement Psalms, Psalm 97 also concludes with a reference to Yahweh's righteous demands (cf. also Ps 132.12ff.).[70]

Thus, even though 93.5 seems not to contain an explicit reference to Yahweh's kingship on Zion, the rest of the Psalm obviously portrays Yahweh as king reigning on his throne. As other Old Testament texts and literature from the ancient Near East make clear, no absolute distinction should be made between Yahweh's heavenly abode and his earthly dwelling in the temple on Zion.[71] The relationship is dialectical, for Yahweh's heavenly rule is reflected in his earthly sovereignty, centered in the temple which unites heaven and earth.

1. 'Rejoicing' and kingship

It is characteristic of these Enthronement Psalms that the announcement of Yahweh's kingship is followed by an exhortation to rejoice. Thus, in 96.10-13, we have the same progression found already in Psalm 93: the proclamation of יהוה מלך, a statement concerning the establishment of the earth (אף תכון תבל בל המוט), and an allusion to Yahweh's demands, here in the form of a promise that Yahweh will judge (דין) the peoples fairly. There then follows an exhortation to rejoice directed toward heaven and earth. Similarly in Psalm 97,[72] the theophanic language depicting the terrifying glory of Yahweh is framed by the introductory proclamation, יהוה מלך with its exhortation to rejoice again directed toward the earth and the islands of the sea, and the statement that Zion has heard and rejoiced (v. 8), as do the daughters of Judah, on account of the judgments of Yahweh. This rejoicing is said, finally, to occur because Yahweh is עליון over all the earth and מאר נעלית over all gods (cf. below on Ps 47). There is thus a chiastic arrangement of the two themes (Yahweh's kingship + rejoicing // rejoicing + Yahweh's kingship) in vv. 1 and 8-9, around the central section of the Psalm.[73]

This theme of rejoicing, and that of the 'new song' (cf. 96.1; 98.2, plus 33.3; 40.4; 144.9; 149.1; Isa 26.1; 42.10), seem to be associated especially with the notion of Yahweh's kingship.[74] For example in Psalm 96, of which we have already noted the conclusion (vv. 10-13), the introductory command to 'sing a new song' is followed by a series of further exhortations to praise, gounded in Yahweh's greatness over against the gods of the peoples (vv. 1-5). The initial section of the Psalm concludes in v. 6 with a series of adjectives describing Yahweh's sovereignty. The second section of the Psalm (vv. 7-13) opens with another series of imperatives, concluding with a command to 'say among the nations, יהוה מלך' (v. 10).

In Psalm 98 the command to 'sing a new song' in v. 1 is followed by a description of Yahweh's faithfulness in securing victory on behalf of Israel in vv. 1b-3. There then follows in v. 4 a command directed to all the earth, exhorting its inhabitants to 'shout for joy (הריעו) before Yahweh'. Verse 5 continues the exhortation to praise and v. 6 concludes this section of the Psalm (vv. 4-6) with an exhortation to 'shout for joy (הריעו) before the king, Yahweh', with trumpets and the sound of a ram's horn. The Psalm then concludes, following a portrayal of the effects of Yahweh's appearance on the sea and the earth, with a final reference to Yahweh's rule (שפט). There are thus connections drawn here among the new song, rejoicing (especially הריע and רנן; Ps 97.8 uses שמח with respect to Zion), and Yahweh's kingship and royal rule.[75]

It is usually acknowledged that Pss 96 and 98 are dependent upon Deutero-Isaiah and thus cannot be pre-exilic.[76] So these two Psalms may provide no independent evidence for a pre-exilic correlation between the themes of rejoicing and Yahweh's kingship or enthronement in the Jerusalem cult. However there is some evidence that there was in the pre-exilic period a connection between Yahweh's kingship and the cultic shout for joy, and a connection between the latter and the celebration of the New Year.[77]

2. *The traditio-historical background*

It is appropriate at this point to digress briefly from the Enthronement Psalms in order to consider more explicitly the traditio-
historical and cultic background of the call to rejoice in these Psalms.
This digression will allow us to focus more clearly on issues that bear
particularly on topics to be taken up later.

It is first of all of some significance that the verb הריע, as well as the
noun תרועה, are used in connection with the Ark.[78] For example in 1
Sam 4.4-5 it is reported that

> The people sent to Shiloh and brought from there the Ark of
> Yahweh of Hosts, Seated Upon the Cherubim. Now the two sons of
> Eli, Hophni and Phineas, were with the Ark. And when the Ark of
> Yahweh came into the camp all Israel gave a great shout and the
> land resounded.[79]

Here the appearance of the Ark is greeted with a shout (הריע) as it
is brought to the field of battle against the Philistines. It is important
to note that it was not the great noise of the Hebrew shouts that
alarmed the Philistines, but, according to the text of vv. 6-7, the
knowledge that this shout was in response to the presence of the Ark,
which meant the presence of God (or 'gods') with the Israelites. It is
also important to note that this story is located in Shiloh where, it is
likely, Yahweh was first explicitly recognized as king, and where he
received the designation ישב הכרובים and perhaps the epithet צבאות as
well (cf. below). Thus, this report brings together the Ark, the
kingship of Yahweh and the joyful shout.

Again in 2 Sam 6, the story of the Ark's entry into Jerusalem, the
journey of the Ark is marked by several celebrations. To begin with,
as the Ark is removed from the home of Abinadab David and his
people 'make merry' (שחק) [80] before Yahweh, who was conceived as
present with the Ark. Such activity is again reported at the end of the
narrative, where David provokes Michal by his insistence upon
'making merry', once again, before Yahweh. But in the middle of the
chapter (vv. 12-15), after the Ark has left the home of Obed-Edom, it
is reported that 'David and the whole house of Israel bore the Ark of
Yahweh with a shout of joy (הריע) and with the sound of a ram's horn
(בקול שופר)' (v. 15). The same terminology is thus used as in Ps 98.6
(see above), where all the earth is exhorted to shout for joy before
Yahweh the king.

a. 'Yahweh of Hosts' and the Shiloh Ark

The beginning of 2 Sam 6[81] is marked by the same epithets attached to the Ark as those found in 1 Sam 4, יהוה צבאות and ישב הכרובים, both of which are, I believe, firmly asociated with Shiloh and with the kingship of Yahweh.[82] It has sometimes been argued that these epithets did not originate in Shiloh, the supposition being that they were retrojections from the Jerusalem temple into an earlier period.[83] Consequently, it has been denied that these epithets entail the conception of Yahweh as king prior to the conquest of Jerusalem. However, it must be noted that the epithet ישב הכרובים is attached to the Ark only in the narratives associated with Shiloh and that it is never used in connection with the Ark in the Solomonic temple. In the temple the cherubim were independent of the Ark and were placed in the *debir*, the inner sanctum, with Yahweh apparently conceived as enthroned upon them (1 Kgs 6.23-28; 8.6-8).[84] Furthermore, the epithet יהוה צבאות is associated with Shiloh apart from the Ark (1 Sam 1.3, 11), suggesting to some that Yahweh was acknowledged as צבאות in Shiloh even before he was associated with the Ark and the epithet ישב הכרובים attached to it.[85] While this seems unlikely, since the context of these two verses makes clear that the title 'Yahweh of hosts' is connected with the shrine, and since it is particularly used in appeals to Yahweh for help (Ps 80), it is nonetheless evident that the title does have an early association with Shiloh.[86] In any event, 1 Sam 4.4 and 2 Sam 6.2 indicate that 'Yahweh of hosts' and 'seated upon the cherubim' were joined specifically in connection with the Ark at Shiloh. That much is clear irrespective of the question whether the two epithets developed independently.[87] There is no ground for supposing that the Jerusalem cult retrojected onto Shiloh an epithet of Yahweh associated with the Ark that was not used in the Jerusalem cult itself. Rather, the narrator in 1 Samuel 4 and 2 Samuel 6 wishes to make clear, as Eckart Otto points out, that the Ark in Jerusalem stands in continuity with the Ark at Shiloh, and for that reason he explicitly calls the Ark by the two epithets which would make that connection obvious.[88]

The association of the epithet ישב הכרובים with the Ark, and both of them with Yahweh and Shiloh, suggests strongly that Yahweh was here conceived as king, and that the Ark was the symbol of his royalty, either as a throne, as a footstool, or as something else related to a throne.[89] It has, however, seemed to some anachronistic to speak of Yahweh as king prior to the monarchy in Jerusalem, because the royal conception of Yahweh should have been modeled on an earthly monarchy. But this 'anachronism' disappears once we recognize that Yahweh was regarded as king already in Israel's earliest pre-monarchic literature. It has also been thought that since the most obvious source of royal imagery and mythology for Israel was Canaanite religion, and since the point of integration for Canaanite mythology into Israelite religion was Jerusalem, the conceptual basis presupposed in the notion of Yahweh as king enthroned upon cherubim would have been lacking in the Shiloh period. However, it must now be conceded that Canaanite influence upon Israelite religion was not limited to, nor was it initiated by, Jerusalem. Furthermore, it is evident that precisely Shiloh was the site of extensive Canaanite influence.

In the first place, Shiloh was the site of an annual wine festival, designated חג יהוה (Judg 21.16ff; cf. 9.27), which is the designation of the Autumn festival in Lev 23.39. It is furthermore likely that this festival was an Autumn New Year festival. The instructions for the sabbatical year celebration in Lev 25.8-9 date the beginning of the year to the Autumn month of Tishri, and other Priestly legislation places this feast at the turn of the year (Exod 34.22; 23.16).[90] This makes it very probable that the feast in Shiloh was an Autumn New Year Feast to celebrate the new wine. That this feast stemmed from the Canaanite milieu is indicated by the name of the first month at Ugarit, *r's yn*, 'first of the wine'.[91] Similarly, in 1 Sam 1.21 Elkanah is described as going to Shiloh to perform the זבח הימים, the annual sacrifice, which is, according to de Moor's reconstruction of the Karatepe inscription, the Phoenician designation of the Autum New Year festival.[92]

Also, according to 1 Sam 1.9; 3.3, the resting place of the Ark in Shiloh was a היכל, which suggests that the conceptions surrounding the Ark in Shiloh were influenced by Canaanite temple notions rather than, or in addition to, Israelite notions of a moveable sanctuary. But even if these texts are anachronistic in their use of the term 'temple', which seems unlikely,[93] the notion of a tent-dwelling for the deity is no less indebted to Canaanite influence than is the notion of a temple, for El, the Canaanite high god, dwelled in a tent shrine.[94]

Excursus: The 'temple' at Shiloh

The problems here are enormously complex. Recently the most common assumption has been that 1 Sam 1.9 and 3.3 are 'anachronistic' in describing the shrine at Shiloh as a היכל.[95] The difficulty exists because of the express statement of 2 Sam 7.6 that Yahweh had not dwelt in a house from the time of the exodus until the writer's present, but had 'moved about (continually—ואהיה מתהלך) in a tent shrine (באהל ובמשכן)'.[96] This assertion is partially substantiated by Ps 78.56-61, in which Yahweh describes his abandonment of Shiloh at the time of the Philistine wars and the loss of the Ark (עוזי ותפארתי). Here God (אלהים עליון) rejects Israel and abandons the משכן שלו, the sanctuary of Shiloh, where he dwelled among his people. Thus there seems to be a flat contradiction between 1 Sam 1.9; 3.3,[97] and 2 Sam 7.6; Ps 78, 56-61. Ps 132.6-7, cited by Cross, is in my view not relevant to the point at issue here.

Virgil W. Rabe has proposed, following a suggestion by his mentor, Cross, that these conflicting traditions should be conflated and that in reality there was at Shiloh a temple together with a tent shrine.[98] Rabe has been followed by Milgrom who believes that Nathan's opposition to the temple was based on the issue of mobility and that Nathan is contradicted by 1 Sam 1-3.[99] The Ark, he believes, was sheltered in a tent and the two should not be separated (as von Rad has argued they should be).[100] This 'tabernacle-tent', which co-existed with the temple at Shiloh, was used in wartime and for peacetime circuits among the people, specifically among the cities of Gilgal, Shechem, Shiloh and Bethal. These cities constituted, according to Milgrom, an early Israelite confederation.[101]

Milgrom's reconstruction is helpful, but I find it improbable that there was such an early confederation of cities, or sanctuaries, which shared a common tent-shrine and Ark. The impression of such a confederation seems to be the product of the Deuteronomistic historian, or his sources, which combined traditions from a number of independent sanctuaries and placed them within a single narrative structure. It is impossible to harmonize satisfactorily the contradictory details, for example, in the Gilgal and Shiloh traditions so as to make it possible to see a movement of the Ark from one sanctuary to the other.[102] As Eckart Otto has pointed out, there is no stage of tradition in Josh 3-6 which does not place the Ark in Gilgal.[103] At the same time the Ark is incontrovertibly in Shiloh at precisely the time, the time of Saul, that Gilgal enjoyed its greatest prominence. This makes it highly improbable that the Ark has moved from Gilgal to Shiloh at some point between the time of Gilgal's initial importance and the time of Saul's kingdom. Furthermore, the terms by which the Ark is known in Gilgal are never used for the Shiloh Ark, and vice versa. Nor do the epithets of Yahweh found in Shiloh ever appear in connection with Gilgal. There appear to be two independent, and perhaps even contradictory and rival traditions associated with Gilgal and Shiloh with little evidence that they constituted part of a larger confederation of sanctuaries.[104] The conflation into one tradition, as we now have it, probably occurred among the theologians of the early royal court, for which the legitimation provided by sacral traditions from earlier sanctuaries continued to be very important.[105]

A view similar to Milgrom's is that of Otto Eissfeldt in his article, 'Kultzelt und Tempel'.[106] He argues that the tabernacle was transformed at Sinai into an oracle tent and that it was there brought into connection with the Ark. The tent continued to be venerated as a relic and was preserved, traveling with the Ark, and both of them were kept together at the temples and sanctuaries they visited. Hence, claims Eissfeldt, there is no contradiction between the traditions of a tent and of a temple at Shiloh, or between the tradition of a temple there and the claims of 2 Sam 7.6. Eissfeldt believes that the tent and its appurtenances were brought to the temple at Shiloh when that temple was adapted to Israelite and Yahwistic worship in the period of Canaanite/Israelite syncretism.

It seems to me that Eissfeldt's view, apart from the problem of the Ark's meeting with the tent at Sinai, is the most cogent. It is extremely difficult to remove either tradition, temple or tent, from the sources, or to attribute either to anachronistic or careless language. Both are part of a pre-Deuteronomistic tradition, according to most,[107] and it is difficult to imagine why a supposed anachronism like that in 1 Sam 1.9; 3.3 would arise, and why it would have been retained in the Deuteronomistic work. That there was an early temple at Shiloh might also be suggested by Judg 18.31, rejecting the emendations proposed by *BH*[3] and *BHS*.[108]

Finally, mention should be made of the study by K.D. Schunck, 'Zentralheiligtum, Grenzheiligtum and "Höhenheiligtum" in Israel'.[109] According to his definition both the sanctuary in Shiloh and the temple in Jerusalem are entitled to the designation היכל because they are central sanctuaries, sites of the Ark, and in Schunck's estimation, centers of administrative authority, rather than border santuaries, which carry the label בית יהוה. Given this character of the terms היכל and בית יהוה, the prohibition of Nathan in 2 Samuel 7 should perhaps be understood along more political lines.[110] This is also the suggestion of Cross, although he understands the political issue to be one of competing ideologies, one a dynastic ideology related to the Ba'al temple, the other a league or covenant ideology, related to the tent of El.[111] Cross's reconstruction of the issue is problematic because it depends in part on early dating of Ps 78, which he simply asserts,[112] and on different political ideologies represented by El and Baal at Ugarit, for which there can be precious little evidence.

In sum, I find no compelling grounds for excising the references to a היכל in Shiloh.

b. *The 'Mighty One of Jacob'*

It is also possible that the epithet אביר יעקב, which means 'the strong one of Jacob',[113] was originally associated with Shiloh and the Ark. In the first place this epithet seems to have a particular connection with the Zion tradition—its five occurrences outside Gen 49.24 are all in Zion texts: Isa 49.26; 60.16; Ps 132.2, 5. In addition, a variant is found in Isa 1.24, אביר ישראל, also in a Zion text (Isa 1.21-26).[114] Secondly, it is difficult to see either element of this epithet stemming originally from Jerusalem. '*br* is not an epithet of either El, whose epithet *tr* is eqivalent to שור in Hebrew, or of Baal in the Ugaritic texts.[115] Nor would 'Jacob' likely be part of a divine epithet originating in Jerusalem, either before or at the time of David. Furthermore, Gen 49.24, the first attestation of this epithet, probably comes from before the monarchy.[116]

In Ps 132.2, 5, besides Gen 49.24 perhaps the earliest of the occurrences of this epithet, it is associated with the Ark.[117] Again, in Isa 1.24 אביר ישראל is in parallel with יהוה צבאות which is, as we have seen, associated with the Ark in Shiloh. Further, references to Jacob, or the God of Jacob, appear with striking frequency in texts related to Zion. Thus in Psalm 24, a Psalm of the procession of the Ark into the temple, the procession is to 'seek the face (or presence) of the God of Jacob'.[118] The Psalm goes on to speak of Yahweh as צבאות and מלך כבוד, both associated with the Ark. In Psalm 46, a Song of Zion, 'Yahweh of Hosts' parallels 'God of Jacob' (v. 8) in a context which also speaks of the dwelling of Elyon (v. 5), as his משכנים/ות. 'God of Jacob' is also used of Yahweh in Ps 76.7, another of the Songs of Zion (cf. Isa 2.3).[119] Again in Ps 84.9-10, in the context of a Zion pilgrimage, 'Yahweh of Hosts' is in parallel with 'God of Jacob'.

Since 'God of Jacob' can be an epithet of Yahweh in connection with Zion, and since 'Jacob' can refer to the people of Yahweh whose center is Zion (cf. Isa 2.5; Ps 79.7, etc.),[120] there do not seem to be clear traditio-historical links between this epithet and the patriarch Jacob, or the tribes earlier associated with him. It would seem that the Jacob terminology, and particularly the epithet אביר יעקב, have come into the Zion tradition through a different route. Given the associations that we have pointed out it would seem reasonable to posit the Ark at Shiloh as the original location of this appellative, as well as the vehicle for its transmission to Zion.

So little is known about this epithet that it is impossible to speak with confidence about its significance. However, its possible association with the Ark and with צבאות suggests that it may have been connected with the kingship notions that gathered around the Ark. This is particularly evident in Ps 132.5-8, where a dwelling (משכנות) for יהוה // אביר יעקב represented by the Ark, and particularly by the הדם רגליו, is sought.[121] Thus, the epithet אביר יעקב would fit well with the two epithets explicitly associated with the Ark, ישב הכרובים // יהוה צבאות. Its connection with Shiloh cannot be proven, but this would seem to provide the most reasonable explanation for a title of clearly northern provenance so firmly anchored in the Zion tradition. At the same time, the occurrence of this epithet in Gen 49.24 in conjunction with the epithet 'Shepherd' applied to Yahweh argues for a background in Canaanite appellations of El.[122]

c. *Yahweh 'Enthroned upon the Cherubim'*
There is very little doubt that the epithet ישב הכרובים is of Canaanite origin and is closely related to the notion of the Ark as Yahweh's throne.[123] In Canaan El is regularly portrayed as sitting on a throne flanked by cherubim and the cherubim were also associated with earthly thrones elsewhere in the Near East.[124] In addition, the epithet of Yahweh, ישב הכרובים, appears to be something like the functional equivalent of Baal's epithet, *rkb 'rpt*, 'rider on the clouds'.[125] It is clear at any rate that both titles are associated with kingship. Thus at CTA 2.4.8. *rkb 'rpt* is in parallel with *zbl b'l*, 'Prince Baal'.[126] Similarly at CTA 4.3.11, *rkb 'rpt* is in parallel with *'liyn b'l*, which is seen to be a royal title by its construction with *zbl* at 6.1.42-43 (cf. also 4.5.122; 5.2.6-7). The Hebrew adaptation of this imagery can be

further seen at Ps 18.11 (= 2 Sam 22.11) where it is said of Yahweh that וירכב על כרוב, 'and he rode upon a cherub'. An even clearer example is found at Ps 80.2, where Yahweh who is ישב הכרובים is urged to 'shine forth' (הופיעה) on behalf of the central Palestinian tribes, Ephraim, Benjamin and Manasseh.[127] The epithet ישב הכרובים is finally brought into explicit relation to the kingship of Yahweh in the Jerusalem cult by Ps 99.1, where it is in parallel with יהוה מלך. There is no agreement about the origin of the other epithet explicitly connected with the Ark, יהוה צבאות, but, as we have suggested above, this epithet too is to be understood against the Canaanite background of the divine council, in which Yahweh, or El, was conceived to exercise administrative and specifically military authority.[128] The connection of 'Yahweh of hosts' with the Ark and the related epithet, 'enthroned upon the cherubim', suggests that it too refers primarily to the kingship of Yahweh rather than to his character as warrior.[129]

Finally, already von Rad saw in the terms נר אלהים at 1 Sam 3.3 an example of Canaanite influence, a suggestion now substantiated by a parallel from Ugarit.[130] Driver thought he had found a Canaanite parallel to the Ephod mentioned in 1 Sam 2.28, but this is a far from certain conclusion.[131]

These examples illustrate quite clearly that Shiloh was a prime site for the integration of Canaanite and Israelite religion. To what degree this was an integration of substance, rather than merely of form, is not our concern here. The point of our discussion has been that the issue of dependence upon Canaanite models for the notion of Yahweh's kingship should not stand in the way of seeing this fundamental notion of the Jerusalem cult, which came to be associated with the symbol of Zion, deriving from the pre-monarchic period, and specifically from Shiloh. As Jeremias has said, the Zion tradition is, in its oldest form, 'an exegesis of the Ark and its tradition', with the help of Canaanite motifs already available at Shiloh.[132]

We have argued that already in Shiloh the notion of Yahweh's kingship is associated with the Ark, as is particularly evidenced by the epithets ישב הכרובים // צבאות, and that the Ark is likely associated with the Autumn celebration of Yahweh's kingship. Further, we have suggested that there is an association of the Ark and the Autumn festival, held at the New Year, with cultic rejoicing (whether the term used is הריע, שמח, שוש, רנן, or עלז).[133] This investigation thus bears on the background and cultic function of the Enthronement Psalms, as these celebrate Yahweh's kingship on Zion.

3. *Yahweh's kingship in the Jerusalem cult*

We have already noted the entrance liturgy in Psalm 24, suggesting that this hymn is associated with the celebration of Yahweh's kingship in the Autumn festival. The language of this hymn is important, in that Yahweh is designated מלך הכבוד יהוה צבאות. Other terms in the Psalm, such as עזוז and גבור, serve to emphasize the martial character of Yahweh associated with the Ark, but the terms כבוד and צבאות are of particular importance in this context. That צבאות was associated with the Ark at Shiloh is virtually certain. However it is important also to recognize the Shiloh-Ark connection of כבוד as well. This connection is made explicit in 1 Sam 4.21, 22. Here it is reported that the wife of Phineas, Eli's son, named her child איכבוד, because

> The glory has left Israel, because the Ark of God was captured . . .
> The glory has left Israel, because the Ark of God was taken.

This identification of the Ark with Yahweh's glory probably reflects the association of the Ark with Yahweh's theophanic appearances,[134] such as that described in Isaiah 6. It is important for us to note, however, that Psalm 24 most likely represents the ritual return of the Ark, signalling the presence of Yahweh, to its place in the temple. It is against this background that Psalm 47, an Enthronement Psalm, should be understood.[135]

It is immediately evident that Psalm 47 is concerned with the kingship of Yahweh.[136] In v. 3 Yahweh is explicitly designated יהוה עליון נורא and, in apposition, מלך גדול over the whole earth. Yahweh is here designated not only the great king, but specifically עליון נורא, 'awesome Elyon'.[137] As J.J.M. Roberts has said,

> Whatever the status of the god Elyon in the Canaanite pantheon, in Israelite thought he was clearly the overlord of the gods. He assigned the nations their repective territories and entrusted them to their national gods (Deuteronomy 32.8), and these national gods were thought of as the sons of Elyon (Ps 82.6).[138]

This identification of Yahweh with Elyon is made the more clear when it is recognized that the traditional translation, 'Yahweh the most high is awesome', misses the parallelism of מלך גדול // עליון נורא. That is, Yahweh is being ascribed two parallel epithets, 'awesome Elyon' and 'great king'.[139] Once this identification is recognized the relation of this verse to Ps 97.9 is clearer. There the pronouncement that Yahweh is exalted (מאד נעלית—an obvious play on עליון) over all gods is prefaced by the statement that 'you, O Yahweh, are עליון' (see above). So here in 47.3 as well, the assertion is being made that Yahweh is the 'awesome Elyon, the great king', and as such has no peer among the gods.

The same claims are made for Yahweh in Ps 48.3, where he is identified as the מלך רב. The point made in this passage, however, is that Mount Zion is precisely ירכתי צפון, that is, the site of the divine king's residence, where he reigns on his holy throne (Ps 47.8).[140] Hence, the pre-eminence of Yahweh as sovereign over all gods is linked to the pre-eminence of Zion as the site of his dwelling. Zaphon is no longer the residence of Baal, but is now equated with Zion, the residence of Yahweh. As Eissfeldt says, 'Baal is dethroned and Yahweh occupies his place'.[141]

To return to Ps 47, the structure indicates quite clearly the liturgical character of this hymn. It is divided into two parts, vv. 2-6 and vv. 7-10. The first section begins with commands to clap hands and shout with the sound of rejoicing (הריעו. . .בקול רנה), and concludes with the report that Yahweh 'went up' (עלה) with a shout (תרועה) and the sound of a trumpet (בקול שופר). Similarly, the second section is introduced by commands to sing praise (זמרו, addressed to the gods) to 'our king', and is concluded, except for v. 10, with the report that God reigns (or has become king—מלך) over all the nations and sits on his holy throne. In both sections the command to shout, or sing, is based on the kingship of Yahweh. In the first section the command is based on the identity of Yahweh as Elyon, the great king. In the second, it is based on the status of God as king of the whole earth.

As we have noted, the background for understanding Ps 47 is found in Ps 24, in which Yahweh's entrance into the temple is symbolized by a procession of the Ark. Here in Ps 47, I am suggesting, we have another example of the Ark's procession into the temple (vv. 6, 9) accompanied by a shout of acclamation and the blowing of the trumpet. As Kraus has pointed out, the conjuction of the deity's entry into the temple and the veneration of the deity is in evidence throughout the Near East.[142] The accompaniment of the Ark's entry into the temple by the shout (תרועה) here, in view of the evidence previously cited, leads to the conclusion that this Psalm of Yahweh's kingship stems from the celebration of that kingship at the beginning of the cultic year in conjunction with the Autumn festival.[143]

We have been reviewing evidence for the connection of the celebration of Yahweh's kingship on Zion with the entry of the Ark into the temple in conjunction wth the Autumn festival and the celebration of the New Year. Part of the evidence with which we have been concerned is the association of joyful celebration and particularly the term הריע // תרועה with the kingship of Yahweh on Zion.[144] We have noted that this term is used particularly in the Jerusalem cult in association with the New Year celebration (Lev 23.24; cf. Lev 25.9; Num 29.1).[145] We are led on the basis of this evidence to agree with Rudolf Schmid, who speaks of the New Year celebration in the context of the Autumn festival as a 'royal festival of God'.[146]

C. THE CELEBRATION OF YAHWEH'S KINGSHIP: SUMMARY

Within the tradition of the Jerusalem cult, then, rejoicing is attached to the celebration of Yahweh's kingship. This kingship is exercised on Zion and it is only natural that the rejoicing over Yahweh's kingship there should be extended to the security of Zion itself. For example, in Ps 48.3 Zion is declared to be

הר קדושו יפה נוף	His holy mountain, beautiful in height,
משוש כל הארץ	The joy of the whole earth.
הר ציון ירכתי צפון	Mount Zion at the heights of Zaphon,
קרית מלך רב	The city of the great king.

The joy associated with Zion is explicitly connected with the presence there of the 'great king', who is Zion's secure refuge (נודע למשגב). The security of Zion, which is the basis of the joy associated with it, derives ultimately from Yahweh's conquest there of the powers of chaos, both cosmic and earthly. Similarly in the Ugaritic texts 'Anat's triumph over the enemies of Baal is celebrated with laughter (ṣḥq)[147] and rejoicing (lbh bšmḥt) over her success. The annual celebration of Yahweh's kingship is thus at the same time a celebration of Zion's security under the protection of her king (cf. Zeph 2.15; Isa 9.3; 24.8).[148]

Likewise, in Jer 8.19-21, the opposite of rejoicing is heard in Judah (קול שועת בת עמי) when it is perceived that Yahweh is not in Zion, nor her king in her midst (v. 19). It is significant to note that this lament by the people includes the observation that harvest is past and summer at an end, and still the people are not saved. The end of harvest and summer would mean that the Autumn New Year is at hand with Yahweh's royal presence in Zion not in evidence.[149] While this text does not explicitly mention the New Year celebration at the Autumn festival, it clearly associates Autumn with the expected presence of Yahweh as king in Zion and the consequent security of the city. Since this expectation is contradicted by contemporary circumstances[150] the joy associated with Yahweh's royal presence on Zion is turned into a lament at his absence in the Autumn season.

There is further evidence from the post-exilic period that there was at least a thematic connection between themes and motifs drawn from the Autumn festival and the celebration of Yahweh's kingship. It is perhaps impossible to prove that this connection stems from an actual liturgical setting in the post-exilic cult, but texts such as Zech 14.16 may suggest this.[151]

A later addition to the basic stratum of Isaiah 24–27, Isa 24.21-23 + 25.6-9 also places the kingship of Yahweh, here given an eschatological projection, in the context of a festival on Zion (בהר חזה).[152] The passage begins by announcing the coming reign of Yahweh on Zion 'in that day'.[153] Punishment will be meted out to the 'host of heaven' (צבא המרום) and the kings of the earth, and Yahweh of hosts will reign in their stead in הר ציון and in Jerusalem. Following this conquest by Yahweh he will hold a feast for 'all peoples' on Mount Zion (25.6). Among the rich things to be consumed at this feast are שמרים, or aged wine, and שמרים מזקקים, or purified wine. The section is closed by v. 9,[154] where the people are finally urged to rejoice (גיל) and be glad (שמח) because Yahweh's anticipated salvation will have dawned.

Thus we have in Isa 24.21-23 + 25.6-9 a rather clear connection between the reign of Yahweh and its celebration with rejoicing in the festival cult. It is also significant that the rejoicing here is done in connection with wine, while in 24.4-13 the desolation of the earth is characterized by the absence, or bitterness, of the new wine. Excepting the eschatological character of this piece, there is rather striking resemblance between it and the ritual character of the earlier texts concerned with Yahweh's kingship. Furthermore, other commentators, notably Wildberger and Millar, have noted the similarity of this text, and perhaps the whole of chapters 24–27, to the Baal epic.[155] Thus in the Baal epic, as is the case here, victory is followed by a feast given by the victorious diety.

Finally, attention could be drawn to other post-exilic texts in which the connection of rejoicing with the security of Zion, in which Yahweh is king, is to be found. Thus, in Isa 30.29 the intervention of Yahweh will produce conditions in which singing and rejoicing, as are appropriate to a feast (הג) on Yahweh's mountain, will be heard. In Isa 35.10 the פרויי יהוה return to Zion with rejoicing (רנה) to be the eternal possessors of joy and rejoicing (ששון and שמחה, cf. 51.11). In Isa 51.3 Yahweh will comfort Zion and give his blessing of fertility on Zion's wastes, with the result that ששון and שמחה will be found in her. Isa 65.18 promises that Yahweh's creation of a new Jerusalem will be greeted with rejoicing (שישו וגילו עדי עד) because he has made Jerusalem גילה and her people משוש.[156]

Within the Old Testament, then, we have a long tradition of the association of rejoicing with the celebration of Yahweh's kingship. In earlier texts we noted that this celebration seems to be located in the Autumn festival, particularly insofar as that festival included the procession of the Ark, as Yahweh's throne, into the temple. Evidence dating as far back as the Shiloh sanctuary also indicates that this festival included the celebration of the New Year. We have also endeavored to show that much of the material associated with Yahweh's kingship in Jerusalem was not created *ad hoc* by the theologians of David's court, nor need its origins be sought in a hypothetical Jebusite tradition, but it was already in existence in association with the Ark at Shiloh. All of this material from the Jerusalem cult tradition is closely related to, one might even say rooted in, its Canaanite milieu. The acclamation of Yahweh's kingship in the New Year festival, in which his conquest of the forces of chaos was celebrated, is nearly identical to Cross's description of the situation in Canaan:

> The Canaanite temple was founded on New Year's day, identified with the foundation of the cosmic temple at creation confirming the victory of the Divine warrior over his enemies who represent chaos and death.[157]

We conclude this section by returning once more to a final Enthronement Psalm, Ps 99. As does Ps 47, this Psalm betrays an association with the traditions of the Ark. This is clear in the first verse, in which Yahweh (יהוה מלך) is called ישב כרובים (see above). The announcement of the rule of Yahweh seated upon the cherubim is accompanied by typical theophanic phenomena, the trembling of the peoples and quaking of the earth.[158] The introductory unit of the

Psalm is concluded by a parallel bi-colon (two non-verbal clauses) in which, significantly for our study, the rule of Yahweh, and his sovereignty over all gods, is exercised in Zion.

יהוה בציון גדול   Yahweh in Zion is great,
ורם הוא על כל אלהים   and exalted is he over all gods.[159]

As we have already noted, the emphasis in the Enthronement Psalms, as particularly demonstrated by Ps 47 (above), is that it is Yahweh who is king, and this emphasis is clearly present here. It is Yahweh in Zion who is גדול and, as we have noted, this adjective is particularly used to emphasize the executive power of Yahweh over other gods. This power is here reinforced by the claim that Yahweh in Zion is exalted over all other gods.

These same themes are continued in v. 5,[160] where the people are exhorted to praise Yahweh (רוממו) and to bow down to his footstool. We have noted earlier the significance of הדם רגל. Here again is a reference to the kingship of Yahweh, as well as a connection with the Ark traditions, in similar combination as in Ps 132.7-8 (see above). Very significant is the conclusion of the Psalm (v. 9), with its virtual repetition of v. 5. The two verses read as follows:

(5) רוממו יהוה אלהינו // והשתחוו להדם רגליו
(9) רוממו יהוה אלהינו // והשתחוו להר קדשו

The verbal agreement between these two verses indicates an intentional balance between the two parts of the Psalm, vv. 1-5 and vv. 6-9. The first part of the Psalm is in the form of a hymn of praise, describing Yahweh's founding act of salvation and concluding with an exhortation to praise in v. 5.[161] The second unit recalls specific times of need in which Moses, Aaron and Samuel called upon Yahweh and were answered from the עמוד ענן, the pillar of cloud (v. 7).[162] There is thus an identificaion made between the obeisance due the footstool of Yahweh in v. 5, which is related to the Ark terminology in v. 1, and the obeisance due Yahweh's holy mountain, Zion, in v. 9.

This text is remarkable in two respects. First of all, the throne of Yahweh is not limited now to the Ark, but is extended to the mountain itself.[163] Secondly, the apparent veneration of Zion is striking.[164] The extension of Yahweh's throne from the Ark, or the הדם רגליו, to Zion is met in similar form in Jer 3.16-18, as well as in Isa 66.1-2. In the Jeremiah passage it is said that the Ark will be forgotten and will not be remade. Instead,

בעת ההיא יקראו לירושלם   At that time Jerusalem will be called
כסא יהוה   'The throne of Yahweh'.

Furthermore, the nations of the earth will gather to Jerusalem, לשם יהוה, and Israel and Judah will gather to their common patrimony in the land. This text clearly represents an exilic or post-exilic development of the assertions in Ps 99,[165] such as is found in Lam 2.1, where Zion is identified as Yahweh's crown (תפארת) and Yahweh's footstool (הדם רגליו). Thus, in the exilic period Zion itself could be identified with the throne of Yahweh and could itself symbolize the presence of God.

This is already strikingly articulated in the singular locution of Ps 99.9,

והשתחוו להר קדשו   Bow down to/at his holy mountain

As we noted above, this does not mean that Zion itself is worshipped, but that the presence of Yahweh is so closely associated with Zion that the exhortations רוממו יהוה אלהינו and השתחוו להר קדשו can be construed in parallel. This theme too receives a further development in the exilic and post-exilic periods. For example, in Isa 60.14 he following is said to Zion:

והלכו אליך שחוח בני מעניך   The children of your oppressors
                                        shall come stooping before you,
להשתחוו על כפות רגליך כל מנאציך   And all of those who spurned you
                                        shall do obeisance at your feet.

Here Zion itself is the object of obeisance on the part of the foreign kings and nations who have been its oppressors. Already in Isa 45.15 it is said that the wealth of various nations will be brought to Zion and that the tall men of Sabea (אנשי מדה) will come to Zion and do obeisance (ישתחוו אליך) and, indeed, they will 'pray' to Zion (יתפללו אליך). Again in 49.23 it is said that kings and queens will lick the dust of Zion's feet.[166]

Thus Ps 99, and the notions expressed there, are not only of importance for the insight they provide into the centrality of Yahweh's kingship on Zion, but for insight into the way in which certain central features of the Zion symbolism were transformed in later periods.

In our study of the kingship of Yahweh on Zion as the central feature of the Jerusalem cult tradition we have concentrated primarily on the Enthronement Psalms, both because the kingship of

Yahweh is obviously prominent within them, and because they locate
the celebration of his kingship so clearly in the ritual of the Jerusalem
cult and its Zion symbolism. It is of course true that Yahweh's
kingship is prominent in relation to Zion in other texts from the
Jerusalem cult. For example, we have already noted that in Ps 29 the
bene Elim, the heavenly council, ascribe kingship to Yahweh. In v. 10
of this chapter it is said that

יהוה למבול ישב // וישב יהוה מלך לעולם

The translation of this verse is disputed, but it seems best to
translate 'Yahweh is enthroned over the flood, Yahweh is enthroned
forever'.[167] The picture here is of Yahweh reigning upon the heavenly
ocean. The roots of this ocean are the primordial mountains, which
are themselves the throne of Yahweh.[168] In Jerusalem this could only
be understood to mean Zion. In the Jerusalem cult the traditions of
El, whose home was at 'the confluence of the subterranean seas',[169]
and Baal, whose home was on the heights of Zaphon,[170] have been
combined. This combination has also resulted in a portrayal of Zion
as not only the site of Yahweh's throne 'on the heights of Zaphon' (Ps
48.3), but also as the site of the fructifying river. Ps 29 seems to
reflect this combination, at least in its Israelite reading,[171] and
conceives the throne of Yahweh, a heavenly throne with its earthly
reflection on Zion, as over the cosmic waters. Thus Yahweh is
portrayed as king in terms which are taken from the portrayals of the
high god in he Ugaritic pantheon, El, and from the storm and warrior
god, Baal.[172]

Ps 46 presents us with similar imagery from which Ps 29 should
probably be understood. Here the primordial mountains are in the
heart of the sea (v. 3), as in Ps 29 and Job 36.30. Furthermore, the
city of God, Zion, is said to be nurtured by a river:

נהר פלגיו ישמחו עיר אלהים   There is a river whose streams
make glad the city of God.[173]

Again the abode of El at the confluence of the subterranean seas is
called to mind, an impression which is strengthened by the
conclusion of the verse which describes Zion as 'the holy habitation
(קרש משכני)[174] of the Most High'. The term עליון is, as we have seen,
synonymous with מלך רב (48.3) and מלך גדול (47.3), all referring to
the supreme deity. In the Ugaritic pantheon this was El, the high
god, whose home is also known to have been a tent shrine.[175] Thus in

Ps 46 as well as in Ps 29 we seem to have the intentional use of well-known imagery which would serve the claims of the Jerusalem cult that the divine king is Yahweh, and he rules in Zion.

We have already seen that Ps 48 makes similar claims (cf. also Ps 76.2-3), as do the Enthronement Psalms which we have been considering. Other Psalms as well made direct or indirect allusion to the kingship of Yahweh on Zion, an exclusive kingship which surpasses or replaces the rule of other deities. From this starting point at the center of the Jerusalem cult's symbolic structure we move to an analysis of those themes that are derivative of this principal theological datum.

Chapter 3

THE EXERCISE OF YAHWEH'S KINGSHIP

Introduction

In the previous chapter we established that the Zion symbolism of the Jerusalem cult tradition was concerned in a fundamental way with Yahweh as king on Zion. We have also set this symbolism within the ritual celebration of Yahweh's kingship and have sought to establish its traditio-historical roots in the kingship traditions particularly associated with the Ark in Shiloh.

Our concern in this chapter is to investigate more closely the meaning of Zion as a symbol that *focuses*, within the tradition of Jerusalem's cult, the theological concerns that lie behind the Songs of Zion and other representative texts. We will thus assume the dominant place of the notion of Yahweh's kingship within this symbolism and will seek to uncover the way in which the exercise of this kingship is conceived. We will begin by discussing the themes of Yahweh as creator and defender, showing that these themes are both interrelated and connected with the notion of Yahweh's kingship. Next, we will deal with the problem of David's election, since Zion and David are often seen as complementary reflexes of the same tradition. Finally, we will discuss the theme of Zion as a symbol of security and refuge.

While the subject of Yahweh as creator and defender is raised explicitly in the first section of this chapter, it will be seen to be an integral part of the third section as well. We may anticipate our conclusion by suggesting that Zion is enabled to symbolize security and refuge because Yahweh reigns there as creator/defender.[1]

The themes addressed in this chapter are obviously relevant to the theology of Isaiah, a prophetic exemplar of the Jerusalem cult tradition and its Zion symbolism. Rather than bringing Isaiah piecemeal into the discussion here, however, we will delay discussion of that book until the next chapter, where it can be treated with greater integrity.

A. YAHWEH AS CREATOR AND DEFENDER

Within the Jerusalem cult tradition Yahweh's kingship is associated with his power as creator and defender. We have already seen this combination of kingship and creation in the Enthronement Psalms considered in some detail above. In Ps 93, for example, the announcement of Yahweh's kingship is followed by his conquest of the waters which threaten Yahweh's throne (vv. 1-4). Again in Ps 29 Yahweh's enthronement is connected, at least implicitly, with his subjugation of the flood.[2] In Ps 24, an entrance liturgy celebrating Yahweh's entrance via the Ark into the temple, the initial declaration is that Yahweh owns the earth:

כי הוא על ימים יסדה   For it was he who founded it upon the waters
ועל נהרות יכוננה   And established it upon rivers (v. 2).[3]

As we noted earlier, this Psalm then goes on to celebrate the entrance of יהוה צבאות the מלך הכבוד into the temple. Here then Yahweh's designation as creator stands in relation to his designation as king in the context of a cultic celebration closely associated with the Ark.[4]

Similarly in Ps 89.9-19 Yahweh's ownership of the earth (לך שמים אף־לך ארץ) is grounded in his creation of the world (תבל, vv. 12-13). Here too this assertion is brought into the context of Yahweh's kingship. The royal associations of Yahweh's 'subjection of the waters' in Pss 24.1-2 and 89.10-11 are clearly evident here and are made explicit in 89.26. Here, in a derivative sense, the representative of Yahweh, David his anointed (v. 21), is secured on his throne through his delegated power to subjugate the waters:

ושמתי בים ידו   And I shall place his hand upon the sea
ובנהרות ימינו   His right hand upon the rivers.[5]

Thus the creation wrought by the cosmic king is administered in the mundane realm through his regent, whose earthly throne is founded in righteousness and justice according to the pattern of Yahweh's heavenly throne (vv. 15, 30-34).[6]

Yahweh's royal function as creator is again clear in Ps 65. Here Zion is explicitly brought into the picture:

לך דמיה תהלה אלהים בציון   Praise is owed to you, oh God, in Zion (v. 2).

The Psalm goes on to speak of creation in traditional language, describing it in terms of the establishing of the mountains (מכין הרים בכחך v. 7—emended) and stilling the raging waters (משביח שאון ימים, v. 8). Psalm 89 does not explicitly designate Yahweh as king, but his kingship is the clear implication of v. 5, which speaks of Yahweh's courts and his holy temple.[7] Furthermore, the blessings of fertility, which are described in this Psalm, are those blessings traditionally mediated through the king (Ps 72.17ff.). According to Kraus, the situation of Ps 65 is 'Proskunesis before the creator of the world and the king of this world . . . who is enthroned on Zion and is honored in hymnic veneration'.[8]

Finally, Theodore H. Ludwig has drawn particular attention to the tradition of establishing the earth (יסד ארץ) and its use within the Jerusalem cult. In addition to some of the material to which we have already drawn attention Ludwig points to Ps 78.69 as an example of the significant relationship between the tradition of Yahweh's dwelling on Zion and his creation activity. Here, in connection with the election of David and Zion in place of the northern tribes, Yahweh's establishing the earth eternally (לעולם ארץ יסדה) is parallel to the claim that he built his sanctuary like the high heavens (ויבן כמו רמים מקדשו). Ludwig concludes

> In the cult tradition, then, the establishing of the temple at Zion is considered to be the same divine activity as the establishing of earth; building the temple is a repetition of the cosmogony.[9]

He further concludes that the particular formula יסד ארץ which occurs in Pss 24, 78 and 89, among those passages that we have mentioned,

> is a distinct earth-creation formula, stemming from cultic traditions having to do with Yahweh's victory over chaotic forces and the ordering of the world as the dwelling of men. This tradition seems to have been particularly at home in the Zion cult.[10]

It is clear then that the theme of Yahweh as creator is an important one within the Jerusalem cult tradition, and that it is connected in a significant way to the theme of Yahweh's dwelling on Zion as king.[11] This is neither surprising nor controversial, given the association of these themes in the Ugaritic literature and their probable impact upon Israel's formulation of its faith. The same is true, of course, of the Enuma Elish, especially 6.1-72, where the creation, accomplished through Marduk's victory over Tiamat, is crowned by the creation of Babylon and the temple Esagila, the dwelling-place of Marduk. As Jacobsen has demonstrated, this myth is of West Semitic origin.[12] The language of creation in Jerusalem probably reflects a mixture of imagery originally applied to Baal on the one hand and El on the other.[13] This in turn may reflect an early association of 'Schöpfung' and 'Chaoskampf'.

While we need not here debate the issue whether or not there was within the Jerusalem cult an original association of 'Schöpfung' and 'Chaoskampf',[14] it is useful at this juncture to point out the link that is made between the themes of Yahweh as creator and Yahweh as defender. The early connection between creation and redemption has also been contested, by Rendtorff and von Rad, who claim that the two themes were first brought together by Deutero-Isaiah.[15] However, this is most unlikely, as we will attempt to show.

In recent Old Testament studies the role of Yahweh as a warrior who fights in defense of Israel has received a great deal of emphasis. Hence it is hardly novel to claim that Yahweh is conceived in the Jerusalem cult as a defender. However it is important to note that this conception is linked with that of Yahweh as creator, and that both of these are seen as functions derivative of Yahweh's status as king on Zion.

It is entirely likely that the conception of Yahweh as a warrior was tied to the conception of him as king already in the premonarchic period. If, as has recently been argued, texts such as Judges 5, Deuteronomy 33, Habakkuk 3, as well as Exodus 15, and perhaps parts of Psalm 68, are from the pre-monarchic era[16] the early linkage of these two conceptions receives considerable support. In these texts Yahweh is depicted as coming, accompanied by theophanic phenomena, from his home in the South to fight on behalf of his people. The references to kingship in these texts are seldom explicit, as they are in Deut 33.5, but the portrayal of Yahweh in command of his hosts clearly suggests royal characteristics.[17] These texts, which describe Yahweh's 'march in the South',[18] appear to stem from experiences among at least some of the Israelite tribes in the region around Kadesh and have now been fitted into the conception of Yahweh as the God who redeemed all Israel from captivity in Egypt and led them in conquest of the prior occupants of Canaan. Yahweh's kingship is won or secured, as it were, through his conquest of Israel's historical enemies.

In the previous section we suggested a different course of development for the notion of Yahweh's kingship in the Jerusalem cult. The conception of Yahweh's kingship here seems to have been drawn from Canaanite mythological traditions associated with the Ark in Shiloh. These conceptions gained a position of dominance in the Jerusalem cult in which the kingship of Yahweh of Hosts was celebrated. Here the conquest of Israel's enemies continued to be rehearsed, but was now placed within the liturgical framework of the celebration of Yahweh's kingship on Zion. This celebration is, as we have already seen, carried out in terms of themes and motifs drawn from the Canaanite background in which Baal's conquest of the forces of chaos was celebrated. The presence of Canaanite traditions in the Jerusalem cult is not an innovation, since the earliest poems themselves reflect such traditions.[19] What is new is the integration of Yahweh's defense of Israel into the celebration of his kingship on Zion.[20] In this integration the defense of Israel is narrated in terms of Yahweh's conquest of chaos, i.e. in his creative activity (Ps 93), while this mythological pattern is itself given a particular historical valence with the incorporation of references, in some cases explicit, to the defense of Israel. This is clearest in Ps 99 (see above), where Yahweh's enthronement on the cherubim, the result of his conquest of chaos (Ps 97), is connected with his intervention on behalf of Moses, Aaron and Samuel in times of historical crisis.[21]

The significance of the integration of the notion of Yahweh as Israel's defender with that of Yahweh as creator and king is that Yahweh's saving activity, or defense, on behalf of Israel is placed within the comprehensive framework of creation. The order wrought by Yahweh in vanquishing his cosmic foes is at the same time an order wrought among the earthly forces with which Israel was confronted. That this particular integration was not the innovation of Deutero-Isaiah or even the Jerusalem court is evident from the early poems of pre-exilic Israel which used the motifs of cosmic struggle to interpret the defense of Israel by Yahweh. Gerhard von Rad claims that

A special feature in Deutero-Isaiah's thought about creation is, of course, that he does not regard creation as a work by itself, something additional to Jahweh's historical acts. Indeed he seems to make no clear distinction here—for him creation is the first of

Jahweh's miraculous historical acts and a remarkable witness to his
will to save.[22]

But already in Exodus 15 the themes of creation and redemption
are woven together in order to interpret the event here celebrated as
involving more than a struggle between opposing armies.[23] It is
rather a cosmic struggle of Yahweh, here with the Sea as his ally,
against the forces of chaos, a struggle within which Israel's defense
against Egypt is secured.[24] It is further significant that this
celebration occurs at Yahweh's sanctuary (vv. 13, 17), the goal of the
'exodus', where Yahweh reigns for ever and ever. (v. 18).[25]

Within the Jerusalem cult the kingship of Yahweh and his creative-
redemptive activity are celebrated in connection with Zion as the
place of Yahweh's dwelling. This is clear from the Psalms which we
considered in the above paragraphs. In Ps 65, for example, Yahweh
who is 'God in Zion' is praised for his activity of deliverance (ישע),
which is then described in creation terminology (vv. 6-9). In Fisher's
terminology it is creation of the 'Baal type', that is, 'Chaoskampf' or
cosmogony. In Ps 74, which recalls both Exodus 15 and Isaiah 51,
God is implored to 'remember Zion' his dwelling-place (v. 2) and is
described as 'king from of old', whose work of salvation (ישועות, v. 12)
is again described in creation terminology. Finally, in Ps 77, where
Yahweh is given the royal title עליון, his deeds (מעלל יה, v. 12) of
redemption (גאלת בזרוע עמך, v. 16) are described in the same mixture
of exodus and creation terminology found in Isa 51.9-11.[26]

It is quite likely that the notion of Yahweh as a warrior who fights
in defense of Israel was already associated with the title יהוה צבאות in
the Shiloh period, and that the notion and the epithet were both
associated with the Shiloh Ark. As we have already seen, the Ark was
also the locus of the notion of Yahweh's kingship. While there is no
explicit testimony to the effect that the Ark was associated with a
creation or cosmogony tradition, this cannot be strictly ruled out,
since expressions such as those in Num 10.35-36 and Ps 132.8 would
seem to presuppose an original 'Chaoskampf'. In Israel this would
have been joined with a 'Völkerkampf' which, as Jeremias has shown
contra Stolz, is a peculiarly Israelite motif.[27] In any event, within the
Jerusalem cult the notion of Yahweh's kingship was closely associated
with his function as creator and defender of Israel. These two
functions were, in fact, two modes of the same activity.[28]

B. ZION AND DAVID

We have thus far claimed that for the Jerusalem cult the presence of Yahweh as king on Zion is the central theologoumenon, closely associated with the interrelated notions of Yahweh as creator and defender. Before describing further the contours of the symbol Zion, as it was employed in the cult tradition of Jerusalem, it is necessary to consider briefly the relation of this symbol, and the tradition in which it was nurtured, to the tradition of Davidic kingship in Jerusalem.

Even a cursory reading of the material from the Jerusalem cult will reveal the significant place of the monarchy in the cult.[29] Furthermore, the pre-exilic form of the Zion tradition continued to have the monarchy as one of its central components. It is important to recognize, however, that David and Zion are the central symbols of two different traditions and cannot simply be identified, or the one reduced to the other.[30]

There is, we repeat, an important place within the Jerusalem cult tradition for the king whose throne is on Zion. In association with Zion the fundamental role of the king is that of executor of Yahweh's rule,[31] expressed most prominently by the terms משפט and צקדה. As the executor of Yahweh's rule the king is his servant[32] and has responsibility for the 'exercise of justice' and the 'ordering of society'.[33]

> Thus the king, in the ancient Near East just as in many other ancient realms, is a power working in parallel with the creator of the cosmos.[34]

Of course, the degree to which the king's power actually corresponds to, or works in parallel with, that of Yahweh varies even within the Psalms,[35] but the foundation of Yahweh's throne (Pss 97.2; 89.15) are also those of the royal throne (Ps 89.30-34). These foundations, embedded in Zion, provide not only the security and promise of each king's reign, but the critical norm by which it is judged.

It is important to recognize, however, that the role of the monarchy within the cult tradition of Jerusalem, especially as it is expressed in relation to the symbol Zion, is part of the general Near Eastern conception of the king and his political, social and cultic significance.[36] This 'royal ideology' is not yet to be equated with the

Davidic tradition, as this emerged in Judah, and it is still possible and important to draw a distinction between the symbols Zion and David and between the traditions in which they functioned.

In the first place the two traditions formed around Zion and David had different traditio-historical origins. The Zion tradition, whatever its indebtedness to previous traditions associated with Jerusalem may have been,[37] is traditio-historically related to the Ark and specifically to the Ark of the Shiloh sanctuary (see above). The Davidic tradition, on the other hand, while very difficult to assess, evidently arose in connection with the problems of legitimation and succession in the Davidic-Solomonic Court.[38]

This is not yet to deny the possibility or the likelihood that the Zion *tradition*, as it is formulated especially in Pss 46, 48, 76, arose in the time of, or as the imperial expression of, the royal court.[39] It is simply to deny that the concerns lying behind these Psalms are the same as those out of which the Davidic covenant tradition arose. If we were to accept that these Psalms were intended to articulate and justify Israelite-Davidic hegemony over neighboring states, this, a common oriental concern of kings, is still quite some way from the problems of *internal* legitimation and succession which lie behind the Davidic tradition as it is expressed in Pss 89, 132 and various other parts of the Old Testament. The symbol Zion is indisputably associated with claims to hegemony, but these claims are made in Pss 46, 48 and 76 quite apart from the Davidic covenant tradition and, indeed, apart from any mention of the king.

Furthermore, within the Jerusalem cult tradition Zion symbolism was able to function independent of any reference to David. This is evident from the fact, just noted, that the three Songs of Zion (Ps 46, 48, 76) make no mention of David, or of an earthly king at all.[40] So if they do reflect a setting in the Davidic kingdom's celebration of its supremacy over neighboring states,[41] this celebration employs the symbol Zion while it excludes that of David.

In addition, the symbol Zion was able to carry significant cultic meaning exclusive of associations with David. Thus the prophet Ahijah, significantly from Shiloh, condemns Jeroboam for erecting sanctuaries in Bethel and Dan, while granting legitimacy to the rebel king's separate, non-Davidic kingdom (1 Kings 11).[42] Northern attachment to Jerusalem as a cult site is, as is well known, attested still after 587 BC (Jer 41.5-8; here too Shiloh is prominent by its mention).[43]

Again, the monarchy is certainly a significant component of the symbolic design of Zion, but this observation must be kept distinct from any claim that there was, at the time of the United Monarchy, a theology of the Davidic covenant that encompassed the Zion tradition as one of its components. As Levenson has pointed out, the Davidic covenant is fairly restricted within the Old Testament, limited principally to two texts, 2 Samuel 7 and Psalm 89, where the issue is succession, not monarchy *per se*.[44] Hence it was possible for the issues of kingship and royal theology to be taken up independent of a specifically Davidic covenant.[45]

Arguments against the dependence of Zion's 'election' on the election of David have also been raised by Rohland,[46] and his objections are, by and large, convincing. However Rohland is in part responsible for introducing confusion into the debate by speaking of Zion's election, and of the Zion tradition as an election tradition. As we have seen above, Zion, in Jerusalem's earliest cultic traditions, is associated with the creation (יסד) of the earth and is itself created by Yahweh (Isa 14.32) as his dwelling-place. This tradition, originating in connection with traditions from the Shiloh Ark in the pre-Jerusalem period,[47] is the basis for the development of an independent Zion tradition. It is in the later literature, principally Deuteronomistic, that Zion is 'elected' as Yahweh's chosen city (cf. 1 Kgs 8.44, 48; 11.13, 32, 36; 14.21; 2 Kgs 21.7; 23.27).[48] This election, furthermore, is to be understood predominantly in a cultic sense and is probably dependent upon the Deuteronomic doctrine of cult centralization in which the cultic site of Yahweh's choice (Deut 12.5ff.; 14.23ff., etc.) is restricted to Jerusalem.[49] The reference in Ps 132.13 to Yahweh's choice (בחר) of Zion clearly reflects the conjunction of David's and Zion's election which was effected by the Deuteronomists.[50]

The notion of Yahweh's election of Zion first gained general prominence, apart from Deuteronomic material, in the post-exilic period, where it is part of Zechariah's message that Jerusalem is, and will continue to be, Yahweh's chosen (1.17; 2.16; 3.2). Originally, however, Zion is simply the place of Yahweh's dwelling created primordially through the defeat of the powers of chaos.[51] Even on the basis of Ps 132, however, Zion maintains a clear theological priority over David.[52] As we have tried to show, this priority not only rests on theological notions introduced into the historical sources, but accurately reflects the historical development of the two traditions.

It is essential once more to point out that the monarchy did play an essential role within the Jerusalem cult tradition, as this tradition employed the Zion symbol. However the tradition of David's election derives from the theological notion of Yahweh's dwelling on Zion (a notion derived from the Ark tradition) and the theme of David's loyalty to this notion.[53] It is thus historically inaccurate to say that, with respect to the development of the tradition, Yahweh's choices of David and Zion were originally connected. This connection, on the contrary, occurs at the earliest in Ps 132, which incorporates notions of conditionality that may not have been present in the earliest traditions of Yahweh's dealings with David,[54] and quite possibly presuppose the conjunction of Davidic and Sinaitic covenants, which did not come about until the time of Josiah.[55]

Recently J.J.M. Roberts has pointed to the prologue of Hammurabi's code as evidence for 'the original linkage of the choice of David and the choice of Jerusalem'.[56] In this prologue the naming of Hammurabi as the guarantor of justice in Babylon by Anum and Enlil is linked to the bestowal of 'Enlil functions' upon Marduk and the exaltation of Babylon, with Marduk as its king.[57] With this prologue Roberts compares Pss 78.6, 132.10-18, and 2 Samuel 7. While this comparison is cogent with respect to the reconstruction of an original oracle authorizing temple construction, some qualification must be made with respect to the biblical texts. In the prologue to Hammurabi's code the city is designated as the site of Marduk's rule, effected by Hammurabi. The city thus receives its divine legitimation from its association with the god's chosen agent.[58] In Ps 132 the logic is completely the reverse. Zion, in this Psalm, is Yahweh's chosen dwelling and his resting place. David receives divine favor by his act of loyalty in securing the *throne* of Yahweh (the Ark) in the *location* which Yahweh has chosen. Thus, even in this Psalm, whose purpose is presumably to celebrate the covenant of Yahweh with David's house in a festal procession of the Ark, the proper theological relationship between David and Zion is maintained. This same relationship can be seen in Ps 2.6.[59]

Our conclusion is, then, that it is improper to speak in the first instance of a tradition of Zion's election. This notion is a secondary development of the Zion symbol. In the second place, the symbol Zion and the network of which it is a part has a traditio-historical origin and development different from that of the Davidic covenant tradition. In the earliest phase of the cult tradition the theology of

Yahweh's dwelling on Zion was governed by the Ark and the traditions associated with it. David's legitimacy was substantially bound up with his role as caretaker of this Ark. It was only in later theological tradition, more precisely that of the Deuteronomists, that his election was made equivalent to an 'election' of Zion.

More important than the question of the origin of Zion as a symbol in relation to the Davidic tradition is the function which the two traditions served within the Jerusalem cult.[60] Here their differences are most apparent. For example, among the crucial concerns of the Davidic tradition are those of legitimation, succession and hegemony.

The issues of legitimacy and succession appear to have been the special concern of Deuteronomic or Levitical circles who were dispossessed as early as Solomon's death by Jeroboam I. Levites from the South appear to have been champions of David from the period of his association with Hebron,[61] where he was first recognized as king. Whatever the source of David's initial support, his legitimacy was argued within the Jerusalem court on the basis of (a) Yahweh's choice of David as the legitimate successor to Saul, and (b) David's loyalty to Yahweh demonstrated by his concern for the 'Ark of God, designated by the name of Yahweh of Hosts, enthroned upon the Cherubim' (2 Sam 6.2).

The choice of David is narrated in the History of David's Rise which is usually thought to begin at 1 Samuel 16 and to end in 2 Samuel 5.[62] This narrative, produced by the Jerusalem court around the time of Solomon, focuses not only on the choice of David, but upon David's conquest of Zion as well (2 Sam 5.7). Thus the issue of legitimacy is broadened to include David's legitimate control of ציון מצדת, 'fortress Zion' (2 Sam 5.7). Significantly, Zion is here identified explicitly, not as the city of God (עיר אלהים, Ps 46.5; עיר אלהינו, Ps 48.2), but as David's city (עיר דוד). Already, therefore, in the earliest period of the 'royal ideology' the symbol Zion is employed by the royal court to enforce claims of legitimacy for the Davidic custody of the traditions associated with the Ark, now localized at a permanent central sanctuary.

Closely connected with the issue of legitimation is that of succession. These issues are evident in the tradition lying behind 2 Samuel 7, which not only grants David legitimate authority over all Israel but establishes a dynasty whereby David's successors would also be heir to the authority granted him. The Davidic covenant tradition is born of this grant of legitimacy and succession. We have already seen how Ps 132, the clearest witness to a Davidic covenant tradition within the Jerusalem cult, employs the symbol Zion to enforce David's legitimacy and Davidic succession (vv. 12, 13).

It is remarkable how far removed are these concerns with legitimacy and succession, which dominate the Davidic tradition, from the concerns of those Psalms which revolve around the Zion symbol. In the Songs of Zion (Pss 46, 48, 76) the symbol Zion is employed in utter detachment from the earthly king.[63] Neither David nor the monarchy itself is even mentioned in these hymns. The only mention of kingship is with respect to the earthly kings who threaten Zion (48.5) and to whom Yahweh is terrible (76.13). Instead, kingship in these hymns is exhausted by Yahweh (48.3) whose city Zion is. It is only in Pss 78 and 132, both closely associated with the Davidic covenant tradition, that Zion is employed in support of explicitly Davidic claims. As Schreiner points out,[64] no king is ever spoken of as 'King of Zion', a title preserved exclusively for Yahweh. As we shall see, Zion as a central symbol is brought into relation to kingship, but not in terms conformable to the special concerns of the Davidic tradition.

Within the Songs of Zion a dominant theme is the inability of Zion's foes to overwhelm it. Otto Eissfeldt noted that, in the case of Ps 76, this theme fits the situation of the United Monarchy and its expanded control of neighboring territory (cf. 2 Sam 8-10).[65] Subsequently Roberts and Clements have noted the compatibility between the claims of the Zion songs, as well as Ps 47, and the claims to hegemony of the Davidic empire.[66] Particularly useful in this comparison is Ps 2, which seems to combine the motif of the 'Völkerkampf', considered to be part of the Zion tradition, with promises to Yahweh's anointed king, spoken of here as the Son of God. Clements goes on from this observation to understand the Zion tradition as simply a component of the larger royal ideology and an instrument of its political claims.

It is necessary, however, to raise some objections to this conclusion. In the first place, we have already argued that the symbols of Zion and David developed along different traditio-historical paths. Secondly, we have argued that these two symbols operate within different designs or complexes reflecting different concerns. Finally, we need to observe the crucial differences between Ps 2 and the Songs of Zion. To begin with, it is not really apposite to speak of a 'Völkerkampf' lying behind Ps 2.[67] Instead of nations assembling to march against Zion we have in Ps 2 a conspiracy on the part of subject rulers to rebel against an authority which has been imposed upon them. This state of affairs is never encountered in the Zion Psalms. Instead of a rebellion (2.1) the Zion Songs envision an attack upon Zion itself (46.7; 48.5), an attack which Yahweh repels. Furthermore, in Ps 2 the power to crush rebellion is delegated to Yahweh's king, which has no parallel in the Songs of Zion.[68]

The real point of contact with the Zion tradition in Ps 2 is encountered in v. 6, where Yahweh announces that he has consecrated (or anointed) his king on Zion, Yahweh's holy mountain. But here again there is a substantial departure from the Songs of Zion, in which the earthly king plays no role whatever.[69] The symbol Zion is here (2.6) employed in the service of the royal theology to enforce claims to hegemony over neighboring kings and nations. Clements is partially correct in his contention that this Psalm bears a 'general similarity' to the Songs of Zion,[70] but is mistaken in concluding that Ps 2 and the Songs of Zion are 'essentially variant expressions of one basic tradition', namely that arising from the imperialistic claims of the United Monarchy.[71]

Within the cult tradition of Jerusalem claims to hegemony, which urge the obeisance of foreign kings, are part of the royal theology which derives its material from the 'oriental *Hofstil*'. That this is so can easily be illustrated from Ps 72, with its expectation that foreign rulers would demonstrate their fealty to the king in Jerusalem by bringing gifts and licking the dust before him (72.9; cf. Ps 2.11, נשקו ברגלו ברעדה).[72] The similarity between Ps 2 and 72.8-11 is much more direct than that between Ps 2 and the Songs of Zion.[73] The symbol Zion, on the other hand, receives its definition from the traditions originally associated with the Ark, as we have already noted. The situation in the United Monarchy, the expansion of Davidic hegemony over neighboring territory and the developing royal theology, did provide the Jerusalem cult with the opportunity to bring Zion into connection with Davidic claims—as happened here in 2.6. However the different origins of the traditions associated with Zion,[74] along with the continued independence of Zion symbolism from Davidic and often even monarchical claims, caution us once more against reducing Zion to a component of royal, or Davidic, theology.[75]

To summarize, the Davidic tradition, as it develops within the Jerusalem cult, has three characteristic concerns: legitimacy, succession

and hegemony. In articulating these concerns the Davidic tradition
sometimes makes use of the symbol Zion. But the overarching design
of which Zion is the central symbol builds on traditional material
which is not dependent upon the Davidic tradition and, in its
application, continues to function independently and, especially in
Isaiah, critically.

C. ZION AS A SYMBOL OF SECURITY AND REFUGE

1. Zion symbolizes security

As the dwelling-place of Yahweh, creator of the cosmic order and
defender of Israel, Zion functions pre-eminently as a symbol of
security. This component of Zion symbolism has been traditionally
viewed as the predominant aspect of the Zion tradition, leading
scholars to speak of the inviolability of Zion/Jerusalem.[76] For our
present purposes it is sufficient to note that the security symbolized
by Zion is rooted first of all in *Yahweh's presence*.[77]

This is made clear in the Songs of Zion themselves. For example,
Ps 46.6 declares that

אלהים בקרבה בל תמוט　　　Elohim is in her midst, she will not
　　　　　　　　　　　　　be moved.

The term מוט is particularly at home in the language of the Jerusalem
cult and refers principally to the quavering of the mountains and the
earth in the presence of the threat of chaos.[78] Thus, in Ps 93.1 the
establishment of the earth by Yahweh means that it is secure and
shall not quaver (similarly Ps 96.10; cf. Isa 54.10). Here in Ps 46 the
security of Zion, grounded in God's presence in her midst, is
contrasted to the quavering (מוט) of the nations (v. 7).[79]

Similarly in Ps 48 it is Yahweh's presence in Zion, his city, that is
the ground of its invincibility against the attacks of the enemy kings
(vv. 5-9). In v. 4 God (Elohim) is said to have proven himself within
Zion's citadels to be her stronghold.[80] The character of Zion's
security is then demonstrated by the repulsion of the kings, who fell
into panic as they saw the city defended by Yahweh.[81]

Again in Ps 76.2-3 the security of Zion, which is here described in
terms of Yahweh's destruction of the implements of war,[82] is
grounded in the presence of Yahweh in the city:

נודע ביהודה אלהים　　　God is known in Judah
בירושלים גדול שמו　　　and in Jerusalem his name is great.
ויהי בשלם סכו　　　His abode is in Salem
ומעונתו בציון　　　his dwelling-place in Zion.

There then follows the typical description of Yahweh's triumph over the hostile forces which would attack Jerusalem.

Thus within the Songs of Zion, the three Psalms most exemplary of the Zion tradition, Zion is first of all a symbol of security—security grounded in the presence of Yahweh in her midst. But this grounding of Zion's security in the presence of Yahweh as king is not limited to the Songs of Zion. It is found in other Psalms that reflect the fundamental notions of the Jerusalem cult. For example, Ps 20.2-3, a Psalm whose precise date and *Sitz im Leben* are a matter of conjecture,[83] invokes the aid (עזר) of Yahweh from the sanctuary on Zion in a time of distress:

יענך יהוה ביום צרה	May Yahweh answer you in the day of distress
ישגבך שם אלהי יעקב	And may the name of the God of Jacob defend you.
ישלח עזרך מקדש	May he send you help from the sanctuary[84]
ומציון יסעדך	And may he support you from Zion.

As v. 7 makes clear, the security symbolized by Zion in vv. 2-3 is to be translated concretely into the victory of Yahweh's anointed. But as v. 8 makes equally clear this victory is to the exclusive credit of the God who dwells on Zion and not to the king and his armaments.[85]

The same notion is expressed in later literature from the tradition of the Jerusalem cult, for example Ps 9.10-13.[86] Yahweh is described here as a stronghold or refuge (משגב) to those who are oppressed (דך). This description is part of a confession in which Yahweh's faithfulness is praised (vv. 10-11; לא עזבת דרשיך יהוה, v. 11b). There follows an exhortation to praise in which it is affirmed that Yahweh dwells (as king) on Zion:

זמרו ליהוה ישב ציון	Sing to Yahweh who reigns on Zion
הגידו בעמים עלילותיו	Tell his deeds among the peoples
כי דרש דמים אותם זכר	For the avenger of blood remembers them,
לא שכח צעקת עניים	He will not forget the cry of the lowly (9.12-13).

Thus Yahweh's presence on Zion imbues it with the power to function as a symbol of security, particularly for the ענײם.[88]

This latter term is of particular importance for the design of the Zion symbolism in the Jerusalem cult. עני and other terms within the general semantic field of 'the poor' have been thought to designate a distinct sociological group or party within Israel,[89] or, on the other hand, to refer to those who suffer some specific and concrete oppression.[90] It is indeed true that in the late period the 'poor' can comprise specific groups of a certain sectarian nature. The Qumran community, for example, referred to itself as 'the poor of the flock' (עניי הצאן, CD 19. 7-9, quoting Zech 13.7). Here the term is used to refer to the community which is separated from the defiled priesthood of Jerusalem.[91] While this late usage surely has its roots within the Old Testament it is hazardous to read the Old Testament references to the poor in terms of later separatist or sectarian tendencies. This is not to deny, however, a certain polemical intention in the use of these terms, particularly in Isaiah.

On the other hand, it may indeed be the case that the poor or lowly are those who suffer from some concrete form of oppression, but the terms certainly have a broader reference which allows them to be used by precisely those in such a state of oppression, and particularly by those who later formed sectarian movements defined by new (in their minds) forms of piety. This broader reference is to be found in our text (Ps 9.12-13). It consists in the belief, tied up in the Jerusalem cult with the symbol of Zion, that only Yahweh who dwells on Zion is the source of security.[92] Within the language of the Jerusalem cult the עניים are those whose only refuge and security is Yahweh. They have no independent power to secure their own salvation or security and thus seek it in the presence of Yahweh who guarantees righteous judgment.[93] John Gray aptly defines the 'poor' as 'those dependent on the grace of God ... and who patiently endured ... ',[94] while Kraus claims that 'the "poor" enjoy unparalleled privileges on Zion, which has its ground solely in that Yahweh is the God of the helpless'.[95]

It is particularly characteristic of these 'poor' that they trust (בטח) in Yahweh alone. In Ps 9.11 this is clearly expressed with reference to the oppressed. In Ps 86.1-2 the petitioner implores Yahweh to hear his case because he is lowly and poor (עני ואביון) and describes himself as Yahweh's servant who trusts (בטח) in him.[96] The posture of trust is described concretely in Ps 40. Here one who is עני ואביון (v. 18) affirms that the one who makes Yahweh his trust is the opposite of the proud (רהבים, v. 5). This contrast of 'the poor and the proud' is further elaborated in Jer 17.5-8, to which Ps 40.5 has a clear relation.[97] According to Jeremiah, one who trusts in human strength (יבטח באדם // שם בשר זרעו, v. 5) is cursed, while the one who trusts Yahweh is blessed (v. 7). In Jeremiah the language is clearly that of Wisdom, but the prophet moves on to tie his observation to the affirmation that Zion, 'the place of our sanctuary', is 'a throne of glory, exalted forever'.[98]

Throughout the literature of the Jerusalem cult the proud or arrogant are described as those who repose in their own security, in direct contrast to the poor. In Ps 10, which forms a unit with Ps 9, the proud person is portrayed as saying in his heart, בל אמוט (v. 6). This is just the opposite attitude of those who trust in Yahweh and who have security in Zion because Yahweh is in its midst and בל תמוט (Ps 46.6).

This range of meaning connected with בטח is evident in other texts as well. For example, the term לבטח is used in Ezek 38.14 to mean 'securely', with reference to the restored community of Israel which, in the face of attack from Gog, dwells under Yahweh's care. In Judg 18.7, 27 reference is made to

העם יושבת / יושב / לבטח
שקט ובטח ואין מכלים דבר בארץ

Boling renders this verse (18.7), referring to the citizens of Laish:

> The folk . . . living securely . . . calm and confident—without anyone perverting anything in the territory or usurping coercive power.[99]

The attitude of the poor is precisely the corollary of those who dwell securely (לבטח). They are those who trust Yahweh for their security and appeal to him for their defense. As von Rad has said,

> In fact, a great number of references understand these poor quite frankly and directly as those who can justifiably expect protection. This state of being poor also includes a defenselessness and helplessness, as a result of which these men who pray designate themselves as cast upon Jahweh alone, as those who seek Jahweh and him alone (Pss 22:27[26]; 69:33[32]) . . . The 'poor man' who commits his affairs to God is the meek one who renounces all claims to conduct his own cause.[100]

It is within this broad framework that references to the poor are to be understood. They are those for whom Yahweh alone is security and it is in him alone that they trust. And it is for them that Zion stands as a symbol of security. In Ps 9/10 Yahweh who is enthroned on Zion is the one to whom the helpless abandon themselves (9.11; 10.14).

We conclude then that Zion is a symbol of security in the first instance because Yahweh is present there. Even after Jerusalem has been destroyed this language can be employed to urge Yahweh to remember Zion his dwelling-place as the symbol of Israel's past and future security (Ps 74.2; cf. Zeph 3.15; Ps 122).[101] But of equal importance, the security to be found in Zion calls forth a particular response, designated as trust. This response is characteristic of the עניים, who, unlike the proud who rely on their own strength, rely on Yahweh alone for their security.[102] In Ps 9 the radical counterpart to the power of Yahweh is the weakness of אנוש (cf. Ps 103.15; Isa 5.15; 40.6; note also Pss 8.5; 144.3; Isa 31.3),[103] and it is specifically the arrogance of the גוים that they do not realize that they are merely אנוש (9.20-21). In ch. 10, appeal to Yahweh by the poor (v. 12) is grounded in his eternal kingship (v. 16) and the confidence that he will intervene for the poor in the face of the tyranny of the אנוש מן הארץ (v. 18).

The contrast in these Psalms between the trust of the עני, who finds security in Yahweh alone, and the proud who rely on their own strength, is even clearer if we follow Ginsberg's suggestion that גוים in Pss 9.16, 18, 20, 21 and 10.16 should actually be read as גאים meaning the 'haughty', or 'proud'.[104] Ginsberg's argument has been expanded by Stanley N. Rosenbaum, who notes that at Qumran 'aleph is often elided since it can be used as a medial *mater lectionis*.[105] Since this is the case, a word written as גים could indicate an original גאים but be read at Qumran as גוים, and 'the haughty' could thus become 'the nations'. Rosenbaum also notes that within the Psalms גאים is often found in parallel with רשעים, but that the latter is not usually found in parallel with גוים. He takes this as further evidence that in Ps 9/10 the equation is not between the wicked and the nations, but between the wicked and the proud.[106] We will see below that 'pride' is considered the fundamental sin in texts related to Zion symbolism, and this pride takes the concrete form of dependence upon one's own resources, or those of an ally, rather than upon Yahweh. Thus Rosenbaum's suggestion also makes sense on other than linguistic grounds.[107]

2. Zion is thus a symbol of security for those who trust alone in Yahweh who dwells there and, by implication, a symbol of judgment against those who seek other sources of security.[108] More specifically, Zion's power as a symbol of security is rooted in Yahweh's *presence as king*.

We have already explored in some detail the centrality of the theme of Yahweh's royal presence on Zion within the tradition of the Jerusalem cult. We have also had occasion to note that the security symbolized by Zion is rooted in Yahweh's kingship on Zion in our discussion of Ps 9.12-13. This theological notion lies behind other texts as well. In Ps 47, for example, the procession of the Ark into the temple is accompanied by the declaration that 'Yahweh is Elyon, the great king'. This declaration is justified by the observation that Yahweh subdued the surrounding nations (v. 4) and reigns over them from his holy throne (v.9). Thus Yahweh can be said to be 'king over all the earth' (v. 8).[109] Zion symbolizes security because Yahweh reigns there as the king who conquered the powers of chaos hostile to cosmic order, and who subdues Israel's potential foes.[110]

We have noted above that Zion as a symbol of security is paramount in Ps 48. But it is important also to note that Zion has this symbolic power not because of some mythological power inherent in the mountain itself, but because it is the site of Yahweh's royal dwelling and hence the site of his defeat of the hostile kings (vv. 5-9).[111] Because the hostile forces have been defeated praise can be offered to Yahweh, and Zion and 'the daughters of Judah' can be glad (vv. 10-12). I see little possibility, nor do I see the value, of identifying the attack of the hostile kings with a specific historical event. That is not to say that the confession of Zion's security (v. 9) does not arise out of historical experience, but this experience is of the continuing security of the city grounded in Yahweh's primordial conquest of his foes.[112]

Finally, evidence for the dwelling of Yahweh on Zion as the theological basis for Zion as a symbol of security is to be found in Ps 80, particularly vv. 2-3.[113] In this lament Yahweh is called upon to 'turn again' (v. 14) and restore Israel (vv. 4, 8, 19) from its deplorable situation to its former glory (vv. 11, 12). The term 'Zion' does not occur in this Psalm, but the language of vv. 2-4 is clearly taken from the tradition of the Ark, which was itself the principal theological source of the Zion tradition.

This tradition is particularly evident in the depiction of Yahweh as 'seated upon the cherubim' in v. 2. We have already shown that this title is associated with the Ark in Shiloh, along with the more common designation of Yahweh as צבאות. Thus it is not surprising that this latter title is used four times in the Psalm (vv. 5, 8, 15, 20),

accounting for over one-quarter of its occurrences in the entire
Psalter. (In vv. 8 and 15 אלהים appears instead of יהוה). These titles,
we have argued, are used particularly in association with the Ark to
designate Yahweh as *king*. It is in his royal function that Yahweh is
here called upon to fight against his foes on behalf of the northern
tribes.[114]

The use of the term הופיעה ('shine forth') here is particularly
instructive. In early Israelite literature (Deut 33.2-5) and in the
Ugaritic texts (*CTA* 3.D.34//3.D.49; 2.1.3) it is 'a term of battle
particularly associated with deity', and 'clearly refers to the conflicts
or battles between the gods'.[115] In Ps 80, as is typical in Israelite
literature, the battle between deities is transposed into a battle
between Yahweh and the enemies of Israel.

Thus the theological notions, and indeed the language of Ps 80.2-3,
are part of the same tradition that forms the theological background
of the use of Zion as a symbol in the tradition of the Jerusalem cult.
In Ps 80, as in Pss 47 and 48, this tradition is utilized to express the
security to be found in Zion, the dwelling-place of Yahweh. Although
Zion is not explicitly mentioned in Ps 80 it is obviously the central
symbol lying behind these expressions. When Yahweh is urged to
'shine forth', it is clearly understood that it is Yahweh who reigns
from Zion who is here called upon as Israel's security, for it is 'from
Zion, the crown of beauty', that Yahweh shines forth (הופיע, Ps
50.2).[116]

3. Zion symbolizes security, which is rooted in Yahweh's presence
there as king and in his power as *creator and defender*.

Earlier we showed that fundamental to the Zion symbolism in the
Jerusalem cult is the belief that Zion is Yahweh's royal residence, and
that his dual function as king is that of creator and defender. We have
further shown that Zion chiefly symbolizes security, and that this
security is rooted theologically in the notion of Zion as the site of
Yahweh's presence as king. Again it is important to note that Zion
conveys such security because Yahweh's rule entails his principal
roles of creator and defender.

This aspect of Zion as a symbol of security can be clearly seen in
Ps 24. As we saw above, Ps 24 is an 'entrance liturgy', celebrating the
ritual return of the Ark, symbolizing the presence of Yahweh, to its
place in the temple on Zion (הר קרש). The introductory unit of the
Psalm proclaims that all the earth belongs to Yahweh because he has

created it (יסדה, vv. 1-2). Following the torah in vv. 3-6, Yahweh's entrance, via the Ark, is announced with the declaration that he is the מלך הכבוד, 'Yahweh powerful and mighty, Yahweh mighty in battle' (v. 8). The Psalm concludes with the question, 'Who is this king of glory?' answered by 'Yahweh of hosts, he is the king of glory' (v. 10).

Yahweh's dwelling on Zion is thus that of the king who is both the creator of the world and the defender of those who stand in his holy place in innocence and purity (vv. 2-3). His dual activity as creator and defender is again illustrated in Ps 89.9-15.[117] Here the defeat of Yahweh's enemies is portrayed in creation language, and it is presumably through his victory over the powers of chaos (Rahab, v. 11) that Yahweh wins or secures ownership of the earth (v. 12). That Yahweh is here conceived as king is indicated by the mention of his throne in v. 15.

While Ps 89 makes no explicit mention of Zion, although that is obviously the location of his throne, his role of defender is explicitly connected with the security of Zion in the Songs of Zion themselves (cf. Pss 46.9-11; 48.5-9; 76.5-7). While Yahweh is portrayed as king and defender in these Psalms, there is no explicit mention of creation. However it is probable that the hostile forces here led by the enemy kings are the counterpart to the forces of chaos which Yahweh has conquered in his primordial act of creation. For example, the term 'rebuke' (גערה) in Ps 76.7 is used frequently in the Jerusalem cult tradition to indicate Yahweh's conquest of chaos in creation. Thus in Ps 18.16 (= 2 Sam 22.16) Yahweh's 'rebuke'[118] laid bare the foundations of the world. That is to say, the waters, symbolic of chaos, responded to Yahweh's rebuke. In Ps 104.7 the waters again respond to Yahweh's rebuke, resulting in the creation of mountains and valleys. And in Isa 50.2 the power of Yahweh to redeem Israel is exemplified by his power as creator, because he is able to dry up the sea by his rebuke.[119] Thus, when the nations are repelled by Yahweh's rebuke, we should understand this as Yahweh's creative power exercised against the hostile forces of chaos on behalf of Zion. Such a parallel between Yahweh's rebuke of the sea and his rebuke of Zion's enemies is to be found elsewhere within the tradition of the Jerusalem cult, in Nahum 1.4, for example, and most clearly in Isa 17.13. There the roaring of the nations is compared to the roaring of 'many waters',[120] and just as the waters responded to the rebuke or 'roar' of Yahweh, so the hostile nations which attack

Zion will flee at his גערה. Similarly, Stolz argues that the Exodus itself, as celebrated in Ps 114, is described in terms drawn from the *Chaoskampf* and Yahweh's 'roar'.[121]

Thus the security symbolized by Zion was not rooted in some mythological power inherent in the mountain itself, but in the theology of Yahweh's kingship on Zion. Zion symbolized security because the divine king who resided there exercised his royalty in his dual activity as creator and defender.

4. *Zion symbolizes refuge*

Since it symbolizes security as the site of Yahweh's royal presence, Zion is also symbolic of refuge.[122] This is immediately clear from the first of the Songs of Zion, Ps 46. The Psalm opens with the declaration that Yahweh is a strong refuge (מחסה ועז) for his people in the face of a trembling and threatening earth (v. 2). The second unit of the Psalm concludes with the description of the 'God of Jacob' as a refuge (משגב) for his people (v. 8). This character of Yahweh is demonstrated through his primordial conquest of the powers of chaos and his presence in Zion, guaranteeing its stability (v. 6). Finally, the Psalm concludes with the confession that God is present for his people as their refuge (משגב, v. 12). Here his character as a refuge is demonstrated through his elimination of wars and ultimate destruction of the military arsenal. Zion's power as a symbol of refuge is thus derived from the presence of Yahweh, the constant defender from the threat of chaos, in its midst.

The character of Zion as a refuge is further developed in Ps 48. Here Zion is identified as the city of Yahweh, the great king, who has shown himself to be a refuge (משגב) within the city. The close association between Yahweh's royal presence in Zion and its power to symbolize refuge is evident at the conclusion of the Psalm (vv. 13-15), where Yahweh himself assumes the attributes of the city. The worshipper is here encouraged to consider the fortress Zion in order to be able to tell the coming generation that זה אלהים (v. 15a).[123] Thus, when in Ps 46.2, 8, 12 Yahweh is declared to be a refuge, this character of Yahweh is understood symbolically in relation to the city itself which both is and symbolizes security and refuge, because it stands as the effect of Yahweh's activity as creator and defender.[124] As Steck has said

> God's character as a defender of the worshipper expresses itself in
> the invincibility of the city (cf. 48.13-14), and the invincibility of

the city is grounded not simply in the thickness of its walls and towers, but in the power of the God who is in its midst.[125]

The development of Zion as a symbol of refuge is most likely associated, traditio-historically, with the Ark sanctuary as a place of refuge—i.e., the site of the Ark was a sanctuary in the true sense of the term.[126] We have already shown that the Zion tradition developed to a great extent out of traditions previously associated with the Ark. In particular we noted that the epithet יהוה צבאות was associated with the Ark at Shiloh and that the name of the patriarch *Jacob* came in a particular way to be associated with Zion (cf. above, ch. 2). It is thus striking that in Ps 46, in the two passages which speak of Yahweh as a refuge (vv. 8, 12), the formulation is repeated:

יהוה צבאות עמנו

משגב לנו אלהי יעקב   (v. 8)

יהוה צבאות עמנו

משגב לנו אלהי יעקב   (v. 12)

Here the epithet 'God of Jacob', which is rooted in the Zion tradition, is in parallel with the designation יהוה צבאות. The same pair of epithets is used in Ps 84, a pilgrimage hymn in praise of the sanctuary at Zion. In v. 9, יהוה אלהים צבאות parallels אלהי יעקב. Furthermore, the pilgrimage hymn in Isa 2.2-4 refers to the goal of this international pilgrimage as the mountain of Yahweh // the house of the God of Jacob.[127]

We may thus conclude that Zion as a symbol of refuge is related to the older traditions of the Ark, which was the goal of Israel's pilgrimage in its early hymnody (Ps 24). The pilgrimage of the faithful was to the site of their security and refuge (cf. especially Isa 30.29).

In the previous section we noted in particular that Zion as a symbol of security was related to the *presence* of Yahweh in Zion as *king*. So too Zion as a symbol of refuge is rooted first of all in Yahweh's presence there. For example, in Ps 11 the speaker begins with the affirmation that he takes refuge (חסה) in Yahweh (v. 1). Verse 2 then describes the violent measures taken by the wicked (רשעים) which stand in contrast to the trust of the righteous (v. 3). In v. 3 the dilemma of the righteous is raised: since they have only their trust in Yahweh to ward off the arrows of the wicked, if the 'foundations' are destroyed, if chaos and violence reign, the trust of the righteous is groundless.[128] This dilemma is resolved in vv. 4ff., where it is asserted that the presence of Yahweh in his temple guarantees the maintenance of the foundations and hence guarantees the vindication of those who seek refuge (חסה) in him over the violence (חמס) of the wicked. In other words, refuge is to be sought in the presence of Yahweh, who can be found in his temple.[129]

Furthermore, Zion as a symbol of refuge is explicitly associated with Yahweh's presence there as *king*.[130] This is stated most explicitly in Zeph 3.12, 15.[131] Verse 12 states that Yahweh will leave in Zion's midst (the verbs are 2nd f.s.) a poor and humble people (עני ודל) and חסו בשם יהוה: 'They will take refuge in the name of Yahweh'.[132] This affirmation is substantiated in v. 15 with the declaration that Zion need no more fear because Yahweh has removed her enemies:

מלך ישראל יהוה בקרבך	The King of Israel, Yahweh, is in your midst,
לא תירא רע עוד	You need fear evil no longer.

5. Just as the power of Zion as a symbol of security is rooted in Yahweh's royal presence and his activity as *creator and defender*, these two aspects of his rule also stand behind Zion as a symbol of refuge.[133]

Yahweh's *creative* activity is revealed especially in the Songs of Zion, in which he is portrayed as victor over the powers of chaos which threaten his people. Since we have dealt with this material above, it is sufficient here to point out that in Ps 46, as well as in 48.9; 78.69; 87.1, 5 and 125.1-2,[134] Yahweh's creative triumph over the hostile powers results in the establishment of Zion, his city. (The verbs are הכון, יסד.) Within Ps 46 the city itself, the site of Yahweh's throne, stands as a symbol of refuge.

We have also indicated that Yahweh's activity as *defender* stands behind Zion as a symbol of security (see ch. 2, above). We may again point to Ps 9.10-11, where Yahweh who dwells in Zion is depicted as a refuge and as a defender of the 'poor' who trust in him. Reference could also be made to Ps 14.6-7, where Yahweh is declared to be a refuge (מחסה) for the poor (עני) and the bestower of salvation upon Israel. This salvation is said to come from Zion, the concrete symbol of refuge.[135]

Before proceeding it is necessary to make a couple of further comments on Zion as a symbol of security and refuge. We have noted especially in connection with Psalms 46 and 48 that the motifs

employed to indicate security and refuge are often ambiguous
between Yahweh and Zion as the referent. This is particularly the
case in Ps 48.13-15.[136] This ambiguity stems, of course, from the
close association between Yahweh and Zion, so that both Yahweh
and Zion can be said to be a refuge (Ps 46.2; Isa 14.32).

This close association, or even ambiguity, between Zion and
Yahweh is perhaps most visible in one feature that appears in several
Psalms that speak of Zion or Yahweh as a refuge, namely their
designation of Yahweh as a 'Rock'. For example, in Ps 18.3 Yahweh is
said by the author to be his rock (סלע) and fortress, his refuge (משגב)
and deliverer. He is then further described as a rock (צור) in whom
the author seeks refuge, or trusts (חסה).[137] The connection between
Yahweh as a rock and the notion of refuge is also to be found in
Psalms 28, 31, 62 and 71. Each of these Psalms is an appeal to
Yahweh for help, expressing the confidence that in Yahweh refuge is
to be found. The designation of Yahweh as a rock is likely due
precisely to his association with Zion, the 'rock' which symbolizes
the presence of Yahweh as the security and refuge of his worshippers.
Yahweh is he who dwells on the 'holy rock',[138] and is himself a sure
rock of refuge. That Yahweh as Israel's refuge is symbolized
concretely by Zion is evident from Isa 30.29, where הר יהוה is in
parallel with צור ישראל.[139] As Kaiser notes,

> The parallelism suggests that the 'rock of Israel' is the holy rock of
> the temple site, on which the altar of burnt offerings stood, and
> which was regarded in Judaism as the stone which kept the
> primeval sea locked up.[140]

Within the Jerusalem cult tradition Yahweh as a 'rock' was
primarily a symbol of refuge, and this symbolism had its physical
pole in Mount Zion.

Special note should be here taken of Dieter Eichhorn's study on
'God as Rock, Fortress and Refuge',[141] in which he draws attention to
the association of Yahweh as 'Rock' and 'Refuge' with the Zion
sanctuary.[142] He says by way of summary that

> The 'holy rock' is the place at which Yahweh reveals himself as the
> one who protects his people and intervenes against the powers of
> chaos and 'the nations' (Pss 46, 48 and 76).[143]

Eichhorn relates this portrayal of Yahweh to Deut 32.15, 18, 30 and
31, which he considers to be the 'programmatic' elaboration of the
themes of 'Rock, Fortress and Refuge', taken by him to be of

Canaanite provenance.[144] One need not accept Eichhorn's suggestion of an institutional 'Mittler' within the Jerusalem cult, although this is not an entirely unlikely suggestion, to benefit from his study of the theme of refuge.

Within the Jerusalem cult tradition, then, Yahweh as a 'Rock' is primarily a symbol of refuge, and this symbolism has its physiological pole in Mount Zion.[145] To refer again to the language of Victor Turner from our introductory chapter, 'Mount Zion' is the 'iconic' symbol vehicle and 'Yahweh as a Rock of Refuge' is part of that set of denotations that constitutes with Yahweh's kingship Zion symbolism's primary range of meaning.[146]

Related to these observations concerning Yahweh as a 'Rock' and Zion as a symbol of refuge is the association of Zion with stability, specifically the 'stability' of those who seek refuge in Zion. Earlier the term מוט was seen to be used especially in connection with the Zion symbol. We went on to point out that the promise of stability is given to those who trust (בטח) or seek refuge (חסה) in Yahweh, preeminently the עניים. We can now expand these observations in connection with Zion as a symbol of refuge. The various thematic associations toward which we have been pointing are clearest in Ps 62. In the opening verses it is declared:

אך אל אלהים דומיה נפשי	On God alone my soul waits in silence,[147]
ממנו ישועתי	From him is my salvation.
אך הוא צורי וישועתי משגבי	He alone is my rock and my salvation, my refuge.
לא אמוט רבה	I shall hardly be moved.[148]

This affirmation is repeated in vv. 6-8, with some modification, followed by the exhortation, 'Trust in him all you people' (v. 9a).[149] This exhortation is based on the observation that Yahweh is a refuge (מחסה) for his people while humankind (בני אדם // בני איש) is a delusion and of no weight, nor worthy of trust (בטח, vv.10-11).[150] The Psalm concludes with the affirmation that power and steadfastness (עז and חסד) are God's.

Here, then, the consistent theological emphases of the symbolism associated with Zion are clear: God alone, specifically the God of Zion, the Rock, is a refuge. This refuge is available to those who trust. It is important in this connection to realize that the term בטח, 'trust', has both a positive and a negative connotation.[151] It is positive in that it is specifically related to the object of trust, and it is negative in that it rules out all other potential objects. Thus the verb has an exclusionary sense that should not be ignored. The positive object of trust, Yahweh in this case, is the power or entity upon which or in whom confidence and reliance are placed. Since the verb thus specifies that which is of life-determining significance for a person or a people it excludes all other possible objects of trust as by definition illegitimate.[152] Within the context of Zion symbolism the emphasis on trust in Yahweh is related quite explicitly to the exclusion of trust in anything else, and specifically it is related to the futility of trust in human power.

This last aspect, the ultimate disillusionment of those who trust in human powers, is related to the emphasis on arrogance as the fundamental sin within the Zion symbolism. We have already suggested this in connection with our discussion of Ps 9/10 above. We can now expand on this by pointing to Ps 75. Here the 'boasters' and the wicked[153] are urged not to boast or to exalt themselves (v. 5). This is then continued in v. 6:

| אל תרימו למרום קרנכם | Raise not your horn against the exalted one |
| תדברו בצור עתק | Nor speak arrogantly against the Rock.[154] |

The Psalm goes on to say that 'exaltation' (הרים) is God's prerogative (vv. 7-8) and the appropriate response of the righteous, who will be ultimately exalted over the 'horns of the wicked', is to 'sing praises in the name of the God of Jacob', whose anchorage in the Zion tradition we have already noted.[155]

In another Psalm from the Jerusalem cult, Ps 15—an entrance liturgy similar to Ps 24—, the behavior of those who have access to Yahweh's 'tent' and his mountain is spelled out with much greater precision.[156] The torah in vv. 2-5a is concluded with the promise that 'the one who does these things shall never be moved' (לא ימוט לעולם, cf. 112.6). This promise may be contrasted to that in Ps 52, where the one (גבר) who refuses to make God his refuge, trusting (במח) rather in his wealth and seeking refuge in it (v. 9), is contrasted to the righteous one who trusts (במח) in the faithfulness of God for ever and stands in the בית אלהים (v. 10). In this Psalm the גבור (v. 3), the mighty man, is caricatured as one who acts arrogantly in seeking refuge in his own strength and cunning, while the righteous is one who trusts only in God. Within the context of the symbolism of Zion

'Man' becomes a symbol of arrogance and, paradoxically, weakness
—one who seeks refuge elsewhere than in the Rock (on) Zion. The
righteous, by contrast, is one who trusts only in God and seeks refuge
in his sanctuary on Zion. It is the poor, the one whose only refuge is
Yahweh on Zion, who stands secure (לא ימוט לעולם).

עצת עני תבישו   You would shame the counsel of the poor,
כי יהוה מחסהו   But Yahweh is his refuge.

Chapter 4

YAHWEH'S EXCLUSIVE PREROGATIVE

Introduction

In the preceding chapters we have emphasized that Zion is the
central symbol of the Jerusalem cult tradition, and that the primary
meaning of this symbol is that Yahweh reigns as king on Zion. This
kingship is concretely exercised in Yahweh's dual role of creator/
defender, in such a way that Zion symbolizes the security and refuge
provided by Yahweh for his people. Given the nature of Israelite
religion, as well as the logic of kingship language itself, it is
understandable that the kingship of Yahweh is an exclusive kingship
shared with no one else. But of equal significance is the recognition
that Yahweh is to be the *only* source of security and refuge and thus
the only object of faith and trust.

In this chapter we will investigate a notion related to Zion
symbolism, a notion based on both Yahweh's exclusive kingship and
his exclusive status as provider of security for his people. This notion
we will term 'Yahweh's exclusive prerogative', for reasons that will
become clear in the course of the investigation. After examining the
development of this notion in the Psalms of the Jerusalem cult we
will turn to the question of its traditio-historical origin. This question
will involve us particularly in a discussion of Isaiah, a prophet who
employs Zion symbolism extensively and particularly in relation to
the notion of Yahweh's exclusive prerogative.

We will devote a substantial amount of space to this chapter
because the importance of the notion here under investigation to
Zion symbolism, or to the Jerusalem cult tradition, has not been
sufficiently appreciated. Furthermore, I believe that an adequate
understanding of Yahweh's exclusive prerogative is vitally important
to a consideration of the contribution that the symbolic design in

which Zion is central can make to a theological appropriation of Old Testament traditions.

A. YAHWEH'S EXCLUSIVE PREROGATIVE
IN PSALMS FROM THE JERUSALEM CULT

1. *Yahweh's Exaltation and Human Subordination*

As we have seen, it was part of the logic of the ascription of kingship to Yahweh that he alone was king and was, by virtue of his monarchical status, the exclusive source of security and refuge. This logic is evident in Ps 82, to choose only one text. This well-known text places Yahweh at the head of the divine council, a position reserved to the head of the pantheon (i.e. the king), for the purpose of demonstrating the subordinate position of all other divine beings over against 'the fact of the total rule of Yahweh in the divine realm'.[1] The Psalm concludes with an appeal to Yahweh to execute judgment on the earth, grounded in the significant confession that he owns all the earth (v. 8). The verb used here is תנחל ב, which is especially appropriate in the designation of a territory owned by a god, in which he 'exercises undisputed power'.[2]

To be sure, the Enthronement Psalms at which we have looked in some detail also have as their central affirmation that it is Yahweh who is king, to the exclusion of any other possible contenders, and it is pointed out there and in other Psalms that Yahweh's kingship involves the subordination of other powers in such a way that Yahweh alone is powerful. To quote Ps 97.9 once more, 'For you, O Yahweh, are *Elyon* over the whole earth, highly exalted over all gods'.

Among the texts that we examined in the previous chapter the conclusion is drawn from Yahweh's exclusive kinghsip and consequent monopoly of power in the cosmic realm, that Yahweh alone is a source of security and refuge. This is perhaps most evident in Ps 9/10 (cf. above, ch. 3). There, particularly in 9.12-13, Yahweh who reigns as king on Zion is portrayed as the defender of his people, especially the 'poor' (עני) who appeal to him.[3] As we pointed out earlier, the 'poor' in the language of the Jerusalem cult tradition are those for whom Yahweh alone is security and refuge. It is of critical importance to recognize that the meaning of עני in this case is not limited to its designation of a particular social class,[4] but is a part of the larger theological claim that Yahweh alone has the prerogative to provide such security and refuge. That this is the case is evident from two further considerations.

a. First of all it is affirmed in 9.11 that the poor on behalf of whom Yahweh provides security and refuge on Zion are those who trust in Yahweh, namely those who 'know his name'.[5] As we have seen, there is in the use of the term בטח an emphasis on the exclusive object of trust.[6] In addition to the texts already referred to, the delimitation of the object of trust is clear in the Deuteronomistic texts in 2 Kgs 18–19. Here in the speech of the Rabshekah the residents of Judah are urged to abandon their exclusive reliance on Yahweh and recognize the superior strength of the king of Assyria. In his opening remarks to Hezekiah the Rabshekah asks him, 'What is this security on which you now rely?'[7] The security referred to here is Egypt, to which Hezekiah has turned in alliance. Rabshekah describes this as trust in false security and proceeds to discourage reliance on Yahweh, on whom the people might stake their security (v. 22), by reminding them that Hezekiah has torn down Yahweh's altars. Thus, according to the Rabshekah, there are three possible objects of trust, Assyria, Egypt, and Yahweh. While he goes on to encourage the belief that the Assyrian king is acting at Yahweh's behest, it is clear from 18.30 that the Rabshekah regards trust in Assyria to be fundamentally incompatible with trust in Yahweh. 'Do not allow Hezekiah to lead you into trusting Yahweh, by saying, "Yahweh will surely rescue us and this city will not be given into the hand of Assyria's king".' The issue, as the Rabshekah goes on to make clear, is purely one of relative power, and the power of Assyria's king has demonstrated itself superior to that of all other gods. Since there is no reason to think that Yahweh will prove any more capable than these other local deities, prudence requires trusting the Assyrian king, not Yahweh.

Similarly, when in Ps 9 the poor are described as those who trust in Yahweh this is to be taken as excluding other possible objects of trust.[8] Referring again to Ps 9/10, it is not only the object of trust that is specified, namely Yahweh enthroned on Zion, but also that which is unworthy of trust. If Ps 82 portrays Yahweh as exercising 'the total rule of Yahweh in the divine realm', then Ps 9/10 excludes one power in particular from consideration as exercising the prerogative of power on earth, namely אנוש, humankind. Ps 9 itself concludes with an appeal to Yahweh to arise and prevent אנוש from prevailing, with the motivation that Yahweh should not ignore the cry of the

עניים (v. 20). This is then followed by the hope that Yahweh will
instill fear in the nations, or the proud,[9] and will thus remind them
that they are but אנוש. Thus, as we have remarked earlier, אנוש,
mortal humankind, is established as a category whose opposite
within the sphere of the exercise of dominion over human affairs is
Yahweh.[10]

b. In the second place, then, the larger theological claim that
Yahweh reserves to himself the prerogative of providing security and
refuge is evident in what we might call the 'anthropology of Zion'. As
is clear from Ps 9/10 this anthropology is concerned to locate אנוש[11]
between two principal poles: on the one hand the poor or innocent
(10.8-9), on the other hand Yahweh. These two poles are those in
relation to which the 'nature' of אנוש can be illuminated because it is
precisely the action of אנוש in tyrannizing and oppressing the poor
that indicates his repudiation of Yahweh. Since it is Yahweh who
provides security and refuge for the poor, the arrogance of אנוש
consists in seeking to create security for himself through his own
power. The arrogance of this behavior is not due simply to its violent
mistreatment of the innocent poor (10.8-9), but to its basis in the
renunciation of Yahweh. The אנוש who tyrannizes the poor is
depicted as arrogant, finding security in himself, because he does not
recognize that Yahweh provides refuge for the poor in Zion and there
provides equitable judgment (9.9). Thus, to tyrannize the poor is to
renounce Yahweh (10.3, 13—נאץ יהוה) precisely because it is to
elevate אנוש, who is like grass (Ps 103.15), to the place of Yahweh as
the only one who legitimately exercises power or justly determines its
exercise.[12] The ultimate basis for this character of אנוש is in his
conviction that 'there is no God' who will call him to account
(10.4, 11).[13]

It is this component of Zion symbolism that we wish to emphasize
here: that Yahweh reserves to himself the exclusive prerogative as the
effective agent in providing security and refuge for his people. That
is, he reserves power to himself in the exercise of his dominion.[14]
That is why all human attempts to insure security which rely on the
power or capacity of humankind are repudiated in the Jerusalem cult
tradition as acts of arrogance and rebellion against Yahweh.[15] Within
the language of the Jerusalem cult the opposite of 'poor' is not 'rich',
but 'proud'.[16]

It is unnecessary to examine every text in which the poor are
opposed to the proud, and the latter are in a fundamental sense the

enemies of Yahweh. I will merely note here a number of passages from the Jerusalem cult tradition or related literature in which this notion is expressed.[17]

Ps. 138.16—Yahweh is 'high', but sees the lowly; the proud he knows only from afar.

Ps 101.5—Yahweh cannot tolerate the proud.

Jer 13.15—Pride is contrasted with giving glory to Yahweh.

Ps 18.28—Yahweh saves the poor but brings down the lofty.[18]

Ps 66.7—Do not let the rebellious exalt themselves.

Ps 94.2-7—The proud and arrogant claim that God is impotent to take note as they arrogantly afflict the poor (cf. Ps 10). Pride is equivalent to a kind of atheism; the poor take refuge in the 'God of Jacob'.

Ps 123—Yahweh's servants are contrasted to the contemptuous proud who scorn the servants of Yahweh, who is enthroned in the heavens.[19]

Zeph 2.10—The pride of Moab and Ammon caused their destruction.

Ps 131.19-24—The righteous are contrasted with the proud, and the faithful are contrasted with those who act arrogantly.

Prov 16.18—Pride precedes destruction and a haughty spirit precedes a fall.

Prov 20.33—'The pride of a man will bring him low, but the lowly in spirit obtains glory.'

These various images are clearly connected in Hannah's Song (1 Sam 2.1-10), where Yahweh is the exalted rock of refuge (v. 2) and hence his people are urged not to speak proudly (גבהה) or arrogantly (עתק), because God shatters the bows of the mighty and he is the one who exalts and humbles (vv. 3-8).[20] From this it is concluded that 'a man does not prevail by his might'[21] and that Yahweh will shatter his adversaries (מריבו, vv. 9, 10).[22]

It is quite evident that the Song of Hannah is related to the Psalms from the Jerusalem cult tradition. One could point to the epithet צור ascribed to Yahweh in v. 2; Yahweh's opposition to arrogance and pride in v. 3; the reference to his breaking the bows of the mighty in v. 4; the creation language in v. 8; the contrast of חסיד and wicked in v. 9; the denial that one triumphs through might in v. 9b;[23] and of course the reference to Yahweh's anointed in v. 10.[24]

The most obvious evidence for the Song's connection with the Jerusalem cult tradition, besides its content, is its partial counterpart in Ps 113. There is dispute about whether the Song[25] or Psalm 113[26] is earlier, but there seems to be general agreement that this poetry is ancient. It may well be that it pre-dates the monarchy and hence is earlier than the development of the Jerusalem cult tradition and the Zion symbolism within it. This is not, however, a refutation of our attempt to relate the notions expressed in the Song of Hannah to the symbolism of Zion within the Jerusalem cult tradition. First of all, it is clear from the later material to which we have already made reference that these notions came to be associated with Zion, whatever their origin may have been. Our argument is not that every component of the theology that came to have Zion as its central symbol *originated* with Zion, or developed first in relation to it. Our argument is simply that Zion *did* function as the central symbol within this complex theology of the Jerusalem cult.

Secondly, the occurrence of these themes within the Song of Hannah, especially if the Song in its original form predates the monarchy, supports the argument made earlier in Chapter 2 that the traditio-historical origin of the Zion tradition is to be found in association with the Ark at Shiloh. Willis claims that the Song of Hannah was originally associated with the Ark and was a 'Song of Victory at the Shiloh sanctuary in connection with some triumph of a tribe or tribes of Israel over some enemy, possibly the Philistines'.[27] The present location of the text, in the midst of a narrative centering on the sanctuary at Shiloh, speaks for its association with that shrine, and hence with the Ark of Shiloh and its connection with the epithets of Yahweh, צבאות and ישב הכרובים (cf. above). These epithets, which emphasize the exaltation of Yahweh as king, are not employed in this text, but the thrust of the Song of Hannah accords well with the notion that Yahweh alone is exalted and his exaltation entails the 'making low' (v. 7) of the arrogant who exalt themselves.[28] This notion was evidently carried with the Ark to Jerusalem, where David's initial attempt at self-exaltation through the construction of a temple was rebuffed.[29]

We may conclude then that the Song of Hannah is a part of the tradition which thrived in the Jerusalem cult and maintained that the poor are vindicated by Yahweh against their common enemy, the proud.[30]

Thus, within the language of the Jerusalem cult tradition there is a clear and consistent emphasis on 'trust' with Yahweh as its exclusive object, and on the proud who are contrasted with the poor. While it is characteristic of the 'poor' that they trust in Yahweh for security and refuge, the proud arrogate to themselves Yahweh's exclusive prerogative and assume the power he has reserved to himself.

In conclusion we may point to Ps 86, where one who is עני and אביון as well as חסיד, describes himself as אליך הבוטח (vv. 1, 2). Pitted against him are the זדים (arrogant, insolent) and the עריצים (tryannical, ruthless) who do not consider God (לא שמוך לנגדם, v. 14b; cf. 54.5). Here is expressed the conviction that trust in Yahweh is the contrary of the arrogant tyranny of those who have no regard for God. This conviction is joined with another in vv. 8-10, that Yahweh is strictly incomparable and he alone is God.[31]

If we return to Ps 9/10 we see in 9.9-13, 20-21; 10.4-6, 16-18 conceptions common to the material from the Jerusalem cult tradition: that Yahweh who reigns on Zion rescues the poor, who trust (only) in him, from the wicked, who are the arrogant usurpers of prerogatives belonging only to Yahweh. They are guilty of the fundamental sin, in connection with the Zion symbol, the failure to recognize that they are merely אנוש.[32]

The exaltation of Yahweh as king on Zion thus has as its corollary the humbling of humankind, whose prerogatives are circumscribed by those of Yahweh.[33] It is important to appreciate the theological scope of this notion before examining (1) its application to more concrete situations and (2) its appropriation of common ancient Near Eastern imagery.

2. *Yahweh's Exclusive Prerogative*

We noted above in discussing Ps 86 that Yahweh's incomparability is extended in this Psalm to include his distinction from the insolent and ruthless oppressors who hate Yahweh's servant (86.16). That is, Yahweh's character is described in this Psalm as being distinct both from other deities and from *human* practitioners of violence. It is this notion, that Yahweh is incomparable to, and thus distinct from, not only divine but human powers as well, that we now take up.

a. *Psalm 118*
This kind of incomparability is stated forcefully in Ps 118, a ritual Psalm from the tradition of the Jerusalem cult.[34] The Psalm opens with a liturgy of thanksgiving and then moves, in vv. 5-21, to an individual hymn of trust.[35] Following the introduction to this hymn

in v. 5, in which the experience of the speaker is briefly summarized,[36] there issues a confession in which the speaker expresses the conviction that

יהוה לי לא אירא	Yahweh is for me, I will not fear.
מה יעשה לי אדם	What can 'man' do to me?
יהוה לי בעזרי	Yahweh is for me as my helper
ואני אראה בשנאי	And I shall gloat over my enemies.
טוב לחסות ביהוה	It is better to seek refuge in Yahweh
מבטח באדם	Than to turst in 'man'.
טוב לחסות ביהוה	It is better to seek refuge in Yahweh
מבטח בנדיבים	Than to trust in nobles.[37]

It is obvious that this Psalm participates in the broad range of notions which we have earlier found to be associated with the symbol Zion in the Jerusalem cult tradition. This is clear first of all in the reference to Yahweh as a refuge. Here, as in Ps 11 and other Psalms referred to above, the speaker is threatened by superior forces who place his life in jeopardy. In the face of these threats Yahweh is a reliable refuge. As in the other Psalms which speak of Yahweh as a refuge, this notion is here bound up very closely with pilgrimage to the house of Yahweh, namely the temple on Zion. Thus, in vv. 19, 20 the speaker requests that the 'gates of victory' (צדק) be opened that he may enter and give thanks to Yah(weh). And in vv. 26, 27 he pronounces a blessing on those who enter the temple and encourages some kind of decoration of the horns of the altar.[38] In other words, the Psalm does not report simply an episode of deliverance on the part of a king or some other individual, but rather, as form and content make clear, confesses that this deliverance testifies to the character of Yahweh *as* a refuge, a refuge to be found in his temple on Zion.[39]

Further, as we might have expected, Yahweh as a refuge is closely connected with trust (בטח). Trust, as we have seen, has not only a positive sense in designating the object of trust, but a negative or restrictive sense in excluding all other potential objects of trust. Given the emphasis in the Jerusalem cult on the 'incomparability' of Yahweh, we should not have been surprised had the Psalm gone on to contrast trust in Yahweh with trust in other gods, or in 'the work of our hands', as it is put in Hosea 14.4. In the speech of Rabshekah mentioned above this is precisely the issue. But, as we went on to note, the incomparability of Yahweh is not limited to his status among other deities, but is applied in numerous texts to his strict

incomparability to potential human objects of trust in such a way
that those who do not recognize this sense of Yahweh's incomparability
exalt themselves (or humanity: אנוש // אדם) to a status reserved
exclusively for Yahweh.

It is in this sense that trust in Yahweh is mentioned in Ps 118, a
sense made explicit in vv. 8, 9, where seeking refuge in Yahweh is
said to be superior to trusting in אדם or in נדיבים.[40] Within the
structure of Ps 118 this confession is grounded in the experience of
the speaker who was surrounded by enemies and was delivered from
them by Yahweh, in whose name he consecrates them.[41] It is stated
explicitly in v. 14 that this deliverance occurred through the power of
Yahweh, not through any human agency, either the speaker's or
anyone else's. As the speaker says in v. 14,

עזי וזמרתי יה	My strength and my song are Yah!
ויהי לי לישועה	And he became my salvation.[42]

The only agency through which this deliverance occurred,
according to the testimony of the Psalm, was Yahweh's 'right hand'
which performs powerfully and is exalted. Victory depicted as won
by Yahweh's right hand is typical within the languages of the
Jerusalem cult and is particularly descriptive of the role of Yahweh as
creator/defender, the dual activity of his kingship. For example, in Ps
89.10-14 Yahweh, who reigns on the throne supported by משפט and
צדק (v. 15), establishes his universal order through the defeat of the
powers of chaos, represented by the sea and the mythical Rahab
(vv. 10-11). The description of his activity is concluded with the
declaration that

לך זרוע עם גבורה	Yours is an arm full of power
תעז ידך	Your hand is mighty
תרום ימינך	Your right hand is exalted (v. 14)

The earliest references to Yahweh's right hand are also set in
mythological contexts in which Yahweh achieves victory over his and
Israel's foes. The earliest such text is Exodus 15, which Ps 118 seems
to have drawn heavily upon.[43] It was Yahweh's right hand that
defeated the enemy, here the particular, historical enemy of
Pharaoh's army, and was thus glorified in power (v. 6). Similarly in
vv. 11-12 it is said that Yahweh, who is incomparable among the
gods, stretched out his right hand and through this act caused the
earth to swallow Pharaoh's chariots and his army.[44]

Again in Deuteronomy 33 Yahweh is depicted as intervening on behalf of Israel and triumphing over their common foes with the power of his right hand. Here that power is elaborated more extensively and is seen to be provided by Yahweh's host, described as 'the warriors of the gods' (33.2).[45] Here too the battle is waged by Yahweh alone through the heavenly forces at his disposal, without any participation by Israel, other than to enjoy the prosperity brought about by Yahweh's victory (33.28).[46]

In Ps 118, then, there is expressed the belief rooted in the oldest of Israel's literature that Yahweh is solely responsible for creating the security and refuge that Israel enjoys. This notion was particularly at home in the Jerusalem cult in whose theology Zion was the central symbol. In one of the Songs of Zion, Ps 48, Zion itself has reason for joy precisely because Yahweh's right hand 'is filled with victory' (צדק, v. 11). Even more to the point, Ps 78.54 claims that Zion itself was the holy territory, or holy mountain that Yahweh's right hand created.[47] Zion, itself the creation of Yahweh's right hand, thus stands as a symbol of Yahweh's power, through which Israel enjoys security and refuge. This power is the prerogative of Yahweh as king on Zion;[48] and it is his *exclusive* prerogative. In the language of Ps 118, it is because Yahweh's right hand brings salvation that it is better to take refuge in Yahweh than to trust in any human help. Just this claim is made in two other Psalms that mention Yahweh's right hand as the exclusive source of victory (Pss 20.7; 44.4), and in other texts associated with the Zion symbolism of the Jerusalem cult.

b. *Psalms 20, 44 and 33*

We have seen that Yahweh who reigns as king on Zion exercises his exclusive prerogative in reserving power to himself, meaning that Yahweh himself is a refuge worthy of trust, while no refuge contrived of human power is, and that the attempts of humans to create their own security are to be regarded as arrogant. This basic conviction of the Jerusalem cult tradition is stated with particular clarity in Ps 20, a royal Psalm with clearly liturgical features.

Psalm 20 is formally divided into three sections: a plea on behalf of the king (2-6); an expression of confidence that the plea wll be heard (7-9); a summary repetition of the plea (10).[49] We noted earlier that the plea on behalf of the king is made on the basis of fundamental notions of the Jerusalem cult in association with the symbol Zion.

This is particularly clear in the use of the name of 'God of Jacob' in v. 2, and in the hope expressed in v. 3 that Yahweh's help would be sent from the sanctuary, which is taken in the parallel portion of the verse to mean that Yahweh's support would come from Zion.

Of particular interest to us is the connection between this use of Zion symbolism and the content of the expression of confidence that the plea will be heard in vv. 7-8.

עתה ידעתי כי הושיע יהוה משיחו
יענהו משמי קדשו בגברות ישע ימינו
אלה ברכב ואלה בסוסים
ואנחנו בשם [ ] אלהינו נזכיר

> Now I know that Yahweh rescues his anointed,
> He answers him from his holy heaven
> With the mighty salvation of his right hand.
> Some with the chariot and some with horses,
> But we are mighty through the name of our God.[50]

In this text there are two important features requiring special note. First of all the salvation performed by Yahweh on behalf of his anointed, i.e. the 'mighty salvation of his right hand', is in v. 3 explicitly connected with Zion. It is from his sanctuary on Zion that Yahweh comes to the aid of his anointed. Zion's power as a symbol of security is thus related concretely to the role or task of the king, whether in a specific situation or as part of the regular ritual. The text does not reveal how this relation was effected liturgically, but the suggestion that a 'fear not' oracle was spoken between verses 6 and 7 is to be taken seriously, since these oracles are common in situations where a leader is confronted with a difficult task, especially in war.[51] In any event the assistance promised is to come from Yahweh, and concretely from Zion.

Secondly, in this text the mighty salvation of Yahweh's right hand is related to the exclusive prerogative of Yahweh in reserving power to himself. That is the force of the confession that it is not through chariots and horses, the typically symbolic instruments of war, that Israel is powerful, but through the name of Israel's God.[52] This point is not made, as in Ps 118, by depicting human help as futile (cf. 60.12-13), or, as in Ps 9/10, by condemning strictly human attempts to provide security as acts of arrogance. Here the point is made by contrasting the success of those who rely on Yahweh for their power to the futility of those who rely for strength on the weapons of war.

All three texts are in agreement, however, that Yahweh reserves to himself prerogatives which may not be usurped by human beings or their instruments.[53]

Psalm 44. A second text which makes the same point in a way similar to Ps 20 is Ps 44.5-9. This text is placed within a community lament which complains to Yahweh that he has sold his people and scattered them among the nations (v. 12). This has often been taken to mean that the Psalm was composed in exile, sometime after 587.[54] However, not only is it unclear that dispersal is to be simply equated with the exile, but the language of dispersal and re-gathering seems to have been part of the royal ideology in both Mesopotamia and Israel.[55] Thus this language may well be traditional language of lamentation. There is good reason to believe that the Psalm is from the pre-exilic period.[56]

The section of the Psalm with which we are concerned, vv. 5-9, is preceded by a historical confession in vv. 2-4, and is followed by the lamentation proper in vv. 10-27. Verses 5-9 themselves are a confession of trust, similar in structure and content to Ps 20.7-8. This confession begins with the identification of Yahweh as King, ordaining salvation for Jacob.[57] This is followed in v. 6 by the statement that it is through Yahweh's name that Israel triumphs over its foes.[58] This triumph through Yahweh's name is then linked causally to the confession in v. 7:

כי לא בקשתי אבטח	Because not in my bow do I trust,
וחרבי לא תושיעני	Nor does my sword save me.

This confession is contrasted in the following verse (v. 8) with the positive affirmation that it was Yahweh who saved Israel from its enemies and put them to shame. The section is drawn to a close with the summary statement that it has been Yahweh in whom Israel boasted and his name that was praised (v. 9). Thus a clear contrast is drawn between trust (בטח) in bows and swords and trust in Yahweh. This contrast is grounded ultimately in the declaration that begins the confession of trust, namely that 'you are my king, O God' (v. 5). While Ps 20.7-8 contrasted power derived from reliance on chariot and horses with help derived from the site of Yahweh's temple on Zion, Ps 44.5-9 contrasts trust in bow and sword with deliverance by Yahweh and victory achieved in his name.[59]

In both of these texts, then, there is a deliberate distinction of Yahweh's power, and the security it provides, from human power and its incapacity to win security or deliverance. In both texts the image of Yahweh's right hand is used to enforce this point. In 20.7 the 'mighty salvation of his right hand' is Yahweh's answer 'from his holy heaven' to pleas on behalf of his anointed. In Ps 44 Yahweh's right hand is not mentioned in the confession of trust, but rather in the historical confession which introduces the community lament. In these verses the speakers refer back to the conquest of the land in terms of the deeds related by 'our fathers' (v. 2). These deeds, specifically driving out the nations from before Israel, were accomplished by Yahweh's 'hand' (v. 3). This historical confession concludes by making clear that this dispossession of the גוים and the establishment of Israel in their place did not occur through Israel's power. Rather, the victory was completely the act of Yahweh (v. 4):

כי לא בחרבם ירשו ארץ	For not by their sword did they possess the land,
וזרועם לא הושיעה למו	Nor did their arm win victory for them
כי ימינך וזרועך	But your right hand and your arm
ואור פניך	And the light of your face,
כי רציתם	Because you favored them.[60]

Since I am drawing attention to these texts in connection with a discussion of Yahweh's exclusive prerogative, and since this discussion follows on our observation regarding the Jerusalem cult tradition's notion of the futility of *human* attempts to create security, it might seem in place at this point to raise the question of human participation in Yahweh's acts of salvation on behalf of Israel. Does Yahweh's exclusive prerogative involve a 'synergism' with human efforts, or does it exclude such participation in principle?[61] At the same time it might seem appropriate to raise the traditio-historical question regarding the relation of these two texts to the tradition of 'Holy War', and to ask whether Ps 20.7-8 and 44.5-9 are brought into relation to Zion from this tradition. Prior to addressing these questions, however, we will look briefly at Psalm 33, which bears on both of them.

Psalm 33 is often thought to be quite late, either because of its form[62] or because of its content, particularly its use of traditional materials.[63]

However, recent studies have shown this Psalm to be a carefully structured unit. Westermann has shown that following an introductory unit in vv. 1-3 the rest of the Psalm through v. 19 is structured around an interpretation of vv. 4, 5. In particular, the two parts of v. 5, 'He [Yahweh] loves צדקה and משפט', and 'the חסד of Yahweh fills the earth', are elaborated in the three central sections of the Psalm; vv. 6-9 and 10-12 elaborate v. 5a, and vv. 10-12 and 13-19 elaborate v. 5b.[64] More recently Jean Marcel Vincent has studied the structure of Ps 33 in greater detail and has shown how the two major parts of the poem, vv. 1-12 and vv. 13-22, correspond to each other.[65] Thus vv. 13-15 correspond to vv. 6-9 in talking about God as creator; vv. 16-19 correspond to vv. 10-12, in drawing certain conclusions from creation regarding threats of disorder; vv. 18-19 are an explication of v. 12 in speaking of Yahweh's people.

Vincent also notes that the poetry of the Psalm contains a number of parallel pairs of words found typically in both Hebrew and Ugaritic poetry.[66] This of itself would not conclusively indicate an early date, but it does indicate that the Psalm was consciously structured with a good knowledge of traditional poetic form. Since there is nothing in the content of the Psalm that demands a late date, and since the structure of the Psalm cannot be used as evidence for a late date, there is no obvious reason why it should be dated to the exile or later.[67]

There is general agreement that the Psalm was used in some liturgical setting, but since so few clues are given in the text itself most of these suggestions consist of simply assigning the Psalm to one of the known or supposed festivals in Israel's cultic year.[68]

For our discussion of Yahweh's exclusive prerogative the critical verses in the Psalm are 16-17. The language here is strikingly close to that of Pss 20.7-8 and 44.5-9.

> אין המלך נושע ברב חיל
> גבור לא ינצל ברב כח
> שקר הסוס לתשועה
> וברב חילו לא ימלט

> No king is saved by the greatness of his army
> No warrior is delivered by the greatness of his strength
> The horse is useless for victory
> And cannot rescue with his great strength.[69]

In this passage human power, that of a king or a warrior, is declared to be futile for precisely its intended pupose, namely for salvation, for security. Even the war horse, the extension of human military power, is useless despite its great strength. In Ps 20.7-8 stength derived from horses and chariots is contrasted with strength derived from Yahweh through the power of his right hand. In Ps 44. 5-9 confidence (בטח) in bow and sword is contrasted with confidence in Yahweh's right hand. Here in Ps 33 this same line of thought is continued, but it is also expanded in such a way that the power of the king himself, and that of his army, is irrelevant to the normal function of just such power. This function, the provision of security, is comprehensively described through the use of three different verbs, ישע, נצל and מלט.[70] The text does not assert that these functions will cease to be performed, only that the king's power, that of his warriors, or that of his war horses, is irrelevant to this performance. The text thus emphasizes in the clearest possible way that Yahweh has exercised his exclusive prerogative by claiming that the power to provide security, which in any monarchical society is the prerogative of the king, is not in fact at the king's disposal. No king has, strictly speaking, the power to provide security; no king, that is, but Yahweh.

In Pss 20 and 44, the texts we examined above, the futility of reliance upon human power for security was contrasted with the reliable power of Yahweh's 'right hand', which, in Ps 44, was credited with freeing Israel and bringing it to the land. In Ps 33 the positive theological affirmation is both different and more elaborate. First of all, the text goes on, after repudiating the power of the king and his army as an instrument of security, to indicate that redemption (נצל)[71] is something accomplished by Yahweh (v. 19). As in our discussion above, where Zion was seen to be particularly a symbol of security for the poor, so here where Yahweh and not the power of the king is seen to provide security, there is a kind of delimitation:

> והנה עין יהוה אל יראיו
> למיחלים לחסדו

> See, the eye of Yahweh is on those who fear him
> On those who wait for this faithfulness.

It is these whom Yahweh delivers from death and preserves during famine (v. 19), those who fear him. Recalling Ps 118.7, we may say that the fear of the power of Yahweh renders unnecessary fear of human power. To quote Walther Zimmerli,

'Fear of God' becomes quite generally a term of the piety that brings people within the orbit of Yahweh's protection: 'In the fear of Yahweh there is confidence and trust, even for God's children he (Yahweh) is a refuge. The fear of Yahweh is a fountain of life, so that one may escape the snares of death' (Prov. 14:26-27). Thus one might almost say: whoever fears Yahweh need have no fear, but whoever does not fear Yahweh must have fear.[72]

The conclusion to this hymn is important (vv. 20-22), summarizing the fundamental stance of those who fear Yahweh,[73] but it is especially important to recognize next the theological context within which the whole of vv. 16-19 has been placed. The immediate context of this section is formed by vv. 13-15, the verses immediately preceding it. This unit, which opens the second half of the hymn, is significant in that it establishes the basis for the repudiation of human power, in this case royal power, in providing security by pointing to the kingship of Yahweh. It is thus similar to Ps 44, which opens the unit proclaiming the futility of trust in bow or sword, the military instruments of security, by affirming that 'you are our king, O God!' (44.5). In Ps 33.13-14, this affirmation of Yahweh's kingship is more elaborate:

משמים הביט יהוה
ראה את כל בני האדם
ממכון שבתו השגיח
אל כל ישבי הארץ

From heaven Yahweh looks down,
He sees all humankind.
From his place of enthronement he peers
At all who dwell on the earth.

Thus the basis for the affirmation of Ps 33.16-17, that royal power is futile in establishing security, is grounded in the fundamental notion of the Jerusalem cult tradition, that Yahweh is king on Zion. While Zion is not mentioned in this text it is obvious that Yahweh's throne is there (v. 14). The phrase 'place of your enthronement' occurs in 1 Kgs 8.13 in the context of Solomon's dedication of the temple in Jerusalem, and that is where Yahweh's throne is in Ps 33. The fact that Yahweh looks down from heaven does not contradict this, since Yahweh's throne, like that of other gods, is on the mountain at the top of which heaven and earth meet.[74] We already noted that in Ps 20.7-8 the futility of reliance upon horses and chariots is based upon the belief that help comes from the sanctuary on Zion (p. 91). The same notion is thus represented here, only in much stronger terms. In Ps 33, Yahweh's kingship on Zion is placed in direct opposition to the power of the king, who is unable to save even himself[75] with the power at his own disposal.

Finally, the second half of this hymn, vv. 13-22, is provided with a comprehensive theological context in vv. 1-12. This context is the creation of the world by Yahweh. The first part of the hymn opens, following the introduction in vv. 1-3, with a reason for praise (introduced by כי), namely the character of Yahweh. A string of adjectives is used to delineate that character: משפט, צדקה, אמונה, ישר, and חסד (vv. 4-5). Then, in vv. 6-9, this character of Yahweh is demonstrated in his creation. The creation itself is said to have been accomplished by Yahweh's word:

$$\text{בדבר יהוה שמים נעשו}$$
$$\text{וברוח פיו כל צבאם}$$

By the word of Yahweh the heavens were made,
And by the wind of his mouth all their host.[76]

It is very important to see the connections made in this section of the hymn between Yahweh's character and the creation which ensues by his word. It is probably that connection which governs the terminology here, since the affirmation that Yahweh's word was the active agent emphasizes precisely the exclusive relationship between Yahweh and his creation. This relationship is exclusive in the sense that the creation is to be seen exclusively as the expression of Yahweh himself. As Vincent says, creation is the 'realization of the love (חסד) of God'.[77]

Talk of God as creator is, of course, especially the concern of the Jerusalem cult tradition and in a text which portrays God as king on his throne it is natural to talk also of God as creator. The language of v. 7, which speaks of Yahweh 'containing' the מי הים and the תהומות, is particularly at home in the Jerusalem cult, as we have seen earlier in our discussion of Yahweh as king and creator. The 'waters of the sea' and 'the great deep' are of course representative of the powers of chaos and it is the work of God as creator that places these powers within the bounds of creation.[78]

However, it is important to note that Yahweh's creation does not mean the establishment of an order of nature which is self-governing and operates in some kind of harmony apart from Yahweh's care, and indeed his intervention. Thus the Psalm moves on to speak in vv. 10-11 of two contrasting sets of plans, those of the nations and those of Yahweh. These verses assert that Yahweh sets aside the thoughts and plans of the nations, but Yahweh's plan stands for ever, and the thoughts of his heart abide 'from generation to generation'. As Kraus says,

> Since the realm of creation is at the same time the realm of Yahweh's sovereignty (v. 10; cf. Ps 24.1-2), the plans of the nations that strive for dominance in history cannot come to fruition (cf. Isa 8.10). The creator of the world is the sovereign Lord of history in every moment. His plan alone prevails (v. 11).[79]

Once again, then, Yahweh's kingship, which is set forth in vv. 13-15, is tied concretely to his dual role of creator/defender. His defense in this case consists of carrying forth his plan, established in creation, consistent with his character described by משפט, צדקה, אמונה, ישר and חסד, against those forces—the nations—which operate differently. It is this activity of defender that links these verses (10-11) with the concluding verse of the first unit:

אשרי הגוי אשר יהוה אלהיו
העם בחר לנחלה לו

> Blessed is the nation whose God is Yahweh
> The people he chose for his own possession.

Israel is blessed because Yahweh has chosen this nation to be his own possession, thus bringing it under the protection of his plan, rooted in his peculiar character expressed in the creation of the world and the conquest of the powers of chaos, cosmic and historical, which pose a threat to that nation. Even within vv. 13-15, following the description of Yahweh enthroned as king, he is described as the sole creator[80] not only of the world, but of the 'heart' of those who dwell within it. For that reason he comprehends the works of the world's inhabitants (v. 15) and thus maintains his prerogative over them. It is only after this assertion, and after the context of Yahweh's creation of the world has been established, that the Psalm declares that kings have no independent power to provide security, even though they possess the personnel and the weapons of war.

Thus, in Ps 33 the exclusive prerogative of Yahweh is grounded immediately in his kingship and then in creation. It is because Yahweh who created the heavens is the king who reigns in heaven (vv. 6, 13) that the plans of nations are thwarted and kings are not independently powerful. It is because this is the case that Israel can confess its blessedness as Yahweh's chosen people and can at the same time wait confidently for Yahweh (vv. 12, 20-22), for the power of kings and their armies is rendered impotent in the face of Israel's God who is truly king, because he is truly creator.[81] Once more we see that the notion of Yahweh as Israel's defender is integrated with the notion of him as creator, both of them unified in his kingship—an exclusive kingship on Zion.[82]

c. *Summary*

We have looked at two groups of Psalms in this section, both of which have to do with the exclusive prerogative of Yahweh. First of all, in Pss 9/10 and 118 we showed that this exclusive prerogative is argued in opposition to the merely apparent power of human beings. In Ps 9/10 the point was made by depicting human claims to power as arrogance against God, because they assumed exactly the opposite posture from that of the poor. While the poor are characterized by trust in Yahweh, the arrogant, who do not recognize that they are merely אנוש, are characterized by their repudiation of Yahweh and their assumption of power in his place. In Ps 118 the point was made by contrasting the impotence of אדם to the power of Yahweh. These two, human power and that of Yahweh, are presented as options for trust. The Psalm emphasizes the futility of trust in the first and the appropriateness of trust in the second. It is because of the power of Yahweh's right hand that the speaker in Ps 118 claims to have no need to fear אדם.

We also saw that the theme of Yahweh's indignation at pride, and his concern and love for the poor, is a constant theme in the Psalms from Jerusalem's cult tradition, and showed that this theme is already in evidence in the Song of Hannah. In this Song the exaltation of Yahweh is pitted against all human self-exaltation and human power is consequently of no avail in achieving security.

In the second group of Psalms the problem of power is addressed more directly. In Pss 20 and 44 the issue is stated in terms of confidence in weapons of war versus confidence in Yahweh, specifically in the power of his right hand. In Ps 33 the power of the king and the warrior, as well as that of the war horse, are brought into the discussion and judged to be inadequate for the provision of security. Yahweh himself is said to be the one who rescues those who fear him.

In all of these Psalms the overarching assumptions behind the statements regarding Yahweh's exclusive prerogative are those peculiar to the Jerusalem cult. Chief among these are the notion that Yahweh is king on Zion, from which he dispenses his help, and that as king he is the creator of the world, the sustainer of its order, and by virtue of this fact the defender of his people. It is important to note, as we remarked in our discussion of Ps 9/10, that Zion, as a symbol of security and refuge provided by Yahweh the king and creator/defender, is at the same time a symbol of the humility[83] which is the appropriate response of those who would claim Zion as their refuge. There is associated with the Zion theology, then, an anthropology of Zion as well.

B. THE ORIGINS OF YAHWEH'S EXCLUSIVE PREROGATIVE

Prior to our discussion of Ps 33 we raised two questions pertaining to the theme of Yahweh's exclusive prerogative. The first question was interpretive: does this exclusive prerogative mean that there was no human participation in Yahweh's acts of salvation? The second question was traditio-historical: does the notion of Yahweh's exclusive prerogative originate in association with Zion symbolism in the tradition of the Jerusalem cult, or does it stem originally from another tradition, such as that of holy war? The first question cannot be answered on the basis of the Psalms texts alone and does not, in any event, seem to be the principal subject addressed in these texts. We will thus delay comment on this question until treating Isaiah, where it is concretely addressed, and restrict ourselves here primarily to the historical question of the origin of the notion itself.

Previous scholarship has centered on two possible sources of what we have called Yahweh's exclusive prerogative. The first of these is the Old Testament tradition of holy war, the second is the broader prophetic tradition. Since we are dealing with this notion in the context of Zion symbolism within the tradition of Jerusalem's cult it is necessary for us to consider whether we should not rather follow other scholars in locating the source of Yahweh's excusive prerogative in either holy war or the prophets. We will examine critically the arguments in favor of these two traditions and then argue for our own conclusion that Yahweh's exclusive prerogative is a notion with its source in the Jerusalem cult tradition. We turn first, then, to holy war as a possible source of the notion.

1. *Holy War*

It might appear most reasonable to assume that the exclusive prerogative of Yahweh originated in the tradition of Israel's holy wars.[84] It is unnecessary for us to arbitrate the numerous points of disagreement in the scholarly debate about holy war in this context. It is sufficient to note that in the texts which von Rad used to demonstrate his thesis of Israel's holy war theology and practice it is characteristic that Yahweh is said to have 'given the enemy into your hand'. That is, in the texts depicting the practice of warfare in the period of the conquest and the period of the judges, victory in war is attributed to Yahweh, who has led Israel in battle. It would make sense then to assume that such texts as Pss 20, 44 and 33, as well as those which downplay human power itself (e.g. 9/10 and 118; 146; 147), derive their theological impetus from the traditions of holy war.

There are, however, two principal difficulties with this position. The first difficulty lies with the contemporary understanding of holy war itself; the second lies with the attribution of Yahweh's exclusive prerogative to the holy war tradition. We will deal with these difficulties in order.

a. In recent scholarship it has been fashionable to distinguish between Yahweh War and Holy War.[85] While the term 'Yahweh War' may be accurately applied to Israel's early experience or tradition of warfare, in the periods of the conquest and the judges, the term 'Holy War' more properly refers to the theologically elaborate schema of holy war characteristic of the Deuteronomistic history.[86] It is important to keep this distinction in mind to avoid the confusion which results when all of the martial imagery occurring in the Old Testament is referred to a supposedly unified tradition of holy war which is its putative source. This occurs, for example, when a subsidiary distinction is not observed, namely the distinction between Yahweh war or holy war and the pervasive motif of the Divine Warrior. While it would not be correct to maintain that these three—Israel's experience in the 'wars of Yahweh', the tradition of holy war and the motif of the Divine Warrior—were unrelated at various points in the history of Old Testament traditions, it would be equally inaccurate to claim that these three can be simply collapsed into each other, so that when we speak of the Divine Warrior we are thereby talking about a holy war tadition or an actual experience of warfare.[87] Rather, we must recognize that talk of Yahweh as Warrior, or as creator/defender, occurs within a wide variety of contexts rooted in various traditions. It is more accurate to view the specific holy war tradition elaborated by the Deuteronomists, in which particularly the exclusivity of Yahweh's action in securing victory is emphasized, as drawing on not only the theme of Yahweh as a Warrior in texts like Exodus 15 and Judges 5, but also on the liturgical traditions of the Jerusalem cult (e.g. Ps 24).[88] In other words, while texts such as Exodus 15 and Judges 5 may provide part of the background for the later Deuteronomistic accounts of Israel's warfare, it is simply inaccurate on traditio-historical grounds to describe this background as 'holy war' and then to conclude that all theological assessments of warfare in, for example, the Jerusalem cult have their roots in Israel's theology of holy war.

b. When the above distinctions are kept in view it becomes increasingly difficult to attribute the exclusive prerogative of Yahweh, as this notion is articulated in the Psalms we have examined, to the influence of a presumed tradition of holy war. This is true in the first place because within those texts which von Rad and others see as portraying Israel's warfare during the period of the judges with the greatest historical accuracy, there is lacking the kind of emphasis on Yahweh's exclusive prerogative found in Pss 20, 33 and 44.[89] It is true, of course, that even within the most historically reliable accounts[90] there is an emphasis on Yahweh as the source of victory, but the lack of human responsibility for this victory is not made the object of theological reflection as it is in Pss 20, 33 and 44.[91] Furthermore, texts such as Exod 14.13-14, 31; Josh 6; Judg 7.2ff.; 1 Sam 17.45-47, etc., which do exhibit such theological reflection, reflect not the period of the wars themselves but a later period in which Israel's wars had become the object of considerable theological elaboration. Gerhard von Rad argues that the context of this theological elaboration was that of 'Solomonic—post-Solomonic humanism', i.e. the Solomonic 'enlightenment'.[92] Fritz Stolz argues in much the same way, but places such elaboration in the traditio-historical context in which Deuteronomic forms of thought and elements of the Jerusalem cult tradition were combined to embrace both exodus and conquest in a unified terminology of warfare.[93] If this argument is correct, as I believe it is, it becomes impossible to look to Israel's holy war tradition for the source of Yahweh's exclusive prerogative, as this notion appears in texts from the Jerusalem cult tradition, since this latter tradition provides certain of the assumptions on the basis of which the holy war tradition is itself formulated.

Furthermore, when in the Deuteronomistic history something akin to Yahweh's exclusive prerogative is developed it is in different terms and with different objectives from those we find in Psalms 20, 33, 44 and 118 (cf. Pss 60, 147). In the Deuteronomic/Deuteronomistic texts the discussion is more properly of Yahweh's 'incomparability',[94] contrasted to other deities, and serves to protect the Yahweh cult from the threat of impurity. Thus in the holy war tradition itself warfare is concerned fundamentally with the continued religious or cultic existence of Israel.[95] The exclusive prerogative of Yahweh, as it occurs in the Psalms, has an entirely different dynamic and does not reflect this primary concern for cultic purity.[96]

On the basis of the preceding paragraphs the conclusion must then be drawn that while Israel's experience of Yahweh as a Warrior lies behind both the notion of Yahweh's exclusive prerogative, found in texts from the Jerusalem cult tradition, and the holy war tradition, it is extremely unlikely that the holy war tradition is itself the source of this notion. Rather, it seems much more likely that the holy war schema of the Deuteronomistic history depends on the ancient tradition of Yahweh as a Warrior as this tradition was incorporated and developed precisely in the Jerusalem cult,[97] and particularly in Pss 20, 33, 44 and 118.

In addition, we may make the form-critical observation that the three Psalms, 20, 33 and 44, all have to do with military situations with explicit reference to the king, whereas in the ancient holy war texts it is the 'Heerbann' that is addressed and is the party active in war. Further, in those texts which address the leader himself, pre-eminently Joshua, the change in emphasis is due in all likelihood to the Deuteronomistic redaction.[98] While this does not rule out the possibility that this change was due simply to the new situation of the monarchy, the fact that the alteration of earlier narratives was undertaken by the Deuteronomists in the seventh century or later argues rather for the conclusion that the influence moved in a different direction.

Finally, the language of these texts (Pss 20, 33, 44, 118) is simply absent from the early narratives. The earliest text which contains similar language is Deut 20.1, which is from the seventh century and is thus almost certainly later than the Psalms we have been considering.[99] On form-critical grounds, then, we are led to conclude again that while both the holy war texts and Pss 20, 33, 44 and 118 are dealing with military situations, or military language, the influence does not seem to run from holy war tradition to the Jerusalem cult.

2. *The Prophets*

It may then be plausibly suggested that the notion of Yahweh's exclusive prerogative derives from the prophets. It has long been noted that the prophets tend to downplay acts of human heroic endeavor in favor of emphasis on God's action and that they particularly seem to take a posture in opposition to Israel's or Judah's preparations for war.[100] This tendency is very apparent in Hosea, for example.

a. *Hosea*
In Hosea 10.13-15 we have language strikingly similar to that found in Pss 20, 33 and 44.

כי בטחת ברכבך	Because you have trusted in your chariots[101]
ברב גבוריך	In the great number of your warriors

This text (10.13b) forms part of an indictment within a larger prophecy of punishment,[102] and is probably to be understood as a further specification of the more general indictment in v. 13a. The punishment is summarized in v. 15b, where Hosea assures the people that the מלך ישראל will be silenced at dawn.[103]

Here, then, the language of Yahweh's exclusive prerogative, as found in the Psalms, is utilized in a prophecy of punishment against the northern kingdom. The language of the text is not in any other way related to the traditions of holy war and there is no reason to see this formulation as dependent upon those traditions. In fact, given the relationship between Hosea and Deuteronomy, the language of this verse is probably most clearly comparable to Deut 20.1-3. In Deut 17.14-17 the people are specifically warned that the king would wish to 'increase horses', which is obviously a reference to the use of horses in chariotry or infantry.[104] Since Hosea 10 issues ultimately in a judgment against the king it is logical to see behind the legislation in Deuteronomy 17 such judgments as those of Hos 10.13b-15.[105]

A similar progression of thought is found in chapter 13 of Hosea. Within the 'plaintiff's speech' in vv. 4-8[106] occurs the declaration that there is no מושׁע but Yahweh. The plaintiff's speech leads then to the 'threat of judgment' in vv. 9-11 and the 'establishment of guilt' in vv. 12-13. Finally, preceding the announcement in 13.15-14.1, there is in 13.14 a 'rejection of false hopes'.[107] Within this structure there is a clear contrast between the declarations of vv. 4-6, which emphasize the exclusivity of Yahweh's relation to Israel as a 'savior', and v. 10, which poses the ironical question,

ואהי מלכך אפוא	But now where is your king
ויושיעך	That he may save you?
וכל שריך	And your princes
לישׁפטוך	That they may help you?
אשׁר אמרת	Of whom you said
תנה לי מלך ושׂרים	Give us a King and Princes![108]

The activity of kings is thus portrayed as opposed to that of Yahweh, and part of his punishment, announced in v. 11, is that the king he gave in anger will be taken away.

Finally, the same set of themes seems to reappear in 14.4. Here, within a summons to return from 'idols', Israel is encouraged to say that

אשׁור לא יושׁיענו	Assyria will not save us.
על סוס לא נרכב	Upon horses we will not ride,
ולא נאמר עוד אלהינו	Nor will we again say 'our God'
למעשׂה ידינו	To the work of our hands.

In this text the two themes mentioned in chapters 10 and 13, Yahweh as Israel's exclusive savior and reliance on armaments for security, are combined, and a third is added, idolatry. We have here some important clues for the origin of the notion of Yahweh's exclusive prerogative.

The first clue is to be found in the connection between reliance on arms of alliances and idolatry. It is important not to confuse the issue here by seeing Hosea's repudiation of Israel's trust in chariots and warriors on the one hand and an Assyrian alliance on the other hand as based on the threat of influence from Assyrian religion on Yahwism in Israel. In the first place, it seems unlikely that alliance with Assyria would have resulted in such an importation of a foreign cult.[109] In the second place, when idolatry or the practice of a foreign cult is attacked in Hosea it is always the cult of Baal, or Canaanite religion, that is under attack, not Assyrian religion.[110]

The point of Hosea's repudiation of reliance on Assyria is rather that such reliance is, like reliance on chariots and warriors, in itself an act of idolatry. From our discussion of the Psalms we learned that בטח has a positive as well as a negative reference, and such a dual reference is clear from Hosea. Trust in chariots and warriors is not compatible with trust in Yahweh. To regard Assyria as a 'savior' is incompatible with belief in Yahweh as savior. These incompatibilities are subsumable under the general religious terminology of idolatry, and all three can be regarded as arrogance in the face of Yahweh's own exclusive prerogative.[111]

Second, we have a clue to the origin of this notion in the connection of Hosea's emphasis on Yahweh's exclusive role as savior and his apparent criticism of kingship. It is not necessary here to debate the issue whether Hosea repudiated kingship in principle, attacked only the northern kings, or sought only to reform kingship as the chief political institution in Israel. It is sufficient merely to note that in 13.10 the institution of kingship is ridiculed as incapable of doing just what kings are supposed to do, namely provide security for the nation. This same incapacity was noted above in relation to Ps 33. In both of these texts the power of the king is insufficient to defend against the enemy. In Ps 33 the enemy is presumably external, but in Hosea 13 it is Yahweh himself, using, to be sure, the Assyrian army.

It should also be noted that Hosea made the same theological move with respect to Israel's kingship as he did with respect to Israel's reliance upon Assyrian strength and upon its own armies: he equated it theologically with idolatry. In 8.4 the making of kings is mentioned in the same breath as the making of idols and both of them have stirred Yahweh to anger.[112]

Thus we have in Hosea the same kind of language reserving the power of salvation and security to Yahweh as we have in the Psalms. In Hosea as in Pss 20, 33 and 44 this reservation is articulated in terms that seem to presuppose some kind of fundamental ascription of kingship to Yahweh, even though this is never made explicit in Hosea.[113] It would then appear reasonable to look to Hosea for the source of the notion that Yahweh reserves the prerogative of power exclusively to himself.[114]

There are, however, some difficulties with this view. In the first place, given the very difficult problem of dating the Psalms, it would be perilous indeed to speak of influence one way or the other between

Psalms 20, 44 and 33 and Hosea. If we are correct in assuming that texts such as Deuteronomy 17 and 20 have been influenced in their formulation at least in part by Hosea it may be safe to assume that Hosea did ultimately have some influence on the Jerusalem court and cult.[115] Still it is difficult to argue that Hosea is the influence behind texts such as the three Psalms we have considered.

Second, Hosea is obviously some distance removed from the Jerusalem cult tradition in language and theology. Furthermore, beyond the absence of any explicit reference to Yahweh as king there is no mention of Zion or use of those motifs and themes that often occur in association with Zion, except for that of Yahweh's exclusive prerogative. In view of the the lack of any other substantive connection between the Zion theology of the Jerusalem cult and the covenant theology of Hosea it would seem unwarranted to find that in this one theological point, the exclusive prerogative of Yahweh, Hosea had been of decisive influence on the Jerusalem cult.

Finally, there is a third problem in finding the origin of this notion in Hosea, namely that it occurs in its most persistent and radical form in the book of Isaiah. Furthermore, in Isaiah it is bound up inextricably wih Zion symbolism. It would appear then that two prophets, virtual contemporaries, rooted in different theological traditions, have both employed a theological notion which is elaborated especially in the Jerusalem cult.[116] This is truly a remarkable fact, leading Stolz to exclaim that

> We have here before us one of those rare cases where a theological frame of reference was of similar significance in the North and also in the South.[117]

In light of this it would seem impossible to derive the notion from the prophets, since Hosea has not demonstrably influenced Isaiah, nor vice versa. Before leaving the issue at that impasse, however, it will pay us to examine the way in which Isaiah articulates this notion in relation to Zion.

b. *Isaiah*
There is a fairly wide range of texts in Isaiah in which the notion of Yahweh's exclusive prerogative appears and in which Isaiah stands sharply opposed to the policies of Judah's kings insofar as these policies include either alliance with another nation or dependence upon armaments for security.[118] The notion is perhaps most clearly

stated in chs. 30 and 31. In the first few verses of ch. 30 (vv. 1-5)
Isaiah inveighs on behalf of Yahweh against the rebellious people:

לעשות עצה ולא מני	Who carry out a plan but it is not mine
ולנסך מסכה ולא רוחי	And conclude an alliance but not of my spirit
למען ספות חטאת על חטאת	To add sin upon sin.

The specifics of the rebellion are spelled out in the following verse.
The alliance not of Yahweh's spirit is with Egypt, and Isaiah
characterizes this activity in terms drawn directly from the Jerusalem
cult:

לעוז במעוז פרעה	To seek the protection of Pharaoh
ולחסות בצל מצרים -	And to take refuge in the shadow of Egypt.

The policy of Judah is thus to ignore the refuge provided by Yahweh
on Zion and to seek it instead in Eygpt. Isaiah goes on to say that this
refuge will prove to be embarrassing (לכלמה) and will result in shame
and reproach (vv. 3, 5).[119]

The same theme is developed using slightly different language in
31.1-3.[120] Here 'those who go down to Egypt for help and rely on
horses' are described as trusting in chariots, 'because they are many,
and in horsemen because they are very strong' (v. 1). In other words,
Judah has chosen to defend itself against Assyrian aggression by
entering into an alliance with Egypt and strengthening its military
forces.[121] This sort of activity is described by Isaiah as an alternative
to reliance upon Yahweh:

ולא שעו על קדוש ישראל	But they did not rely upon the Holy One of Israel
ואת יהוה לא דרשו	Nor did they seek Yahweh.

In view of the threat faced by Judah in the form of advancing
Assyrian troops the defensive measures taken by Hezekiah and the
royal court would seem to be prudential, and indeed wise. Isaiah
deals with this apparent wisdom implicitly in v. 2 by stating that 'he
[Yahweh] too is wise and he brings evil, and his words he will not
annul'.[122] That is, Yahweh too partakes of wisdom and his wisdom is
not abrogated by the constraints of the present situation in which
that wisdom appears insufficient to the demands of political reality.
The end of this verse (v. 2) contains the threat that Yahweh will 'arise

against the house of evil-doers and against the helpers of those who work iniquity'. The evil-doers and workers of iniquity are clearly the people of Judah here (cf. 1.4), not the Egyptians. Of interest in this text, in addition to its posing of Yahweh's wisdom against that of Judah's rulers, is the turn of cultic language to condemn the political decision described in v. 1.[123] Depending on armaments and foreign alliances is here described in the cultic language of evil and iniquity often reserved to condemn idolatry (cf. 1 Sam 15.23). Thus Isaiah combines reliance on foreign alliances and armaments with sinfulness in much the same way as Hos 14.4.

This section (31.1-3) concludes with an elaboration of that notion which forms the basis of the הוי-oracle in vv. 1-2. This notion is the apparently self-evident one that the Egyptians are אדם and not אל, and that their horses are בשר and not רוח (v. 3a). We need not probe deeply into the anthropology that lies behind the terms בשר and רוח to understand the contrast established here. The terms אל and רוח are paired against אדם and בשר simply to indicate that the latter pair are the embodiment of weakness, while the former pair are the embodiment of power.[124] We are prepared for this understanding from our examination of Ps 9/10, in which the power of Yahweh as king on Zion is contrasted with those humans whose weakness indicts their tyranny as arrogance. It is the prayer of that Psalm that Yahweh will act in such a way that the nations (or the insolent) will know that they are nothing but אנוש (9.21). The same thought lies behind Isa 31.3, where the power of Yahweh who is אל and רוח is contrasted the impotence of the heavily armed Egyptians, who are but אדם and בשר.

In these two passages (30.1-5; 31.1-3) Isaiah draws from language associated with Zion in the tradition of Jerusalem's cult and employs it in a concrete and specific way against the military policy of Hezekiah in the face of Assyrian aggression. The assumption of this application is that Yahweh's plan and wisdom are contrary to the plans and wisdom of the Jerusalem court.[125] Further, the plans of this court are doomed to fail because they rely on human power, or the power of armaments, rather than the power of Yahweh. There is here in Isaiah the same coordination between Yahweh's exaltation and human powerlessness that we have seen in other texts in the symbolic design whose central symbol is Zion. The exclusive prerogative of Yahweh seems to be rooted in this coordination, especially as this is developed in Isaiah.

This development is carried out with utter clarity in Isa 2.6-22. While this chapter has seldom been given the attention usually reserved for texts such as 30.1-5; 31.1-3 and 30.15-17 in considering Isaiah's exegesis of Yahweh's exclusive prerogative, it represents, I believe, the basic assumptions lying behind this exegesis.[126] This text occurs within a section of Isaiah concentrating to a large degree on judgments against the haughtiness of Judah (2.6-4.1 + 5.8-24/25). In its present form the text consists of three units. In the first unit Yahweh's rejection of his people is introduced (vv. 6-8).[127] The reasons for this rejection are given in 6b-8 and consist of a combination of idolatrous practices and the abundance of military hardware in the land.[128] In v. 9 the results of this rejection, based on 6b-8, are spelled out: אדם is humbled and איש is brought low. The prophet's address to Yahweh ends with the plea that the people not be forgiven.[129] The first unit is then concluded with an address to the people, who are urged to seek refuge in the rock and dust from before the terror of Yahweh (vv. 10-12). This warning is based on the approaching humiliation of all who are presently 'proud',[130] which is to take place 'in that day' when he alone will be exalted.

In the second unit, vv. 12-19, this 'day' is elaborated in a description of the day of Yahweh. In vv. 12-16 the various objects against which this day is directed are enumerated, while in vv. 17-19 the results of Yahweh's exaltation are described. These results are three: the pride of אדם will be shattered, the idols will disappear and the people will hide in caves to escape the terror of Yahweh. A third, concluding unit in vv. 20-22 describes the elimination of idols 'in that day', the attempt to hide from Yahweh's wrath and, in v. 22, a concluding exhortation to 'turn away from אדם', because he is unworthy, by implication, of consideration.

There seems to be a consensus among contemporary scholars that this text has undergone considerable editing during the course of its transmission and that its present form represents the concerns of the post-exilic period.[131] It may be that vv. 20-22 are later additions, but I believe that vv. 6-19 are a self-contained unit stemming from Isaiah. There are two aspects of this text that call forth the objection that they reflect post-exilic concerns. The first of these is the mention of idols in various parts of the text.[132] It is objected that idolatry was brought into this text at a later date and that originally it mentioned only the presence of armaments in Judah.[133] We have already seen, however, that the conjuction of armaments and idolatry was made in

Hosea, that is, at a time contemporaneous with Isaiah (cf. Isa 31.2). In Hos 14.4 the dependence upon Assyria, use of war horses and idolatry are mentioned in the same breath. The point of both texts, Hosea and Isaiah 2, is not that weapons or alliances are idols, but that all of these constitute the 'work of your hands' (Hos 14.4; Isa 2.8), which is an alternative to reliance on Yahweh, and thus constitute an offense against his exclusive prerogative. Just such an understanding is present also in Hab 2.18, where the worthlessness of an idol (פסל) is due to its status as something formed by a craftsman (יצר). The irony of this is drawn out by Habakkuk who notes that the craftsman trusts (בטח) in that which he himself formed by making dumb idols (אלילים; cf. also Hab 1.11, 16). It is by implication foolish to trust in what you have yourself made and such trust is an offense against Yahweh.[134] In Isaiah this offense is described in terms of arrogance, the arrogance of human efforts to achieve security. It is thus simply to misunderstand the nature of the prophetic polemic against 'horses and chariots' to assume that the mention of idolatry is a shift to cultic concerns, and thus constitutes an addition to a text originally dealing with more characteristically prophetic issues.[135]

A second aspect of Isa 2.6-22 that has been described as stemming from post-exilic concerns is the language of reversal, specifically the assurance that what is now proud shall be brought low[136] or humbled. We have already seen, however, that far from being only the concern of the post-exilic period or 'a central theme of apocalyptic',[137] this theme is the explicit concern of Psalms from the Jerusalem cult tradition and is found in its earliest form in the Song of Hannah which is at least as early as the Jerusalem cult itself. In a prophet whose theological roots are in that tradition it should be expected that this theme would play a predominant role, and that expectation is not disappointed.[138]

We began our discussion of Isaiah 2 by noting that in vv. 6-22 the coordination of Yahweh's exaltation with human powerlessness or humility is carried out with utter clarity. This clarity is served by the placement of Yahweh's exaltation and the consequent humiliation of human arrogance in the context of the Day of Yahweh.[139] It is not possible here to debate the complex issue of the origin of this motif, but it is important to note that it is used here in Isaiah to emphasize the solitary exaltation of Yahweh and the consequent humbling of everything else.[140] In vv. 10 and 19 this exaltation of Yahweh is described in kingship terms ('splendour of his majesty') and it makes sense to associate Yahweh's day with his theophanic exaltation as king on Zion. John Gray has argued, in fact, that the Day of Yahweh in Isaiah 2 must be connected with Yahweh's manifestation as king in chapter 6.[141] And we should also point out that the 'ships of Tarshish' mentioned in 2.16 appear with the same meaning in Ps 48.8, where Yahweh's theophany destroys them and the efforts of the hostile kings to assail the city of Yahweh, the great king. The ships of Tarshish do not refer to the 'occupation of Ezion-geber on the Gulf of Aqaba',[142] but are used 'as a metaphor for human arrogance'.[143] Thus the 'Day of Yahweh' in Isa 2.6-22 seems to indicate that day on which Yahweh alone is exalted and imposes his rule on the earth, with catastrophic effects on all that is high and lifted up, all that is arrogant, and upon all human efforts to find security in weapons, idols or anything of their own making. It would seem, then, that Gray is correct in associating the Day of Yahweh, at least in Isaiah 2, with Yahweh's kingship, a kingship that is always exclusive.

Our interest, however, is not in debating the origin of the Day of Yahweh motif, but in the origin and meaning of Yahweh's exclusive prerogative. In Isa 2.6-22 we have a text in which the horses and chariots, the military armaments, that fill the land of Judah are brought into explicit connection with the exaltation of Yahweh on his day and the consequent humiliation of all forms of arrogance,[144] including the arrogance of worshipping idols. Yahweh's exaltation is here described in theophanic language with its roots in the traditions of Jerusalem's cult[145] using themes we found to be present earlier in texts from the same tradition. We would agree with Stolz, then, that

> It is clear that the theological schema of God's (exclusive) power and human powerlessness is already at home in the pre-exilic cult of Jerusalem.[146]

We would only add that the schema of God's exclusive prerogative in Isa 2.6-22 is part of Isaiah's application of the symbolic design constructed around the symbol Zion, which is for Isaiah the site of Yahweh's dwelling (8.18).

Isaiah 2, we suggested above, presents in brief the assumptions lying behind Isaiah's exegesis applied to concrete situations in Isa 30.1-5 and 31.1-3. There are two more passages which seem to provide us with what we might designate as premises that mediate between the assumptions laid out in Isa 2.6-22 and the specific applications recorded in 30.1-5 and 31.1-3. The two texts that provide such premises are 28.12 and 30.15, which Hermann Barth considers to be Isaiah's own retrospectives on Yahweh's message proclaimed through him.[147]

In Isa 30.15 the prophet quotes the words of Yahweh directed toward his people, and specifically to the rulers of Judah:

| בשובה ונחת תושעין | You will be saved through turning and rest |
| בהשקת ובבטחה תהיה גבורתכם | In quietness and trust consists your strength. |

The major difficulty in these lines is the understanding of שובה, which I have translated 'turning'. The substantives in the rest of the verse would seem to weigh against such a translation and 'quietness' or 'stillness' might seem a more appropriate translation. Hermann Barth translates the term with 'Nichtstun', arguing that it means a turning away from all activity, not only from war, and toward reliance exclusively on Yahweh.[148] Dahood derives the term from שוב as a by-form of ישב and translates 'sitting still'.[149] While it is clear from the rest of v. 15 that Isaiah is counselling quietness and rest in the face of Assyrian aggression, it seems simplest to agree with Wildberger that the term should be translated 'returning' or 'turning', as would be suggested by its root שוב.[150] The point being made, it would seem, is that turning to Yahweh precisely entails quietness, repose and trust in the face of Assyrian forces. Wildberger points to Isa 9.12 and 30.1 for support of his view that שוב is best translated 'Umkehr'.[151] In these passages Yahweh reproaches the people for not turning to him in a threatening situation and for relying on their own strength, or that of the Egyptians, instead. In other words, we should not see (re)turning to Yahweh as something other than rest, quietness and trust in a pressing political and military situation. As 30.1 makes clear, failure to rely on Yahweh, as opposed to an Egyptian alliance, is sin and turning away from sin involves concretely a change in political strategy. That is, repentance and turning to Yahweh is, according to Isaiah, a strategy for meeting the real demands of the situation and is defined by rest, quietness and trust. So just as reliance on armaments and foreign alliances can be discussed in the same breath as idolatry, repentance can be discussed in the same breath as the recommended political strategy.

That *strategy* is precisely what Isaiah is talking about here is clear from the context. In vv. 15c-16 Isaiah describes the option which the people took, namely to rely on their own military power, and the results of this option, namely destruction. The strategic option described here is thus the same one chosen by Judah as described by Isaiah in 30.1-5 and 31.1-3, as we saw earlier. In both of these texts Isaiah outlines the disastrous results of the strategy of reliance upon armaments and foreign alliances. In 30.15 he also lays out a positive strategy for dealing wih a threatening situation, and it is to return to Yahweh, i.e. to rest, be quiet and trust. In that strategy alone Judah will find success.[152]

The second text that provides a mediating premise in the form of a retrospective on Isaiah's message, is found in Isa 28.12. In its present form the text reads

זאת המנוחה	This is the place of rest,
הניחו לעיף	Give rest to the weary,
וזאת המרגעה	And this is the place of repose,
ולן אבוא שמוע	But they were unwilling to listen.

The similarity of this text to 30.15 is clear. There is one critical problem to be dealt with, however, and that is the apparent imbalance in the two lines. We would expect, in other words, that the second clause beginning with זאת would be followed by an imperative built on the *hiphil* of רגע, just as in the first line the זאת clause is followed by the *hiphil* of נוח. This would resemble more closely the structure of 30.15. Recently J.J.M. Roberts has observed that the LXX of 28.12 skipped over הניחה, apparently because of haplography with the immediately preceding המנוחה. He then suggests that the MT reflects a similar haplography, in which the verb הרגיעו has dropped out of the MT because of the similarity of the immediately preceding המרגעה. Since an object would be required for this verb he suggests further that לאביון was lost because of its similarity to the following אבוא ולא.[153] If Roberts's suggestions are accepted the verse would now read,

> This is the place of rest,
> Let the weary rest,
> And this is the place of repose,
> Let the needy repose.[154]

Whether this text-critical correction is accepted or not, the meaning of the verse is still clear, that 'this' is the place of rest and repose and requires that the weary be offered rest themselves.

Isa 28.12 is particularly significant in our discussion because of the association of rest and repose with Zion. It is evident that in this verse 'this' refers to a particular location, namely Zion.[155] This is clear from a comparison with Psalm 132, where Zion is designated as Yahweh's dwelling place (מנוחה//מושב, v. 14), and this is quite specifically associated with Zion as the מנוחה of the Ark of Yahweh (vv. 7, 8). The point made here in Isa 28.12 is that Zion is the site of Yahweh's sovereign rule and that is the basis for the security of Yahweh's people. The strategy they should pursue, if one can speak in those terms here, is one of giving rest to the weary, and perhaps repose to the poor. The context of this verse makes clear that the people have chosen a different strategy, rejecting and ridiculing the words of the prophet and opting to depend for their security on other arrangements (v. 15).[156]

Isa 28.12 may then be profitably compared with 14.32, in which Isaiah claims that

| כי יהוה יסד ציון | Yahweh has founded Zion |
| ובה יחסו עניי עמו | And in it[157] the poor of his people find refuge. |

In this text Isaiah challenges the leadership of Jerusalem to reject the invitation of the Philistines to join an alliance against the Assyrians and bases this challenge explicitly on his understanding of the Zion symbol: Zion has been founded as a refuge for the poor. We have already noted the significance of עני/ענו within other texts from the Jerusalem cult tradition. Here it is sufficient to refer to our earlier discussion and to quote Barth, who says

> That Isaiah develops the refuge quality of Zion precisely with
> reference to [the poor] is to be seen in connection with the
> particular relation of the עניים to Yahweh in the sphere of the
> Jerusalem tradition: the oppressed state in which they find
> themselves prevents them from arrogance and pride and clarifies
> for them their radical dependence upon Yahweh.[158]

To draw the strands of our argument together, we saw first of all that Isaiah evokes one of the fundamental notions of the Jerusalem cult tradition, that Yahweh alone is exalted and that his exaltation requires the humility of all else. In chapter 2 this is developed in relation to the Day of Yahweh, which is his exaltation against all that is proud. In Isa 30.15 and 28.12 the premises are given which allow this fundamental notion to be applied to the concrete political situation faced by Judah, that if an impending conflict with Assyria. In these texts the strategy that corresponds to Yahweh's exaltation against pride is quietness and rest. This rules out dependence upon armaments or alliances, and requires, on the other hand, a particular disposition of trust and concern for the poor. Isaiah himself connects this explicitly with the nature of Zion itself, which Yahweh founded as a refuge for the poor. The fundamental position of Isaiah's salvation message is then that Yahweh associates himself with Zion as the place of security and peace for those who do not attempt to secure their own or Jerusalem's defense through 'practical', military means, leaving the matter of security absolutely in the hands of Yahweh.[159] Yahweh associates his offer of salvation in 30.15 with a corresponding disposition on the part of the people, and in 28.12 he associates his help with the location of Zion, not with the citizens of Judah and Jerusalem who were quite certain of Yahweh's presence with them.[160] In 14.32 the emphasis on the עניים, corresponding to the עיף and perhaps the אביון in 28.12, makes clear that in Isaiah's view those who respond to Yahweh in faithlessness and pride have no refuge in Zion, but it will be a place of refuge and security for those who, because they are neither arrogant nor proud, expect help only from Yahweh.[161]

It is clear, then, that in the passages from Isaiah which we have considered the notion of Yahweh's exclusive prerogative is associated explicitly with the symbol Zion. The way in which Isaiah wove this symbol and this notion together in the fabric of his theology is especially apparent in Isa 28.16. Since this verse appears in close connection with 28.12, which we considered above, it is appropriate that we look at v. 16 in this context.

Given the textually complicated nature of this verse it is necessary first to deal with some of the critical problems. To begin with, the first words of the Yahweh speech in v. 16 present a problem. The speech begins with הנני ('look, I . . . ') followed by a third person perfect verb, יסד ('he founded'). This has been altered in most versions to a participle, מיסד or יוסד, and almost all commentators follow this emendation.[162] However, it cannot be denied that the third person perfect is the more difficult reading, and Irwin suggests that this should be left intact, reading the construction as a relative clause without a relative pronoun, modifying the suffix of הנני.[163] This makes a difference in translation, since presumably the stone would have been placed, or be in the process of being placed, if a perfect verb were read. On the other hand the later versions, such as 1QIs[a] and LXX, would have had good reason, given their interpretive interests, to read this as a future event. Thus it seems likely that the perfect is the original reading here.

There have been myriad proposals for understanding what this stone may be.[164] However, I would propose following the suggestion of Gesenius–Kautzsch that we read the ב on בציון as *beth essentiae*, in which case the phrase would be translated, 'he placed Zion as a stone', or 'founded Zion as a stone'.[165] There is no way to settle the issue grammatically, but it seems to me that this reading would accord well with Isaiah's Zion theology expressed elsewhere in the book. We have already noted that 14.32 describes Zion as a place of refuge and it seems that here in 28.16 it is described as a stone, a sure foundation, to contrast with Sheol in the verse immediately preceding.[166] It remains true, of course, that Israel's 'rock' is Yahweh, and thus no independent security is granted to Zion apart from him, but the criteria for finding Zion a refuge have already been set out in numerous passages (7.9; 28.12; 30.15, etc.), as they are also in this verse. Zion is a refuge for the poor and weary whose faith is in Yahweh. To regard Zion as a stone would mean, for those whom Isaiah addressed, renouncing all effort to seek security elsewhere.

It is also hard to determine just what is meant by a 'stone of testing'. As Dahood has pointed out, the stereotyped phrase אבן פנת which occurs in Ps 118.22, Job 38.6 and Jer 51.26, is here broken up and separated by בחן.[167] It would seem natural at first to regard this word as having the normal meaning of the verb 'to test', taking it as either passive ('tested') or active ('for testing'). E.E. LeBas takes the verb as having an active sense, comparing this passage with Zech 3.9; 4.7, 9; Ps 118.32. According to LeBas the reference here is to a pyramidal apex-stone used to test the accuracy of a pyramid by applying the stone to the summit.[168] S.H. Hooke disagreed and saw the stone as representative of the purified, tested remnant of Israel.[169] Probably both of these interpretations are straining too much toward the allegorical.

Ludwig Köhler, on the other hand, argued in 1947 that בחן is a technical term for building material, and he has been followed by most scholars since. If the term does refer to building material it is also probable that it was chosen for its secondary associations with

testing, with the distinction between active and passive voices left
ambiguous.[170]

The last line of v. 16 is very difficult. It is evident that פנת is in the
construct state, but the following word, יקרת, is an adjective, also
apparently in construct. This has led some to suppose that יקרת is a
substantive, perhaps another technical architectural term.[171] Irwin
suggests, on the other hand, that we should not be troubled by an
interruption of the construct chain, but should regard יקרת as an
adjective modifying פנת, whose genitive is מוסד.[172] The translation
offered by the RSV would then be correct in rendering the line, 'a
precious cornerstone of sure foundation'.[173]

There is also some disagreement about what is meant by the
'cornerstone'. It has been suggested that this stone is actually the
keystone, not the cornerstone.[174] The references in Ps 118.22 and
Zech 4.7 to the ראש פנה and the אבן ראשה have led others to believe
that a capstone or a stone in the parapet of a house is intended
here.[175] It is likely, however, that 'cornerstone' is a more adequate
translation in Isa 28.16. In the first place, the parallelism with
'foundation' would indicate that this is not a capstone or keystone.
Secondly, the Greek translation, ἀκρογωνιαιος means 'at the
extreme angle', and the ἀκρογωνιαιος λίθος is 'the corner foundation-
stone'.[176] Thirdly, recent comparisons with Mesopotamian temple
construction have suggested that the language of this verse is
associated with the ritual laying of the cornerstone. Under the
cornerstone of a temple was placed a 'foundation document', which
reported the acts of the king in the service of his god. When a new
temple was constructed this foundation document was searched for
by the later king who was building the new temple, or restoring the
old one. The cornerstone of a former temple building had to be
removed before construction on the new temple could begin. It is
possible that such a temple ritual is the background for Isa 28.16.[177]
The cornerstone was particularly visible, and thus hewn from
precious stone, and was perhaps inscribed with a dedicatory message.
At any rate, the stone here associates Yahweh's promises with the
security of Zion as a stone of firm foundation.

The verse concludes wth a cryptic phrase, reminiscent of Isa 7.9b
and Hab 2.4b. This phrase crystallizes the message of salvation that
Isaiah is proclaiming in this chapter. The message is that whoever
believes, i.e. relies on Yahweh's promise of salvation, will not be in
haste. One who has faith will not try to force the immediate

materialization of this salvation by other means.[178] This is a conclusion that is consistent with the message of Isaiah in association with Zion elsewhere in the book. It is significant that this statement (28.16c) occurs in this context, because it forms a programmatic statement for the new 'structure' to be erected on Zion. We should certainly not miss the radical nature of Isaiah's message here and in the following three chapters. It is very likely that Isaiah is implying nothing less than a total judgment upon the ruling house of Judah and a new beginning on new foundations with a new cornerstone.[179] The temptation is strong to identify this new structure with the remnant, the 'true Israel', who trust Yahweh rather than weapons.[180] It may be legitimate to do so, but all that Isaiah tells us explicitly is that Yahweh is creating something that consists in security for those who trust (האמין).[181] So this message of salvation is at the same time a message of judgment on Jerusalem's leaders who choose other means of security. Their refuge and shelter (v. 15) will be swept away and overwhelmed (v. 17). The standards of the new structure will be משפט and צדקה in contrast to Lie and Deception.

The context in which Isa 28.16 was written was most likely that of the invasion of Sennacherib in 701 BC. As we noted earlier, in 30.4 Isaiah mentions the Egyptian officials of Zoan and Hanes, which implies that the 25th Egyptian Dynasty (Ethiopian) had succeeded in bringing the local dynasts under their centralized control. This happened, most likely, around 711 or 710 BC.[182] It was this development in Egyptian unification that led Hezekiah to change Judah's consistent policy toward Assyria and withhold tribute, imposed after Sargon II's earlier campaigns against Ashdod. This military-political context should warn us against spiritualizing Isaiah's message in 28.16, and the surrounding chapters.[183] He is talking not only of an attitude of faithful trust, but is recommending to Jerusalem's leaders a policy to be followed in dealing with the most crucial political issues.[184] Zion as the location of refuge and the foundation of security, is bound up inextricably with this recommended policy. As the rest of ch. 28 makes clear (vv. 21-22), Zion's 'inviolability' is applicable to the leadership of Judah only upon condition of faithfulness to Yahweh's word. Although Isaiah sees clearly that Jerusalem is doomed to destruction because of her rulers' reliance on the wisdom of her wise men (29.14b), he sees just as clearly that this doom does not mark the end of Yahweh's promise to his people nor of his commitment to Zion. While Judah's 'Hauptstadt' may be violated, the 'heilige Stadt Jahwes' is indeed inviolable.[185]

Thus we have in Isa 28.16 a further example of the way in which Isaiah articulated the notion of Yahweh's exclusive prerogative in connection with the symbol Zion, and applied this notion to the circumstances of Judah's political conflicts with Assyria. What emerges from this text with remarkable clarity is the dialectical nature of Zion symbolism in Isaiah. As we saw in the Psalms from the Jerusalem cult the presence of Yahweh as king on Zion carried with it not only the promise of security but also the demand for trust, or faith.[186] We noted that particularly in Pss 20, 33, 44 and 118 trust in Yahweh is contrasted with other potential objects of trust which are revealed as impotent. In these Psalms Yahweh's exclusive prerogative is thus clarified or explicated in relation to other presumed sources of power which are seen in reality to be powerless. In ch. 28 Isaiah not only connects Yahweh's exclusive prerogative to the Zion symbol, and derives from this combination the demand for faith on the part of Judah's leaders,[187] but he also makes the presence of faith, defined as the recognition of Yahweh's exclusive prerogative, a descriminatory instrument on the basis of which Yahweh decides the fate of Judah. That is to say that while Yahweh makes unconditional promises regarding his intention to defend Zion, these promises can be turned precisely against the leaders of Judah who, if they act faithlessly and turn to Assyria or Egypt for deliverance, become the enemies of Yahweh and are thus the objects of his saving action on behalf of Zion. Thus Yahweh, who characteristically battles the hostile forces assembled against Zion, can himself become the leader of these forces brought against the city to purge from its midst those who have become its true enemy.[188] Yahweh's enemy is thus defined simply as anyone who makes plans contrary to *his* plan, that Zion should be a refuge for the poor[189] who rely solely on the exercise of his exclusive prerogative for their security. So (1) those who rely on any other power for their security and (2) those who try to battle against Zion are equally in opposition to Yahweh's plan and are hence his enemy. They are instances of the arrogance against which Yahweh is exalted in his day (2.6-22).[190]

It is in this light that those Isaianic texts characteristically seen as expressing Zion's inviolability are to be understood. While this notion is often thought to lie behind a number of texts in Isaiah 1–39[191] it is stated with seeming explicitness and clarity in Isa 8.9-10; 17.12-14. We urged above that Isaiah 2 should be seen as presenting the assumptions lying behind Isaiah's exegesis of Yahweh's exclusive prerogative. We then considered Isa 30.15 and 28.12 to present mediating premises between Isaiah 2 and Isaiah's political counsel in 30.1-5 and 31.1-3. Finally, Isa 28.16 was seen to bring together the assumptions of Isaiah's exegesis of Yahweh's exclusive prerogative with the mediating premises of 28.12 and 30.15, into a combination in which faith—reliance upon Yahweh alone—becomes a discriminatory instrument whereby Yahweh's action is decided.[192] All of these texts are used by Isaiah in the development of his 'Gegenwartskritik' of Judah,[193] a critique directed fundamentally against the pride of Judah's leaders, as well as Assyria's. Pride was, as we have seen, the counterpoint to faith in the Jerusalem cult tradition. In texts such as 8.9-10 and 17.12-14, however, Isaiah grants insight into the basis for faith in the first place. These texts thus present the theological rationale for Isaiah's call to faith and his insistence on Yahweh's exclusive prerogative.

In recent years critical opinion has tended to deny that these texts (along with 10.33-34; 14.24-27, etc.) are from Isaiah of Jerusalem. The problem is that they seem to speak of almost certain salvation for Zion, or Judah, while Isaiah seems to anticipate the almost total destruction of Judah-Jerusalem.[194] Thus Barth, followed by Clements, believes that these texts come from a period in which 'the hope of the downfall of Assyria is sufficiently strong as to appear imminent, and the sense that the grip of Assyria upon Judah is now almost non-existent', and 'Judah no longer has anything to fear from Assyria'.[195] This position does not, it seems to me, do justice to Isaiah's message, nor does it rest on adequate critical grounds.

In the first place, it must be noted that Isaiah's proclamation that Judah had nothing to fear from Assyria took place just at the height of Assyria's power (e.g. chs. 28-31). Similarly, in 7.1-17 Isaiah counselled against alliance with Assyria just at the time when Assyria seemed to be in the best position to help in the face of the apparently superior forces of Syria and its ally, Israel.[196] Furthermore, it appears to be an unwarranted truncation of Isaiah's message if his demand for faith is not allowed to be supplemented with expressions that define what it is Ahaz and Hezekiah are encouraged to have faith in.[197]

We are justified, I believe, in seeing Isa 8.9-10 and 17.12-14 as providing the rationale for Isaiah's demand for faith. They do this primarily by drawing on the tradition of Zion symbolism provided in the Jerusalem cult tradition, especially in the songs of Zion (Pss 46,

48, 76), in which Zion's security is grounded in Yahweh's commitment
to it as the site of his kingship.[198]

רעו עמים וחתו
והאזינו כל מרחקי ארץ
התאזרו וחתו // התאזרו וחתו
עצו עצה ותפר
דברו דבר ולא יקום // כי עמנו אל

> Look with despair and be dismayed, O peoples
> Give ear, all the far reaches of the earth
> Gird yourselves and be dismayed
> Gird yourselves and be dismayed
> Take counsel together that it may be annulled
> Discuss the matter, but it will not stand
> Because God is with us.

This text (Isa 8.9-10) is presently situated in a very significant
position between 8.5-8, in which Ahaz's refusal to take Isaiah's
counsel and rely on the exclusive prerogative of Yahweh for his and
Judah's security results in the punishment of the land of עמנו אל, and
8.11-15, in which Isaiah's policy is differentiated from that of Ahaz
and is governed by the fear of Yahweh of hosts, not of Rezin and
Pekah. In this central position the text presents the set of theological
convictions that determine Isaiah's message and should have
determined Ahaz's policy.

In a detailed study of these verses Magne Saebø has suggested that
the initial word of v. 9, ורעו, should be taken as an imperative of רוע,
instead of from רעע, and translated 'raise a battle cry'.[199] He thus
concludes that these two verses have their background in holy war
tradition.[200] However, it is dubious to suggest that רעו is from the
root רוע, since (a) this would be the only instance of that root in the
qal, and (b) the form of the imperative here indicates a geminate root,
not a hollow or middle weak root.[201] There is no difficulty in
rendering the imperative 'look with despair', in which case it would
be a good parallel to the following imperative תאזינו. We would also
question whether it is apt to refer to holy war traditions as the
background of these verses. Rather, we should look to the traditions
of the Jerusalem cult in which the attack of hostile forces against
Zion is repulsed by Yahweh. In Ps 46.5-8, for example, the faith that
the forces of chaos will be defeated is grounded in the confession that

'Yahweh of hosts is with us', a virtual parallel to Isa 8.10.[202] We would agree with Saebø that the 'Vorstellungskreis' of these verses is Exod 15.14-16, but we would see these latter verses related to the tradition of the Jerusalem cult that Yahweh as king exercises his dual role of creator/defender in defeating the forces of chaos, whether these forces be cosmic or historical.

The same is true, we would argue, with respect to 17.12-14.

> Ah! the tumult of many nations:
> They roar like the roaring of the seas
> And the uproar of the peoples.
> They roar like the uproar of the mighty seas.
> He rebukes them, and they flee away.
> They are chased like the chaff on the mountains before the wind,
> And tumbleweeds before the storm.
> At evening, look! Terror. Before morning they are no more.
> This is the portion of those who plunder us,
> And the lot of those who rob us.[203]

It is unnecessary to comment extensively on these verses. While the context is not as instructive as that of 8.9-10, it is clear that in 17.12-14 Isaiah is still interested primarily in providing the theological background to his call to faith. That background is simply the theological design of Zion symbolism in the Jerusalem cult. Thus the tumult and the roar of the nations is comparable to the roar of the chaos waters in Ps 46.4 (cf. ch. 3) which also in that Psalm are brought into relation to the roaring of the nations. In both instances, Psalm 46 and Isaiah 17, it is Yahweh who repels the threat of cosmic and historical chaos. In Isa 17.13 it is his rebuke, or 'roar', that repels these forces, just as in Ps 76.7 it was the roar of the God of Jacob that stopped rider and horse. We saw earlier that in the language of the Jerusalem cult Yahweh's roar was at the same time the creative force behind the conquest of chaos and the protection of that creation against the threat of nations.[204] In Isaiah 17 it is this theological understanding that Isaiah urges upon his audience in an effort to deter them from the fatal mistake of making common cause with the forces of chaos. These forces, are, according to Isaiah, no threat to Yahweh and if Judah recognizes his exclusive prerogative it will be protected by his creative power.[205]

Isa 8.9-10 and 17.12-14 have sometimes been denied to Isaiah because they are almost purely mythological and make no specific reference to an enemy of Judah.[206] While acknowledging that they are mythological and do not specify the nation(s) hostile to Judah, I would maintain that this is no argument against either their Isaianic provenance or their theological importance. The fact that they do not specify the foe is inconsequential since Isaiah is here clearly employing liturgical language and forms[207] similar to Pss 46, 48 and 76, as well as Ps 2, in which no foe is specified. What is expressed in these two liturgical pieces (8.9-10; 17.12-14) is both the futility and needlessness of reliance on foreign alliances, grounded in the superiority of Yahweh and his commitment to his city.[208] Seen in this light there is no contradiction between the faith expressed here and the expectation expressed elsewhere that Judah will reject this faith and suffer the destructive consequences of repudiating Yahweh's exclusive prerogative.[209]

The logic of Isaiah is perhaps clearest in this regard in Isa 7.1-9, a final text to consider in our discussion of Yahweh's exclusive prerogative in Isaiah.[210] This text and its various literary, formal and traditio-critical problems have been discussed in such detail by others that it is unnecessary to survey them here. The point we wish to make can be stated most clearly by arguing against two recent scholarly positions that have come to govern interpretation of it. These are (1) that Isaiah's counsel to Ahaz is determined by his understanding of the Davidic covenant (2 Samuel 7), and (2) that the כי clauses in vv. 8a, 9a are to be read as the subject of v. 7b, so that what 'will not stand nor shall it be' (7b) is that the head of Aram is Damascus, etc. (8a).

The first view was put forth perhaps most vigorously by Ernst Würthwein in 1954.[211] Würthwein rejects the earlier position of Gressmann that Isaiah is encouraging Ahaz in 7.1-9 to forego all defensive measures[212] and suggests rather that Isaiah is urging Ahaz to take up the battle against Syria and Israel with confidence. This confidence, argues Würthwein, is based on the Davidic covenant elaborated in 2 Samuel 7. Evidence for this is derived from the presence of the verb אמן in Isa 7.9, which is said to be reminiscent of 2 Sam 7.16, etc.[213] Rather than warning Ahaz to assume a posture of passivity, Isaiah in 7.3 (cf. 8.6-7) is counselling Ahaz not to worry about the water supply for the coming battle. What Isaiah warns Ahaz against is not preparation for battle but alliance with Assyria. This warning is not based on the notion of Yahweh's exclusive prerogative but on the recognition that such a military alliance would bring with it the imposition of Assyrian worship, principally that of Shamash, on the Yahwist cult of Jerusalem. The question then is one of covenant and the fear of syncretism as a threat to this covenant of Yahweh with the house of David. Würthwein concludes his exposition by making the standard suggestion that the text of vv. 8 and 9 should be expanded to read, 'but the head of Judah is Jerusalem and the head of Jerusalem is the Davidic house'.[214] Thus a non-existent text is invented to provide evidence for the argument on the basis of which it was created. The argument thus supported is that Isaiah encourages Ahaz to trust in the promise of a secure Davidic house, and Isa 7.7-9 'actualizes' the prophecy of Nathan.[215]

This argument strikes one as specious. In the first place there is precious little evidence from chapters 1–39 that Isaiah based any hope for salvation on Yahweh's promises to the Davidic house. Apart from chapter 7 only 9.6 would seem to support such an argument and the mention of David in this verse has been seen by some as a secondary expansion.[216] Second, the term אמן in 7.9b has as its immediate background not 2 Samuel 7, but Isa 1.21-26, where Jerusalem is called קריה נאמנה in vv. 21, 26.[217] F.M. Cross has shown that the phrase נאמן ביתד in 2 Sam 7.16, (cf. 1 Sam 2.35; 25.28 and 1 Kgs 11.38) is 'characteristic of the Deuteronomistic idiom'[218] and it is thus far more likely that נאמן is from Isaiah and that this language found its way secondarily into the Deuteronomistic prose of 2 Samuel 7.[219] Third, the theory that alliance with Asyria would necessarily have meant the imposition of the Assyrian cult can no longer be maintained with certainty after the historical research of Morton Cogan.[220] The threat of syncretism as a basis upon which to reject alliances is simply not part of Isaiah's argument here or elsewhere. Fourth, what Isaiah means to offer Ahaz is not a utopian form of political practice, or an unrealistic military policy, but precisely a realistic policy based on the reality that Yahweh governs the world of both Judah and Assyria, and on the promise of Yahweh to be Zion's security. This promise is put to Judah and confronts the leadership with a choice between it and the more 'realistic' prospects of reliance on Assyria and the armaments of war. Jerusalem and its king, and indeed the royal house, are secure just to the extent to which they accept Yahweh's promise to make them so. Isaiah is not a utopian, he is a realist. He rejects the pseudo-realism of Judah's political leaders in favor of the concrete realism of Yahweh of Hosts.[221] Fifth, the argument that the text of 7.8-9 should be expanded to conform to what Würthwein and others presume it must say is simply no argument at all. The text is comprehensible as it stands, as I hope to show in dealing with the second argument, i.e. that the כי clauses in vv. 8a, 9a should be read as the subject of v. 7b.

The way that Isaiah argues elsewhere (e.g. chs. 28; 30; 31) leads me to believe that the כי clauses in Isa 7.8a, 9a are to be read causally,[222] following the clause in 7.5 introduced by יען כי. This fits well with 7.7b, since the imperfect verbs there are third feminine singular, in agreement with an implied subject, עצה (יעץ in 7.5a). That is, the plan of Aram (and Ephraim) will fail *because* the head of Aram is Damascus, etc. This is the position of Wildberger as well.[223] However, Wildberger interprets vv. 8a, 9a as meaning that the plan of the two foes of Judah will fail because 'they lack divine legitimation', and he refers to Hos 8.4, as well as to 3.4; 5.1; 7.5; 8.10 and 10.3, 7.

I disagree with Wildberger for two reasons. In the first place, the Hosea texts, except for 3.5, which is late,[224] have nothing to do with the exclusive legitimacy of Davidic kingship.[225] In any case, all of Hosea's discussion of Israel's kings would tend to undermine, rather than strengthen, the claims of the Davidic court as well.[226]

Secondly, the כי clauses in 7.8a, 9a are most naturally understood against the background of language found in Isa 31.2-3 (cf. above) and also in 10.5-15 and 14.4b-21. Particularly in the first two of these passages a contrast is drawn between plans which are contrary to Yahweh's. In 31.2-3 the wisdom of Judah's leaders is contrasted to the superior wisdom of Yahweh. The wisdom of the leaders is faulted because it does not take into account that the Egyptians are 'flesh' and not God. Thus the plan of Judah to defend itself through Egypt's strength will not succeed. Similarly in 10.5-15 the wisdom of Yahweh (v.13) annuls the plans of the Assyrians (cf. 17.13) to conquer Jerusalem through their own power. Assyria's self-reliance is characterized as foolishness because it arrogates to Assyria a wisdom and an understanding that belong exclusively to Yahweh.[227] This kind of arrogance, which is in direct opposition to the 'anthropology of Zion' (see above), is described in detail in Isa 14.14b-21, especially vv. 12-14.[228] The verses that follow, 14.24-27, emphasize that it is only Yahweh's plans that ultimately prevail in the course of history and that is precisely because there is no earthly power whose planning can contravene his.[229]

Seen against this background the language of 7.8a, 9a, together with v. 5, means simply that the plan of Aram and its ally will fail because Yahweh has other plans. The 'evil plan' (v. 5) cannot succeed because the head of Aram is merely Damascus and its head merely Rezin; likewise Ephraim. What Ahaz is asked to believe (v. 9b) is not that the head of Jerusalem is the Davidic house, or some such, but that Yahweh, whose exclusive prerogative it is to provide security, is sufficient for the defense of Zion. The responsibility of Ahaz is exhausted in faithfulness (vv. 9b + 4a) because Yahweh who reigns as king (6.5) on Zion (8.18) is in his presence the guarantee of Zion's security (8.9-10). Of course, should Ahaz decide to rest his security in military preparation or alliance with Assyria, Yahweh's presence becomes a threat (7.9bβ) and a 'stumbling block' (8.15) to Jerusalem (1.18-20) and to the *Davidic house* (7.2, 13). The import of 7.9b is thus virtually identical to that of 28.16c: to believe or trust is not to be in haste. In the context of ch. 7 being in haste means preparing for war and turning to the Assyrians for help, while in ch. 28 it means turning to the Egyptians. In both cases it means attending to all the apparently necessary preparations except the only one which would truly provide security (22.5-15).[230] Faith, on the other hand, means reliance upon Yahweh alone and the abandonment of all that infringes upon his exclusive prerogative. As Odil Hannes Steck says,

> Thus those scholars are likely correct who already insist that for Isaiah 7 'faith' means concretely here total passivity over against those defensive measures which in fact seek to place Yahweh's assurance in question and to displace Yahweh's power to defend.[231]

While 'passivity' does not quite convey what is urged by Isaiah, it does highlight the seriousness with which Isaiah took the notion of Yahweh's exclusive prerogative.

Conclusions: Isaiah
Within the structure of Isaiah's message, as we have examined it above, the notion of Yahweh's exclusive prerogative plays a central theological role. It is not developed by Isaiah as an independent theologoumenon, but arises most clearly in the context of concrete application to the problem of Judah's continued survival in the face of two international threats, the Syro-Ephraimite War and Assyrian hegemony over the West. At the same time the notion of Yahweh's

exclusive prerogative rests on clearly stated theological assumptions, namely the exaltation of Yahweh, as depicted most explicitly in 2.6-22, and Yahweh's commitment to Zion's security as stated in 8.9-10 and 17.12-14.[232] We have also seen that Isaiah provides mediating premises between these theological assumptions and the application of them in chs. 30 and 31. Such mediating premises are found in 28.12 and 30.15 and provide answers to the question of what measures should be taken to insure Zion's security. These measures are restricted in these texts, in sum, to (a) trusting Yahweh to exercise his prerogative and (b) making Zion what it was intended to be, a place of rest for the weary or poor. This posture of trust is then defined, in chs. 7 and 28, in terms of faith, which serves in both chapters as a discriminatory instrument on the basis of which Yahweh's action toward Jerusalem is determined.

Isaiah's message, and the central place of the notion of Yahweh's exclusive prerogative within it, can be diagrammed thus:

Assumptions	*Assumptions*
Yahweh's exaltation	Zion's security
Isa 2.6-22	Isa 8.9-10; 17.12-14

Yahweh's exclusive prerogative
Isa 30.1-5; 31.1-3

Required Posture	*Discriminatory*
Trust: 30.15; 28.12	*instrument*
Concern for poor:	Presence of faith
14.32; 28.12	Isa 7.9b; 28.16

As our discussion has shown, Isaiah develops the notion of Yahweh's prerogative in very close association with the symbol Zion. It is because Yahweh is exalted as king on Zion that Zion is secure, and it is because Yahweh as king assumes all responsibility for Zion's security that the responsibility of Jerusalem's leaders is exhausted in trusting in Yahweh and making of Zion that for which it was founded, namely a refuge for the poor.[233] It is important to note as well that the exclusive prerogative of Yahweh is connected in Isaiah as in the Psalms with what we have called 'the anthropology of Zion'. That is, in the language of the Jerusalem cult and its Zion symbolism, the exaltation of Yahweh entails at the same time the humility of all humankind, and indeed the humiliation of all that is proud.[234] It is for this reason that it is not only unnecessary for Ahaz and Hezekiah to engage in military and diplomatic preparations to defend Jerusalem from foreign aggression, but it is a positive affront to the exaltation of Yahweh as king on Zion and thus forbidden by Yahweh through Isaiah. In other words, Isaiah's development of Yahweh's exclusive prerogative in association with the Zion symbol is not simply the artificial conjunction of a theme with an appropriate symbol, but is the consistent, reflective exegesis of that symbol within the tradition of the Jerusalem cult itself.[235]

Given the nature of Isaiah's total involvement with the Jerusalem cult tradition and his elaboration of Zion symbolism in such a complex fashion, it is not surprising that his language reflects so closely that of the Jerusalem cult, and especially the Songs of Zion (Pss 46, 48, 76). We thus conclude that for Isaiah the notion of Yahweh's exclusive prerogative was bound up with his exegesis of the Zion symbol as the central symbol of the Jerusalem cult tradition.[236]

c. *Conclusions: the Prophets*

We have examined several texts in Hosea and Isaiah to determine whether the notion of Yahweh's exclusive prerogative, which we discovered in Psalms from the Jerusalem cult tradition, had its origin within the prophetic tradition. This now seems to be unlikely, since both Hosea and Isaiah, operating out of distinct theological traditions, make use of this notion. Hosea, on the one hand, uses this notion to condemn Israel's alliances with other nations and reliance upon their armaments, which he associates explicitly with idolatry. His use of the notion of Yahweh's exclusive prerogative thus bears some resemblance to the use of the notion of Yahweh's incomparability by the Deuteronomists, a tradition upon which Hosea undoubtedly had a major influence.

Isaiah, on the other hand, makes use of the notion of Yahweh's exclusive prerogative as part of the larger Jerusalem cult tradition associated with the Zion symbol. He too condemns alliances with other nations and reliance upon armaments, but he places this condemnation in the larger context of a theology of Yahweh's exaltation as king on Zion which he promises to defend against hostile forces. Isaiah too may associate this notion with the condemnation of idolatry, if v. 18 or v. 20 is originally part of ch. 2. However Isaiah is not primarily concerned, as Hosea is, with a polemic against Baalism but rather with idolatry as an affront to Yahweh's exaltation.

Still, it is important to note the strong similarity between Isaiah and Hosea in their use of the notion of Yahweh's exclusive prerogative. As we noted above, Hosea does not seem to equate reliance upon Assyria with idolatry because such an alliance would entail incorporation of the Assyrian cult, but rather because reliance upon Assyria as a 'savior' is incompatible with belief in Yahweh as savior. It is thus significant that Isaiah and Hosea, contemporaries in the South and North respectively, not only use the same imagery associated with a notion they hold in common, but use it in nearly identical ways and with a nearly identical theological dynamic.

Given this state of affairs it would seem that we must deny that the notion of Yahweh's exclusive prerogative originated with the prophets.[237] Rather, we should consider briefly whether some common origin can be posited for the use of the notion in two prophets otherwise unrelated to each other, and whether this common origin can be linked in some way to the Zion symbolism of the Jerusalem cult tradition.

3. *A Common Background*

a. In the preceding pages we have considered two possible origins of the notion of Yahweh's exclusive prerogative, namely holy war and the prophets. We rejected the possibility that this notion originated in Israel's holy war tradition, in part because that tradition as it is elaborated in the Deuteronomic literature seems to be influenced *by* that notion rather than providing the background *for* it.[238] We further rejected the possibility that the prophets were the originators of this notion, since this explanation could not account for the simultaneous appearance of the notion in Isaiah and Hosea, who worked in different geographical and traditio-historical contexts. This has led us to consider the possibility that there is a common background to the use of the notion of Yahweh's exclusive prerogative in both Isaiah and Hosea, as well as in the Psalms of the Jerusalem cult. While we cannot go into this question in depth here, it is important to explore it briefly since I believe that it helps to illuminate some of the issues discussed earlier in Chapter 2. In short, we will be suggesting that the common background to the notion of Yahweh's exclusive prerogative is the same as the background of the Jerusalem cult tradition itself, and hence of the design of Zion symbolism within that tradition.

We begin by noting that in Hosea the reservation of the power of salvation and security to Yahweh, what we have called Yahweh's exclusive prerogative, is linked to Hosea's criticism of kingship.[239] We are leaving aside the question whether Hosea rejected kingship completely or merely wished to critique some aspect of it. Of interest to us is simply the fact of Hosea's linkage of this criticism with the notion of Yahweh's exclusive prerogative. We note further, as above, that the institution of kingship in Israel is ridiculed as incapable of performing the principal function of kingship, providing security in the face of threatened external aggression.[240] Finally, Hosea equates the making of kings with idolatry in 8.4, an equation applied elsewhere to reliance upon Assyrian strength for deliverance. The premise behind all of this is that Yahweh alone is savior and he rises in opposition to any rival pseudo-saviors.

While the language of Isaiah is somewhat different, there being no apparent criticism of kingship as such,[241] Isaiah does critique the practice of kingship in Judah since it is arrogant in its refusal to accord Yahweh his exalted status. This refusal is apparent to Isaiah in the reliance upon armaments (2.8; 30.16) and foreign alliances (30.1-5; 31.1-3) as opposed to trust in Yahweh (7.9b; 28.16). Isaiah in his critique makes explicit reference to the kingship of Yahweh, while such explicit reference is lacking in Hosea.[242] Nonetheless both prophets pose the sovereignty of Yahweh in opposition to idolatrous practices which include foreign alliances and dependence upon their power for deliverance.

b. If we concentrate for the moment on Hosea, what can we posit as the background of his polemic agaist Israelite kingship on the basis of the exclusive sovereignty of Yahweh, i.e. his exclusive status as 'savior'? Given the northern provenance of the traditions from which Hosea works it is not surprising that there seem to exist certain structural relationships between his argument and that of the sources lying behind the account of the origin of kingship in Israel found in 1 Sam 8–12.[243] While this account poses certain critical traditio-historical problems it is clear that it contains evidence of an early opposition to the institution of the monarchy.[244] Texts such as 1 Sam 8.1-7; 10.17-18; 12.12 state this opposition most clearly.[245] In these texts the desire for a king on the part of the people is portrayed as a rejection of Yahweh's kingship[246] in favor of a human deliverer. The primary motivation ascribed to those desiring a king was that they wanted to be like the surrounding nations,[247] while the primary evidence of this motivation was their request for a king. While Hosea does not employ the same language as the earliest sources of 1 Sam 8–12, we can recognize the same structure in his arguments: the people are prone to idolatry, and this is evidenced by their repudiation of Yahweh in favor of the apparent security of alliances and armaments, as well as in their turn to Baal.

The critical problems are no less serious in the book of Judges than in 1 Sam 8–12, but there seems to be good reason to believe that in the speech of Gideon (Judg 8.22-23) and in Jotham's fable (9.8-15) we have evidence of criticism of the tendency toward monarchy already in the pre-monarchic period.[248] We mention these texts only to make clear that criticism of kingship appears to depend upon the prior notion of Yahweh's kingship. As Benjamin Uffenheimer says, 'the repudiation of kingship in those days meant the rejection of any earthly sovereignty', and entailed the prior conception of Yahweh as king.[249] If this view is correct it means that the opposition to, or criticism of, kingship in the account of the founding of the monarchy in 1 Sam 8–12 rests on a tradition dating from the period of the judges according to which the kingship of Yahweh meant concretely that the human exercise of sovereignty in the form of kingship was excluded on theological grounds. Whether or not Hosea accepted such a fundamental critique is, as we have noted, open to debate. But it is clear from the text of Hosea that Yahweh's sovereignty did entail certain constraints upon the exercise of leadership in Israel, and specifically it excluded alliances and dependence upon armaments as impinging upon Yahweh's exclusive sovereignty.

c. On the basis of what we have found thus far it would seem reasonable to suggest that the background to Hosea's use of the notion of Yahweh's exclusive prerogative is to be located in the notion of Yahweh's kingship, which was used to critique the institution of monarchy in the tenth and probably the eleventh centuries BC. However, this raises yet another tradito-historical problem. For example W.H. Schmidt has agreed that the background to the criticism of kingship found in 1 Sam 8–12 is to be found in the notion of Yahweh's exclusive 'Herrschaft', but believes that this notion was the basic tenet of the tradition that later developed into Israel's holy war schema in the hands of the Deuteronomists.[250] That is, he rejects the conclusion that the idea of Yahweh's exclusive sovereignty, as expressed primarily in what he calls the 'Yahweh War or Exodus tradition', implies Yahweh's kingship, since the combination of the origially independent Yahweh war-exodus tradition and the tradition of Yahweh's kingship occurred much later in the history of traditions.[251]

This analysis is, however, misleading at a couple of points. First of all, we have already argued that the criticism of kingship in 1 Sam 8–12 presupposes as its necessary premise the kingship of Yahweh, traces of which are also found in early traditions from Judges. But, secondly, we are not reduced merely to asserting this, but can find evidence for the pre-monarchic notion of Yahweh's kingship precisely in the traditions from the pre-monarchic period in which Yahweh's deliverance of the people from Egypt is conceived as the action of a divine king and warrior acting against the forces hostile to him and his people. Chief among this evidence is Exodus 15, which is both undeniably early and portrays Yahweh acting in royal fashion.[252] It is thus necessary to correct Schmidt's analysis by insisting that the notion of Yahweh as king was the very foundation upon which the theme of the Divine Warrior was formed, and from which the tradition of holy war later developed.[253]

d. We have thus cleared the way for considering the kingship of Yahweh as the background to the use of the notion of Yahweh's exclusive prerogative in Hosea. This does not yet, however, explain the dilemma with which we began this discussion, namely the use of this notion in Hosea *and* Isaiah, since they worked in different geographical and traditio-historical contexts. To pursue such an explanation we refer now to our earlier contention, that the locus of the celebration of Yahweh's kingship and the traditio-historical origin of the Zion symbolism of the Jerusalem cult in the pre-monarchic period was the sanctuary of the Ark in Shiloh.

In Chapter 2 we argued that the twin epithets of Yahweh, צבאות and ישב הכרובים, are both essentially royal epithets attached to Yahweh in connection with the Ark at Shiloh. We argued further for the strong possibility that already in Shiloh the Ark was associated with the celebration of Yahweh's kingship in the context of the New Year celebration of the Autumn festival. It is probable that the tradition of Yahweh's kingship as it developed at Shiloh occurred in the encounter of Yahweh with Canaanite deities,[254] and that Yahweh's kingship was conceived in terms of El as the head of the divine council.[255] The status of Yahweh as supreme over all gods was further emphasized in the Jerusalem cult when he was described as

Elyon, as in Ps 47.3 and 97.9. When this insistence on the sovereignty of Yahweh as king is combined with the probability that Shiloh exercised a kind of cultic monopoly among the Israelite tribes in at least a part of the pre-monarchic period,[256] we have further historical grounds for arguing that Shiloh was the context in which Yahweh's kingship was elaborated in association with the Ark and where the exclusivity of Yahweh's kingship was spelled out.

While we have in Shiloh the probable background to the theology of Yahweh's kingship as this is formulated in the theology of the Jerusalem cult, we have not yet spelled out a plausible historical relationship between this theology and the criticism of the monarchy in 1 Sam 8-12. Some suggestions along this line need to be made, even though the evidence is necessarily sparse, since the Jerusalem cult theology is typically understood as the embodiment of the monarchicalism against which the critical texts protest. Such a historical connection has been suggested by Martin A. Cohen, who argues that during the pre-monarchic period Israel was led by the *'zeqenim'*, or elders, who opposed the usurpation of power by kings. The institution which they utilized to limit the monarchy in this fashion was 'the Yahwistic priesthood at Shiloh'.[257] Secondly, it is significant that Abiathar, the priest brought to Jerusalem by David, was probably a descendant of Eli, the priest of Shiloh, and functioned by virtue of his Levitical status as a custodian of the Ark.[258] It is thus historically probable that the traditions of the Shiloh Ark were brought to Jerusalem through Abiathar and were then used by David in the justification of his kingdom.[259] While this arrangement must have worked under David, despite the degree to which it may have compromised old Shilonite notions, it was clearly unsuccessful under Solomon.[260] It was upon Solomon's accession that Abiathar was expelled to Anathoth and Cohen suggests that it was precisely the attempts by Abiathar to limit the power of the king on the basis of the Shilonite traditions that led to his expulsion by Solomon, who wanted to establish a more unlimited form of monarchy.[261] Cohen goes on to point out that these two events, Solomon's accession and the consequent expulsion of Abiathar, help to explain the appearance of Ahijah, a prophet from Shiloh, who is credited with legitimating the division of the northern tribes from the monarchy in Jerusalem.[262]

e. If this historical reconstruction is substantially correct, as I believe it is, we may propose the following development for the notion of Yahweh's exclusive prerogative. First of all in Jerusalem, where the traditions from Shiloh were taken up into the theology of the Jerusalem cult, the notion of Yahweh's kingship became attached, through the presence of the Ark, to Mount Zion. While the newly formed Zion symbolism could be brought into the service of the royal ideology, as in Ps 2, it continued to function independently of this ideology, even to the extent of placing constraints upon the practice of kingship, as happens in Isaiah. Most importantly, the Zion symbolism derived from the traditions of the Ark in Shiloh emphasized the exaltation of Yahweh as king which is seen to entail his singular status as savior. The notion of Yahweh's exclusive prerogative is then precisely derived from the exercise of his prerogative as king and hence as the exclusive refuge of his people.

It is unlikely that Hosea inherited his language, or his use of the notion of Yahweh's exclusive prerogative, directly from Isaiah or the Jerusalem cult. Rather, we would argue, it is more likely that Hosea was part of that tradition with its roots in the Shiloh sanctuary which continued to flourish in the North. Here too the kingship of Yahweh was celebrated and was brought to bear in a critical fashion on the movement toward monarchy as attested in 1 Sam 8.7; 12.12. A substantial argument can be made for placing Hosea within the stream of tradition stemming from Shiloh and preserved by Levitical circles in the North.[263] Whether or not Abiathar played a role in the formulation of these traditions upon his removal from Jerusalem cannot be said with certainty, but it is interesting to note that Akio Tsukimoto, following the analysis of the Yahwist by Odil Hannes Steck, associates Abiathar with the 'Landjudäertum' which he believes was responsible for the composition of the primeval history in Genesis 1–11.[264] These chapters, according to Tsukimoto, were designed as a polemic agaist the arrogance of the monarchy under Solomon with its ideology formulated by the Zadokite priesthood.[265]

Whether or not this account of the origin of Genesis 1–11 can be sustained, we would maintain that the exclusive kingship of Yahweh with its traditio-historical roots in Shiloh forms the basis of the notion of Yahweh's exclusive prerogative as this prerogative is expressed in Psalms from the Jerusalem cult (20, 33, 44, 118, etc.), the book of Isaiah and Hosea. Thus it was possible for a prophet in the South, who worked from the Jerusalem cult tradition with its emphasis on Zion as the site of God's royal rule, and a prophet in the North, who worked from the tradition of Yahweh's covenant with his people redeemed from Egypt, to draw on the same tradition of

Yahweh's kingship in formulating his exclusive prerogative in the provision of security and refuge for his people. For both prophets, and for the Psalms, any efforts on the part of the people to secure themselves by any other means constituted an affront to his prerogatives as king and was, as such, an act of idolatry.

4. *The Ancient Near Eastern Context*

Our purpose in this section is simply to place the language of Yahweh's exclusive prerogative in a broader context as this is supplied primarily by royal inscriptions. We have already argued that this notion has a traditio-historical background in the Ark sanctuary at Shiloh and its Yahweh-kingship theology, but the ancient Near Eastern texts may help us by providing a context for understanding the particular language in which this notion was expressed, and may help us to appreciate its significance.

a. Some twenty years ago I.L. Seeligmann wrote a long and insightful article on the problem of the relationship between human activity and divine assistance within the biblical tradition.[266] In the course of his study he noted that a certain flexibility existed, in both Greek and Assyrian historical texts, between the ascription of deeds to human agents and to the gods. This fact in itself is not surprising, nor had it gone previously unnoticed.[267] What is interesting for our study is the similarity of the language of some of these texts to that of Yahweh's exclusive prerogative in texts associated with Zion symbolism in the Old Testament. For example, Ashurbanipal claims that

> Tirhakah, without the permission of the gods, marched forth to seize Egypt. . . . The power of Assur, my lord, he despised and trusted in his own might. The evil treatment which my father had given him had not penetrated his mind, so he came and entered Memphis.[268]

Approximately ten years later Manfred Weippert called attention to similar Mesopotamian texts in a critical study of von Rad's thesis of a uniquely Israelite cultic institution of holy war.[269] He there refers to another text of Ashurbanipal, in which the king makes the pious claim that he relied on the power of the Ishtars, rather than his own:

> Not by my own power,
> Not by the stength of my bow—

By the power of my goddesses
Did I subdue the lands under the yoke of Assur.[270]

Ashurbanipal furher testifies that 'they trusted in their own power, but I trusted in Assur, my Lord'.[271]

Weippert also refers to a text from Esarhaddon which displays a certain relationship to Israelite holy war texts, especially in that Esarhaddon proceeds to battle only after receiving a positive oracle and then relies completely on the power of Assur to bring him victory. The victory is accomplished, according to Esarhaddon, by the 'terror (-inspiring sight) of the great gods, my lords', which overwhelmed the enemy.[272] Similar texts from Egypt have been brought to light by Fritz Stolz, who refers especially to texts from Amenhotep III (*ANET*, p. 245), and from Rameses II (*ANET*, p. 257a), in which both Pharaohs are victorious through the miraculous appearance of their own divinity.[273]

> Then the great princes of every land heard of the mysterious qualities of his majesty. Then they were dismayed and afraid, and the terror of his majesty was in their hearts, while they lauded his glory and gave praise to his beautiful face, . . . [*making offer*]ing to him with their children, namely the great lords of Retenu and of strange countries—no matter which—in order to appease the heart of the Bull and to beg peace from him.[274]

There is thus clear evidence that in the ancient Near East, as well as in Israel, thought was given to the nature and extent of divine participation in victories won over human enemies. There is in these Mesopotamian and Egyptian texts an explicit concern to attribute to the deity the power and the responsibility for providing security, and in this respect they are comparable to those texts we have examined in dealing with Yahweh's exclusive prerogative.[275]

b. There is, however, one crucial difference which bears on our investigation. In each of the texts from Mesopotamia and Egypt mentioned above the explicit purpose is the exaltation of the king. For example, in the first text quoted above, the words immediately preceding the quotation are 'the kings of the rising and setting sun came and kissed my feet'. The rest of the text praised the power of Ashurbanipal in subduing his foes, including the recalcitrant Tirhakah of whom the Assyrian king finally says that 'the fear and terror of my sovereignty overwhelmed him'.[276]

Similarly in the text cited by Weippert, in which Ashurbanipal credits his victory to the Ishtars, the exaltation of the goddesses (obverse, line 1) is at the same time the exaltation of the kings: 'Who from the house of succession *have magnified* my kingship' (line 10).[277] The result of this exaltation is that the defeated kings bring gifts to the king (reverse, line 7) and 'with prayer and entreaty they kiss my feet' (line 10). The same is true in the Esarhaddon text (*ANET*, p. 289b), where the presence of Ishtar with Esarhaddon leads those who have refused to recognize his kingship to exclaim, 'This is our king', and they too kissed his feet in recognition of his sovereignty (p. 290a).

The situation is, if possible, still clearer in the Egyptian texts, because the Pharaoh himself is the embodiment of deity. Thus it is the glory of the divine Pharaoh himself that inspires awe in his enemies and results in their capitulation to his strength. On the basis of this evidence Stolz concludes that in Egypt and in Mesopotamia

> the thought is the same, that the royal function interjects the power
> of the deity into the historical realm, so that it is really—as in
> myth—the deity alone who wins victory.[278]

While it is also characteristic of the texts from the Jerusalem cult tradition which reflect the notion of Yahweh's exclusive prerogative that he alone wins victory, this victory is never said to result in the exaltation of the king, nor is the participation of the king in this victory ever described.

There are, of course, texts in the Old Testament that match very closely the notions expressed in the Near Eastern texts cited in this section, namely those texts such as Pss 2, 18, and 110 that derive from the royal ideology in Jerusalem. In these texts the exaltation of Yahweh is clearly associated with the exaltation of the king, and imagery is used that is strikingly close to that of the Near Eastern texts. For example in Ps 2.11-12 there is a reference to the formerly hostile nations kissing the feet of Yahweh's king.[279] To this may be compared the reference in Ps 72.9 to the kings of the nations licking the dust as they bow in submission to the king in Jerusalem, and Ps 110.1, where Yahweh makes the king's enemies the footstool of his feet.[280] In Ps 18 the king clearly expresses his dependence on Yahweh (vv. 21-25), but just as clearly it is the king himself who is empowered to destroy his enemies by using the weapons of war (vv. 35-43).

c. While these texts representative of the royal ideology are thus comparable to similar texts from the ancient Near East, there is a clear distinction between them and those texts from the Jerusalem cult tradition that employ the notion of Yahweh's exclusive prerogative in relation to Zion symbolism. While this distinction is clear in Pss 20, 33, 44 and 118, it is brought into radical focus by Isaiah.[281] In Isaiah this notion is brought to bear in a critical fashion on the actions of the kings themselves so that the action of Yahweh is not coordinated with that of the kings, as in Ps 18, but is contrasted to it.[282] For Isaiah, Yahweh is not the power that guarantees the success of Ahaz's or Hezekiah's military preparations; rather, those preparations are themselves the guarantee of Yahweh's judgment.

Two recent studies have attempted to deal with this notion, specifically as it is articulated by Isaiah, in relation to a 'double-causality concept' in the action of the king and of Yahweh.[283] It seems to me, however, that this concept is inappropriate and misleading, especially in relation to Isaiah, in that it tries to explain the peculiar counsel of Isaiah on the basis of some theory of human action to which Isaiah must have been committed. Isaiah's message is really not that complicated. He does not rule out Yahweh's cooperation in the conduct of military campaigns, for he makes quite explicit claims that Assyria's campaign against Judah is precisely at Yahweh's behest and under his guidance (ch. 10). Rather than engaging in action-theoretical reflection about synergism, Isaiah instead delivers himself of clear instruction about what kinds of action are appropriate given the nature of Yahweh and his commitment to Zion. The action required, according to Isaiah, is caring for the poor and the practice of social justice. It is this kind of action that is 'synergistic' with Yahweh's protection of Zion's security. Alliances and material preparations for war are, on the other hand, *not* synergistic because they work against Yahweh, not in concert with him. Thus for Isaiah it is the *kind* of action that is at issue, not *whether* action is permissible.[284] Synergism is not a univocal concept.

While the literature of the Near East is thus helpful in providing language comparable to that found in Old Testament texts which speak of Yahweh's exclusive prerogative, it is necessary at the same time to recognize the different emphasis of the language in Assyrian or Egyptian texts as compared with the Old Testament. While in the Near Eastern texts the language is always employed in the interests of glorifying the king, in the Zion texts of the Old Testament it is always Yahweh who is glorified, never the king. This difference is also obvious when it is recognized that the Egyptian and Assyrian texts are all first-person reports of the king, while in the Old Testament the king is either addressed or spoken of in the third person.[285] It seems clear, then, that the way in which the Old Testament uses the language of 'exclusive prerogative' has been decisively modified by the emphasis within the Jerusalem cult and its traditions on Yahweh's kingship.

5. Conclusions

a. We began this section by posing the question of the origin of the notion of Yahweh's *exclusive prerogative*. In an attempt to answer this question we looked first to the tradition of holy war and then to the prophets, the two sources most often posited as the source of the notion with which we are dealing. We rejected holy war as the source, because that tradition draws on the notion of Yahweh's exclusive prerogative, as well as other traditions, in its development of a holy war schema. In short, it is dependent upon the notion we have investigated, rather than being the source of it.[286] We also rejected the prophets as the source, because it is impossible to establish any traditio-historical interdependence between Isaiah and Hosea, the earliest prophetic texts in which this notion appears.[287]

b. In our discussion of the prophets, and particularly Isaiah, it became clear that the notion of Yahweh's exclusive prerogative is dependent upon earlier traditions, namely those traditions stemming from the Ark sanctuary of Shiloh which emphasized the kingship of Yahweh and consequently his exclusive status as savior and sovereign over Israel. In Isaiah this notion is bound up so completely with the symbol Zion that the symbol itself entails or evokes the entire range of notions inherited by Isaiah from the Jerusalem cult, chief among which is the notion of Yahweh's kingship. To return to the language of Victor Turner introduced in the introduction of this monograph, in Isaiah the symbol Zion has among its 'denotations' the kingship of Yahweh, and among its 'designations' the notion of his exclusive prerogative.[288]

We can say, then, that for Isaiah the source of the notion of Yahweh's exclusive prerogative was the Zion symbolism of the Jerusalem cult. With respect to the Psalms (20, 33 and 44) and Hosea, we can say that the source of the Jerusalem cult tradition itself, insofar as this tradition was rooted in the Yahweh-kingship theology of the Ark, was their source (through a vastly different traditio-historical process) for the notion of Yahweh's exclusive prerogative.

c. Among the texts that are part of the Jerusalem cult tradition we can be even more explicit in claiming the symbol Zion as the source of the notion of Yahweh's exclusive prerogative and his consequent disapproval of reliance upon armaments, as this is expressed in Pss 20, 33 and 44, and in Isaiah. This claim is based on the statements of Pss 46.10 and 76.4:

> He [Yahweh] makes wars to cease to the end of the earth.
> The bow he smashes and the spear he cuts in two.
> The wagons[289] he burns with fire.
>
> There [in Zion] he shattered the flames of the bow;[290]
> the shield, the sword and (the weapons of) war.

It has sometimes been claimed that these two texts are extraneous to the Zion tradition and do not constitute a part of the *Völkerkampf* motif with which they are connected in these Psalms.[291] This argument is dubious, on the face of it, since the only real instances of the *Völkerkampf* in pre-exilic texts are these two Psalms and Ps 48, in addition to Isaiah. In other words, apart from Ps 48 all of the pre-exilic texts that clearly attest a *Völkerkampf* also relate it either to Yahweh's destruction of weapons of war or to their prohibition.[292] We have then a very important connection in Ps 46 between the theophany of Yahweh in v. 7, which overcomes the threat of the hostile forces, and v. 10, which portrays Yahweh as establishing a universal peace and destroying the equipment of war.

The significance of Yahweh's victory over the hostile forces of chaos in Ps 46 does not come to an end with the declaration of v. 10, however, but is continued in v. 11. The meaning of this verse may not be apparent form the RSV translation, 'Be still, and know that I am God', which makes it seem identical to Hab 2.20, 'Let all the earth keep silence'. The verb in Ps 46.11 is not from חסה, as is the interjection הס in Hab 2.20, but from רפה. In the *hiphil* this verb means to 'desist' or stop doing something, a meaning conveyed by Kraus's translation, 'Lasst ab'.[293] The significance of this verse is recognized by Dahood, who translates the first verb 'be still', but notes its meaning as 'namely, do nothing'.[294] Dahood unnecessarily restricts the range of this command to 'do not enter into military alliances with other nations, since Yahweh controls history',[295] whereas the connection with v. 10 makes clear that it is the waging of war or the preparation for war generally that is in view in v. 11. In other words, the action of Yahweh in defeating the forces of chaos at Zion is tied in Ps 46 to the elimination of war and its equipment, and to the appropriate response on the part of Zion's people, namely to desist and recognize that Yahweh is God.[296]

Thus the exclusive prerogative of Yahweh is established in Ps 46 through his creative power in establishing Zion over against the powers of chaos that threaten it. War and its equipment are recognized as threats, then, not only against the created order established by Yahweh, but against his stature as 'God, exalted among the nations' (Ps 46.11b). The theology of Ps 46 is then virtually identical to that of Ps 33, where Yahweh's role as the creator who defeats chaos is tied to his kingship and both of them are the presupposition of his exclusive prerogative.

d. We have already cited Robert Bach's attempt to deny Yahweh's destruction of weapons to the symbolism associated with Zion. He assigns it rather to the prophetic re-interpretation of the Yahweh war tradition.[297] We mention Bach's argument again only because it stands in diametrical opposition to our own conclusions. Bach begins his investigation by listing a number of Old Testament texts that speak of Yahweh destroying weapons and then seeking a common origin for this language. He fails, however, to draw the necessary distinctions in the way this language is used and the different traditio-historical backgrounds that it assumes.

For example, he begins by referring to texts such as Hos 1.4-5 and Jer 49.35, which simply state that Yahweh destroys the 'bow' of Israel and Elam respectively. This is nothing more than a claim that Yahweh removes the military power of the two nations, and it has no traditio-historical relation to Pss 46.10 and 76.4.[298] Bach also fails to recognize that Hos 2.20, which also speaks of the removal of weapons from the land, is rooted in the covenant tradition with parallels in the Near Eastern language of treaty-curses. This would have been clear had Bach referred to the study of Delbert Hillers, in which he showed that the language of Lev 6.6, 25, which is most closely related to Hos 2.20,[299] closely resembles treaty-curses from Northwest Semitic texts.[300] For example, in the Sefire treaty text the wish is expressed that if the treaty is violated,

Just as (this) bow and these arrows are broken, so may 'Anahita and Hadad break [the bow of Mati'el] and the bow of his nobles.[301]

An Esarhaddon treaty expresses a similar wish:

May they break your bow . . . May they reverse the direction of the bow in your hand.[302]

By ignoring this traditional language of the Near East, Bach is forced to conclude that texts such as Hos 2.20 and Ps 46.10 are derivative of an earlier form of the tradition, which he finds in Mic 5.9-10. This text can be ascribed to the eighth-century Micah, however, with no certainty at all[303] and is more likely dependent upon Isa 2.7. It is obvious, however, that texts such as Pss 46.10, 76.4, and Isa 2.7 are not dependent upon a treaty context and are thus not part of the same tradition-history as either Hos 2.20, or Hos 1.4-5 and Jer 49.35.

We may be helped in understanding the language of Pss 46.10 and 76.4 by keeping in mind that we are dealing here with the language of kingship. This is perhaps most clearly evident in a comparison of these texts with the much later Zech 9.9-10.[304] Here the approach of Zion's king, whose identity need not be debated here, is accompanied by the announcement that Yahweh will 'cut off' the horse and chariot from Ephraim and Jerusalem, and that the 'bow of battle' will be cut off when peace is declared to the nations and the dominion of Yahweh's king will be universal.

This text participates in the general Near Eastern belief that the accession of the king inaugurated a new age of peace. This is well illustrated by a text of Ashurbanipal detailing the universal response to his installation as king.

At the proclamation of my honored name, the four regions of the world were glad and rejoiced. The kings of the Upper and Lower seas, vassals subject to my father, sent me tidings of their joy at my assumption of the kingly office. The hurled weapons of the enemy sank to the ground. The well-organized enemy broke their battle line. Their sharp lances came to a stop, they brought their drawn bows to rest. The wicked, who were planning war upon those who were not subject to them, sank down exhausted. In city and in home, a man took nothing from his neighbor by force. In the whole land, no gentleman did any evil. The one traveling by himself, traveled the farthest road in safety. There was no thief, nor shedder-of-blood. No deed of violence was committed. The lands were quiet. The four regions of the world were in perfect order, like the finest oil.[305]

In Pss 46.10 and 76.4 universal peace is announced as a result of Yahweh's triumph over his enemies, the enemies of Zion, by which his kingship and Zion's security are established. This, we conclude, is the origin and the basis for the notion of Yahweh's exclusive prerogative as this prerogative is expressed in the Psalms from Jerusalem's cult, and radicalized in the prophecy of Isaiah of Jerusalem.[306]

Chapter 5

CONCLUSION

A. SUMMARY OF RESULTS

As suggested by the title of this monograph our study has intended to investigate the theological dimensions of Zion symbolism, and the structure and character of the investigation are determined by that intention. This means, on the one hand, that the investigation of Zion symbolism here undertaken has been guided not by the traditio-historical development of the 'Zion tradition' or Zion mythology, but by the nature of Zion as a symbol, as this is elaborated in the theology of the Jerusalem cult tradition. It also means, on the other hand, that the tradition of the Jerusalem cult has provided the context, the 'evocative field', for our investigation since this tradition forms the design within which Zion functions as the central symbol. The primary advantage of this procedure is its ability to move beyond strictly historical questions regarding the origin of Zion as a discrete tradition in Israel's theological inventory to a consideration of its place in a theological structure of definite parameters.

We began our discussion with the assumption that the scholarly debate about the origin of the Zion tradition and the degree of its dependence on mythological traditions already at hand in Jerusalem, whatever its usefulness to a traditio-historical account of the faith that came to expression in Jerusalem may be, is inadequate to a theologically responsible account of the Zion symbol's significance in the articulation of this faith. Our investigation has left aside the apparently insoluble problem of possible Jebusite contributions to the Zion symbol itself and has made the integral function of the symbol within a theological tradition the starting-point of the discussion. By making this the starting-point rather than the conclusion of the investigation we have been able to raise the more theologically interesting question of the traditio-historical roots of the themes and notions which are basic to the larger Jerusalem cult tradition within which Zion is already firmly embedded in its earliest attestations. The traditio-historical questions thus play a subsidiary role in the study and are raised only insofar as they may enlighten our understanding of the network of symbolic relations in which Zion is dominant, and help us to make distinctions between this network and others, such as that sponsored more properly by the Davidic-Solomonic court and its dynasty, in which the central symbol becomes the Davidic kingship. While both of these networks are composed of traditions from the Jerusalem cult the dominant symbol, David or Zion, determines the theological valence of the symbolic network by determining—precisely *as* the dominant symbol—the nature of the relationship among all the symbols in the network or design.

This procedure has enabled us to see that the central theological notion evoked by the symbol Zion is the kingship of Yahweh, and this notion is thus the principal focus of the monograph itself. We have found that the ritual setting within which the iconic and cognitive poles of the symbol Zion are held together is the celebration of Yahweh's kingship on Zion in the Autumn festival in conjunction with the New Year. Our investigation has shown that this celebration is itself dependent upon the earlier Autumn festival at Shiloh which apparently participated in the wider Canaanite practice of conjoining celebration of the New Year with the kingship of the deity. In Shiloh the kingship of Yahweh was articulated in terms of his status as head of the 'host' or council and explicitly in connection with his enthronement over the Ark. In other words, the kingship of Yahweh, as celebrated in the Jerusalem cult tradition, is not an *ad hoc* innovation of the Jerusalem cult, but is instead the development in a particular way of traditions located in Shiloh and connected specifically with the Ark.

As we might have expected from other Near Eastern literature, the celebration of Yahweh's kingship in the Jerusalem cult is expressed in terms of the conquest of chaos, i.e. in the language of creation. When this activity of creation was examined in terms of the Zion symbolism of Jerusalem's cult two important discoveries were made. First of all, Yahweh's activity as creator is a function of his status as king. Yahweh's kingship is established in a primordial conquest of the powers of chaos, symbolized by the unruly waters that pose themselves against the created order. As king, Yahweh continues to exercise responsibility for the maintenance of this order against the threat of chaos, and the powers of chaos are just those cosmic and historical forces that threaten the cosmic and historical order of Yahweh's creation. Second, the historical order of Yahweh's creation is symbolized by Zion, which was established or created by Yahweh.

We have further discovered that this latter point is itself important in at least two respects. First, the security of Zion is grounded in its creation by Yahweh as the site of his royal residence. As the Songs of Zion make clear, the threat to Zion by cosmic and historical forces is ephemeral because Yahweh, the great king, is Zion's defender. Secondly, just as the status of Yahweh as king is the ground of Zion's security against all external threats, so his status as king is also the ground for the exclusion of all internal efforts to provide for the security of Jerusalem by means independent of trust in Yahweh as the creator and hence defender of the city. We will return to this point below.

Previous scholarship, which has tended to subsume the symbol Zion under the category of Davidic kingship, has failed to account for this specifically political dimension of Zion theology. Our procedure has enabled us to differentiate the network of symbolic relations in which Zion is the central symbol from the contours that this network assumes when the earthly kingship itself is elevated to a position of symbolic dominance. While we have shown that this distinction is defensible on purely traditio-historical grounds, it is equally important to note that the two symbols—Zion and David—are central to two networks of different theological and political character. When Zion is subsumed under David the responsibility for security is shared between the earthly and heavenly kings. In the symbolic design in which Zion is central, however, the political responsibility of earthly kingship or leadership assumes a different character. When this distinction is ignored the specific theological character of Zion symbolism is missed and Zion is relegated to a component in the structure of the legitimacy, succession and hegemony of the Davidic dynasty.

Part of the theological and hence ethical-political dimension of Zion symbolism was brought to light in our discussion of Zion as a refuge. Zion symbolizes refuge, it was argued, because Yahweh's role as king includes the provision of security for his people, security available only at Zion. It is at this point that the specific ethical dimension of Zion symbolism is highlighted, since the availability of security in Zion is made conditional on the posture of the community. In the texts this conditionality is expressed in terms of faith or trust. These terms are not left without definition in the Jerusalem cult tradition, but are connected concretely with the corporate response to Yahweh's promise to be the savior of his people. The posture of trust is further defined by the term 'poor', which was seen to describe the community or those within the community who seek refuge in Zion, leaving to Yahweh the prerogative he claims to be the defender of Jerusalem. At the same time, the community of the 'poor' distinguished by its faith or trust, and its willingness to seek refuge only in Yahweh on Zion, is contrasted with the 'proud' whose oppression of the poor is an internal parallel to the external forces of chaos who appear to threaten the security of Jerusalem. Faith is thus established as a criterion for evaluating the internal and external policies of Judah's leadership, an evaluation conducted in its most extensive form by Isaiah.

The theological dimension of faith or trust that is a part of Zion symbolism helps to form a bridge between the iconic component of Zion as a symbol of security and refuge on the one hand, and the cognitive component of Zion symbolism on the other. We explicated the principal features of this cognitive component in terms of Yahweh's exclusive prerogative, which formed the substance of our investigation in Chapter 4. This investigation began by examining the traditional arguments for deriving this notion from either Israel's holy war tradition or the prophets. We found these arguments less compelling than our own conclusion that Yahweh's exclusive prerogative is a notion drawn from the Jerusalem cult tradition itself. While we sought to show that there continue to be certain traditio-historical links between the notion of Yahweh's exclusive prerogative and the primary denotation or set of denotations of Zion as a symbol, namely the kingship of Yahweh, it is just as important to note that these two notions continue to function in relation to each other within the network of symbolic relations constituted by the Jerusalem cult tradition, with Zion as its central symbol.

We have seen that this relationship between Yahweh's kingship on Zion and his exclusive prerogative is not only a central component of certain poems from the Jerusalem cult but is at the same time the theological foundation of a number of prophetic passages. This is especially true of Isaiah. While previous scholarship has noted the 'utopian' character of Isaiah's political counsel and has sought to ground it in the prophet's appropriation of either a Zion mythology or the promises to David, we have shown that Isaiah's political understanding represents a theologically consistent exegesis of the Zion symbolism of the Jerusalem cult. Thus, for Isaiah the security of Jerusalem is grounded in the kingship of Yahweh on Zion and is dependent upon the acknowledgment of Yahweh's exclusive prerogative. Hence, security is not something intrinsic to Jerusalem by virtue of its location, but is rather the result of Yahweh's royal presence and is available insofar as Judah and its leaders exercise faith, by resisting the temptation to seek security through armaments and alliances that would infringe upon a prerogative exclusively Yahweh's. Within the structure of Isaiah's message, then, Yahweh's exclusive prerogative is entailed in his kingship, and faith is again that dimension of Zion symbolism connecting its iconic (security) and cognitive (kingship—exclusive prerogative) poles. Isaiah's utopianism is not derived from a myth of Zion's inviolability or from the tradition of promises to David, but is really a coherent attempt to make political strategy realistic in terms of Yahweh's sovereignty over the forces of chaos, as this sovereignty was explicated in the tradition of the Jerusalem cult.

B. CONCLUSIONS AND IMPLICATIONS

Thus far in this concluding chapter we have attempted to show that an investigation of Zion as a theological symbol in the Jerusalem cult tradition calls for a reappraisal of the theological character of this symbol as it has been understood in previous Old Testament scholarship. We have thus far been addressing problems and issues in the academic discipline of Old Testament studies. However, a conclusion to an exegetical inquiry may also suggest how the results achieved in the course of the investigation may be of importance to a wider community of interest. In the remainder of this chapter I want to pursue this second course. While the hermeneutical dimensions of *explicatio* and *applicatio* are not discrete activities that follow on one another as separate methodological steps, in what follows I shall turn explicitly to the question of application by offering what I take to be the contributions of the preceding investigation to this wider community of interest.

The community addressed here is the North American Christian community, specifically that portion of this community that considers it important to bring biblical interpretation to bear on the general question of the shape of Christian faithfulness in this age. I specify the community of interest in this way for a simple reason:

> God reveals himself to human beings who are preoccupied with their own concrete situation. We can only understand and appreciate the word of God if we take that fact into account. Only in connection with the problems that are embodied in the questions of the community can we comprehend who exactly this responding God is. If we fail to understand the situation and problems of the community, we cannot possibly come to know that God.[1]

The author from whom this quote is taken, Juan Luis Segundo, is a theologian whose community comprises the oppressed Christians of Latin America, specifically Uruguay. I want to make it clear that the community addressed in this conclusion is a very different community, comprising North Americans who enjoy, by and large, positions of wealth, prestige and hence power. It is to this community that I wish to offer the resources of Zion symbolism discovered in the preceding investigation.

1. *Exodus*

In the recent past there has been no shortage of studies on the topic of what we might call the application of the Bible to public life.[2] It is perhaps not surprising that in many of the studies that seek to draw on the Bible as a source of moral vision, or even as a source of ethical norms, the Old Testament tradition of the Exodus is viewed as articulating the fundamental value framework by which a particularly Christian approach to ethical and political issues should be shaped. This view is due in part, of course, to the conviction commonly held by scholars that the Exodus was the primary datum of Israel's faith and that the Pentateuch itself grew up around this central tradition and central experience.[3] But the historical development of the Old Testament is often not the primary issue in the choice of this one tradition or theme as central. It is actually not at all difficult to see why the Exodus serves in this foundational capacity. It is the story of God's powerful intervention on behalf of a group of slaves in liberating people to pursue life in their own land under his protection. Thus, when Ronald Sider wishes to lay a biblical foundation for his study of Christian responsibility to the poor and hungry he turns first to the Exodus, claiming that

> The Exodus was certainly the decisive event in the creation of the chosen people. We distort the biblical interpretation of this momentous occasion unless we see that at this pivotal point, the Lord of the universe was at work correcting oppression and liberating the poor.[4]

Given this character of the Exodus it is not surprising that it is the dominant theme in the use of the Old Testament by theologians of liberation.[5] Gustavo Guttierez demonstrates the usefulness of this theme for a Christian understanding of liberation:

> The liberation of Israel [the Exodus] is a political action. It is the breaking away from a situation of despoliation and misery and the beginning of the construction of a just and fraternal society. It is the suppression of disorder and the creation of a new order.[6]

The most sustained exploration of the value of the Exodus to Latin American theologians of liberation has been provided by J. Severino Croatto, who explains why precisely the Exodus has this value by saying that

> For us . . . the Exodus is established as a *radical* datum, exceedingly profound, *in which* both Israel and we ourselves must interpret God and ourselves. The Exodus becomes an inexhaustible 'reservoir-of-meaning'. For this reason its 'donation-of-meaning' is unlimited, whence its unique hermeneutical possibilities for Latin American theology.[7]

It is perhaps unnecessary to quote other writers. Suffice it to say that the Exodus is *the* Old Testament theme or metaphor most often drawn upon to support the claims of Christian theologians that the Bible, and in this case, the Old Testament, bears on contemporary ethical and political problems in a particular way; namely, in favor of social change or social transformation toward more just and equitable relationships, in which the poor and oppressed are protected from the power of the rich.

2. Zion

It is not my purpose in this context to offer a critique of the use particularly by Latin American theologians of the Exodus as a starting-point for addressing the situation of oppression in which they work.[8] Rather, I want to treat a problem that has emerged in contemporary Old Testament scholarship based in part on the very power of the Exodus to evoke, or to form the normative basis of, a moral vision appropriate to the application of the Old Testament and even the whole Christian gospel to the contemporary situation. The problem of which I speak is that the Exodus is often seen as providing a radical critique not only of the exploitation and oppression of the poor in modern society, but also of a substantial portion of the Old Testament itself. This problem has emerged in an acute fashion in contemporary Old Testament scholarship, in which the Old Testament is sometimes conceived as containing broadly two distinct traditions or streams of tradition.[9] For convenience we may refer to these as the Mosaic and the Jerusalem traditions.

These two traditions are usually characterized as follows. The Mosaic tradition is historical in character: It centers on the particularity of Israel's history, on episodes in the lives of individual patriarchs and their families, on the liberation from Egypt, the occupation of Canaan and various episodes in the history of Israel and Judah during the period of the monarchy. It is also covenantal in character, emphasizing the relationship of Yahweh and Israel governed by Torah, a conditional covenant whose stipulations carry the sanctions of punishment and removal from the land.

The Jerusalem tradition, on the other hand, is cosmic in character: it centers on the creation of the world, and on the establishment of Zion as the site of Yahweh's dwelling. It speaks of covenant and election in unconditional terms, as promise: Yahweh's solemn promise to defend Jerusalem against attack and to maintain the Davidic dynasty. While the Mosaic tradition tends to conceive of God's presence dialectically, as the God who hides his face, who appears and then recedes, the Jerusalem temple conceives God's presence as constant. While the Mosaic tradition focuses on *liberation* through the defeat of Israel's historical enemies, the Jerusalem tradition focuses on *creation* through Yahweh's conquest of the powers of chaos. And finally, it is said, the Mosaic tradition is composed of theological notions and historical traditions indigenous to Israel, while the Jerusalem tradition owes its character to Canaanite society and its mythology.

When the Mosaic tradition, in which the Exodus is located, and the Jerusalem tradition are contrasted in this way it is easy to see why the Exodus is not only preferred over the Jerusalem tradition as a more appropriate source of moral vision, but is prone to become the normative basis from which the Jerusalem tradition is judged to be a reflex of the pagan religion against which Moses and his followers protested. That this statement is not hyperbolic is evidenced by George Mendenhall's claim that

> What we can now prove is the fact that the cultic/political system of Jerusalem during the Monarchy had nothing to do with the Yahwist revolution and was actually completely incompatible with that religious movement. Further, we can prove that almost every item concerning the Monarchy in the biblical record . . . justifies the conclusion that during Solomon's regime the Jerusalem state became a very typical Syro-Hittite political system.[10]

On the basis of Mendenhall's historical judgments Walter Brueggemann proceeds to draw a contrasting theological profile of the two traditions that compete for space in the Old Testament.

> . . . The Mosaic tradition tends to be a movement of protest which is situated among the disinherited and which articulates its theological vision in terms of a God who decisively intrudes, even against seemingly impenetrable institutions and orderings. On the other hand, the Davidic tradition tends to be a movement of consolidation which is situated among the established and secure and which articulates its theological vision in terms of a God who faithfully abides and sustains on behalf of the present ordering.[11]

Given this characterization of the two traditions Brueggemann designates the Mosaic tradition the 'liberation trajectory' and the Jerusalem tradition the 'royal trajectory'.[12] Having applied these value-laden labels to the two traditions, he then proceeds to differentiate their spheres of interest by saying that the Mosaic trajectory 'focuses on the justice and righteousness of God's will', an interest by implication lacking in the royal trajectory, which 'is never primarily concerned about such matters'.[13] The reason that the royal trajectory of the Jerusalem tradition lacks an interest in justice is that it is based in 'creation faith', which embraces 'more of the imperial myths of the ancient near east' and breaks 'with the scandalous historical particularity of the Moses tradition'.[14]

The Zion symbolism that we have investigated in this study is an inextricable part of the Jerusalem tradition, as we have sought to show throughout. This being the case, if we are to accept

Brueggemann's characterization it would seem to follow that Zion symbolism's contribution to contemporary theological reflection should be limited to that of a negative example—a foil against which the brilliant theological and ethical clarity of the Exodus could be played off. That I do not intend to follow this strategy should be clear from the preceding investigation of Zion symbolism itself. What we have in fact found in this symbolism is anything but what Brueggemann's studies would lead us to expect. What we have found in the Zion symbolism of the Jerusalem cult tradition is a constant, pervasive concern for justice, a consistent and radical criticism of royal attempts to pervert justice, a theologically motivated attempt to ground this justice in the action and character of God and a sustained emphasis on the poor as the particular concern not only of Yahweh himself but also of the very symbolism of the Jerusalem cult which Brueggemann characterizes as even indifferent to the poor and to justice. Perhaps the most striking of Brueggemann's claims is that the Mosaic tradition emphasized 'singular reliance on Yahweh', while the Jerusalem tradition encouraged 'a more prudent embrace of the gifts of culture'.[15] Since we have just devoted a chapter to an examination of the Jerusalem cult's notion of Yahweh's exclusive prerogative we could be expected to take some exception to Brueggemann's claim.

One problem with Brueggemann's analysis is that it is not sufficiently nuanced to allow for any differentiation within the 'Jerusalem tradition'. Had he drawn distinctions among the various components of this mass of material he might have been able to distinguish between 'liberating' and 'oppressing' strands of the larger tradition without disqualifying everything non-Mosaic as non-liberating. Part of the problem with Brueggemann's argument is procedural. It is striking that he is unable to cite any texts which articulate the position that he characterizes as the royal trajectory except those texts that portray prophets arguing against kings or their representatives. In other words, the primary evidence on which he draws for his characterization of the Jerusalem tradition is drawn from those sources which are at least ostensibly arguing against it. While this is an illegitimate historical method it is also part of an inappropriate hermeneutical method. On the one hand, Brueggemann draws on texts from the 'liberation trajectory' to portray clearly a tradition, perhaps even a *theology* of covenant. On the other hand he draws from these and other texts to portray a *practice*, namely royal practice, and infers from it a theology or a tradition. That is, he imputes to the Jerusalem tradition a theology nowhere advocated in the texts.

There are two significant points at which Brueggemann departs from this procedure, and both of them tell against his argument. In the one instance he refers to Ps 72, conceding that it offers hope of 'a humane reality in a social world of hostility', but concluding that it really presupposes a 'management mentality' that counts against liberation.[16] He fails to note either that the Psalm is concerned from beginning to end with justice, or that this justice is in the specific interest of the poor and oppressed. Secondly, in a series of instances cited by him to show how prophets from the Mosaic tradition confronted the kings of Israel and Judah with radical criticism, he seems to run aground on Isa 7.1-9.7. He tries to rescue the argument by claiming that Isaiah's critique is really not so radical as Amos's. Brueggemann is forced into this reservation because Isaiah's message is clearly formulated wholly in terms of the Jerusalem trajectory. He tries to obviate this by claiming that

> The confrontation of Isaiah and Ahaz (Isa 7.1-9.7) is somewhat different because Isaiah is not so unambiguously placed in the Mosaic trajectory, though of course he does affirm a transcendence beyond royal perception in his use of the key words 'glory'. . . and 'holy'. . .[17]

What Brueggemann ignores is that precisely the reason Isaiah is able to confront Ahaz with such a radical critique is that he is rooted so firmly in the Jerusalem tradition and its theology of creation, which includes among its presuppositions the exaltation of Yahweh as king, and indeed his glory and holiness which are most apparent in his theophanic appearance in that favored of all Jerusalem institutions, the temple.[18]

3. *Creation*

It cannot be denied that in the hands of the royal court Zion symbolism could serve as an instrument for the legitimation of royal prerogatives and dynastic succession. But in our investigation we have also seen that the same symbolism could also serve purposes quite different from those the kings might have found useful. It is my conviction, already stated, that the critical use made of Zion symbolism in the Psalms and in Isaiah is available to us today. In the remarks that follow I want to indicate in a broad and perhaps oblique fashion how Zion symbolism and the theology it focuses may contribute to the reflection of the North American theological community.[19]

In the first place the Zion symbolism of the Jerusalem cult tradition places the historical particularity of Israel's experience with Yahweh as its liberator and judge within the cosmic framework of universal creation. Within this cosmic framework Yahweh is conceived as king—as the only king—to whom not only Israel, its priests and leaders are subject, but the king to whom all kings and all gods on heaven and earth are subject. In my judgment it is not adequate to the testimony of the Old Testament texts themselves to regard creation theology as either an interpolation of pagan theology into the more properly historical theology of Israel, or as a mere set of deductive inferences made by the Old Testament tradents on the basis of their historical experience of Yahweh. Whatever the psychological or traditio-historical processes whereby creation came to be articulated in the Old Testament tradition, the theological confession of Yahweh as king and creator stands as the presupposition to the particular history of Israel in the context of the world history of which it was a part.[20]

The creation theology in which Zion symbolism participates places *all* particular histories within the universal framework of God's good and just creation. It is not merely the prolegomenon to Israel's history, nor the first of Yahweh's historical acts with Israel as its object. Rather, creation theology places the liberation of Israel within the context of God's cosmic plan—within a universal 'world order'—to which all other plans, those of Israel, Egypt, Assyria, Babylon and their kings are subject.

Secondly, because Yahweh is king and creator/defender, according to the Zion symbolism of the Jerusalem cult, he exercises a monopoly on imperial power. It is this monopoly of power that we have termed Yahweh's 'exclusive prerogative'. In the texts which we have examined, this exclusive prerogative was seen to be directed against the attempts of Israel and Judah to find security in international alliances and military armaments. But Yahweh's exclusive prerogative is also violated in the 'perversion of power', as Croatto puts it, practiced by the socially and politically powerful who are 'crushing my people, by grinding the face of the poor' (Isa 3.15, RSV).[21]

It is important that both of these, creation and Yahweh's exclusive prerogative, be seen together. In the theology of the Jerusalem cult it was through Yahweh's conquest of chaos that his kingship, and hence his exclusive prerogative, was established. This conquest of chaos was not limited to the defeat of powers hostile to Yahweh and his people but resulted positively in the creation of a world-order which is good (Genesis 1) and just (Psalm 99).[22] It is not only the origin of this world-order for which Yahweh is responsible, but its maintenance and even its re-creation as well (Isa 65.17). For that reason Yahweh opposes all that perverts this world-order, such as injustice against the poor who have a refuge in Zion, or stands in opposition to his exclusive prerogative, such as dependence upon arms and alliances for security. Indeed, the particular history of Israel and its relation to other nations of the Near East can be viewed as Yahweh's action in accordance with the world-order which he established. If Israel was intended to be the historical exemplar of the justice of God's creation, then his interventions of judgment can be seen as judgments against the perversion of this created order through the practice of idolatry, oppression or injustice. Conversely, when the nations of the Near East arrogate to themselves the power to 'plan' the destruction of his people, God asserts his prerogative in saving his people from the perverted power of their enemies.[23]

It must be emphasized that the world-order of God's good and just creation is offered in the traditions of the Jerusalem cult as a statement of the way things really are. It is not offered as a wish for the way things could be, or a hope for what they will become, but as a positive affirmation of what is 'really real'.[24] In the real world Yahweh is Lord and King and his exclusive prerogative is exercised. It does not matter that other, alternative realities have been proposed by kings who believe that peace and security depend on power under their control, or by 'the wicked', who tyrannize the poor without fear of retribution (Ps 9/10). The realities presumed by kings and tyrants are false realities, just as idols are false gods, and all are subject to the judgment of God who is the Lord of creation.

Thirdly, we have seen in our investigation that there is a human component to the Zion symbolism, what we have called 'the anthropology of Zion'. It is related to Yahweh's exaltation as king and forms the appropriate response to his kingship, namely a posture of subordination and trust. This subordination is not merely an act of obeisance to a monarch, but a reasonable response to the recognition that this posture is the one appropriate to the way the world really is according to the theology of creation. Given that Yahweh is king and the creation is an expression of his justice, subordination to his order is not an abdication of either responsibility or human prerogatives. It is rather the recognition that human responsibility is nothing other than the practice of justice which conforms to the just order of creation.

The positive side of subordination is trust, or faith. Trust, as we have seen, is involved with the recognition of Yahweh's exclusive prerogative and the consequent recognition that human activity that encroaches on this prerogative is doomed, because it is unrealistic—it presupposes a reality in which Yahweh is not king. For Isaiah, at least, this was not an abstract notion, nor one reduced to a mere disposition. He translated trust in Yahweh into concrete counsel to a king faced with the responsibility of making strategic decisions in the face of a complex political problem. When Isaiah met Ahaz inspecting his defensive resources he gave the king strategic advice: 'Take heed, be quiet, do not be afraid, and do not let your heart be faint' (7.4, RSV). This strategic counsel was not based upon a naive pacifism, but on the belief that Yahweh is king and that trust in military arms and alliances for security is idolatrous and foolish. That Isaiah's counsel was unrealistic is a judgment based on a view of reality to which Isaiah could not subscribe. The choice of what is really real, and hence what policy is realistic, is not a choice limited to Ahaz. In the language of the Jerusalem cult tradition it is a continuing choice between faith and pride.[25]

4. The order of the real world

If the Exodus tradition offers to the oppressed Christians of Latin America a paradigm of liberation, the Zion symbolism of the Jerusalem cult tradition offers to the North American Christian community a paradigm of a different character.[26] It is a paradigm in which especially the perversion of power is condemned as an arrogant act of idolatry which is incommensurate with faith in Yahweh the creator. Furthermore, the paradigm offered by Zion symbolism condemns the justifications we offer for the perversion of power by appeal to the realities of the world, a world in which humankind, not Yahweh, is king. Finally, the paradigm of Zion symbolism condemns absolutely and without equivocation the reliance upon the perversion of power for the creation of our own security.[27]

It may be thought by some that the monarchical image of God in Zion symbolism is inappropriate, if not irrelevant, to the present era, in which images of a suffering God seem so much more pertinent. For that reason it is important to make clear that the emphasis on Yahweh's kingship in Zion symbolism does not mean 'the theological legitimation of imperial monarchy and the exercise of absolute power in the political sphere'.[28] It means, in fact, the precise opposite. The notion of God as king in the context of Zion symbolism, when interpreted in a manner that follows the clues of the texts themselves, is counter to any human form of dominion in which the prerogatives of God are contravened and humankind itself is seen to be both the executor of power and the legislator who determines the norms of its execution. The 'exercise of absolute power in the political sphere' entails in its very conception the repudiation of God's kingship and at the same time, at least by implication, a repudiation of the world-order which is his creation in favor of an alternative world-order in which humankind is both creator and redeemer. The notion of God's kingship entailed in the doctrine of creation is thus incompatible with the practice of tyranny in the world, and the Zion symbolism of the Jerusalem cult tradition offers a powerful critique of any and all forms of imperial monarchy, whether or not they invoke divine sanction.

It is indisputable on historical grounds that nations and kings have legitimated the practice of tyranny and oppression by appeal to divine kingship. A rejection of this appeal on biblical grounds must not proceed by removing, denying or tempering the Old Testament language of divine kingship, but rather by emphasizing just this language and its exegesis within the biblical tradition itself. It is just because God exercises the royal prerogative exclusively that no other attempts, human or divine, to exercise this prerogative are legitimate.[29]

It may also be thought that what we have called the 'anthropology of Zion', the belief that divine exaltation entails human subordination, is inappropriate to the nobility and freedom of persons, and that it undermines the achievement and realization of full personhood and its creative potential. However, this criticism also seems to miss the point. To quote Karl Barth:

In relation to God the creature is lowly and dependent and relative. But this position of lowliness and dependence and relativity in relation to God does not involve a degradation or depreciation or humiliation of the creature. To be lowly before God is its exaltation ... It is the glory of the creature to be lowly in relation to God. For when it is relative to Him, it participates with all its activities and effects in His absoluteness. To be able to serve Him alone with all its activities and in all its joint-effects, to be in His hands and under His control only as a means, an instrument, the clay of the potter—this is its direct and original glory.[30]

In the language of Zion symbolism, human subordination and humility before the kingship of God 'is the glory of the creature' because this subordination occurs in the recognition that in his royal activity of creation God establishes a good and just world-order over which he is Lord. Theologically considered this means that human projects are appropriate and can 'succeed' only insofar as they acknowledge that order of God's creation. Furthermore, this means that any alternative order proposed by humankind or presupposed in the projects of humankind must be critically tested against the world-order of God's good and just creation. For biblical theology this does not mean a turn to natural theology, for we are not speaking here of a close reading of nature to see what possibilities are there revealed. Rather, we are speaking of rigorous and critical interpretation of the theology of creation articulated in the Zion symbolism of the Jerusalem cult tradition.[31] According to this symbolism, as we have interpreted it in the previous chapters, we must realize that the world-order most often presupposed by the proposals and actions of nations and individuals in the contemporary world is not real. This is essentially the message of Isaiah to Ahaz and Hezekiah. The kings proposed a certain course of action appropriate to the common understanding of the world, of what was real, among nations of the Near East, including Judah. The response of the prophet was that the kings' projects were bound to fail because they were not realistic. The kings' projects assumed that security for Jerusalem and Judah could be obtained through a system of alliances and adequate military armaments which would cumulatively supersede the estimated strength of those forces hostile to Judah. The projects were based, according to Isaiah, on the false assumptions that (a) in the real world the plans of nations determine how history will turn out; (b) it would be unrealistic to depend entirely on the promises of God for the defense of his people.

The prophet's message was based, as we have seen, on a view of reality in which God is exalted and humankind is humbled. According to this view of reality the full potential of human existence can only be realized when the arrogance of human exaltation is sacrificed to the sovereignty of God and life is pursued in conformity to the justice[32] of God's creation. In this world-order the widow, the orphan and the poor are not to fear the arrogant and powerful, because Zion, the center of God's creation and symbol of its order, is created as their refuge (Isa 14.32)

In summary, the monarchical language of Zion symbolism does not legitimate 'imperial monarchy', it prohibits it. The subordination of humankind in the face of Yahweh's exaltation does not limit or suppress human realization and responsibility, it sets forth the parameters of the real world and its just order in which authentic humanity can be achieved.

It would seem that the contributions of Zion symbolism to the life of the Christian community in North America, as I have here outlined them, are primarily negative. I wish, however, to conclude this conclusion on a positive note.

If I have interpreted the Zion symbolism of Jerusalem's cult tradition correctly, it is fundamentally a theology of creation. Furthermore, this creation theology wishes to assert that it is pre-eminently through creation, rather than nature or history, that God is related to the world.[33] This claim, if true, is theologically and morally significant. It means at the very least that since creation is by definition a universal category, the possibilities open to all humankind are determined not by history or by nature, but by creation.

We know that at various points in human history we have been told that it is impossible to have a world without slavery, for the inferiority of some peoples to others is part of the essential fabric of history, or it is grounded in the immutable order of nature. We have been told that the idea that men and women could govern themselves in a democracy is impossible, for the monarchy is part of the essential fabric of history, or it is grounded in the immutable order of nature. We have been told that it is impossible for women to hold positions of significance or assume equal responsibility with men, for the domination of women by men is part of the essential fabric of history, or it is grounded in the immutable order of nature. In the present day we are being told that a world without poverty is impossible, for poverty is part of the essential fabric of history—the poor we have always with us, or it is part of the immutable order of nature. And we are being told that a world without war is impossible, for war is an essential part of the fabric of history, or it is part of the immutable order of nature. However, at the very heart of the 'Jerusalem tradition' is the affirmation that our vision of what is *possible* is to be determined not by history or by nature, but by *creation*.

The vision here offered on the basis of Zion symbolism is not simply a romantic image of a carefree world in which there is no evil and humankind is really a pacific creature, of pure heart and gentle demeanor. Rather, what is offered in the Zion symbolism investigated in this study is a moral vision based on possibilities grounded in the justice of God and thus in the cosmic order of his creation. It is a vision that compels us as Christians to transcend the limited possibilities unfolded by history and revealed by nature, and to offer to the world the example of life pursued beyond the historical and natural limitations of death itself. It is thus a vision based not on human possibilities, but on God's. It is a vision based on faith in God the king and creator who raised Jesus from the dead and pronounced a divine 'No!' to moral visions limited to 'human potential', moral visions inadequate to the challenges of this critical age.

The conviction has grown out of the preceding investigation that it is only within the comprehensive, cosmic scope of Zion and its theology of creation that we have available this radical, new (yet unspeakably ancient) vision of the good and just order of Yahweh's creation, empowering us to envision a world in which even war itself is no longer deemed a necessity, and a world without war (if not without conflict) is envisioned as a possibility, because in Zion the city of God it is said,

> Come, behold the works of the Lord,
> How he has wrought desolations in the earth.
> He makes wars to cease to the end of the earth;
> He breaks the bow, and shatters the spear,
> He burns the chariots with fire!
> Be still, and know that I am God,
> I am exalted among the nations,
> I am exalted in the earth! (Ps 46.8-10, RSV)

NOTES

Notes to Chapter 1

1. For a comprehensive analysis of traditio-historical research see Douglas A. Knight, *Rediscovering the Traditions of Israel* (SBLDS, 9; Missoula: Scholars Press, revised edition, 1975).

2. Cf. the essays in the volume edited by Douglas A. Knight, *Tradition and Theology in the Old Testament* (Philadelphia: Fortress, 1977).

3. Gunkel, *Genesis, übersetzt und erklärt* (HKAT, 1/1; Göttingen: Vandenhoeck & Ruprecht, fourth edition, 1917).

4. The work of von Rad and Noth is evaluated by Knight in *Rediscovering the Traditions of Israel*, pp. 97-176.

5. Von Rad, *Old Testament Theology*, 2 vols., trans. by D.M.G. Stalker (New York: Harper & Row, 1962, 1965). Cf. Bernhard W. Anderson, 'Tradition and Scripture in the Community of Faith', *JBL* 100 (1981), pp. 5-21; Walther Zimmerli, 'Alttestamentliche Traditionsgeschichte und Theologie', in *Studien zur alttestamentlichen Theologie und Prophetie: Gesammelte Aufsätze* II (TBü, 51; München: Chr. Kaiser, 1974), pp. 9-26.

6. On the characteristics of a tradition see Knight, *Rediscovering the Traditions of Israel*, p. 26.

7. Cf. von Rad, *Old Testament Theology* I, pp. 175-79.

8. See for example the study by Bernhard W. Anderson, 'Exodus Typology in Second Isaiah', in *Israel's Prophetic Heritage: Essays in Honor of James Muilenburg*, ed. by B.W. Anderson and Walter Harrelson (New York: Harper & Row, 1962), pp. 177-95.

9. Cf. Odil Hannes Steck, 'Theological Streams of Tradition', in *Tradition and Theology in the Old Testament*, pp. 183-214, especially pp. 184-85. I am dependent on Steck for what follows as well.

10. *Ibid.*, p. 190.

11. See the analysis of Steck's method in Knight, *Rediscovering the Traditions of Israel*, pp. 187-89.

12. Steck, 'Theological Streams of Tradition', p. 193.

13. 'Die Stadt auf dem Berge', *EvT* 9 (1948/49), pp. 439-47; also in *Gesammelte Studien zum Alten Testament* (TBü, 8; München: Chr. Kaiser, 1958), pp. 214-24.

14. 'Jerusalem und die israelitische Tradition', *OTS* 8 (1950), pp. 28-46; also in *Gesammelte Studien zum Alten Testament* (TBü, 11; München: Chr. Kaiser, 1960), pp. 172-87. See also the article by K.L. Schmidt from the same year, 'Jerusalem als Urbild und Abbild', *Eranos-Jahrbuch* 18 (1950), pp. 207-

48. Schmidt's essay deals primarily with post-OT developments.

15. 'Die Bedeutung der Erwählungstraditionen Israels für die Eschatologie der alttestamentlichen Propheten' (Dissertation: Heidelberg, 1956). Also noteworthy is the article of the previous year by H. Schmid, 'Jahwe und die Kulttraditionen von Jerusalem', *ZAW* 67 (1955), pp. 168-97.

16. Rohland, 'Bedeutung der Erwählungstraditionen', p. 142. These motifs are also enumerated by J.J.M. Roberts, 'The Davidic Origin of the Zion Tradition', *JBL* (1973), pp. 329-44. Cf. also R.E. Clements, *Isaiah and the Deliverance of Jerusalem* (JSOT Supplement Series, 13; Sheffield: JSOT Press, 1980), pp. 72-89.

17. Rohland, 'Bedeutung der Erwählungstraditionen', p. 142. Hans Martin Lutz (*Jahwe, Jerusalem und die Völker: Zur Vorgeschichte von Sach 12,1-8 und 14,1-5* [WMANT, 27; Neukirchen-Vluyn: Neukirchener Verlag, 1968]) notes the variations among (1) the 'Völkersturm', in which the nations storm Zion's gates; (2) the 'Völkerkampf', in which Yahweh battles against the nations; (3) Yahweh's own battle against Jerusalem (note ch. 4, *passim*).

18. 'Die Völkerwallfahrt zum Zion', *VT* 7 (1957), pp. 62-81.

19. 'Sancta Civitas, Jerusalem Nova: Eine formkritische und überlieferungs-geschichtliche Studie zu Is 2', *TTS* 15 (1862), pp. 17-33, especially p. 28. See Walther Eichrodt, 'Prophet and Covenant: Observations on the Exegesis of Isaiah', in *Proclamation and Presence: Essays in Honor of G. Henton Davies*, ed. by J.L. Durham and J.R. Porter (Richmond: John Knox, 1970), p. 178, note 23.

20. Rohland, 'Bedeutung der Erwählungstraditionen', p. 174, note 2. See also Isa 45.14-17; 49.22-23.

21. For a very helpful overview of the motifs in the Zion tradition see Bertil Albrektson, *Studies in the Text and Theology of the Book of Lamentations* (STL, 21; Lund: CWK Gleerup, 1963), pp. 219-30.

22. Gunkel included Ps 122, while recognizing that it was different in form from the others. Cf. Hermann Gunkel and Joachim Begrich, *Einleitung in die Psalmen: Die Gattungen der religiösen Lyrik Israels* (Göttingen: Vandenhoeck & Ruprecht, 1933), p. 42.

23. *Ibid.*, p. 80.

24. *Ibid.*, p. 81.

25. *Ibid.* He placed Ps 132 in the same *Sitz im Leben*.

26. *Ibid.*

27. A comprehensive review of the historical and eschatological inter-pretations of these Psalms can be found in E. Lipiński, *La Royauté de Yahvé dans la Poésie et la Culte de l'Ancien Israël* (Brussel: Paleis der Academien, 1965), pp. 20-43. The most important criticism of Gunkel was that of Mowinckel in *Psalmenstudien II: Das Thronbesteigungsfest Jahwäs und der Ursprung der Eschatologie*, published in 1961 as part 2 of volume 1 (Amsterdam: P. Schippers, 1969), see especially pp. 63-64. The work was originally written in 1920.

28. See for example Gunther Wanke, *Die Zionstheologie der Korachiten in ihrem traditionsgeschichtlichen Zusammenhang* (BZAW, 97; Berlin: Alfred Töpelmann, 1966), p. 13. Odil Hannes Steck (*Friedensvorstellungen im alten Jerusalem* [ThSt, 111; Zürich: Theologischer Verlag, 1972], p. 9, note 5) maintains that they do constitute a specific *Gattung*, on the basis of a common structure, cultic setting and intention. Jörg Jeremias argues that the Psalms do have a common structure and set of notions, but different *Sitze im Leben* ('Lade und Zion: Zur Entstehung der Zionstradition', in *Probleme Biblischer Theologie: Gerhard von Rad zum 70. Geburtstag*, ed. by Hans Walter Wolff [München: Chr. Kaiser, 1971], pp. 183-98, especially pp. 190-91).

29. Clements, *Isaiah and the Deliverance of Jerusalem*, p. 88.

30. Steck, *Friedensvorstellungen*, p. 5. The Psalms representative of these categories are listed and briefly discussed in footnotes 5-8, on pp. 5-6 of *ibid.* The Psalm types are conveniently laid out in Bernhard W. Anderson, *Out of the Depths* (Philadelphia: Westminster, 1974), pp. 169-72.

31. 'The Davidic Origin of the Zion Tradition'.

32. Huber denies that Isaiah taught the 'inviolability' of Zion, although such a notion was abroad in Judah, as demonstrated by Mic 3.11 (*Jahwe, Juda und die anderen Völker beim Propheten Jesaja* [BZAW, 137; Berlin: de Gruyter, 1976], pp. 238-39). He seems to follow Wanke (*Die Zionstheologie*, pp. 107-108) in dating Pss 46, 48 and 76 after Isaiah. Clements, on the other hand, admits that these Psalms, or the notions expressed in them, are earlier than Isaiah (*Isaiah and the Deliverance of Jerusalem*, pp. 87-88), but denies that they depict a coherent 'Zion ideology'. Both authors seem to introduce a red herring here by reducing the Zion tradition to a belief in the inviolability of Zion (John H. Hayes, 'The Tradition of Zion's Inviolability', *JBL* 82 [1963], pp. 419-26), while Clements adds as a defining characteristic 'a special sacred mountain mythology associated with Mount Zion' (p. 88). These features, if they are associated with Zion at all, are certainly not the sum of the Zion tradition, or, more specifically, of the theological tradition that has Zion as its central symbol. Thus what Clements has to say on this point is true, but trivially so.

33. Schmid, 'Jahwe und die Kulttraditionen von Jerusalem'; Josef Schreiner, *Sion-Jerusalem Jahwes Königssitz: Theologie der heiligen Stadt im Alten Testament* (SANT, 7; München: Kösel-Verlag, 1963); von Rad, *Old Testament Theology*, vol. II, translated by D.M.G. Stalker (New York: Harper & Row, 1965), pp. 155-58, 293-94; Lutz, *Jahwe, Jerusalem und die Völker*; Schmidt, 'Jerusalemer El-Traditionen bei Jesaja', *ZRGG* 16 (1964), pp. 302-13; *Alttestamentlicher Glaube in seiner Geschichte* (Neukirchener Studienbücher, 6; Neukirchen-Vluyn: Neukirchener Verlag, second edition, 1975), pp. 207-16; Clements, *God and Temple* (Philadelphia: Fortress, 1965), pp. 41-48.

34. Roberts, 'The Davidic Origin of the Zion Tradition', pp. 339-44; 'The Religio-Political Setting of Psalm 47', *BASOR* 220/21 (1975/76), pp. 129-32;

'Zion in the Theology of the Davidic-Solomonic Empire', *Studies in the Period of David and Solomon* (ed. Tomoo Ishida; Winona Lake: Eisenbrauns, 1982), pp. 93-108.

35. Clements, *Isaiah and the Deliverance of Jerusalem*, pp. 72-89. Richard Clifford believes that the Zion tradition is indebted to Jebusite tradition, but suggests that the Baal traditions associated with Zion were combined with El traditions associated with Yahweh at the time of David (*The Cosmic Mountain in Canaan and the Old Testament* [HSM, 4; Cambridge, MA: Harvard University Press, 1972], p. 140). Eckart Otto also believes that there was a combination of Davidic innovation and old Canaanite tradition associated with Jerusalem in the Zion tradition. Cf. 'Silo und Jerusalem', *TZ* 32 (1967), pp. 65-77; 'El und JHWH in Jerusalem: Historische und theologische Aspekte einer Religionsintegration', *VT* 30 (1980), pp. 316-29. Otto's view of the motivation behind the Davidic court's theologizing is, however, quite different from that of Roberts. See also J. Alberto Soggin, 'Der offiziell geförderte Synkretismus in Israel während des 10. Jahrhunderts', *ZAW* 78 (1966), pp. 179-204.

36. David L. Eiler, 'The Origin and History of Zion as a Theological Symbol in Ancient Israel' (Dissertation: Princeton Theological Seminary, 1968). While the scope of this study is quite different from his, I am greatly indebted to Eiler at a number of points. A similar approach to the traditio-historical questions is taken by Jörg Jeremias, 'Lade und Zion'.

37. Noth, 'Jerusalem und die israelitische Tradition'; Otto Eissfeldt, 'Jahwe Zebaoth', in *Kleine Schriften III*, ed. by Rudolf Sellheim and Fritz Maass (Tübingen: J.C.B. Mohr, 1966), pp. 103-23; 'Silo und Jerusalem', *ibid.*, pp. 417-25. Cf. also the later articles by Eissfeldt in *Kleine Schriften VI*, ed. by Sellheim and Maass (Tübingen: J.C.B. Mohr, 1979), 'Kultzelt und Tempel' (pp. 1-7), and 'Monopol-Ansprüche des Heiligtums von Silo' (pp. 8-14).

38. See the articles cited in note 35, above. Eiler also believes that 'Jebusite El Elyon mythology' was part of the Zion tradition ('Zion as a Theological Symbol', p. 147), but the Jebusite contribution is not as central for him as for Otto. Eiler himself is indebted to the dissertation of T.E. Fretheim, 'The Cultic Use of the Ark of the Covenant in the Monarchial Period' (Dissertation: Princeton Theological Seminary, 1967).

39. Cf. A.F. Kirkpatrick *The Book of Psalms* (Cambridge: Cambridge University Press, 1902), especially pp. 253-55, on Ps 46.

40. For the term 'Jerusalem cult tradition', see Odil Hannes Steck, 'Das Problem theologischer Strömungen in nach-exilischer Zeit', *EvT* 28 (1966), pp. 445-58; 'Theological Streams of Tradition', in *Tradition and Theology in the Old Testament*, ed. by Douglas A. Knight (Philadelphia: Fortress, 1977), pp. 183-214. The term was apparently coined by Schmid, 'Jahwe und die Kulttraditionen Israels'.

41. For such a review see John Skorupski, *Symbol and Theory* (Cambridge:

Cambridge University Press, 1976). A survey of the understanding of symbols among anthropologists is provided by Raymond Firth, *Symbols: Public and Private* (Ithaca: Cornell University Press, 1973), especially pp. 92-126, 165-206.

42. Firth, *ibid.*, pp. 245-46.

43. Skorupski, discussing the theories of Parsons and Beattie.

44. See Clifford Geertz, *The Interpretation of Cultures* (New York: Basic Books, 1973), especially the Introduction; Gibson Winter, *Liberating Creation: Foundations for Religious Social Ethics* (New York: Crossroad, 1981), pp. 54-91.

45. Cf. Victor Turner, 'Symbols and Social Experience in Religious Ritual', in *Worship and Ritual in Christianity and Other Religions*, Studia Missionalia 2 (1974), pp. 1-21. Turner prefers 'vocal' to 'valent', because while the latter refers specifically to motivation, the former includes cognition as well (pp. 7-9).

46. Turner, *ibid.*, p. 8. See his earlier work, *The Ritual Process: Structure and Anti-Structure* (Ithaca: Cornell Paperback, 1977); *Drama, Fields, and Metaphors: Symbolic Action in Human Society* (Ithaca: Cornell University Press, 1974); 'Sacrifice as Quintessential Process: Prophylaxis or Abandonment?', *HR* 16 (1977), pp. 189-215.

47. The term 'symbolic design' is taken from Bernhard W. Anderson, 'The Messiah as Son of God: Peter's Confession in Traditio-historical Perspective', in *Christological Perspectives: Essays in Honor of Harvey K. McArthur*, ed. Robert F. Berkey and Sarah A. Edwards (New York: Pilgrim, 1982), pp. 157-69. Anderson relates the term to Steck's 'theological streams of tradition' (see above, note 40).

48. Peter Slater, *The Dynamics of Religion: Meaning and Change in Religious Tradition* (New York: Harper & Row, 1978), pp. 30, 40. The use of the term 'structure', which is mine, not Slater's, may obscure the dynamic quality of symbolic systems within the same culture or religious tradition. In addition to the term 'central symbol', the roughly synonymous terms 'master symbol' (attributed by Firth to C. Wright Mills [*Symbols*, p. 86]), 'dominant symbol' (Turner) and 'emphatic symbols' (Firth, *Symbols*, p. 91) are in use. Firth emphasizes again that it is not symbols *per se* that are central, master, dominant or emphatic, but symbolic relations. That is so because 'it is the conceptualization of the object in a given relation that is important ... Dominant refers to relations, not to objects' (*ibid.*, pp. 245-46).

49. *Rethinking Symbolism*, trans. by Alice L. Morton (Cambridge Studies and Papers in Social Anthropology; Cambridge: Cambridge University Press, 1977), especially pp. 120-22. A problem in need of further investigation is the relation between knowledge mediated by symbols from 'the stock of knowledge at hand', 'common sense knowledge', available in the 'everyday world', and the knowledge mediated by symbols from specific traditions (the terms in quotes are those of Alfred Schütz, quoted by Rolf Eickelpasch,

Mythos und Sozialstruktur [Studien zur Sozialwissenschaft, 7; Düsseldorf; Bertelsmann Universitätsverlag, 1977], pp. 95-98). Rolf Knierim raises the issues, without speaking of symbols, in his essay, 'Offenbarung im Alten Testament', in *Probleme Biblischer Theologie*, pp. 206-35. On the 'knowledge' provided by Zion symbolism, John J. Schmitt says that the Zion Songs allude to 'a common story or drama', which the people who heard these hymns knew well. 'The story placed its hearers at the center of a universe of meaning and security. It placed them in the city of God' ('The Zion Drama in the Tradition of Isaiah ben Amoz' [Dissertation: University of Chicago, 1977], p. 11).

50. Turner, 'Symbols and Social Experience', p. 9.

51. Geertz, 'Ethos, World View, and the Analysis of Sacred Symbols', in *The Interpretation of Cultures*, pp. 126-41; the quote is from page 126. It is also true of symbols and symbolic designs that they undergo change and transformation. Cf. Slater, *The Dynamics of Religion*, and Eickelpasch, *Mythos and Sozialstruktur*, pp. 95-98.

52. This has been done, in part, by Alan Robinson, 'The Zion Concept in the Psalms and Deutero-Isaiah' (Dissertation: University of Edinburgh, 1974).

Notes to Chapter 2

1. Richard J. Clifford prefers 'cosmic mountain to 'sacred mountain', in *The Cosmic Mountain in Canaan and the Old Testament* (HSM, 4; Cambridge, MA: Harvard University Press, 1972). Cf. Robert L. Cohn, 'Jerusalem: The Senses of a Center', *JAAR* 46 (1978), pp. 1-26; *The Shape of Sacred Space: Four Biblical Studies* (AAR Studies in Religion: Chico, CA: Scholars Press, 1981).

2. This is particularly true of the notion of Zion's supposed inviolability. Note especially the connection in Ps 46.6 between Yahweh's presence and the security of Zion. Even in such texts as Mic 3.11 and Jer 7, in which the notion of inviolability is attested, the important factor is the presence of Yahweh, not some independent notion of the mountain's sacral character. Cf. R.E. Clements, *God and Temple* (Philadelphia: Fortress, 1965), p. 71.

3. *Ibid.*, p. 76. Note also the comments of Odil Hannes Steck, *Friedensvorstellungen im alten Jerusalem* (ThSt, 111; Zürich: Theologischer Verlag, 1972), p. 14, note 15; Jörg Jeremias, 'Lade und Zion: Zur Entstehung der Zionstradition', in *Probleme Biblischer Theologie, Gerhard von Rad zum 70. Geburtstag*, ed. by Hans Walter Wolff (München: Chr. Kaiser, 1971), pp. 183-98, especially p. 191.

4. Note El's *hdm* in *CTA* 4.4.29. Here it appears to be connected with El's royal function as giver of decrees. Cf. David L. Eiler, 'The Origin and History of Zion as a Theological Symbol' (Dissertation: Princeton Theological

Seminary, 1968), pp. 37, 122; Hans-Joachim Kraus, *Worship in Israel: A Cultic History of the Old Testament*, trans. by G. Buswell (Richmond: John Knox, 1966), pp. 105-12.

5. Martin Metzger, 'Himmlische und irdische Wohnstatt Jahwes', *UF* 2 (1970) pp. 139-58, especially p. 157. See also *CTA* 4.1.34, noted by Paul Hanson in 'Zechariah 9 and the Recapitulation of an Ancient Historical Pattern', *JBL* 92 (1973) pp. 37-59, especially p. 41, note 3. Cf. H.-J. Kraus, *Die Königsherrschaft Gottes im Alten Testament: Untersuchungen zu den Liedern von Jahwes Thronbesteigung* (BHT, 13; Tübingen: J.C.B. Mohr, 1951), pp. 51-54.

6. Mowinckel, *Psalmenstudien*, 2 vols. (Amsterdam: Paul Schippers, 1961). *Psalmenstudien II: Das Thronbesteigungsfest Jahwäs und der Ursprung der Eschatologie*, is part 2 of volume I. A discussion of Mowinckel's work can be found in R.E. Clements, *One Hundred Years of Old Testament Interpretation* (Philadelphia: Westminster, 1975), pp. 83-98. Cf. also Arvid S. Kapelrud, 'Sigmund Mowinckel and Old Testament Study', *ASTI* 5 (1967), pp. 4-29. For a bibliography of studies on the problem of translation see Jarl H. Ulrichsen, 'JHWH MALAK: Einige Sprachliche Beobachtungen', *VT* 27 (1977), pp. 361-74, especially p. 361, note 1. Cf. also J. Alberto Soggin, 'Gott als König in der biblischen Dichtung: Bemerkungen zu den *yhwh mlk* Psalmen', in *Proceedings of the Fifth World Congress of Jewish Studies*, ed. by Pinchas Peli (Jerusalem: World Union of Jewish Studies, 1969), pp. 126-33; J.D.W. Watts, 'Yahwe Mālak Psalms', *TZ* 21 (1965), pp. 341-48.

7. *Psalmenstudien II*, pp. 6-10. Cf. also Mowinckel, *The Psalms in Israel's Worship*, 2 vols., trans. by D.R. Ap-Thomas (Nashville: Abingdon, 1962), I, p. 107; II, pp. 222-24. In *Psalmenstudien II* Mowinckel included Ps 100 among the Enthronement Psalms, but he omitted it in the later work.

8. Hermann Gunkel and Joachim Begrich, *Einleitung in die Psalmen: Die Gattungen der religiösen Lyrik Israels* (Göttingen: Vandenhoeck & Ruprecht, 1933). Cf. Kraus, *Worship in Israel*, pp. 16-17.

9. Note also the comments of Aubrey Johnson, *Sacral Kingship in Ancient Israel* (Cardiff: University of Wales Press, second edition, 1967), pp. 61-62, note 1.

10. A useful summary of Gunkel's position can be found in G.N.M. Habets, 'Die grosse Jesaja-Apokalypse (Jes 24-27): Ein Beitrag zur Theologie des Alten Testaments' (Dissertation: Bonn University, 1974), pp. 321-23. Apparently the first to make this connection was Paul Volz, *Das Neujahrfest Jahwes* (Tübingen: J.C.B. Mohr, 1912).

11. *The Psalms in Israel's Worship*, II, p. 228.

12. Tübingen: J.C.B. Mohr, 1927.

13. Cf. Johnson, *Sacral kingship*, p. 65, note 1; W.H. Schmidt, *Königtum Gottes in Ugarit und Israel* (BZAW, 80; Berlin: Alfred Töpelmann, second edition, 1966), pp. 76-77; Diethelm Michel, Studien zu den sogenannten Thronbesteigungspsalmen', *VT* 6 (1956), pp. 40-68. Josef Schreiner presents

arguments against the festival in *Sion-Jerusalem: Jahwes Königssitz: Theologie der heiligen Stadt im Alten Testament* (SANT, 7; München: Kösel-Verlag, 1963), pp. 191-216.

14.   BHT, 13; Tübingen: J.C.B. Mohr, 1951.

15.   In his commentary on the Psalms Kraus recognizes at least Psalms 93 and 99 to be pre-exilic. See his arguments in *Psalmen*, 2 vols. (BKAT 15; Neukirchen-Vluyn: Neukirchener Verlag, fourth edition, 1972), pp. 647-48, 682-83. The volumes are paginated sequentially, so I will make no distinction between volumes I and II in these notes.

16.   See above, note 10. Cf. also Claus Westermann, *The Praise of God in the Psalms*, trans. by Keith R. Crim (Richmond: John Knox, 1965), pp. 145-51.

17.   Habets, 'Die Grosse Jesaja-Apokalypse', p. 237. This objection, and others listed here, are raised by Roland de Vaux, *Ancient Israel*, II (New York: McGraw Hill, 1965), pp. 504-506.

18.   *Die Psalmen, Teil II. Beitrag der Ugarit-Texte zum Verständnis von Kolometrie und Textologie der Psalmen* (AOAT, 207/2; Neukirchen-Vluyn: Neukirchener Verlag, 1979). *Teil I* has not yet been published.

19.   *Ibid.*, p. 491.

20.   *Ibid.*, p. 461.

21.   Schmidt, *Königtum Gottes*, pp. 74-79; de Moor, *The Seasonal Pattern in the Ugaritic Myth of Ba'lu* (AOAT, 16; Neukirchen-Vluyn: Neukirchener Verlag, 1971), pp. 25-28. Apparently Schmidt ignores the evidence de Moor credits him with collecting, because he translates, 'It is *Yahweh* who is king'.

22.   De Moor, *The Seasonal Pattern*, pp. 56-57, 77-80.

23.   *Ibid.*, p. 61.

24.   Loretz, *Die Psalmen*, p. 491. Loretz is not, of course, the first to draw such a comparision.

25.   W.G. Lambert, 'The Great Battle of the Mesopotamian Religious Year: The Conflict in the Akitu House (A Summary)', *Iraq* 25 (1963), pp. 189-90; J.A. Black, 'The New Year Ceremonies in Ancient Babylon: "Taking Bel by the Hand" and a Cultic Picnic', *Religion* 11 (1981), pp. 39-60. From the earlier literature cf. S.A. Pallis, *The Babylonian Akitu Festival* (Copenhagen: A.F. Horst, 1926); Heinrich Zimmern, *Das babylonische Neujahrfest* (Leipzig: J.C. Hinrichs, 1926).

26.   It is unclear whether Loretz believes the pre-exilic festival celebrated a primordial conquest or an annual enthronement.

27.   Loretz, *Die Psalmen*, pp. 491-92. Loretz's dating is based on the mechanical application of a metrical scheme derived from the poetic texts at Ugarit (cf. Loretz, 'Die Analyse der ugaritischen und hebräischen Poesie mittels Stichometrie und Konsonantenzählung', *UF* 7 [1975], pp. 261-64), and on what I consider to be an untenable view of the development of Israelite religion, i.e. that Yahweh's universal sovereignty was a late theological development.

28. Johnson, *Sacral Kingship*, pp. 61-62; A.A. Anderson, *The Book of Psalms*, 2 vols. (NCB; London: Oliphant's, 1972), pp. 34-35, 666-67.

29. Johnson, *Sacral Kingship*, e.g. p. 135.

30. *Ibid.*, p. 101.

31. *Ibid.*, p. 102. A summary of Johnson's reconstruction, with his own modifications, can be found in John H. Hayes, *Introduction to Old Testament Study* (Nashville: Abingdon, 1979), pp. 315-16. Johnson's position is too often caricatured and the differences between him and other 'patternists' is neglected. See H.H. Rowley's comments in *Worship in Ancient Israel* (London; SPCK, 1967), pp. 191-92.

32. Michel, 'Thronbesteigungspsalmen', p. 68. He translates 'It is Yahweh who exercises kingship'.

33. Niek Poulssen, *König und Tempel im Glaubenszeugnis des Alten Testaments* (SBM, 3; Stuttgart: Verlag Katholisches Bibelwerk, 1967), p. 137, note 158. Poulssen cites Deut 33.5; Ps 114.1-2; Isa 24.23; 52.7 as requiring an ingressive sense. Cf. E. Gerstenberger, 'Psalms', in *Old Testament Form Criticism*, ed. by John H. Hayes (TUMSR, 2; San Antonio: Trinity University Press, 1974), p. 214.

34. Cf. A.S. Kapelrud, 'Nochmals Jawä mālāk', *VT* 13 (1963), pp. 229-31; A.A. Anderson, *Psalms*, pp. 34-35. Ulrichsen, 'JHWH MALAK', argues that word order is irrelevant and only the context can determine the translation. Further, since in the Enthronement Psalms it is not a matter of the beginning of a reign, but of the new year, the Ugaritic evidence is not conclusive. The ingressive-durative contrast is not relevant, he argues, because the perfect verb can have both senses. The various pieces of syntactic evidence are collected by Kraus in *Theologie der Psalmen* (BKAT, 15/3; Neukirchen-Vluyn: Neukirchener Verlag, 1979), p. 107.

35. Cf. Steck, *Friedensvorstellungen*, pp. 15-17; Fritz Stolz, *Strukturen und Figuren im Kult von Jerusalem* (BZAW, 118; Berlin: de Gruyter, 1970), p. 174, on Ps 104.

36. Kraus, *Worship in Israel*, pp. 66-68; Johnson, *Sacral Kingship*, pp. 57-59. Cf. also Kraus, *Theologie der Psalmen*, p. 105; Kjell Aartun, 'Studien zum Gesetz über den grossen Versöhnungstag Lev 16 mit Varianten. Ein ritualgeschichtlicher Beitrag', *ST* 34 (1980), pp. 73-109, especially p. 95.

37. This is admitted by Georg Fohrer (*History of Israelite Religion*, trans. by David E. Green [Nashville: Abingdon, 1972], p. 204), although Fohrer considers this to count against the probability of a New Year celebration in connection with the Autumn festival. Mowinckel vehemently denies that he is inventing an otherwise unattested festival. See, among other places, *He That Cometh*, trans. by G.W. Anderson (Nashville: Abingdon, 1956), p. 139, note 1; *The Psalms in Israel's Worship*, I, p. 121, note 51.

38. Cf. de Vaux, *Ancient Israel*, II, pp. 495-96, John H. Eaton, *Kingship and the Psalms* (SBT, 2/32; London: SCM, 1976), pp. 103-104; Clements, *God and Temple*, pp. 69-70; Frank M. Cross, *Canaanite Myth and Hebrew Epic* (Cambridge, MA: Harvard University Press, 1973), p. 105 and note 48,

p. 123 and note 37; Simone Springer, *Neuinterpretation im Alten Testament* (SSB; Stuttgart: Katholisches Bibelwerk, 1979), p. 55. I do not agree with Cross that the Shiloh festival was held in the Spring. See below.

39. See especially John H. Hayes, *Introduction to Old Testament Study*, pp. 315-16. For the presence of covenant renewal in this festival see, among others, Cross (note 38, above); Arthur Weiser, *The Psalms: A Commentary*, trans. by H. Hartwell (OTL; Philadelphia: Westminster, 1962), *passim* and cf. Albrecht Alt, 'The Origins of Israelite Law', in *Essays on Old Testament History and Religion*, trans. by R.A Wilson (Garden City, NY: Anchor Books, 1968), pp. 164-67.

40. Martin Noth especially has emphasized the importance of Israel's historical traditions among the influences on the Jerusalem cult. See 'God, King, and Nation in the Old Testament', in *The Laws in the Pentateuch and Other Studies*, trans. by D.R. Ap-Thomas (Philadelphia: Fortress, 1966), pp. 145-78. The essay was originally published in *ZTK* 47 (1950), pp. 157-91.

41. *Worship in Israel*, p. 208.

42. Much the same thing is claimed by W.R. Millar, *Isaiah 24-27 and the Origin of Apocalyptic* (HSM, 11; Cambridge, MA: Harvard University Press, 1976), p. 89. Cf. Gerstenberger, 'Psalms', p. 215. Soggin argues that the designation of Yahweh as king virtually requires some festal celebration of that designation ('Gott als König', pp. 130-31).

43. Cf. Kraus, *Psalmen*, pp. 647-48, on Ps 93 (and note *ibid.*, p. xliii). He notes that pilgrimage and prostration before Yahweh, as in Pss 95.6; 96.9; 99.5, in addition to 99.3, belong most likely in the festival of tabernacles (cf. Zech 14.16), which would explain the reference to Yahweh's testimonies in 93.5. Cf. Deut 31.10ff. See also Albrecht Alt, 'The Origins of Israelite Law', pp. 164-67. Alt believed that the Autumn festival, which was also a New Year festival, only included the proclamation of law and covenant renewal in sabbatical years (p. 167, note 20). Mowinckel (*The Psalms in Israel's Worship*, I, pp. 94-95) argues for the early association of Exodus and Covenant with the Autumn festival, and the latter with the New Year celebration. D.J.A. Clines ('The Evidence for an Autumnal New Year in Pre-Exilic Israel Reconsidered', *JBL* 93 [1974] pp. 22-40; 'New Year' in *IDBS*, pp. 625-29) claims that the only evidence linking enthronement to the Autumn festival is Zech 14.16, from the post-exilic period. One has to ask why these would first come to be joined in this period. Cf. Rowley, *Worship in Ancient Israel*, p. 192.

44. For a helpful discussion of these texts and the royal ritual see T.N.D. Mettinger, *King and Messiah: The Civil and Sacral Legitimation of the Israelite Kings* (ConBOT, 8; Lund: CWK Gleerup, 1976), pp. 99-105.

45. For a delimitation of this category cf. Gerstenberger, 'Psalms', p. 216; Mettinger, *King and Messiah*, pp. 99-100. Gillis Gerleman argues that Ps 110 is not a Psalm of royal enthronement in 'Psalm 110', *VT* 31 (1981), pp. 1-19.

46. Otto Eissfeldt, *The Old Testament: An Introduction*, trans. by P.R.

Ackroyd (New York: Harper & Row, 1965), p. 110.

47. Gerstenberger, 'Psalms', p. 216. On the question of 'Hofstil', see K.H. Bernhardt, *Das Problem der altorientalischen Königsideologie im Alten Testament* (VTS, 8; Leiden: E.J. Brill, 1961). For a contrasting view see Mettinger, *King and Messiah*. Cf. Victor Maag, 'Malkut JHWH', *VTS* 7 (1959), pp. 129-53, especially p. 149.

48. This was argued already by Martin Buber in 1932, in the first edition of *Königtum Gottes* (Heidelberg: Lambert Schneider, third edition, 1956), translated as *Kingship of God*, by Richard Scheimann (New York: Harper & Row, 1967). In 1940 J. Schmidt claimed that 'in no case . . . can the status of Yahweh as sovereign in the time before the formation of Israel as a settled people be doubted, even if the title 'king' is not attested in this era', in *Alttestamentliche Abhandlungen* 13 (1940), p. 49 (quoted in Habets, 'Die grosse Jesaja-Apokalypse', p. 408, note 95). In 1905 Hugo Gressmann found traces of a cult of Yahweh as king, but connected this with the earthly kingship of Gideon (*Der Ursprung der israelitisch-jüdischen Eschatologie* [FRLANT, 6; Göttingen: Vandenhoeck & Ruprecht, 1929], pp. 228-30). On Gressmann see J. de Fraine, 'La Royauté de Yahvé dans les Textes concernant l'Arche', *VTS* 15 (1966), pp. 139-49, especially p. 135. De Fraine himself sees the kingship of Yahweh in pre-monarchic Israel in association with the deposit of the tables of the law in the wilderness Ark. Cf. also de Vaux, 'Les Chérubins et l'Arche d'Alliance, les spinx gardiens et les trônes divins dans l'ancien Orient', in *Bible et Orient* (Paris: Les Editions du Cerf, 1967), pp. 231-59; 'Arche d'Alliance et Tente de Réunion', *ibid.*, pp. 261-76 ('Ark of the Covenant and Tent of Reunion', in *The Bible and the Ancient Near East*, trans. by Damian McHugh [New York: Doubleday, 1971], pp. 136-51). For a recent discussion of the issues see Walter Dietrich, 'Gott als König', *ZTK* 77 (1980), pp. 251-68.

49. See below, ch. 3. In Ps 99.4 the MT has ועז מלך, which RSV renders 'and the king's strength', in the margin. As Kraus notes, this is impossible in the context. He punctuates עז as an adjective (*Psalmen*, p. 681). It is possible that עז goes at the end of v. 3, 'Holy is he, and mighty' (Anderson, *Psalms*, p. 694). Dahood also reads an adjective ('the strongest king'), but does not alter the punctuation (*Psalms II* [AB; Garden City, NY: Doubleday, 1974], p. 369). In any case, the reference is clearly to Yahweh (although Loretz says it is a 'Messianic gloss' [*Die Psalmen*, p. 74]).

50. Ps 89 may indicate that at some point the enthronement of Yahweh and the king were drawn together, perhaps on a single occasion. The date of Ps 89 is contested. Cross claims that it is early (*Canaanite Myth*, p. 97, note 25). W.H. Schmidt argues that it is exilic or post-exilic ('Kritik am Königtum', in *Probleme Biblischer Theologie*, p. 446, note 15). James M. Ward places it in the divided monarchy, perhaps after 800 BC ('The Literary Form and Liturgical Background of Psalm 89', *VT* 11 [1961], pp. 320-39, especially p. 339, note 1).

51. Simone Springer claims that in the early monarchic period Yahweh was honored as king only indirectly through the veneration of the earthly king who represented Yahweh in the Autumn festival. She further claims that it was only in the late monarchic period, after the fall of the North and the centralization of the cult in Jerusalem, that Yahweh was honored as king directly in the Autumn festival. She demurs from calling this an enthronement festival (*Neuinterpretation im Alten Testament*, pp. 74-75, on Ps 99, which she places in the late monarchic period). On the basis of contacts with 1 Kgs 8.1-13 she puts Pss 24 and 47, together with Ps 29, in the Autumn festival (*ibid.*, pp. 52-54). However, Springer fails to account for the veneration of Yahweh as king in the pre-monarchic period, as well as for the absence of any mention of the earthly king in the Psalms she studies (24, 29, 47, 99). Further, Solomon's role in 1 Kgs 8.1-13 does not allow for any conclusions regarding the king's role in the celebration of Yahweh's kingship.

52. See especially the references to Kapelrud and Anderson in note 33, above.

53. Cf. Kraus, *Psalmen*, pp. 197-205, on 'Die Kulttraditionen Jerusalems', and *Theologie der Psalmen*, pp. 103-25, on 'Der Gottesdienst in Jerusalem'. I will argue below that 'creation' would be a better term than 'choice'.

54. Just as the celebration of Good Friday and Easter does not imply the periodic return of Jesus to the grave. This objection seems to me simply to misunderstand the nature of ritual, on which see Roy A. Rappaport, 'Liturgies and Lies', in the *Internationales Jahrbuch für Wissens- und Religionssoziologie*, X, *Beiträge zur Wissenssoziologie*, ed. by Günter Dux and Thomas Luckman (Opladen: Westdeutscher Verlag, 1976), pp. 75-104. Helmer Ringgren makes a similar point in *The Faith of the Psalmists* (Philadelphia: Fortress, 1963), p. xv; cf. H.H. Rowley, *Worship in Ancient Israel*, pp. 184-85, note 2.

55. As suggested, e.g., by Johnson, *Sacral Kingship*, pp. 65-68, 87-88; Mowinckel, *The Psalms in Israel's Worship*, I, p. 177; cf. John Gray, 'A Cantata of the Autumn Festival: Psalm 68', *JSS* 22 (1977), pp. 2-26. Psalm 47 may combine a processional and an enthronement, suggesting a liturgical setting in which the two took place. See below.

56. See especially Cross, *Canaanite Myth*; Patrick D. Miller, *The Divine Warrior in Early Israel* (HSM, 5; Cambridge, MA: Harvard University, 1975); R.N. Whybray, *The Heavenly Counsellor in Isaiah 40.13-14* (SOTSMS, 1; Cambridge: Cambridge University Press, 1971); Max E. Polley, 'Hebrew Prophecy Within the Council of Yahweh, Examined in its Ancient Near Eastern Setting', in *Scripture in Context: Essays on the Comparative Method*, ed. by Carl D. Evans, William W. Hallo and John B. White (PTMS, 34; Pittsburgh: The Pickwick Press, 1980), pp. 151-56.

57. Miller, *The Divine Warrior*, p. 35.

58. The title 'Yahweh of Hosts' may particularly reflect these notions. See J.P. Ross, 'Yahweh Seba'ot in Samuel and in Psalms', *VT* 17 (1967), pp. 76-

92, especially pp. 83-84. At Ugarit one of the functions of the *bene Elim* is to ascribe kingship, as they do in Ps. 29. Cf. Clifford, *Cosmic Mountain*, p. 47. H.L. Ginsberg first suggested that Ps 29 was originally a Baal hymn, according to Cross, *Canaanite Myth*, p. 152, note 22. See Cross's treatment in *ibid*., pp. 152-63.

59. Accepting the rendering of *dyknnh* as 'who appointed him', as in J.C.L. Gibson, *Canaanite Myths and Legends* (Edinburgh: T.&T. Clark, second edition, 1978), p. 54, note 4.

60. As does Johnson, *Sacral Kingship, passim*; cf. Rowley, *Worship in Ancient Israel*, pp. 191-202. That the king played some role within the cult is evident, but the nature of this role and its relation to the celebration of Yahweh's kingship remain uncertain.

61. It would seem probable that at least Pss 24, 68 and 132 are related to this festival. On the other hand, there is no obvious reason why the Songs of Zion (46, 48, 76) should be placed at some specific point within the same celebration, as Johnson (*Sacral Kingship*, pp. 85-90, 92-95) and Mowinckel (*The Psalms in Israel's Worship*, II, pp. 244-45) have argued.

62. Dahood, *Psalms II*, pp. 339, 342; Shenkel, 'An Interpretation of Psalms 93.5', *Biblica* 46 (1965), pp. 401-16. Cf. also Joachim Becker, *Israel deutet seine Psalmen* (SBS, 18; Stuttgart: Katholisches Bibelwerk, 1967), pp. 73-74.

63. *Psalms II*, p. 339.

64. Shenkel, 'Psalms 93.5', pp. 408-409.

65. *Psalms II*, p. 342.

66. *Ibid*., p. 343. Dahood also takes נואה as a *qal*, third singular, rather than as an adjective, and translates it 'to praise or laud'.

67. Dahood is forced to change the verb to a plural to conform to his earlier revision of the text (*ibid*., p. 342).

68. See above, note 43, and cf. Kraus, *Psalmen*, p. 650. Cf. also Ps 81, especially v. 4 (*ibid*., pp. 351-52).

69. *Ibid*., p. 648. The verb שפט in 96.13 and 98.9 may be better translated 'to rule', rather than 'to judge'. Cf. Schmidt's treatment in *Königtum Gottes*, pp. 36-43, especially pp. 38-40.

70. Ps 47 also makes mention of God's holy throne, which would correspond to לביתך נאוה קדש in 93.5; cf. 47.8. Dahood's contention that 93.5 refers to Yahweh's heavenly throne is dubious in light of such references as 99.9 (*Psalms II*, p. 343).

71. See above, note 5, and cf. de Moor, *Seasonal Pattern*, pp. 60-61.

72. Although this Psalm *may* be post-exilic (note its use in 1 Chr 16; cf. Kraus, *Psalmen*, pp. 671-72), that does not affect our use of it here.

73. On the relation of this Psalm to other 'storm theophany' Psalms in the Old Testament, and their relation to Canaanite patterns and motifs, see Cross, *Canaanite Myth*, pp. 156-63. The pattern of this Psalm is 'the return of the Divine Warrior to take up kingship' (p. 162).

74. In Ps 144.9 the association is indirectly with David's kingship. This Psalm, perhaps a royal Psalm from the late monarchic period (Kraus, *Psalmen*, pp. 941-42), is unrelated formally to the Enthronement Psalms and represents a combination of earlier independent forms, such as lament and thanksgiving.

75. Cf. also Ps. 95.1 (rejoicing and shouting for joy), together with v. 3 (Yahweh is a great God // great king over the whole earth). According to the Mishnah this is a New Year Psalm. Cf. Weiser, *The Psalms*, p. 625. Note also Aartun, 'Gesetz über den grossen Versöhnungstag', p. 87.

76. Dahood objects to this dating for Ps 96 (*Psalms II*, p. 357), suggesting instead that both Deutero-Isaiah and Ps 96 'were heir to a common literary tradition long existent in Canaan'. That is undoubtedly the case, but dependence upon Canaanite tradition is no criterion for dating, as Isa 27.1 should amply demonstrate. Cf. also Loretz, *Die Psalmen*, pp. 502-506.

77. On the 'New Song' as related to the pre-exilic festival see Millar, *Isaiah 24-27*, pp. 111-12. He says that 'the New Song would have a solid foundation in the procession of the Ark to the temple. We argue, then, that we have here the shout of victory in praise of Yahweh, the victorious king' (p. 112). Millar's comment is made on the basis of the same evidence we have cited. Cf. also E. Lipiński, *La Royauté de Yahwé dans la poésie et le culte de l'ancien Israël* (Brussels: Paleis der Academiën, 1965), p. 259.

78. For much of the following discussion I am dependent upon Rudolf Schmid, 'Opfer mit Jubel. Die *zibhe t^eru'a* von Ps 27.6', *TZ* 35 (1979), pp. 48-54. Cf. also Helmer Ringgren, *Israelite Religion*, trans. by David E. Green (Philadelphia: Fortress, 1966), pp. 191, 327. The earlier work by Paul Humbert, *La 'Terou'a': Analyse d'un rite biblique* (Neuchâtel: Université de Neuchâtel, 1946), pp. 7-9, connected this term originally with holy war, and with the Ark as a war palladium. The terms in the general semantic field of 'rejoice' are investigated by Dorothea Ward Harvey, '"Rejoice Not, O Israel!"' in *Israel's Prophetic Heritage: Essays in Honor of James Muilenburg*, ed. by B.W. Anderson and Walter Harrelson (New York: Harper & Row, 1962), pp. 116-27. Cf. also the earlier study by Humbert, '"Laetari et exultare" dans le vocabulaire religieux de l'Ancien Testament', *RHPR* 22 (1942), pp. 185-214.

79. On the text see P. Kyle McCarter, *I Samuel* (AB; Garden City, NY: Doubleday, 1980), p. 103; Eckart Otto, *Das Mazzotfest in Gilgal* (BWANT, 107; Stuttgart: W. Kohlhammer, 1975), p. 355; Hans Joachim Stoebe, *Das erste Buch Samuelis* (KAT 8/1; Gütersloh: Gerd Mohn, 1973), p. 156. It seems that צבאות is a fixed epithet and should be retained in 4.4 and 2 Sam 6.2. On the other hand, it is unlikely that ברית was associated with the Ark in Shiloh. Cf. Otto, *Mazzotfest*, pp. 351-61. 'Resounded' is the most fitting translation for הום. Cf. McCarter, *I Samuel*, pp. 103-106.

80. On the background of this term see Harvey, '"Rejoice Not!"'.

81. On the problem of the Ark Narrative, its origin, purpose, extent and

specifically the inclusion of 2 Sam 6 within it, see Stoebe, *Das erste Buch Samuelis*, pp. 127-28; Patrick D. Miller and J.J.M. Roberts, *The Hand of the Lord: A Reassessment of the 'Ark Narrative' of 1 Samuel* (Johns Hopkins Near Eastern Studies; Baltimore: Johns Hopkins University Press, 1977); John T. Willis, 'Samuel Versus Eli, I. Sam. 1-7', *TZ* 35 (1979), pp. 202-12; Georg Fohrer, 'Die Ladeerzählung', *JNWSI* 1 (1971), pp. 23-31.

82. See e.g. Tomoo Ishida, *The Royal Dynasties in Ancient Israel* (BZAW, 142; Berlin: de Gruyter, 1976), pp. 37-39. See also the literature cited in ch. 1, above. Full bibliographical data on the topic can be found in H.J. Zobel, '*'aron'*, *TDOT* I (1974), pp. 363-74. See also Otto, *Mazzotfest*, pp. 351-61. The connection of 'Yahweh of Hosts' with the Ark was proposed by E. Kautzsch in *ZAW* 6 (1886), pp. 17-22, according to Wildberger, *Jesaja 1-12* (BKAT, 10/1; Neukirchen-Vluyn: Neukirchener Verlag, 1972), p. 27. The definitive treatment is still Otto Eissfeldt, 'Jahwe Zebaoth', in *Kleine Schriften III*, ed. by Rudolph Sellheim and Fritz Maass (Tübingen: J.C.B. Mohr, 1966), pp. 386-97.

83. For example, Johann Maier, *Das altisraelitische Ladeheiligtum* (BZAW, 93; Berlin: Alfred Töpelmann, 1965), pp. 56-62. See most recently Frank Crüsemann, *Der Widerstand gegen das Königtum: Die antiköniglichen Texte des Alten Testaments und der Kampf um den frühen israelitischen Staat* (WMANT, 49; Neukirchen-Vluyn: Neukirchener Verlag, 1978), pp. 76-78.

84. Joseph Gutman, 'The History of the Ark', *ZAW* 83 (1971), pp. 22-30, especially p. 26; Otto, *Mazzotfest*, p. 357. Gutman suggests that there really was no Ark in Solomon's temple, it having lost its sacral character under Solomon's administration, which abandoned earlier ties with the tribes and hence did not need the ligitimation of the Ark as David had. But if the description in 1 Kgs 6 and 8 is historically accurate Solomon may have tried to mediate two rival Ark traditions, those of Gilgal and Shiloh (see below). Fohrer's argument, that the two epithets derived from Baalat rather than Shiloh, seems contrived (*History of Israelite Religion*, p. 110).

85. So Otto, *Mazzotfest*, pp. 354-56, following Kurt Galling, 'Die Ausrufung des Namens als Rechtsakt in Israel', *TLZ* 81 (1956), pp. 65-70. Galling claims that the background of 2 Sam 6.2 is a legal transfer of the Ark, but see Clements, *God and Temple*, pp. 32-34. The origin of the name צבאות cannot be treated here. Cross may be correct in regarding 'Yahweh' as originally a verbal element in the name אלהים יהוה צבאות, 'God who creates armies' (*Canaanite Myth*, pp. 60-75), although the construction *rsp ṣb'i* in the Ugaritic texts might suggest that צבאות is a genitive. Cf. J.C. de Moor, review of P.D. Miller, *Divine Warrior*, p. 21; William J. Fulco, *The Canaanite God Resep* (AOS; New Haven: American Oriental Society, 1976), p. 42. The question is probably moot, since the term 'hosts' had probably become an abstract plural by the time of Isaiah, even if it once had a concrete referent (Walter Dietrich, 'Gott als König', pp. 253-54). Miller argues that the proper methodological approach to determining the term's meaning is not context,

but a reconstruction of the term's origin (*The Divine Warrior*, p. 152). The reason context is insufficient, he claims in circular fashion, is that it does not reveal anything about the term's origin. Cf. also the study by Matitiahu Tsevat, 'Yhwh Seba'ot', in *The Meaning of the Book of Job and Other Biblical Studies: Essays on the Literature and Religion of the Hebrew Bible* (New York: KTAV, 1980), pp. 119-29. He construes the relation between the two terms as appositional, not genitive: 'Yahweh, i.e., armies'. Tsevat's essay was first published in *HUCA* 34 (1965), pp. 49-58.

86. Wildberger notes that the epithet 'Yahweh of hosts' is used in the books of Kings only in 1 Kgs 18.15; 19.10; 2 Kgs 3:14, i.e. in a specifically northern cycle of traditions, making it very difficult to suppose that the title originates in Jerusalem and is retrojected into earlier Shilonite narratives ('Gottesnamen und Gottesepitheta bei Jesaja', in *Jahwe und sein Volk: Gesammelte Aufsätze zum Alten Testament* [TBü, 66; München: Chr. Kaiser, 1979], pp. 224-30).

87. It is possible that the original title was 'El of hosts, enthroned upon the cherubim'. Cf. Clements, *God and Temple*, p. 34, note 4; Eissfeldt, 'Jahwe Zebaoth', p. 120.

88. Otto, *Mazzotfest*, p. 358.

89. For the various views on the relation of the Ark to Yahweh's throne see Otto, *ibid*. pp. 359-60, note 7.

90. Cf. Mowinckel, *The Psalms in Israel's Worship*, I, pp. 120-23; de Moor, *Seasonal Pattern*, pp. 55-61. The difficulties are discussed by de Vaux, *Ancient Israel*, pp. 190-93.

91. De Moor, *New Year With Canaanites and Israelites*, I, (Kamper Cahiers, 21; Kampen: Uitgeversmaatschappij, 1972), p. 6.

92. *Ibid.*, p. 10; cf. I, pp. 29-30. De Moor's reconstruction is based on the Hieroglyphic-Luwic version of the text (I, p. 29, note 121). For the Phoenician text see *KAI* #26, A.II.17–III.2; cf. also #26, C.IV.3-4. De Moor claims Henri Cazelles in support of his reconstruction. Cf. also J. Coert Rylaarsdam, 'Booths, Feast of', in *IDB* I, pp. 455-58, especially p. 456.

93. One must ask why the Deuteronomistic editors of 1 and 2 Samuel would allow this anachronism to stand in light of the supposedly polemical context of 2 Sam 7.6. See below.

94. Cf. *CTA* 3.E.13-17; 6.1.32-36; 17.5.31-33; 15.3.18-19, and the comments of Cross, *Canaanite Myth*, pp. 36-39; Clifford, *Cosmic Mountain*, pp. 51-54, 177-78. See also Cross, 'The Priestly Tabernacle in the Light of Recent Research', in *Temples and High Places in Biblical Times* (Jerusalem: Hebrew Union College–Jewish Institute of Religion, 1981), pp. 169-80, especially pp. 171-72.

95. Haran, 'Shiloh and Jerusalem: The Origin of the Priestly Tradition in the Pentateuch', *JBL* 81 (1962), pp. 14-24; *Temples and Temple Service in Ancient Israel* (Oxford: The Clarendon Press, 1978), pp. 201-202; Cross, *Canaanite Myth*, p. 73, note 114.

96. See above, note 94, and below, note 175.

97. Cf. also Judg 18.31 and 1 Sam 1.7, 24, which speak of a 'house of God in Shiloh' and a 'house of Yahweh' or a 'house of Yahweh (of) Shiloh'. Both a בית יהוה and a היכל would indicate a place where Yahweh dwells and the terms are in that sense identical, as is indicated by their interchangeability with reference to the Jerusalem temple. See Haran, *Temples and Temple Service*, pp. 13, 34; Peter Welten, 'Kulthöhe und Jahwetempel', *ZDPV* 88 (1972), pp. 19-37, especially pp. 29-30, note 43; Yohanan Aharoni, 'Arad: Its Inscriptions and Temple', *BA* 31 (1968), pp. 2-32, especially pp. 19-21. 1 Sam 1.9 and 3.15 assume a solid structure at Shiloh.

98. Virgil W. Rabe, 'Israelite Opposition to the Temple', *CBQ* 29 (1967), pp. 228-33; see especially p. 230.

99. Milgrom, *Studies in Levitical Terminology, I: The Encroacher and the Levite, The Term 'Aboda* (Berkeley: University of California Press, 1970), p. 69.

100. See Gerhard von Rad, 'The Tent and the Ark', in *The Problem of the Hexateuch and Other Studies*, trans. by E.W. Dicken (Edinburgh: Oliver and Boyd, 1966), pp. 103-24. Cf. the earlier study by R. Hartman, 'Zelt und Lade', *ZAW* 37 (1917/18), pp. 209-44.

101. Milgrom, *Studies in Levitical Terminology*, p. 70, note 254.

102. On the diversity among the Ark traditions see Stoebe, *Das erste Buch Samuelis*, pp. 158-66.

103. Otto, *Mazzotfest*, pp. 351-61.

104. *Ibid.*, pp. 362-63. Joseph Blenkinsopp reconstructs the rivalries in a different manner. See his *Gibeon and Israel: The Role of Gibeon and the Gibeonites in the Political and Religious History of Early Israel* (SOTSMS, 2; Cambridge: Cambridge University Press, 1972), p. 94, and ch. 6, *passim*. According to Eissfeldt, who draws on Joshua 22 and the excavations at Deir 'Alla, the rivalries were quite ancient. Cf. 'Monopol-Ansprüche des Heiligtums von Silo', in *Kleine Schriften VI*, ed. by Rudolf Sellheim and Fritz Maass (Tübingen: J.C.B. Mohr, 1979), pp. 8-14.

105. It is probably inadequate to see the Deuteronomic conception of the Ark as a simple 'demythologizing' of earlier Ark traditions, as is commonly done. See, e.g., R.E. Clements, 'Deuteronomy and the Jerusalem Cult Tradition', *VT* 15 (1965), pp. 300-12. Cf. Stoebe, *Das erste Buch Samuelis*, p. 156. Deut 10.1-5 may contain an older tradition of the (or an) Ark, from which the later, characteristically Deuteronomic conceptions developed. See von Rad, *Deuteronomy: A Commentary*, trans. by Dorthea Barton (OTL; Philadelphia: Westminster, 1966), p. 79.

106. 'Kultzelt und Tempel', *Kleine Schriften VI*, pp. 1-7.

107. Although the present form of the chapter is said by Cross to be a Deuteronomistic creation (*Canaanite Myth*, p. 252). Psalm 78 also is widely thought to reflect Deuteronomic influence. Cf. H. Junker, 'Die Entstehungszeit des Ps 78 und des Deuteronomiums', *Biblica* 34 (1953), pp. 487-500; R.P. Carroll, 'Psalm 78: Vestiges of a Tribal Polemic', *VT* 21 (1971), pp. 113-50.

108. Cf. Robert G. Boling, *Judges* (AB; Garden City, NY: Doubleday, 1975), pp. 266-67. There is a large bibliography of studies on 2 Sam 7. For the older literature see J. Alberto Soggin, *Das Königtum in Israel* (BZAW, 104; Berlin: Alfred Töpelmann, 1966); Mettinger, *King and Messiah*. In addition, note especially Konrad Rupprecht, *Der Tempel von Jerusalem* (BZAW, 144; Berlin: de Gruyter, 1977), pp. 62-77; Eckhard von Nordheim, 'König und Tempel. Der Hintergrund des Tempelbauverbotes in 2 Samuel 7', *VT* 27 (1977), pp. 434-53; Ilse von Löwenclau, 'Der Prophet Nathan im Zwielicht von theologischer Deutung und Historie', in *Werden und Wirken des Alten Testaments. Festschrift für Claus Westermann*, ed. by Rainer Albertz (Göttingen: Vandenhoeck & Ruprecht, 1980), pp. 202-15.

109. Schunck, *Numen* 18 (1971), pp. 132-40.

110. Since it is apparently not the case that Yahweh never had a 'house' prior to Jerusalem, perhaps the emphasis in 2 Sam 7.6 is on the mode of dwelling rather than on the edifice. Cf. Rupprecht, *Der Tempel*, pp. 69-70; contrast Cross, *Canaanite Myth*, p. 245. Michilo Ota has a different understanding of the issues, somewhat along the lines of Hartmut Gese's earlier study (Ota, 'A Note on 2 Samuel 7', in *A Light Unto My Path: Old Testament Studies in Honor of Jacob M. Myers*, ed. by Howard N. Bream, Ralph D. Heim and Carey A. Moore [Philadelphia: Temple University Press, 1974], pp. 403-408; Gese, 'Davidsbund und Zionserwählung', in *Vom Sinai zum Zion: Beiträge zur biblischen Theologie* [BEvT, 64; München: Chr. Kaiser, 1974], pp. 113-29).

111. Cross, 'The Priestly Tabernacle in the Light of Recent Research', p. 43.

112. *Ibid.*

113. Nahum M. Sarna, 'The Divine Title "abhir ya'aqobh"', in *Essays on the Occasion of the Seventieth Anniversary of the Dropsie University*, ed. by Abraham I. Katsch and Leon Nemoy (Philadelphia: Dropsie University, 1979), pp. 389-96, especially p. 396.

114. *Ibid.*, p. 389, note 2. Sarna explains the variation of the epithet here as 'conditioned by the fossilized epithet יהוה צבאות אלהי ישראל', found in Isa 21.10; 37.16. However, it would seem that 'Yahweh of Hosts' is the original form, with 'God of Israel' added later as an interpretive element. Cf. Wildberger, *Jesaja*, pp. 27-29.

115. *Ibid.*, p. 394. Cf. pp. 392-95 for earlier literature attempting to identify the epithet with either Baal or El. '*br* does appear in association with Baal, but not as an epithet of him (*CTA* 12.1.32; 10.3.21). At the same time it does seem likely that the term as a designation of the deity has a Canaanite background (Cross, *Canaanite Myth*, pp. 4-5). Sarna takes אביר as simply a parallel form of אביר.

116. Cf. David Noel Freedman, 'Divine Names and Titles in Early Hebrew Poetry', in *Magnalia Dei: The Mighty Acts of God. In Memoriam G. Ernest Wright*, ed. by F.M. Cross, W.E. Lemke and P.D. Miller (Garden City, NY: Doubleday, 1976), pp. 55-102, especially p. 96.

117. Cf. Terrence E. Fretheim, 'Psalm 132: A Form-Critical Study', *JBL* 86 (1967), pp. 289-300, especially p. 291. Note also Schreiner, *Sion-Jerusalem*, pp. 177-78, and note 17. Schreiner and Fretheim both suggest a relationship with the Ark. Alt had argued that the 'Mighty One of Jacob' was venerated in a confederation of six tribes that included Judah, and thus the epithet originated in the South. But Schreiner points out that the only early attestation of the epithet puts it among the northern tribes, in the area where the Ark was kept for some generations. Schreiner also points to the terminology of Ps 132.5, which corresponds to Ps 78.60, in speaking of the sanctuary at Shiloh as a משכן.

118. Reading with LXX; cf. Kraus, *Psalmen*, p. 193. Dahood changes the suffix of the MT פניך to an emphatic particle, כי, interposed between the genitive and the construct. See *Psalms I*, p. 152.

119. See Wildberger, *Jesaja*, p. 86.

120. There are instances in which 'Jacob' may refer to the North. Cf. Henri Cazelles, 'Qui aurait visé, à l'origine, Isaïe II 2-5?', *VT* 30 (1980), pp. 409-20. But when Jacob is in parallel with Israel (e.g. Ps 78.71) the terms seem to refer either to South and North respectively, or to the people of God generally, as in Isaiah 40–48. Jeremiah 30.10 and 31.7 present a different point of view; both terms refer to the North (cf. Wilhelm Rudolph, *Jeremiah* [HAT, 12; Tübingen: J.C.B. Mohr, third edition, 1968], pp. 177-79).

121. Note also that the notion of Yahweh's kingship is associated with the title 'God of Jacob' in Pss 24, 46, 75, 76, etc.

122. Cf. Ringgren, *Israelite Religion*, p. 21.

123. See especially de Vaux 'Les Chérubins', and his *The Early History of Israel*, trans. by David Smith (Philadelphia: Westminster, 1978), p. 468.

124. Cross, *Canaanite Myth*, p. 69; McCarter, *I Samuel*, pp. 105-96; T.H. Gaster, 'Angels', in *IDB*, I, pp. 128-34, especially p. 131. See also de Vaux, 'Les Chérubins'; Eissfeldt, 'Jahwe Zebaoth'. According to Cross, the cherubim throne 'is ultimately derived from the typical iconography of 'El' ('The Priestly Tabernacle in the Light of Recent Research', p. 173).

125. See Eckart Otto, 'Silo und Jerusalem', *TZ* 32 (1976), p. 75; Stoebe, *Das erste Buch Samuelis*, p. 158; Fohrer, *History of Israelite Religion*, p. 105.

126. The connection of *zbl* with kingship is evident not only in this connection, but also at CTA 6.1.42-43 (*zbl b'l arṣ*); 13.26 (*zbl mlk*); and 2.1.24-25 (*kḫt zblkm*, 'your princely thrones'). Cf. *UT* #815. Note also the name Jezebel in Hebrew, and the use of the term in 1 Kgs 8.12-13. Cf. also Moshe Held, 'The Root ZBL/SBL in Akkadian, Ugaritic and Biblical Hebrew', *JAOS* 88 (1968), pp. 90-96.

127. See further, Ps. 68.1-5, and cf. the comments of Kraus in *Psalmen*, p. 710, on Ps 104.3. Psalm 80, an Asaph Psalm, may well be from the North (see the comments of Anderson, *Psalms*, p. 581; Martin J. Buss, 'The Psalms of Asaph and Korah', *JBL* 82 [1963], pp. 382-92).

128. Cf. Wildberger, *Jesaja*, pp. 28-29. Shiloh may have been a center of

E1 worship and it is possible that the combination of E1 and Baal mythology which is found in Jerusalem occurred already at Shiloh.

129. Contrast the emphases of Ross ('Jahwe Ṣeba'ot in Samuel and Psalms', *VT* 17 [1967], pp. 76-92) with those of Miller (*The Divine Warrior*, pp. 145-55). Unfortunately, Miller's only comment on Ross's study is that 'his approach has too many problems and does not lay out any fruitful directions to follow' (*ibid.*, p. 257, note 265). Miller is correct in emphasizing the martial character of Yahweh of hosts, but this character is to be understood as a component of Yahweh's kingship. Cf. the related discussion by Waldemar Janzen ('God as Warrior and Lord: A Conversation with G.E. Wright', *BASOR* 220/221 [1975/76], pp. 73-76), whose concerns, but not conclusions, I share.

130. Von Rad, 'The Tent and the Ark', p. 116. The text is printed in *UT* #1126.6, and is apparently an order or invoice for temple supplies. The relevant line reads *kd smn lnr 'ilm*. Both the transcription—*lnr ⁱm* (sic)—and the citation—1126.2 (sic)—are incorrect in Otto, 'Silo und Jerusalem', p. 75, note 70.

131. *Canaanite Myths and Legends* (Old Testament Studies, 3; Edinburgh: T.&T. Clark, 1956), p. 102, cf. p. 136, note 17.

132. Jeremias, 'Lade und Zion', p. 197. Cf. Eiler, 'Zion as a Theological Symbol', pp. 69-70, 117.

133. Cf. Jean M. Vincent, *Studien zur literarischen Eigenart und zur geistigen Heimat von Jesaja, Kap. 40–55* (BBET, 5; Frankfurt: Peter Lang, 1977), pp. 60-61, on Isa 42.10-17.

134. On the usual distinction between the Ark as Yahweh's permanent presence and the Tabernacle as the place of his occasional visitations, see de Vaux, 'Ark of the Covenant and Tent of Reunion'.

135. Mowinckel claims that Pss 24 and 47 reflect the Ark processional, 'in which the king Yahweh is borne to the temple on his palladium, the Ark' (*Psalmenstudien II*, pp. 3-4). Lipiński relates Ps 24.7-10 closely to 1 Sam 4.21-22, described as a ritual return of the Ark to the sanctuary in Shiloh. He also notes the close association of 'the king of glory' with 'Yahweh of hosts', and stresses the importance of this background for understanding Ps 47. See *La Royauté de Yahwé*, pp. 405-407.

136. In addition to the commentaries see especially J.J.M. Roberts, 'The Religio-Political Setting of Psalm 47', *BASOR* 221 (1976), pp. 129-32. Roberts proposes that the occasion of the Psalm is 'a cultic celebration of Yahweh's imperial accession, based on the relatively recent victories of David's age, which raised Israel from provincial obscurity to an empire of first rank' (p. 132). The date of the Psalm is very difficult to assess, especially since the notion of Yahweh's universal sovereignty is known already in the pre-monarchic period. Roberts's dating is based in part on the presence of foreign princes at this celebration, indicated by v. 10. This would suggest the period of the United Monarchy, when Israel enjoyed its most extensive

hegemony. He takes עַם in v. 10 as עַם in the dative sense, which is known from Ugaritic, and the ל with אלהים in the same verse as an emphatic. He also emends מגני to מגן. However, nothing stands in the way of regarding עַם as 'people', taking it in apposition with נדיבי, referring to the leaders and the people of Israel. This is the sense of the word in Num 21.18, where it is in parallel with שרים. This would allow the retention of מגני and make the expression in v. 10 parallel to that in v. 9, both expressing Yahweh's universal sovereignty (taking the *lamedh* in the possessive sense). If this reading is followed, the dating of the Psalm is much less certain.

137. *Ibid.*, pp. 129-30. Cf. also Roberts, 'The Davidic Origins of the Zion Tradition', p. 342.

138. 'Psalm 47', p. 130. On this point and the following see Kraus, *Psalmen*, pp. 198-99.

139. Roberts, 'Psalm 47', p. 130.

140. Clifford points out that מלך רב is the equivalent of Assyrian *sarru rabu*, 'the suzerain, the great king' (*Cosmic Mountain*, p. 145, note 63).

141. Eissfeldt, *Zeus Kasios und der Durchzug der Israeliten durchs Meer* (BRGA, 1; Max Niemeyer, 1932), p. 20. Eissfeldt also associates this theme with the use of the title 'Elyon' (p. 19). Cf. W.H. Schmidt, *Königtum Gottes*, p. 33; Kraus, *Psalmen*, pp. 95-96. Note again that in the Jerusalem cult motifs associated with Baal and with El have been combined.

142. Kraus cites a hymn of Nabonidus to Shamash as an example (*Psalmen*, p. 352; cf. *SAHG*, p. 288), and suggests that closer parallels are to be found in the 'Syrian-Canaanite' sphere (p. 353).

143. A.A. Anderson, *Psalms*, p. 360.

144. The term is also associated with earthly kingship, as 1 Sam 10.24 makes clear. Note also 1 Kgs 1.39 and Ps 89.16. Cf. Schmid, 'Opfer mit Jubel', p. 50; Arvid S. Kapelrud, *The Message of the Prophet Zephaniah: Morphology and Ideas* (Oslo: Universitetsforlaget, 1975), pp. 39-40, 70-71.

145. Both Humbert ('"Laetari et exultare"') and Harvey ('"Rejoice Not, O Israel"') point out that the term שמח, 'to rejoice', occurs in connection with the festival cult, as might be expected, and especially in connection with the harvest (cf. Deut 12.7; 14.22-29, etc.). The term גיל, also meaning 'rejoice', similarly occurs in connection with harvest festivals in both Israel and Canaan. Within the Jerusalem cult these terms and others such as שוש and עלז are used in the celebration of Yahweh's theophanic appearance as king (cf. Ps 68.4). It should not be argued that the prominence of rejoicing in connection with both the harvest and the celebration of Yahweh as king strictly proves a connection between the two, but there does seem to be some evidence for a continued association between the Autumn festival and Yahweh's kingship (Johnson, *Sacral Kingship*, pp. 47-58), and at least in the post-exilic period these two are explicitly related (Zech 14.16). It is also likely that the Baal epic locates the celebration of the New Year and the construction of Baal's temple in an Autumn festival (cf. Gibson, *Canaanite*

Myths and Legends, pp. 6, 13). On the problems involved see de Moor, *Seasonal Pattern*, pp. 55-61. Note that *smh // gyl* at 3.E.28-29 in connection with the building of El's *bht // hkl*.

146. 'Opfer mit Jubel', p. 51.

147. Cf. Harvey, '"Rejoice Not, O Israel"', on the verb *śḥq*. The text is *CTA* 3.B.23-27.

148. Note that Tukulti-Ninurta describes the temple of Ishtar as 'her joyful dwelling' after his accession and rebuilding of the temple. Cf. A.K. Grayson, *Assyrian Royal Inscriptions*, I (RANE; Wiesbaden: Otto Harrassowitz, 1972), #728, #742.

149. On the date of the harvest in Israel see H.N. Richardson, 'Harvest', *IDB*, II, p. 527. Wheat would have been harvested in early summer.

150. The circumstances are perhaps those of 587, according to John Bright (*Jeremiah* [AB; Garden City, NY: Doubleday, 1965], pp. 65-66). J.A. Thompson agrees with Bright (*Jeremiah* [NICOT; Grand Rapids: Eerdmans, 1980], p. 304), while Rudolph suggests that the reference is general, not to a specific time or event (*Jeremiah*, pp. 113-15).

151. Recently Helmer Ringgren and John H. Eaton have remarked on the liturgical character of Deutero-Isaiah, particularly the latter chapters. Both suggest the Autumn festival as the setting for this material. Ringgren, 'Zur Komposition von Jesaja 49-55' in *Beiträge zur alttestamentlichen Theologie. Walther Zimmerli zum 70. Geburtstag*, ed. by H. Donner, R. Hanhart and R. Smend (Göttingen: Vandenhoeck & Ruprecht, 1977), pp. 371-76. Eaton, *Festal Drama in Deutero-Isaiah* (London: SPCK, 1979), pp. 38-89. Cross also notes the ritual character of these texts without dealing with the question of a cultic setting, in *Canaanite Myth*, pp. 105-11. G. Hylmö was the first to note the liturgical character of Isa 24-27, according to Wildberger, *Jesaja 13-27* (BKAT, 10/2 [Neukirchen-Vluyn: Neukirchener Verlag, 1978), p. 885. Cf. also Millar, *Isaiah 24-27*, p. 105.

152. For the connection between 24.21-23 and 25.6-8 see Wildberger, *Jesaja*, pp. 899-900, 960. Wildberger's commentary is paginated sequentially and I will not distinguish between volumes I and II in these notes.

153. It now seems likely that the notion of 'Yahweh's day' derived from the Jerusalem cult. See M. Weiss, 'The Origin of the "Day of the Lord"— Reconsidered', *HUCA* 37 (1966), pp. 29-60. Cf. Kapelrud, *Zephaniah*, pp. 80-87.

154. I follow Millar here in taking v. 9 with 25.6-8. See *Isaiah 24-27*, pp. 42-43. Whether or not v. 10a goes with vv. 6-9, as suggested by *BHS*, remains unclear. It is possible that vv. 10b-12 have been appended to the preceding by a redactor who wanted to make a polemical point against Moab, but this is not certain either.

155. Wildberger has also drawn attention to the Rephaim texts in *Jesaja*, p. 962, as well as to other, more wide-ranging parallels from Germanic mythology. The Rephaim text cited by Wildberger is apparently *CTA* 22.13-

17; he follows Aistleitner's translation in *Die mythologischen und kultischen Texte aus Ras Schamra* (Budapest: Akademiai Kiado, second edition, 1964), pp. 85-86. Aistleitner himself based his translation on the reconstruction of the text by Ch. Virolleaud, 'Les Rephaim. Fragments de Poèmes de Ras Shamra', *Syria* 22 (1941), pp. 1-30. Virolleaud found in this text an enthronement ritual of Baal. That interpretation is now in considerable doubt; cf. Conrad E. L'Heureux, *Rank Among the Canaanite Gods, El, Ba'al, and the Repha'im* (HSM, 21; Cambridge MA: Harvard University Press, 1979), pp. 144-45, 148-52. The point does not really affect Wildberger's interpretation of Isa 25.6-8, however.

156. In Isa 66.5 שמח ('joy') clearly reflects the dual sense of vindication and security as does the term at Ugarit (cf. *CTA* 6.1.32-43; 3.B.25-27; 3.E.28-29; 18.1.8-9).

157. 'The Priestly Tabernacle in the Light of Recent Research', p. 170.

158. As Kraus notes, the imperfect verbs in Ps 99.1 should be taken as declaratives, not optatives, as in RSV (*Psalmen*, p. 681). The verb נוט is a *hapax* in Hebrew, but is known in its D-Stem at Ugarit. Cf. *CTA* 4.7.35, where, at the voice of Baal, *bmt. 'ar[ṣ] ttṭn*.

159. The reading of several Hebrew and Greek manuscripts, אלהים for עמים, is to be preferred. This reading avoids the simple repetition of עמים in vv. 1 and 2, and gives force to the claim that Yahweh is 'great' and 'exalted'. Further, the occurrence of similar claims in 95.3, 96.4 and 97.9, as noted in *BHS*, lends support to the argument that Yahweh's supremacy over the gods is being claimed here. That claim is at the heart of all the Enthronement Psalms. Dahood recognizes this, but instead of reading אלהים he reads עמים as a divinity (*Psalms II*, p. 268). If יורו is taken as a jussive (v. 3) there is no difficulty in connecting this with אלהים as its antecedent. The gods are exhorted to praise Yahweh in Ps 47 (cf. Roberts, 'Psalm 47', p. 130), and in 97.7 it is said that all gods will bow to him. Cf. also Ps 29.1-2; Deut 32.43 (Roberts, *ibid.*).

160. On v. 4, see above, note 49.

161. My formal analysis of this Psalm differs somewhat from those of Westermann (*The Praise of God in the Psalms*, pp. 149-50) and Kraus (*Psalmen*, pp. 681-82). Rather than seeing v. 9 as forming an *inclusio* with v. 5, and framing vv. 6-8, I would note the repetition of קדוש הוא in vv. 3 and 5, as does Kraus, and would see the exhortation to praise in v. 5 as a conclusion to the first section. Similarly, v. 9 concludes the second section and is itself concluded by a variation on the phrase 'holy is he' of vv. 3 and 5.

162. Cf. Frank Crüsemann, *Studien zur Formgeschichte von Hymnus und Danklied in Israel* (WMANT, 32: Neukirchen-Vluyn: Neukirchener Verlag, 1969), pp. 195-99, on the formal relations of the latter half of this chapter.

163. If the Ark was lost during the reign of Manasseh, as proposed by Menahem Haran ('The Ark and the Cherubim. Their Symbolic Significance

in Biblical Ritual', *IEJ* 9 [1959], pp. 30-38, 89-94; *Temples and Temple Service*, pp. 277-84), this Psalm may reflect theological developments following that event. However, as Jeremias suggests, the Ark itself may have lost its independent significance after its transfer to Zion, which then inherited the sacral notions formerly associated with the Ark (cf. 'Lade und Zion'). Artur Weiser, commenting on Jer 3.16, speaks of a 'spiritualization' here, in that the presence of God attaches no longer to the Ark, but to Jerusalem itself. He says that the text is from Jeremiah, not a redactor (Weiser, *Das Buch des Propheten Jeremia* [ATD; Göttingen: Vandenhoeck & Ruprecht, 1955], p. 37). In any event, this does not suggest the inheritance or development of a 'sacred mountain mythology', since Zion's sacral character is limited to its place as Yahweh's abode. It is in relation to Yahweh's holiness that Zion can be called his holy mountain.

164. The verb חוה in the *eshtaphal* (שחה—*hithpalel* in some lexica) with the preposition ל regularly means 'to bow down to', and derivatively 'give obeisance to', or 'to venerate', as seen clearly, for example, in Gen 27.29; Exod 32.8; Ps 45.12. When it means 'bow down before', the preposition לפני is used, as in Gen 18.2; 1 Sam 25.41; 2 Chr 32.12. The preposition אל is used with the verb to mean 'bow down at or toward' in Pss 5.8; 138.2. In Lev 26.1 על is used, and in several instances the simple directive ה־ is used without a preposition. Among the dozens of instances of the construction השתחוה ל, only in Pss 99.5 and 132.7 could it have been a locative sense, meaning 'at' or 'before'. While it is clear that neither the Ark nor Zion is to be worshipped, their association with the presence of Yahweh makes it possible to speak of 'bowing down' to them.

165. Cf. Bright, *Jeremiah*, pp. 26-27; Thompson, *Jeremiah*, pp. 202-203. Weiser's argument (*Jeremia*, pp. 35-36) that this passage is from Jeremiah and represents competing understandings of the Ark in the priesthood of Jerusalem in the monarchy is unconvincing, since it seems to presuppose an exilic situation. Likewise, Rudolph's argument (*Jeremiah*, p. 25) that this text is comparable to 14.21, which is from Jeremiah, fails to note the elaboration in 3.16 of the simple assertion in 14.21 that Yahweh's throne was being dishonored in the events of that period.

166. אפים ארץ ישתחוו לך // ועפר רגליך ילחכו

167. Dahood takes למבול as 'from the flood', meaning that this is a reference 'not to the flood in the days of Noah, but to the motif of the struggle between Baal, lord of the air and genius of the rain, and Yamm, master of the sea and subterranean waters' (*Psalms I*, p. 180). He refers to *CTA* 2.4.9-10 (= *UT* 68.9-10, 32) for parallels, as well as to Pss 92.9-10; 93.2-3. That the reference to the flood is not to the Noahic flood was shown already by Joachim Begrich ('MABBUL, Eine exegetisch-lexikalische Studie', in *Gesammelte Studien zum Alten Testament* [TBü, 21; München: Chr. Kaiser, 1964], pp. 39-54. The referent seems to be the heavenly ocean above the firmament, in which the foundations of Yahweh's temple were

placed (Anderson, *Psalms*, p. 238; Begrich, 'MABBUL', pp. 47-49; cf. Pss 148.4; 104.3). Dahood argues that the preposition here must mean 'from', and Cross seems to agree in a couple of footnotes, but then translates the passage, 'Yahweh sits enthroned on the Flooddragon' (*Canaanite Myth*, p. 147, note 4; contrast pp. 95, note 19, 97, note 24), with reference to *RS* 24.245, published in *Ugaritica V*. Ps 93.2 expresses 'from eternity' with מעולם. In Ps 29 Yahweh's connection with the flood is already expressed in v. 3, and v. 10 seems to indicate that he will reign over the flood forever. Cf. further, Siegfried Mittmann, 'Komposition und Redaktion von Psalm 29', *VT* 28 (1978), pp. 172-94, especially pp. 189-90; Johannes Schildenberger, 'Psalm 29: Ein Hymnus auf den machtvollen Gott zu Beginn eines neuen Jahres', *Erbe und Auftrag* 57 (1981), pp. 5-12.

168. Cross, *Canaanite Myth*, pp. 147-48, note 4, on Job 36.10. Cross follows Marvin Pope in emending כסה (*piel*, 'to cover') to כסאו 'his throne', translating 'the roots of the sea are his throne' (Pope, *Job* [AB; Garden City, NY: Doubleday, 1965], p. 275).

169. Pope, *ibid.* Cf. also his *El in the Ugaritic Texts* (VTS, 2; Leiden: E.J. Brill, 1955), pp. 61-81; Harmut Gese, *Die Religionen Altsyriens* (Die Religionen der Menschheit, 10/2; Stuttgart: W. Kohlhammer, 1970), p. 98.

170. See especially Roberts, 'The Davidic Origins of the Zion Tradition'. Attempts to prove an original connection between El and Zaphon have been unsuccessful.

171. We have already noted the suggestion that Ps 29 was originally a Canaanite hymn. Cf. further, F.M. Cross, 'Notes on a Canaanite Psalm in the Old Testament', *BASOR* 117 (1950), pp. 119-21.

172. El apparently shares some characteristics of a warrior. Cf. P.D. Miller, 'El the Warrior', *HTR* 60 (1967), pp. 411-31. Still, it is possible to distinguish Baal as *the* warrior god in Ugaritic mythology.

173. Dahood takes נהר פלגיו with v. 4, changing סלה to a verb, which he translates 'to heap up' (*Psalms I*, p. 280). Clifford (*Cosmic Mountain*, pp. 149-50, note 68) follows Dahood, saying that since vv. 3-4 speak of the 'threatening waters of chaos' נהר must continue the threatening tone. This completely misses the point of the contrast between the threatening waters of chaos and the waters of the stream by which Zion is made glad. There is thus no need to follow Dahood's emendation. On the possible relation of Ps 46.5 to Isa 9.6, the waters of Shiloah, see most recently John Day, 'Shear-Jashub (Isaiah VIII 3) and "the Remnant of Wrath" (Psalm LXXVI)', *VT* 31 (1981), pp. 76-78, especially p. 78, note 3.

174. Taking the plural here as that of 'local extension' (*GK* #124b). The construction is the same as in Ps 132.5. The suggestion to take קדש as *piel*, based on the Vulgate and LXX, is not convincing, since עליון and נהר make for an awkward parallelism. It is better to read with MT, taking the entire final phrase in apposition with עיר אלהים.

175. See above, note 94 and, in addition, *CTA* 4.4.20-26, with the

comments of Cross, *Canaanite Myth*, pp. 36-38; Clifford, 'The Tent of El and the Israelite Tent of Meeting', *CBQ* 33 (1971), pp. 221-27; *Cosmic Mountain*, pp. 51-54.

Notes to Chapter 3

1. For a recent theological exposition of creation as the context of Yahweh's historical activity see Rolf Knierim, 'Cosmos and History in Israel's Theology', *HBT* 3 (1981), pp. 59-123.

2. See above, ch. 2, and cf. Loren R. Fisher and Brent Knutson, 'An Enthronement Ritual at Ugarit', *JNES* 28 (1969), pp. 157-67, especially p. 158 and note 7.

3. Cf. Mitchell Dahood, *Psalms I* (New York: Doubleday, 1965), p. 176; Aubrey Johnson, *Sacral Kingship in Ancient Israel* (Cardiff: University of Wales, second edition, 1967), p. 97. On the parallel of *ym // nhr* at Ugarit see *CTA* 2.4.12-13; 3.D.34-44, where *ym* and *nhr* are opponents of Baal. Cf. also Loren R. Fisher, 'Creation at Ugarit and in the Old Testament', *VT* 15 (1965), pp. 313-24; 'From Chaos to Cosmos', *Encounter* 26 (1965), pp. 183-97 (especially pp. 188-89).

4. In addition to the literature already cited in relation to the Ark, see Otto Eissfeldt, 'Die Lade Jahwes in Geschichtserzählung, Sage und Lied', in *Kleine Schriften V*, ed. by Rudolf Sellheim and Fritz Maass (Tübingen: J.C.B. Mohr, 1973), pp. 77-93.

5. On the motif of the waters in the creation texts see A.H.W. Curtis, 'The "Subjugation of the Waters" Motif in the Psalms: Imagery or Polemic?', *JSS* 23 (1978), pp. 245-56.

6. According to Fisher's definition this is creation 'of the Baal type'. See 'Creation at Ugarit'. For a critique of Fisher's terminology cf. Arvid S. Kapelrud, 'Creation in the Ras Shamra Texts', *ST* 34 (1980), pp. 1-11; 'The Relationship Between El and Baal in the Ras Shamra Texts', in *The Bible World: Essays in Honor of Cyrus H. Gordon*, ed. by Gary Rendsburg, Ruth Adler, Milton Arfa and Nathan H. Winter (New York: KTAV, 1980), pp. 79-85. Cf. also the contrasting essays of Dennis J. McCarthy, 'Creation Motifs in Ancient Hebrew Poetry', *CBQ* 29 (1967), pp. 87-100; J. Alberto Soggin, 'God the Creator in the First Chapter of Genesis', in *Old Testament and Oriental Studies* (BibOr 29; Rome: Pontifical Biblical Institute, 1975), pp. 120-29.

7. Cf. John Gray, *The Biblical Doctrine of the Reign of God* (Edinburgh: T. & T. Clark, 1979), pp. 42-45.

8. Hans-Joachim Kraus, *Psalmen* (BKAT, 15; Neukirchen-Vluyn: Neukirchener Verlag, fourth edition, 1972), p. 450.

9. Theodore M. Ludwig, 'The Traditions of Establishing the Earth in Deutero-Isaiah', *JBL* 92 (1973), pp. 345-57. The quote is from p. 354.

Ludwig also draws attention to Pss 24 and 89, as well as to Ps 102, which is later.

10. *Ibid.*, p. 355. On enthronement and kingship see the comments of Sigmund Mowinckel, *The Psalms in Israel's Worship*, I, trans. by D.R. Ap-Thomas (Nashville: Abingdon, 1962), p. 122.

11. Cf. also Ps 134, and note the essay of Norman C. Habel, '"Yahweh, Maker of Heaven and Earth": A Study in Tradition Criticism', *JBL* 91 (1972), pp. 321-37.

12. Thorkild Jacobsen, 'The Battle Between Marduk and Tiamat', *JAOS* 88 (1968), pp. 104-108. For a different view of creation and kingship see Carroll Stuhlmueller, 'Yahweh King and Deutero-Isaiah', *BR* 15 (1970), pp. 32-45.

13. On El as creator see Rolf Rendtorff, 'El, Ba'al und Jahwe', *ZAW* 78 (1966), pp. 277-92; Robert Oden, 'Ba'al Šamem and 'El', *CBQ* 39 (1977), pp. 457-73; Patrick D. Miller, 'El, the Creator of Earth', *BASOR* 239 (1980), pp. 43-46.

14. Westermann denies such a connection in *Genesis* (Biblischer Kommentar, 1/1; Neukirchen-Vluyn: Neukirchener Verlag, 1974), pp. 36-52. Stolz claims to find such connections in Israel and the Near East, in *Strukturen und Figuren im Kult von Jerusalem* (BZAW, 118; Berlin: Walter de Gruyter, 1970), pp. 46, note 158, and 167-75.

15. Rolf Rendtorff, 'Die theologische Stellung des Schöpfungsglaubens bei Deuterojesaja', *ZTK* 51 (1954), pp. 3-13; Gerhard von Rad, *Old Testament Theology*, II, trans. by D.M.G. Stalker (New York: Harper & Row, 1965), pp. 240-41.

16. For the basic approach cf. Douglas Stuart, *Studies in Early Hebrew Meter* (HSM, 13; Missoula: Scholars Press, 1976). A critique of Stuart's method is provided by Alan Cooper, *BASOR* 233 (1979), pp. 75-76.

17. See Patrick D. Miller, *The Divine Warrior in Early Israel* (HSM, 5; Cambridge, MA: Harvard University Press, 1973), p. 81. Miller notes that the role of Yahweh in Deut 33.2-5 is comparable to that of Enlil in the Mesopotamian pantheon.

18. See Richard J. Clifford, *The Cosmic Mountain in Canaan and the Old Testament* (HSM, 4; Cambridge, MA: Harvard University Press, 1972), pp. 114-20. On the possible associations with Kadesh see Eduard Meyer, *Die Israeliten und ihre Nachbarstämme* (Halle: Max Niemeyer, 1906), especially p. 60.

19. Cf. the summary discussion in Frank Moore Cross, *Canaanite Myth and Hebrew Epic* (Cambridge, MA: Harvard University Press, 1973), pp. 162-63. It would appear that even in Israel's earliest poetry characteristics of El and Baal have been combined.

20. As suggested earlier, I consider it likely that substantial integration in this direction already occurred in connection with the Ark at Shiloh. Cf. Eiler, 'Zion as a Theological Symbol'. This would especially be the case if

there were tendencies toward cult centralization at Shiloh, as argued by Eissfeldt, 'Monopol-Ansprüche des Heiligtums von Silo', in *Kleine Schriften VI*, ed. by Rudolf Sellheim and Fritz Maass (Tübingen: J.C.B. Mohr, 1979), pp. 8-14.

21. Cf. Miller, *Divine Warrior*, pp. 120-21.

22. *Old Testament Theology*, II, p. 240.

23. The combination of creation and redemption in Exodus 15 was already noted by Fisher, 'Creation at Ugarit'.

24. As Childs says, 'The victory at the sea simply illustrates those same attributes which are continually celebrated throughout the Psalter' (*The Book of Exodus* [OTL; Philadelphia: Westminster, 1974], pp. 250-51). We might add that it is particularly in the Psalms celebrating Yahweh as king and creator that these attributes are noted.

25. Since the site of Yahweh's sanctuary is not named in this hymn there has been considerable speculation about it. The debate is summarized by Freedman in 'Early Israelite History in the Light of Early Israelite Poetry', in *Unity and Diversity: Essays in the History, Literature, and Religion of the Ancient Near East*, ed. by Hans Goedicke and J.J.M. Roberts (Baltimore: Johns Hopkins University Press, 1975), pp. 3-35, especially pp. 5-9. I cannot accept Freedman's conclusion that Sinai is the site of the sanctuary.

26. On Yahweh as creator and redeemer in Ps 95 see G. Henton Davies, 'Psalm 95', *ZAW* 85 (1973), pp. 183-95; Charles B. Riding, 'Psalm 95.1-7c as a Large Chiasm', *ZAW* 88 (1976), p. 418. Riding seems to strain the text to achieve an A:B::B:A pattern of the themes of creator and redeemer in Ps 95. As the text makes clear, Yahweh's kingship is also assumed (cf. Kraus, *Psalmen*, p. 661). The expression in v. 2 (נקדמה פניו בתודה) connects the Psalm with the Jerusalem temple.

27. Jeremias, 'Lade und Zion: Zur Entstehung der Zionstradition', in *Probleme biblischer Theologie. Gerhard von Rad zum 70. Geburtstag*, ed. by Hans Walter Wolff (München: Chr. Kaiser, 1971), p. 189 and note 25; *Theophanie: Die Geschichte einer alttestamentlichen Gattung* (WMANT, 10; Neukirchen-Vluyn: Neukirchener Verlag, 1965), pp. 73-95. Stolz's argument can be found in *Strukturen und Figuren*, pp. 72-85. Jeremias believes, however, that Wanke has disproven Gunkel's argument that the *Völkerkampf* of Israel is merely a historicized *Chaoskampf* (Wanke, *Die Zionstheologie der Korachiten in ihrem traditionsgeschichtlichen Zusammenhang* [BZAW, 197; Berlin: Alfred Töpelmann, 1966]). Nor does Jeremias agree with most previous scholarship that the *Völkerkampf* is taken from Jebusite tradition. Finally, Georg Molin, 'Das Motiv vom Chaoskampf im alten Orient und in den Traditionen Jerusalems und Israels' (*Memoria Jerusalem: Freundesgabe Franz Sauer*, ed. by J.B. Bauer and J. Marböck [Graz: Akademische Druck-u. Verlagsanstalt, 1977], pp. 13-27) argues that there is no *Chaoskampf* in the Old Testament. He manages this conclusion by restricting the motif so completely that even the Ugaritic struggle between Baal and Yam is excluded.

28. The unique contributions of Deutero-Isaiah should not be minimized. It is possible that in his formulation he drew on traditions from the Priestly tradents. Cf. Bernhard W. Anderson, 'Exodus and Covenant in Second Isaiah and Prophetic Tradition', in *Magnalia Dei: The Mighty Acts of God. In Memoriam G. Ernest Wright*, ed. by F.M. Cross, W.E. Lemke and P.D. Miller (Garden City: Doubleday, 1976), pp. 339-60.

29. The issue has been explored traditio-historically by Niek Poulssen, *König und Tempel im Glaubenszeugnis des alten Testamentes* (SBM, 3; Stuttgart: Verlag Katholisches Bibelwerk, 1967).

30. This has been argued by, among others, Th.C. Vriezen, 'Essentials of the Theology of Isaiah', in *Israel's Prophetic Heritage: Essays in Honor of James Muilenburg*, ed. by B.W. Anderson and Walter Harrelson (New York: Harper & Brothers, 1962), pp. 128-46. For the opposing view see Ronald E. Clements, *Isaiah and the Deliverance of Jerusalem* (JSOT Supplement Series, 13; Sheffield: JSOT Press, 1980), ch. 4.

31. See, most recently, John Gray, 'Sacral Kingship in Ugarit', *Ugaritica* VI (1969), pp. 289-302.

32. Gray, *The Reign of God*, p. 78.

33. Cf. Johnson, *Sacral Kingship*, p. 7; Keith W. Whitelam, *The Just King: Monarchical Judicial Authority in Ancient Israel* (JSOT Supplement Series, 12; Sheffield: JSOT Press, 1979), pp. 29-37.

34. Victor Maag, 'Kosmos, Chaos, Gesellschaft und Recht nach archäisch-religiösem Verständnis', in *Kultur, Kulturkontakt und Religion: Gesammelte Studien zur allgemeinen und alttestamentlichen Religionsgeschichte*, ed. by O.H. Steck and H.H. Schmid (Göttingen: Vandenhoeck & Ruprecht, 1980), pp. 329-41. The quote is from p. 336.

35. Werner H. Schmidt, 'Kritik am Königtum', in *Probleme Biblischer Theologie*, pp. 440-61.

36. For contrasting views of this conception see Ivan Engnell, *Studies in Divine Kingship in the Ancient Near East* (Uppsala: Almqvist & Wiksell, 1943), and Henri Frankfort, *Kingship and the Gods: A Study of Ancient Near Eastern Religion as the Integration of Society and Nature* (Chicago: University of Chicago Press, 1948).

37. J.J.M. Roberts denies that there was a substantive relation to earlier Jerusalem traditions ('The Davidic Origin of the Zion Tradition', *JBL* 92 [1970], pp. 329-44). Eckart Otto believes that the Zion tradition incorporated aspects of the 'El religion' indigenous, according to his reconstruction, to Jerusalem ('El und JHWH in Jerusalem: Historische und theologische Aspekte einer Religionsintegration', *VT* 30 [1980], pp. 316-29; *Jerusalem: Die Geschichte der Heiligen Stadt von den Anfängen bis zur Kreuzfahrerzeit* [Urban Taschenbücher, 308; Stuttgart: W. Kohlhammer, 1980], pp. 25-33).

38. For a summary of these issues see T.N.D. Mettinger, *King and Messiah: The Civil and Sacral Legitimation of the Israelite Kings* (ConBOT, 8; Lund: CWK Gleerup, 1976), p. 254.

39. See the essays of Clements (above, note 30), Roberts (above, note 37) and Otto ('El und JHWH').

40. Cf. Eiler, 'Zion as a Theological Symbol', p. 193. Clements claims that Ps 48.2 is evidence that the Songs of Zion are related to the royal Psalms and are not about Zion but about the Davidic dynasty (*Isaiah and the Deliverance of Jerusalem*, pp. 87-88). I cannot follow this conclusion.

41. Eissfeldt suggests such a setting for Ps 76 ('Psalm 76', *Kleine Schriften III*, ed. by Rudolf Sellheim and Fritz Maass [Tübingen: J.C.B. Mohr, 1966], pp. 448-57; cf. 'Jahwes Königsprädizierung als Verklärung national-politischer Ansprüche Israels', *Kleine Schriften V*, pp. 216-21). Eissfeldt seems too eager to interpret the Songs of Zion in light of Ps 2. Cf. J.J.M. Roberts, 'The Religio-Political Setting of Psalm 47', *BASOR* 220/221 (1975-76), pp. 129-32.

42. See the comments of G.N.M. Habets, 'Die grosse Jesaja-Apokalypse (Jes 24–27): Ein Beitrag zur Theologie des Alten Testaments' (Dissertation: Bonn University, 1974), pp. 238, 413, note 151.

43. Cf. Roland de Vaux, 'Jerusalem and the Prophets', in *Interpreting the Prophetic Tradition*, ed. by H.M. Orlinsky (Cincinatti: Hebrew Union College, 1969), pp. 275-300, especially pp. 385-86.

44. Jon Levenson, 'The Davidic Covenant and its Modern Interpreters', *CBQ* 41 (1979), pp. 205-29.

45. *Ibid.*, p. 217. Cf. also Moshe Weinfeld, 'Covenant, Davidic', *IDBS*, pp. 188-92. He argues that the 'Davidic dynasty cannot be separated from Zion' (p. 189). This is true, but may not be converted into the claim that Zion cannot be separated from the Davidic dynasty, as in fact it can be. Note also how McCarthy shows that the Davidic tradition simply applied to itself the appropriate promises attached to Zion (Dennis J. McCarthy, *Old Testament Covenant: A Survey of Current Opinions* [Growing Points in Theology; London: Basil Blackwell, 1972], p. 51). It is not clear, however, that McCarthy fully appreciates the breadth of Zion symbolism.

46. Edzard Rohland, 'Die Bedeutung der Erwählungstraditionen Israels für die Eschatologie der alttestamentlichen Propheten' (Dissertation: Heidelberg University, 1956), pp. 120-23.

47. Cf. de Vaux, 'Jerusalem and the Prophets', p. 286.

48. All of these texts are from the Deuteronomist(s). 1 Kgs 8.44, 48; 2 Kgs 21.7 are said by Gray to be later additions to the basic Deuteronomistic text (John Gray, *I & II Kings* [OTL; Philadelphia: Westminster, second edition, 1970], pp. 226, 705). Cross says the same of 2 Kgs 23.27 (*Canaanite Myth*, p. 287).

49. Cf. Helga Weippert, 'Der Ort, den Jahwe erwählen wird, um dort seinen Namen wohnen zu lassen', *BZ* 24 (1980), pp. 76-94. She misses the cultic issues at stake in 1 Kings 11-14, and perhaps over-emphasizes the political role of Jerusalem in these texts (cf. p. 82).

50. Contrast Cross (*Canaanite Myth*, pp. 96-97, 232-33) and Mettinger

(*King and Messiah*, p. 256) on Ps 132. The primarily cultic provenance of the *election* of Jerusalem/Zion is indicated clearly in 2 Kgs 21.7, regarding Manasseh, and 23.27, regarding Josiah, but harking back to Manasseh. The importance of David and Solomon, and their 'anti-types' Hezekiah and Josiah, is principally that of cult guardians: David originated the cult, Solomon built the temple, Hezekiah and Josiah reformed the cult. This kingly role is reflected in the history itself and in Ps 132, and it is with respect to this role that the tradition of the dual election of Zion and David comes to be formed.

51. This theme is joined to that of Zion's election in Ps 78, which many, myself included, hold to be Deuteronomic. See especially Ps 78.67-69. On the Deuteronomic provenance of Ps 78 see H. Junker, 'Die Entstehungszeit des Ps 78 und des Deuteronomiums', *Biblica* 34 (1953), pp. 487-500. Albright, following Eissfeldt, dated the Psalm in the monarchy, around the tenth century (*Yahweh and the Gods of Canaan* [London: Athlone, 1969], p. 17, note 41, and p. 25, note 56).

52. Ps 132 may indeed pre-date Deuteronomy. However, the conditional elements in v. 12 and the reference to the priests in v. 16 may suggest influence from Deuteronomy 17, where the king is subject to Torah administered by the Levitical Priests.

53. Ronald E. Clements, *God and Temple* (Philadelphia: Fortress, 1965), p. 55: 'It can no longer be maintained that it [Zion] became Yahweh's abode because the temple was built there. Rather the reverse was the case and the temple was built there because Mount Zion had become Yahweh's abode.' Cf. also p. 48.

54. See above, notes 38 and 45. Cross maintains that conditionality was an original aspect of the Davidic covenant, an aspect lost under Solomon (*Canaanite Myth*, pp. 260-64; 'The Priestly Tabernacle in the Light of Recent Research', in *Temples and High Places in Biblical Times* [Jerusalem: Hebrew Union College—Jewish Institute of Religion, 1981], pp. 169-80).

55. L. Rost, 'Sinaibund und Davidsbund', *TLZ* 72 (1947), pp. 129-34; A.H.J. Gunneweg, 'Sinaibund und Davidsbund', *VT* 10 (1960), pp. 335-41; Poulssen, *König und Tempel*, pp. 27-142.

56. J.J.M. Roberts, 'Zion in the Theology of the Davidic-Solomonic Empire', *Studies in the Period of David and Solomon*, ed. by Tomoo Ishida (Winona Lake: Eisenbrauns, 1982), p. 105.

57. The text is in *ANET*, p. 164.

58. In any event, Marduk's 'triumph, above and below', is attributed to Hammurabi (*ANET*, p. 178).

59. We omit 2 Sam 7 from consideration, since it is concerned with the two 'houses'—of David and of Yahweh—and makes no mention of Zion. On Ps 78, see above, note 51.

60. The questions here are, as elsewhere, complex and we can only sketch briefly a couple of points of importance to our later considerations.

'Function' here must be inferred from use within various strata of the literature.

61. See Joseph Blenkinsopp, *Gibeon and Israel* (SOTSMS; Cambridge: Cambridge University Press, 1972); Timothy Polk, 'The Levites in the Davidic-Solomonic Empire', *SBTh* 9 (1979), pp. 3-22.

62. Rolf Rendtorff, 'Beobachtungen zur altisraelitischen Geschichtsschreibung anhand der Geschichte vom Aufstieg Davids', in *Probleme biblischer Theologie*, pp. 428-39; T. Veijola, *Die ewige Dynastie. David und die Entstehung seiner Dynastie nach der deuteronomistischen Darstellung* (Helsinki: Suomalainen Tiedeakteneia, 1975), pp. 98-99. Contrast Mettinger, *King and Messiah*, pp. 33-47.

63. This refers, of course, to the content of the Psalms and does not concern the possible use of these or other Psalms in connection with the king in the context of some cultic celebration. There is no compelling reason, however, to locate these Psalms in some *Sitz im Leben* of a specifically royal character.

64. Josef Schreiner, *Sion-Jerusalem Jahwes Königssitz: Theologie der Heiligen Stadt im Alten Testament* (SANT, 7; München: Kösel-Verlag, 1963), pp. 129-30.

65. See above, note 41.

66. Note also Eissfeldt, 'Jahwes Königsprädisierung' (note 41, above). He includes Pss 2, 46, 47 and 82 among those which articulate Davidic/Solomonic claims to hegemony. Without noting the differences between Pss 2 and 46 he assumes that the latter presupposes the same royal theology (and indeed the king himself) as does the former. It may be that Ps 46 contains 'national-political claims of Israel', but it is essential not to confuse the theological bases of these claims in Ps 46 with those in Ps 2.

67. Contra Stolz, *Strukturen und Figuren*, pp. 88-89, and many others.

68. The rebellion (רגש) of the nations in 2.1 is different from the roaring and raging of the sea (המה, חמר) in 46.4, or from the raging of the nations in 46.7 (המה).

69. There does not seem to be any critical difference in date between Ps 2 and the Songs of Zion. All could easily come from the United Monarchy.

70. *Isaiah and the Deliverance of Jerusalem*, p. 79.

71. *Ibid.* It may be important to recall that theological criticism of the imperial monarchy was present from the beginning, as we shall see in ch. 4. It would not be impossible to conceive of the Songs of Zion as theological attempts to modulate the claims of the monarchy, especially since the kingship of Yahweh is stressed, while that of the earthly kings goes unmentioned. The kingship of Yahweh *is* used to critique the monarchy elsewhere.

72. Kraus, *Psalmen*, pp. 11-12.

73. As suggested in ch. 1, it is in the post-exilic period that the themes of fealty to the king and the 'Völkerkampf' are brought together in the

'Völkerwallfahrt' motif; i.e., in a period when there was no longer an earthly king.

74. See especially Jörg Jeremias, 'Lade und Zion'.

75. Kraus sees in Ps 2.6 reference to the dual election of Zion and David, as in Ps 132. However Mettinger has shown on the basis of 2 Sam 7 that the Son of God theology in Ps 2 is earlier than the dynastic theology of Ps 132 and the later redaction of 2 Sam 7. The language of election is completely absent in Ps 2, particularly regarding Zion. Cf. Hans-Joachim Kraus, *Die Königsherrschaft Gottes im Alten Testament: Untersuchungen zu den Liedern von Jahwes Thronbesteigung* (BHT, 13; Tübingen: J.C.B. Mohr, 1951), pp. 65-70; Mettinger, *King and Messiah*, pp. 258-59.

76. Cf., among others, John Bright, *Covenant and Promise: The Prophetic Understanding of the Future in Pre-Exilic Israel* (Philadelphia: Westminster, 1976), pp. 67-69; J.H. Hayes, 'The Tradition of Zion's Inviolability', *JBL* 82 (1967), pp. 419-26.

77. ' . . . It is not some immanent mightiness of the city of God that makes Jerusalem an inviolable bulwark, but alone the presence of Yahweh' (Kraus, *Psalmen*, p. 345).

78. Cf. Pss 60.4; 82.5, and see H. Schmid, 'Jahwe und die Kulttraditionen von Jerusalem', *ZAW* 67 (1955), p. 183; Schreiner, *Sion-Jerusalem*, pp. 220-21.

79. Reading with the MT. Cf. Kraus, *Psalmen*, p. 339. Contrast Dahood, *Psalms I*, p. 281. Dahood points to the term *ttt* at *CTA* 3.D.30 as a cognate of Hebrew מוט. There the context is the fear of 'Anat at the approach of Gupn and Ugar, the foes of Baal. A closer parallel is perhaps to be found at *CTA* 4.7.29-30, where the earth shakes (*tttn*) when Baal utters his voice. Note also Pss 99.1; 29.1-11.

80. Translating, 'God has proven himself within her citadels to be a stronghold'. Dahood regards the ב on ארמנותיה to be either *essentiae* or *emphaticum* (*Psalms I*, p. 29). However there is no other instance of Yahweh being described as a citadel in the Old Testament, whereas in v. 14 Zion's citadels are explicitly mentioned. There is thus little reason to follow Dahood. אלהים should rather be taken as a *casus pendens* (GK #143).

81. Interpreting v. 6 to mean that the kings recognized that the city was protected by God's glory. Cf. Kraus, *Psalmen*, p. 358. Yahweh's theophany may be simply presupposed by the text.

82. On Robert Bach's argument that this motif does not originally belong in the context of Zion symbolism, see below, ch. 4.

83. Cf. Kraus, *Psalmen*, pp. 163-64. The two most prevalent explanations are that the Psalm is set 'in a service of intercession on the eve of war' (Arthur Weiser, *The Psalms: A Commentary* [OTL; Philadelphia: Westminster, 1962], p. 205. This is the position of Gunkel and Mowinckel; cf. *The Psalms in Israel's Worship*, p. 225), or that it is a part of the royal festival of Yahweh, in which kingship was celebrated (cf. Weiser, p. 206). Even if the Psalm can

be located in a specific occasion, such as that proposed by A.A. Anderson (*The Book of Psalms* 2 vols. [NCB; London: Oliphants, 1972], pp. 173-74) it is probable that it is part of the cultic repertoire which could be drawn upon in relevant situations (Mowinckel, *Psalmenstudien*, 2 vols. [Amsterdam: P. Schippers, 1961], II, part I [*Psalmenstudien III*], p. 73).

84. The Syriac reads 'his sanctuary'. Kraus adopts this reading but ascribes it to the LXX (*Psalmen*, p. 120). In his translation of the passage Dahood reads with the MT, but in his notes argues for the pronoun, taking the *waw* from ומציון as originally a pronoun suffixed to מקדוש (*Psalms I*, p. 127).

85. The language of vv. 2-3 is clearly from the Jerusalem cult and is elsewhere related specifically to Zion (cf. Pss 46.8, 12; 48.4; Zech 9.10).

86. This Psalm is usually thought to be part of a unit with Ps 10, with the date uncertain. Cf. Robert Gordis, 'Psalm 9-10: A Textual-Exegetical Study', in *The Word and the Book: Studies in Biblical Language and Literature* (New York: KTAV, 1976), pp. 114-32 (= *JQR* 48 [1957], pp. 104-22).

87. The term is ישב, which, as Dahood notes, is used in its 'pregnant sense', meaning 'to reign' (*Psalms I*, p. 57).

88. The *qere* here is עניים instead of the *kethib* ענוים. Although there is a history of discussion regarding possible differences in meaning between these two forms (עני/ענו), the current consensus is that the difference is purely dialectical. Cf. R. Martin-Achard, 'elend sein', *THAT* II (1976), pp. 341-50; and especially Kjell Aartun, 'Hebräisch 'ānāw', *BO* 28 (1971), pp. 25-26.

89. Cf. Martin-Achard (previous note) and the literature cited by Kraus, *Psalmen*, p. 83; *Theologie der Psalmen* (BKAT, 15/3; Neukirchen-Vluyn: Neukirchener Verlag, 1979), pp. 188-89. Note also the important study by Antonin Causse, *Du groupe éthnique à la communauté religieuse* (Paris: Alcan, 1929). Causse's work is evaluated by S.T. Kimbrough, *Israelite Religion in Sociological Perspective: The Work of Antonin Causse* (SOR, 4; Wiesbaden: Otto Harrassowitz, 1978); see especially pp. 81-89.

90. The work of Hans Birkeland ('*Ani und 'Anaw in den Psalmen* [1933]) was unavailable to me, but is discussed in Kraus, *Psalmen*, p. 82. The stereotypical cultic language in which these expressions occur, and their corporate reference, should serve to qualify any individualistic interpretation of them.

91. Joseph A. Fitzmyer, *Essays on the Semitic Background of the New Testament* (Missoula: Scholars Press, 1974), p. 47. The term האביונים is also a designation of the Qumran community (cf. 1QpHab 12.3, 6, 10, etc.; Leander Keck, 'The Poor Among the Saints in Jewish Christianity and Qumran', *ZNW* 47 [1966], pp. 54-78).

92. Cf. Ps 147.3, 10-11. To the extent that Yahweh is a refuge and security for the poor the designation עני does denote a form of piety in opposition to either the wicked or the arrogant—those who oppress the poor and/or find

other means of security besides trust in Yahweh. Still, even in the post-exilic literature the 'material-sociological' meaning of ענּי is not completely left behind (cf. Martin-Achard, p. 343).

93. Kraus, *Psalmen*, p. 190.

94. Gray, *The Reign of God*, pp. 99-100. Gray's remarks are made with reference to Ps 69.33-36. He believes that the poor are represented by the king who is responsible as God's regent for their protection. Cf. also J. de Fraine, *L'Aspect Religieux de la Royauté Israélite* (AnBib, 3; Rome: Pontifical Biblical Institute, 1954), pp. 375-76, 381, discussing Ps 92. Keith Whitelam suggests that this royal responsibility derives from that originally ascribed to the *paterfamilias* in the pre-monarchic period (*The Just King*, p. 42). This may describe the social developments in Israel, but ancient Near Eastern parallels suggest that responsibility for the poor was a standard obligation of the king (Kraus, *Psalmen*, pp. 82-83).

95. Kraus, *Psalmen*, p. 83.

96. G.J. Botterweck, "ebhyon', *TDOT* 1 (1974), pp. 27-41.

97. Georg Braulik, *Psalm 40 und der Gottesknecht* (Forschung zur Bibel, 18; Würzburg: Echter Verlag, 1975), pp. 120-21.

98. Reading מרום for מרוֹם, with LXX. On the 'blessing' of one who trusts in Yahweh, see Claus Westermann, 'Der Gebrauch von 'srj im Alten Testament', in *Forschung am Alten Testament. Gesammelte Studien II*, ed. by Rainer Albertz (TBü, 55; München: Chr. Kaiser, 1974), pp. 191-95, especially pp. 193-94.

99. Robert G. Boling, *Judges* (AB; Garden City: Doubleday, 1975), pp. 260, 263. He evidently reads עצר as עֹצֶר, 'coercion', retaining מכלים as *hiphil* of כלם, 'to humiliate (by defeat)', according to *BDB*. Commenting on Zech 2.9, C. Jeremias says that 'because Jerusalem is completely unfortified and must rely entirely on Yahweh's defense, it is urged to "have faith", even if the express concept is not present...'. (*Die Nachtgesichte des Sacharja. Untersuchungen zu ihrer Stellung im Zusammenhang der Visionsberichte im Alten Testament und zu ihrem Bildmaterial* [FRLANT, 117; Göttingen: Vandenhoeck & Ruprecht, 1976], p. 175).

100. *Old Testament Theology*, I, trans. by D.M.G. Stalker (New York: Harper & Row, 1962), p. 401.

101. In Ps 122 the 'house of Yahweh', indicating Yahweh's presence, is the goal of the pilgrimage. In v. 7 the language of Ps 48.4 is recalled.

102. The term בטח has a positive and a negative or exclusionary force. It is positive in denoting the object of trust, and negative in excluding any other object. Thus in various places in the Old Testament trusting in someone or something besides Yahweh is seen as implicitly a rejection of him. Cf. E. Gerstenberger, 'Vertrauen', *THAT*, I (1971), pp. 303-305. See also the extensive essay by B. Beck, 'Kontextanalysen zum Verb *bṭḥ*', in *Bausteine Biblischer Theologie: Festschrift für G. Johannes Botterweck* (BBB, 50; Köln: Peter Hanstein, 1977), pp. 71-98.

103. Cf. Botterweck, note 96, p. 347.

104. See H.L. Ginsberg, 'Some Emendations in Psalms', *HUCA* 22 (1950-51), pp. 97-104.

105. Stanley N. Rosenbaum, 'New Evidence for Reading GE'IM in Place of GOYIM in Pss 9 and 10', *HUCA* 45 (1974), pp. 65-70. See especially p. 66. Rosenbaum is relying on the prior analyses of Kutscher and Talmon (*ibid.*, p. 66, notes 6 and 8).

106. *Ibid.*, p. 70.

107. Gordis regards the enemies in Ps 9/10 as internal, enemies of the 'humble and poor', constituting a distinct group. Therefore he does not emend 'nations' to 'haughty'. In regarding the *goyim* as domestic, however, Gordis has recourse to a rather strange notion of 'fluid personality, so richly documented in the Bible' ('Psalm 9-10', p. 117).

108. See especially Kraus, *Theologie der Psalmen*, pp. 190-92. He cites comparative material from Egypt.

109. I take 'our heritage' and 'pride of Jacob' to refer to Zion/Jerusalem. Cf. Clements, *God and Temple*, p. 55, note 1; Schreiner, *Sion-Jerusalem*, p. 198. In Canaan *ǵr nḥlty* 'is a mountain possessed inalienably, in patrimony, with the possible overtone of possession by conquest' (Clifford, *Cosmic Mountain*, p. 72). Exod 15.16-18 would suggest the same meaning. In Ps 47.5 this would most naturally refer to Zion. As noted earlier, 'Jacob' is a frequent designation of the South and is used in the traditions associated with Jerusalem. The land of Canaan is probably included in Ps 47.5 by extension (A.A. Anderson, *Psalms*, p. 363).

110. On this cosmic order see H.H. Schmid, *Gerechtigkeit als Weltordnung* (BHT, 40; Tübingen: J.C.B. Mohr, 1968).

111. Note Knierim, 'Cosmos and History', p. 86. Knierim shows that Israel's trustful attitude toward the cosmic order is based upon Yahweh as the object of that trust. Similarly with respect to Zion, we may differentiate between Zion as a concrete symbol of security and Yahweh as the object of trust. It is this trust in Yahweh that is the basis of Zion's power to evoke the attitude of trust. Clements (*God and Temple*, pp. 48-49) tries to distinguish between Israel's 'historical' traditions and the 'mythological' traditions of a holy mountain. However, the real distinction is between historical and cosmic traditions [the distinction is not one of mutual exclusion]. It is much more helpful in the long run to inquire after the theology associated with the Ark and its later association with Mount Zion than to try to separate Israelite historical from Canaanite mythological traditions. One is thus spared the difficulty of inventing a Jebusite mythology for which there is no non-Israelite evidence. This is not to deny, of course, that the notion of Yahweh's royal dwelling on Zion is mythological. It is merely to affirm that this mythology is rooted in earlier traditions of Israel. On the problem of history and myth as categories in biblical scholarship see J.J.M. Roberts, 'Myth Versus History: Relaying the Comparative Foundations', *CBQ* 38 (1976), pp. 1-13.

112. See our investigation of the Enthronement Psalms in ch. 2. Clements (*Isaiah and the Deliverance of Jerusalem*, p. 79) argues that Ps 48 and the other Songs of Zion are part of the royal ideology, and are not about the inviolability of Zion. Thus this latter notion could not have been of influence on Isaiah's preaching. He claims further that we lack 'a clear indication that Jerusalem was held to be different, and more privileged, than any other city of Israel' (*ibid.*, p. 78). It is very difficult, in the light of the three Psalms here in question, to make sense of this claim. Jerusalem was different, it is explicitly stated, because Yahweh dwells there (cf. Ps 87.2: 'Yahweh loves the gates of Zion more than all the habitations of Jacob'). Whether these Psalms were 'about' Zion or something else is strictly irrelevant to that point. The subject in any event is not Zion's inviolability but Yahweh's faithfulness and power.

113. The Psalm itself is a community lament of uncertain provenance. Given the references to Ephraim, Benjamin and Manasseh, the Psalm could be, in its original form, from the North. Note also the references to the cherubim and the title 'Yahweh of Hosts'. Cf. Kraus, *Psalmen*, p. 556.

114. The title 'shepherd' (v. 2) is of course a royal designation as well.

115. Miller, *Divine Warrior*, p. 77. Miller also notes the similar context of Ps 80 (p. 78). Cf. Thomas W. Mann, *Divine Presence and Guidance in Israelite Traditions: The Typology of Exaltation* (The Johns Hopkins Near Eastern Studies; Baltimore: Johns Hopkins University Press, 1977), p. 253.

116. It is possible that at least the first two verses of the Psalm (Ps 80) reflect a background in Shiloh. In its present form the Psalm may be compared with Isaiah, noting especially the titles ascribed to Yahweh and the use of the vine imagery.

117. The actual unit may be vv. 6-19. Cf. E. Lipiński, *Le Poème royal du Psaume LXXXIX* (Cahiers de la Revue Biblique, 6; Paris: Gabalda, 1967). Lipiński does not regard these verses as part of the original Psalm, a position I find unconvincing.

118. The term should probably be translated 'roar' in the light of the Ugaritic evidence. Cf. Dahood, *Psalms I*, p. 110, referring to the earlier article by H.G. May, 'Some Cosmic Connotations of *Mayim Rabbim*, "Many Waters"', *JBL* 74 (1955), p. 17, note 32. Interestingly, at *CTA* 2.4.28, Athtart 'roars' in response to Baal's conquest of Yam/Nahar, his traditional enemy and the symbol of the unruly waters of chaos.

119. גערה as indicative of Yahweh's creative power over the sea is also seen in Job 26.11-12 and Ps 106.9.

120. On this term see Curtis, 'Subjugation of the Waters', pp. 1-2.

121. Fritz Stolz, *Jahwes und Israels Kriege: Kriegtheorien und Kriegserfahrungen im Glauben des alten Israels* (ATANT, 60; Zürich: Theologischer Verlag, 1972), pp. 164-65. Cross implies that this Psalm is very early, perhaps set in the Gilgal cult (*Canaanite Myth*, pp. 138-39, 164).

122. 'Refuge' is an appropriate translation of primarily three terms: מחסה,

משגב and מעוז, each having, of course, its own nuances. Cf. L. Delekat, 'Zum Hebräischen Wörterbuch', *VT* 14 (1964), pp. 7-66 (especially pp. 28-31).

123. זה אלהים is difficult. It is often taken as 'this is God's' (Dahood, *Psalms I*, p. 293). This is based on passages such as Judg 5.5, where זה סני is rendered 'He of Sinai', or 'the one of Sinai' (Boling, *Judges*, p. 108). Here זה is regarded as the equivalent of the pronoun *du* of Northwest Semitic (William Moran, 'The Hebrew Language in its Northwest Semitic Background', *The Bible and the Ancient Near East: Essays in Honor of William Foxwell Albright*, ed. by G. Ernest Wright [Garden City, NY: Anchor Books, 1965], pp. 59-84, see especially p. 69; F.M. Cross, 'Yahweh and the God of the Patriarchs', *HTR* 55 [1962], pp. 236-56). However, given the following clause it seems best to regard the זה in an explicative sense (*WHS* #114; cf. *BHS* #23a). Schreiner captures the sense well by translating, 'So ist Gott' (*Sion-Jerusalem*, p. 232).

124. This is perhaps clearest in the use of the term 'Rock' as a title of Yahweh. See below.

125. Odil Hannes Steck, *Friedensvorstellungen im alten Jerusalem* (ThSt, 3; Zürich: Theologischer Verlag, 1972), pp. 23-24, note 38; cf. also p. 37, note 87.

126. Eiler, 'Zion as a Theological Symbol', p. 210. Cf. Schreiner, *Sion-Jerusalem*, pp. 220-21. As Kraus points out, the term מחסה (Ps 46.2, etc.) is used primarily in the Psalms to indicate the 'refuge function of the sanctuary' (*Psalmen*, p. 342).

127. On the title 'God of Jacob' here see Hans Wildberger, *Jesaja 1-12* (BKAT, 10/1; Neukirchen-Vluyn: Neukirchener Verlag, 1972), pp. 84-87; 'Gottesnamen und Gottesepitheta bei Jesaja', in *Jahwe und sein Volk: Gesammelte Aufsätze zum Alten Testament* (TBü, 66; München: Chr. Kaiser, 1979), pp. 223-25.

128. Kraus, *Psalmen*, p. 90. On the text of v. 1 see *ibid.*, p. 88.

129. According to Clements (*God and Temple*, p. 68) Zion is meant here in 11.4. Cf. Ps 9, discussed above.

130. Alfons Deissler has noted a connection between trust in Yahweh and his designation as king, pointing especially to Pss 44.5-6; 46. He believes that Zion as the seat of royal vengeance attracted the notion of trust to it. This may be so, but it should not overshadow the importance of Zion as the site of the Ark sanctuary, the symbol of Yahweh's royal presence prior to the institution of royal vengeance (Deissler, 'Das Israel der Psalmen als Gottesvolk der Hoffenden', in *Die Zeit Jesu: Festschrift für Heinrich Schlier*, ed. by G. Bornkamm and Karl Rahner [Freiburg: Herder & Herder, 1970], pp. 15-37).

131. These passages are probably post-exilic but reflect notions developed in the pre-exilic cult (cf. especially the Songs of Zion). See, however, Arvid S. Kapelrud, *The Message of the Prophet Zephaniah: Morphology and Ideas* (Oslo: Universitetsforlaget, 1975), pp. 38-40. He believes that 3.11-12 are from Zephaniah.

132. For the meaning of חסה see especially Delekat, pp. 28-31. He notes that the verb with the prepositon ב *always* refers to refuge in the sanctuary (p. 29).

133. Cf. especially Dieter Eichhorn, *Gott als Fels, Burg und Zuflucht: Eine Untersuchung zum Gebet des Mittlers in den Psalmen* (Europäische Hochschulschriften, 23/4; Bern: Herbert Lang, 1972), pp. 107-108. Eichhorn points to the designation of Yahweh as מחסה in the Psalms and prophetic literature and claims that it appears 'in the immediate horizon of the cultically celebrated and historically anticipated powerful revelation of Yahweh on Zion on behalf of his people' (pp. 112-13).

134. Steck, *Friedensvorstellungen*, pp. 23-24, note 38. Steck also alludes to Pss 24.2 and 104.6, 9 in this context.

135. *Ibid.*, p. 37, note 87. Steck notes the frequency with which the Psalms of Lament make reference to the notion of Zion as a refuge. It is not unexpected, of course, that laments would speak of refuge. What is interesting is the predominance of motifs from the Zion symbolism of the Jerusalem cult tradition within these laments. As Steck says, they begin from the observation that the fate of the individual is in contrast to the 'comprehensive work of peace of Yahweh from Zion' (p. 37). Cf. further Walter Beyerlin, *Die Rettung der Bedrängten in den Feindpsalmen der Einzelnen auf institutionelle Zusammenhänge untersucht* (FRLANT, 99; Göttingen: Vandenhoeck & Ruprecht, 1970), pp. 20-21.

136. See above, ch. 2, on Ps 99.9.

137. On the text see F.M. Cross and D.N. Freedman, *Studies in Ancient Yahwistic Poetry* (SBLDS, 21; Missoula: Scholars Press, 1975), p. 140. Besides 2 Sam 22, this portion of the Psalm also has a parallel in Ps 144.

138. Hans Schmidt, *Der Heilige Fels in Jerusalem: Eine archäologische und religionsgeschichtliche Studie* (Tübingen: J.C.B. Mohr, 1933), pp. 40-57, 89-98. See also Kraus, *Psalmen*, p. 142. Jer 21.13 refers to Zion as צור המישור. Cf. John Bright, *Jeremiah* (AB; Garden City, NY: Doubleday, 1965), pp. 140-41; J.A. Thompson, *The Book of Jeremiah* (NICOT; Grand Rapids : Eerdmans, 1980), pp. 471-72; Wildberger, 'Gottesnamen', pp. 244-45.

139. Wildberger, "Gottesnamen', pp. 244-45, Cf. also Wildberger, *Jesaja* (BKAT, 10/13-15; Neukirchen-Vluyn: Neukirchener Verlag, pp. 1219-21).

140. Otto Kaiser, *Isaiah 13-39: A Commentary*, trans. by R.A. Wilson (OTL; Philadelphia: Westminster, 1974), p. 308. Kaiser refers to an earlier article by J. Jeremias, published in 1926.

141. *Gott als Fels, Burg and Zuflucht*.

142. He follows the study of Hans Schmidt (above, note 138).

143. *Gott als Fels, Burg und Zuflucht*, p. 91.

144. *Ibid.*, pp. 42-54.

145. See further, Isa 17.10; 26.4. One may include Ps 75.6 in this discussion if the emendations of Dahood (*Psalms II* [AB; Garden City, NY: Doubleday, third edition, 1974], p. 212) or Kraus (*Psalmen*, p. 520) are

accepted. They translate בצואר עתק as 'the Ancient Mountain' and 'Rock', respectively.

146. Victor Turner, 'Symbols and Social Experience in Religious Ritual', in *Worship and Ritual in Christianity and Other Religions*, Studia Missionalia 23 (1974), p. 8.

147. On the text here see A.A. Anderson, *Psalms*, p. 451.

148. I am taking רבה ... לא as 'hardly'. Cf. *BHS* #93k.

149. Following the LXX. Cf. Kraus, *Psalmen*, p. 435.

150. On the possible wisdom elements in this Psalm see Roland Murphy, 'A Consideration of the Classification "Wisdom Psalms"', *VTS* 9 (1962), pp. 156-67; F. de Meyer, 'La Dimension sapientiale du Psaume 62', *Bijdragen* 42 (1981), pp. 350-65. See especially Murphy, 'Wisdom Psalms', p. 165.

151. See B. Beck, 'Kontextanalysen zum Verb *bṭḥ*'. The verb's connection with Zion is noted on p. 86, with reference to Ps 91. See also p. 95, and cf. Gerstenberger, 'Vertrauen', pp. 303-304.

152. It should also be recognized that בטח and האמין are theological synonyms. See Gerhard von Rad, *Der Heilige Krieg im alten Israel* (Göttingen: Vandenhoeck & Ruprecht, third edition, 1958), p. 57. Gerstenberger (note 151) also includes חסה within this semantic range (pp. 303-304).

153. Dahood, *Psalms II*, p. 211.

154. Taking למרום in v. 6a as 'the most high', with Dahood, *Psalms II*, p. 212. On the basis of Ps 94.4, however, I take עתק as 'arrogantly'. Note the common emphases in Pss 75 and 94.

155. The specific character of Yahweh as the one who exalts may form at least part of the theological quality of Israel's view of kingship as this was distinct, for example, from Egyptian views. Cf. Manfred Görg, *Gott-König-Reden in Israel und Ägypten* (BWANT, 105; Stuttgart: W. Kohlhammer, 1975); see the summary on p. 271.

156. See Aubrey Johnson, *The Cultic Prophet and Israel's Psalmody* (Cardiff: University of Wales Press, 1979), pp. 93-102.

Notes to Chapter 4

1. Patrick D. Miller, *The Divine Warrior in Early Israel* (HSM, 5; Cambridge, MA; Harvard University Press, 1973), p. 67.

2. Cf. Richard J. Clifford, *The Cosmic Mountain in Canaan and the Old Testament* (HSM, 4; Cambridge, MA: Harvard University Press, 1972), pp. 71-72. Clifford says that in the Ugaritic texts the *nḥlt* of Mot is 'where Mot exercises undisputed power over Baal and Baal's messengers' (*ibid.*).

3. For the location of this Psalm in the Jerusalem cult see W. Beyerlin, *Die Rettung der Bedrängten in den Feindpsalmen der Einzelnen auf*

institutionelle Zusammenhänge untersucht (FRLANT, 99; Göttingen: Vandenhoeck & Ruprecht, 1970), pp. 20-21.

4. Clearly the material-social referent is not deleted from this term even when used in this theological sense. See the conclusion of Ps 10, where Yahweh is urged to prevent the continued tyrannization of the orphan and the oppressed by אנוש מן הארץ (v. 18).

5. On this phrase cf. Kraus on Ps 91.14 (*Psalmen* [BKAT, 10; Neukirchen-Vluyn: Neukirchener Verlag, fourth edition, 1972], p. 639). The phrase occurs in 91.14 with a meaning similar to that in 9.11. See also 5.12, where the petitioner appeals to Yahweh his king (v. 3) to intervene against his enemies, and concludes by affirming that those who take refuge in Yahweh, and love his name, will rejoice and sing for joy. On the use of 'name' as a designation of Yahweh's power see Walter Zimmerli, *Old Testament Theology in Outline*, trans. by David E. Green (Atlanta: John Knox, 1978), p. 78; Otto Procksch, *Theologie des Alten Testaments* (Gütersloh: C. Bertelsmann, 1949), pp. 229, 430.

6. Cf. above, ch. 3, as well as E. Gerstenberger, 'Vertrauen', *THAT* I (1971), pp. 303-304.

7. 2 Kgs 18.19. Literally, 'what is this trust (בטחון) which you now trust (בטח) ?'

8. As noted above, he verb חסה, 'take refuge', may be included with האמין as part of the same semantic field with בטח. It is significant that all three of these verbs appear in the context of Zion symbolism.

9. Cf. above, ch. 3.

10. It is interesting that immediately preceding Ps 9, Ps 8.5 marvels at the glory and honor of אנוש and affirms that dominion has been given to אנוש. However, this dominion is severely restricted (vv. 8-9) and the Psalm concludes with praise for the splendor of Yahweh's name, as it begins. On the other hand, Ps 12, following the hymn of refuge in ch. 11, pits the poor, whom Yahweh will help, agaist the בני אדם, characterized by boasting and wickedness.

11. The term used in Ps 9/10 is אנוש, but what is said of אנוש here is said of אדם elsewhere. Cf. Fritz Maass, '"nosh', *TDOT* I (1977), pp. 345-48.

12. In the Psalms אנוש is used almost exclusively to indicate either human *weakness* (Pss 73.5; 90.3; 105.3; 144.3) or human *arrogance*, displayed in violence against one who is innocent (Pss 55.14; 56.2; 66.12, and Ps 9/10).

13. On the text of v. 4 cf. Kraus, *Psalmen*, p. 76; Weiser, *The Psalms: A Commentary*, trans. by H. Hartwell (OTL; Philadelphia: Westminster, 1962), p. 148. Dahood seems to miss the significance of the verse by translating גבה as 'the Lofty One', referring to God (*Psalms I* [AB; Garden City, NY: Doubleday, 1965], p. 62). Gordis takes God as the subject of בל ידרש, 'God does not exact retribution' ('Psalm 9-10: A Textual-Exegetical Study', in *The Word and the Book: Studies in Biblical Language and Literature* [New York: KTAV, 1976], p. 123).

14. Within German scholarship the terms used are 'Alleinmächtigkeit' and 'Alleinwirksamkeit'. I take the latter to mean 'the exclusive prerogative of Yahweh as the sole effective agent', and the former I am taking to mean 'the reservation of power to Yahweh'. I shall use the English term 'exclusive prerogative' to refer to both German terms.

15. Cf. John Barton, 'Ethics in Isaiah of Jerusalem', *JTS* 32 (1981), pp. 1-18, especially p. 7.

16 It is important to keep in mind here that we are still dealing with aspects of Zion symbolism. It is precisely Yahweh as king and creator on Zion who reserves power to himself, and it is as king and creator that he provides security and refuge. It is obvious that the use of the title 'king' in reference to Yahweh is highly reflective in the Old Testament traditions and is not an accidental appellation, but part of a highly elaborated theology. This is clear from the Psalms and obvious in Isaiah.

17. The terms used for 'poor' include עני/ענו, אביון, דל, שפל, דך, עבד, etc.; those for 'proud' include גבה, רום, גאה, גאון, גאוה, גאה, עתק, זד, etc.

18. On the text see F.M. Cross and D.N. Freedman, *Studies in Ancient Yahwistic Poetry* (SBLDS, Missoula: Scholars Press, 1975), p. 150.

19. Cf. Dahood, *Psalms III* (AB; Garden City: Doubleday, 1970), pp. 208-10.

20. Cf. above, ch. 3, note 145 on Ps 75.6. Robert Bach takes no note of this passage in his study of the motif of Yahweh breaking the bow ('"... der Bogen zerbricht, Spiesse zerschlägt und Wagen mit Feuer verbrennt"', in *Probleme Biblischer Theologie. Gerhard von Rad zum 70. Geburtstag*, ed. Hans Walter Wolff (München: Chr. Kaiser, 1971), pp. 13-26.

21. כי לא בכח יגבר איש (v. 9b). Cf. Zech 4.6.

22. Stoebe regards this Song as much later than do American scholars (Hans Joachim Stoebe, *Das erste Buch Samuelis* [KAT, 7/1; Gütersloh: Gerd Mohn, 1973]). According to Stoebe the Song of Hannah presupposes the content of the two Samuel books and is hence later than they (p. 107). He also regards the formulation in Ps 75.6 to be earlier than that found in the Song of Hannah (p. 102). This is contradicted, however, by the studies of John T. Willis ('The Song of Hannah and Psalm 113', *CBQ* 35 [1973], pp. 139-54) and David Noel Freedman ('Psalm 113 and the Song of Hannah', *Eretz Israel* 14 [1978], pp. 56*-69*). Both Stoebe and de Boer find wisdom influences in the Song of Hannah (P.A.H. de Boer, 'Einige Bemerkungen und Gedanken zum Lied 1. Samuel II 1-10', in *Beiträge zur alttestamentlichen Theologie: W. Zimmerli zum 70. Geburtstag*, ed. by H. Donner, R. Hanhart and R. Smend [Göttingen: Vandenhoeck & Ruprecht, 1977], pp. 53-59). De Boer points also to the 'Deuteronomistic' formulation of v. 9, 'böser Tat folgt böser Lohn' (p. 56), and believes that the Song of Hannah shows some influence from Deutero-Isaiah, although he seems to regard vv. 1-3 as earlier. We would only comment that the theological background to wisdom's pronouncements is the creation horizon of the

Jerusalem cult tradition. Wisdom presupposes a cosmology. Thus it should not be surprising that the Deuteronomistic history, which has other points of contact with wisdom, makes extensive use of creation language (cf. Moshe Weinfeld, *Deuteronomy and the Deuteronomic School* [Oxford: Clarendon Press, 1972], pp. 32-45).

23. For the ancient Near Eastern background see Manfred Weippert, '"Heiliger Krieg" in Israel und Assyrien: Kritische Anmerkungen zu Gerhard von Rads Konzept des "Heiligen Krieges im alten Israel"', *ZAW* 84 (1972), pp. 460-93. The reference in Zech 4.6 is usually seen in a negative light; that is, Zerubbabel is understood to be reprimanded for his forceful attempts at rebuilding the temple (cf., e.g., Margaret Barker, 'The Two Figures in Zecharia', *HeyJ* [1977], pp. 38-46). Understood against the Near Eastern references this needs correction. This was pointed out to me by a student, David Hymes.

24. Some have sought to eliminate this reference to the king in the original version of the Song. Cf. Willis, 'The Song of Hannah'; Norman Gottwald, *The Tribes of Yahweh: A Sociology of the Religion of Liberated Israel, 1250-1050 BCE* (Maryknoll: Orbis, 1978), pp. 534, 773, note 453. Albright attempted to turn it into a reference to the kingship of Yahweh (*Yahweh and the Gods of Canaan* [London: Athlone, 1968], pp. 20-22).

25. Besides the references in the previous note, cf. the analysis of P. Kyle McCarter, *I Samuel* (AB; Garden City, NY: Doubleday, 1980), pp. 75-76, and note 7.

26. Freedman ('Psalm 113 and the Song of Hannah') claims that Ps 113 is from the twelfth century and hence earlier than the Song of Hannah, which is monarchical. He bases his dating on prosody and the absence of titles attached to Yahweh in Ps 113. Unfortunately Freedman mentions Willis's treatment only in passing.

27. Willis, 'The Song of Hannah', p. 151. Gottwald seems to follow Willis but takes the imagery of the Song of Hannah altogether too literally. He argues that the poetry 'refers' to the overthrow of Canaanite overlords by peasants of the region and substantiates this argument by pointing to the reversal language of the Song, claiming that it is not part of royal ideology (*Tribes of Yahweh*, pp. 534-40). While that may be true, it is certainly a part of Zion symbolism in the Jerusalem cult, which cannot simply be equated with royal ideology. Albright dates the Song of Hannah early, partially on the basis of a comparison with Deuteronomy 32, a poem which we would follow Eichhorn in relating to the Jerusalem cult (*Yahweh and the Gods of Canaan*, pp. 20-22; on Eichhorn, see above, ch. 3, note 133).

28. Among all the texts from the Jerusalem cult tradition Isaiah 2 states most clearly and most forcefully the notion that Yahweh's exaltation means that the proud and their works are brought low. Within the Song of Hannah this notion is not contradicted in v. 7 ('he also exalts'), because as v. 8 makes clear, it is precisely the poor and oppressed who are raised up or exalted.

29. On 2 Sam 7 see the Excursus in ch. 2. Cf. also Thomas W. Mann, *Divine Presence and Guidance in Israelite Traditions: The Typology of Exaltation* (The Johns Hopkins Near Eastern Studies; Baltimore: Johns Hopkins University Press, 1977), pp. 219-20. As Mann and others have made clear, this theological notion was modified by the Solomonic court in the interests of the dynasty, whose paradigmatic text is now Ps 89. Mann has shown that in the royal ideology it is the king who is exalted while prior to that it was the people who were exalted. If the dynastic edition of 2 Sam 7 comes from Solomon's court, as Mettinger has argued, this may well mark the break between the royal ideology and the Jerusalem cult's development of Zion symbolism (Mettinger, *'King and Messiah: The Civil and Sacral Legitimation of the Israelite Kings'* [ConBot, 8; Lund: CWK Gleerup, 1976]).

30. We have already referred to Freedman, Willis and Gottwald, who believed that the Song of Hannah in its present form, namely with v. 10 included, comes from the monarchy. All three reject Albright's suggestion that מלכו in v. 10 should be vocalized *molko* and rendered 'his kingdom', because this 'jars with the parallel "his anointed"' (Gottwald, *Tribes of Yahweh*, p. 773, note 453). Cf. Albright, *Yahweh and the Gods of Canaan*, p. 18. However, משיחו may have a corporate reference, making it an apt parallel to 'his kingdom'. In Hab 3.13 משיחו is in parallel with עמך, 'your anointed//your people'. The concluding unit of the Song of Hannah, vv. 9-10, begins with reference to 'Yahweh's faithful', reading the plural of the Qere, and this would have a fitting parallel in 'your anointed', referring to Yahweh's kingdom. Cf. Albert E. Glock, 'Early Israel as the Kingdom of Yahweh. The Influence of Archaeological Evidence on the Reconstruction of Religion in Early Israel', *CBQ* 41 (1970), pp. 558-605.

31. C.J. Labuschagne, *The Incomparability of Yahweh in the Old Testament* (Pretoria Oriental Series, 5; Leiden: E.J. Brill, 1966), adequately describes the Psalm's emphasis on Yahweh's incomparability among the gods (pp. 119-20). However, he fails to note the structural relation between the confession of God's incomparability in vv. 8-13 and the lament in vv. 14-17. Thus the rhetorical question in v. 8 ('Who is like you among the gods, O Adonai?') is related to the affirmation in v. 15 ('But you, O Adonai, are merciful and gracious'). In between, God is contrasted not only with other gods, but with the insolent and ruthless folk of v. 14. Yahweh's incomparability is thus extended considerably.

32. Above, ch. 3, we noted with Steck (*Friedensvorstellungen im alten Jerusalem* [ThSt, 111; Zürich: Theologischer Verlag, 1972]) how frequently themes and motifs from the hymns of the Jerusalem cult tradition are found in individual laments. In this connection note especially Pss 12; 17; 53; 55; 56; 71; 140; 142. In all of these Yahweh is the active agent in restoring 'peace' on behalf of the petitioner by removing the wicked, often defined as the proud (Steck, p. 71).

33. This does not mean, of course, that the theology associated with the symbol Zion entails a view of humanity as merely weakness. It means rather that people are 'blessed' so long as their strength is in Yahweh (Ps 84.6; 86.16). What this theology establishes is simply a different relationship between 'glory' and how it is achieved. While it may seem obvious that glory is achieved through human effort and strength, the theology of Zion maintains that glory is achieved only as a gift of God to those who are blameless (Ps 84.12). For that reason Ps 84 can conclude that one who trusts in Yahweh of Hosts is blessed. Zion theology does not contest the common assumption that 'glory' is a good thing; rather, it proposes an unusual way of achieving it.

34. Kraus, following Gunkel–Begrich (Hermann Gunkel and Joachim Begrich, *Einleitung in die Psalmen: Die Gattungen der religiösen Lyrik Israels* [Göttingen: Vandenhoeck & Ruprecht, 1933], section 7.7) calls this a liturgy for a festival of thanksgiving (*Psalmen*, p. 802), setting it within the context of Torah-liturgies such as Pss 15 and 24 (cf. 118.19-20, 26-27). Mowinckel also associates the Psalm with Pss 15 and 24, suggesting that Ps 24 is set at the outer gate, while Ps 118 is set at the inner gate of the temple (*The Psalms in Israel's Worship*, 2 vols., trans. by D.R. Ap-Thomas [Nashville: Abingdon, 1962], I, p. 180). In *Psalmenstudien II* he suggests the enthronement festival as the setting of both Pss 24 and 118 (*Psalmenstudien*, 2 vols. [Amsterdam: P. Schippers, 1961], I, part 2, pp. 121-25). Cf. also Aubrey Johnson, *Sacral Kingship in Ancient Israel* (Cardiff: University of Wales Press, second edition, 1967), p. 124, note 1. Dahood also suggests a liturgy, but rejects a ritual interpretation, since vv. 5-18 are the 'king's description of the battle in which through divine intervention he escaped sure death' (*Psalms III*, p. 155). Why the king must be the speaker, and why this excludes ritual, are both unclear to me. The date of the Psalm is uncertain, though there is no reason to follow Kirkpatrick in dating it to the post-exilic period; he associates it with the Feast of Tabernacles described in Nehemiah 8 (444 BC, Kirkpatrick, *The Book of Psalms* [Cambridge: Cambridge University Press, 1901], p. 693) and notes other proposals ranging to 165 BC. To the other extreme, Dahood notes certain points of comparison with Exodus 15 and suggests an early date, believing that vv. 10-12 indicate that the Philistines were in mind (1 Sam 18.25-27; Dahood, pp. 157-58). It is best to say simply that the Psalm is pre-exilic (Mowinckel, *The Psalms in Israel's Worship*, I, p. 170).

35. Kraus, *Psalmen*, p. 804.

36. 'I called to Yah(weh) from imprisonment, from a broad expanse Yahweh answered me.' On the translation see Dahood, *Psalms III*, p. 156.

37. In v. 7 בעזרי is to be taken as *beth essentiae* with the participle (cf. *WHS* #249; Exod 18.4). Kraus refers to *GK* #119i (*Psalmen*, p. 801). Dahood translates 'my Great Warrior' (*Psalms III*, pp. 154). In the second part of the verse, אראה is translated by Dahood as 'I will gloat over', and I have followed

his translation (*Psalms III*, p. 129, on Ps 112.8). Cf. also Aubrey Johnson, *The Cultic Prophet in Ancient Israel* (Cardiff: University of Wales Press, second edition, 1962), p. 190, note 5. Dahood also points to the word play between ירא and ראה. In v. 8 4QPs[b] reads לבטח instead of לחסות and is followed by LXX and Syriac. However, the LXX reads ἐλπιζειν in both parts of v. 9, and is obviously attempting to balance both parts of each verse.

38. Kraus, *Psalmen*, p. 809; Dahood, *Psalms III*, p. 160. What role the king plays in the cult here is a matter of speculation. Cf. Jean de Fraine, *L'Aspect religieux de la Royauté Israélite* (AnBib, 3; Rome: Pontifical Biblical Institute, 1954), pp. 331, 341.

39. We refer again to Delekat's conclusion that חסה ב־ always refers to refuge in the sanctuary ('Zum hebräischen Wörterbuch', *VT* 14 [1964], p. 29).

40. It seems better to render נדיבים as 'nobles' rather than 'princes', since the latter is not strictly parallel to אדם. The contrast here is not between Yahweh and those who occupy some status or office, but between Yahweh and human beings, as in Ps 146. 3-4: 'do not trust in nobles, in a son of man in whom there is no help. His spirit returns to the ground. In that day his plans perish'. On נדיב cf. Gottwald, *The Tribes of Yahweh*, pp. 538-40.

41. This must be the meaning of v. 10 (cf. Dahood, *Psalms III*, p. 157). The verb must be a *hiphil* of מול, 'cause to be circumcised', or 'circumcise'. In any event, this should not be seen as a contradiction or qualification of the confession that Yahweh won the victory alone, since to my knowledge circumcision has never been used as a military strategy outside of Gen 34. Kraus offers no etymology for the verb and merely translates it as 'abwehren' (Kraus, *Psalmen*, p. 800).

42. As proposed by *BHS*, the final *yodh* of זמרתי was lost through haplography with יה.

43. Cf. above, note 37, and note Ps 118.14//Exod 15.2. The text in Ps 118 even goes so far as to repeat the haplography of final *yodh* on זמרי, although in Exodus 15 this could be attributed to the early orthography (cf. Cross and Freedman, *Ancient Yahwistic Poetry*, p. 55).

44. On the exclusivity of Yahweh's action in this poem (Exodus 15) see Millard Lind, *Yahweh is a Warrior: The Theology of Warfare in Ancient Israel* (Scottdale, PA: Herald Press, 1980), ch. 3. For a positive review of Lind's treatment see Patrick D. Miller in *BA* 44 (1980), pp. 188-89. The 'right hand' brings salvation also in *CTA* 2.1-39.

45. Cf. A.F.L. Beeston, 'Angels in Deuteronomy 33.2', *JTS* 2 (1951), pp. 30-31. Beeston is followed by Miller, *The Divine Warrior*, p. 79. The decision is to take אשד in 33.2 as cognate with Sabaean *'sd*, meaning warrior.

46. The relation of Exodus 15 and Deuteronomy 33 to the Jerusalem cult tradition is complicated. We can say that they share the same conception of theophany and a common set of motifs (cf. Steck, *Friedensvorstellungen*, p. 42 and note 112).

47. זה הר here must mean Zion. This Psalm follows no strict chronology and the fact that Shiloh is mentioned later, and then Zion, does not contradict the identification of 78.54 with Zion. קנה is here rendered 'created', since this sense is clear in v. 69. On this verb see Normal C. Habel, '"Yahweh, Maker of Heaven and Earth"—A Study in Tradition Criticism', *JBL* 91 (1972), pp. 321-32; Patrick D. Miller, 'El, the Creator of Earth', *BASOR* 239 (1980), pp. 43-46.

48. Cf. especially Ps 146, which, although late, combines the notions of several Psalms of the pre-exilic Jerusalem cult. Yahweh is king on Zion, he is the creator of heaven and earth, he is the exclusive object of trust, and he brings justice to the poor or oppressed.

49. On the setting and date of the Psalm see above, ch. 3, note 82.

50. In v. 8 יהוה is omitted to preserve balance between the two lines; cf. v. 6. The name יהוה is missing in the Targum and in LXX[a], according to *BHS*. I have followed Dahood in taking נזכיר from זכר 'male' (*Psalms I*, p. 129). The meaning is virtually the same as the *hiphil* of גבר. Thus the LXX reading is inconclusive.

51. It has also been suggested that vv. 7ff. follow a 'cultic theophany', as presented in Ps 18.6ff. (Weisser, *Psalms*, pp. 207-208). A comparison could also be drawn with Habakkuk 3, especially Habakkuk's response in v. 16. These two suggestions (a 'fear not' oracle or a theophany) do not necessarily exclude each other. While it is true that 'fear not' oracles often, or usually, occur in situations of war 'and confrontation with a difficult task' (Weinfeld, *Deuteronomy*, p. 45, note 5), they are also found in theophanies (cf. Judg 5.23; Dan 10.12). See Ludwig Köhler, 'Die Offenbarungsformel "Fürchte dich nicht!" im Alten Testament', *STZ* 36 (1919), pp. 33-39; J. Kenneth Kuntz, *The Self-Revelation of God* (Philadelphia: Westminster, 1967), pp. 65-68. Cf. Edgar W. Conrad, 'Second Isaiah and the Priestly Oracle of Salvation', *ZAW* 93 (1981), pp. 234-46. Fear is engendered not only by threat of war or a difficult task, but by the presence of holiness (Lev 19.30; 26.2; cf. Exod 19).

52. It is important to note that in this text, in which the king is the dominant subject, it is the speakers, not the king, who are said to be powerful. This is presuming that *nazkir* is taken as suggested above, note 41.

53. Cf. Johnson, *Sacral Kingship*, p. 113, on Ps 89.

54. See the discussion of possible dates in Kraus, *Psalmen*, p. 325; Kirkpatrick, *The Book of Psalms*, p. 235.

55. See the discussion of this theme by Geo Widengren, 'The Gathering of the Dispersed', *SEÅ* 41-42 (1976/77), pp. 224-34. On the policies of deportation and resettlement under Assyria see Hayim Tadmor, 'Assyria and the West: The Ninth Century and its Aftermath', in *Unity and Diversity: Essays in the History, Literature and Religion of the Ancient Near East*, ed. by Hans Goedicke and J.J.M. Roberts (The Johns Hopkins Near Eastern Studies; Baltimore: Johns Hopkins University Press, 1975), pp. 36-48.

56. Especially vv. 5-9 would be ill-fitting in the exilic period.

57. Dahood takes ישועות as 'savior', which one would expect to be in the participial form (*Psalms I*, p. 256). I am reading מצוה in v. 5, with LXX and Syriac.

58. The speakers are plural in vv. 5-6, 8-9, but v. 7 is in the singular. This could indicate that the king is speaking in v. 7, but this conclusion is not required.

59. In the Near East the bow seems to have stood for power, political and sexual. Cf. Delbert Hillers, 'The Bow of Aqhat: the Meaning of a Mythological Theme', in *Orient and Occident: Essays in Honor of Cyrus Gordon*, ed. by Harry A. Hoffner (AOAT, 22; Neukirchen-Vluyn: Neukirchener Verlag, 1973), pp. 71-80.

60. For 'light' as a symbol of salvation, particularly in connection with Zion, see Isa 60.1, which is addressed to Zion; cf. Isa 58.8-10.

61. Cf. Lind, *Yahweh is a Warrior, passim*; Miller, *The Divine Warrior*, pp. 155-60. The term 'synergism' is von Rad's (*Der Heilige Krieg*, p. 13).

62. Kraus calls it an 'alphabetizing' Psalm because it has twenty-two verses (*Psalmen*, p. 261). For a discussion of the date of the Psalm see Jean Marcel Vincent, 'Recherches exégétiques sur le Psaume XXXIII', *VT* 28 (1978), pp. 442-54, especially p. 451.

63. Cf. Mowinckel, *Psalmenstudien II*, p. 192; von Rad, *Der Heilige Krieg*, p. 82.

64 Claus Westermann, *The Praise of God in the Psalms*, trans. by Keith R. Crim (Richmond: John Knox, 1965), p. 125. I am not in agreement with the comments Westermann makes with respect to the relation of his two types of Psalms of Praise, declarative and descriptive, nor with the treatment of creation on which he bases this relation. See *ibid.*, p. 126 and note 78, commenting on von Rad's 'Das theologische Problem des alttestamentlichen Schöpfungsglaubens', in *Gesammelte Studien* (TBü, 8; München: Chr. Kaiser, 1965), pp. 136-47.

65. Vincent, 'Recherches exégétiques', pp. 442-54. Vincent argues for an early date for the traditional material used in the Psalm, particularly in vv. 6-8, 10-12 and 13-17, and places the later redaction of the Psalm in the time of Micah and Isaiah (p. 454).

66. *Ibid.*, p. 445.

67. See to the contrary von Rad, *Der Heilige Krieg*, pp. 82-83. He believes that in this Psalm and others the living tradition of holy war has atrophied and the motifs of that tradition have become 'doctrines of faith'. This decision is based on the judgment that historical narration precedes the formulation of the presuppositions on which it was composed. This is not an adequate criterion for dating.

68. Thus A.A. Anderson places it in the 'Autumn festival', while Weiser assigns it to the 'covenant festival which was celebrated at the New Year' (Anderson, *Psalms*, p. 260; Weiser, *Psalms*, p. 289). Given our earlier

comments on the 'new song' in the celebration of Yahweh's kingship, a combination of these two suggestions may be correct. See above, ch. 2.

69. On נושע in v. 16, cf. Magne Saebø, *Sacharja 9–14: Untersuchungen von Text und Form* (WMANT, 34: Neukirchen-Vluyn: Neukirchener Verlag, 1969), pp. 185-86.

70. E.g., in 2 Sam 19.10 'the king [David] is credited with delivering (נצל) Israel from the enemy and rescuing (מלט) the people from the Philistines. The royal function of deliverance is also described in 1 Sam 30.8, 18, as well as in other texts. The king saves (ישע) his people as a part of his royal responsibility according to Ps 72.4, 12-13, which includes נצל among his royal duties. Cf. also 1 Sam 23.2. A foreign king (perhaps Adad-Nirari III?) is described as a savior in 2 Kgs 13.5, and this title is commonly applied to judges in the pre-monarchic period. Stolz believes that the emphasis on Yahweh as the bringer of ישועה, not Israel's own strength, comes from holy war tradition ('*jš' hi.* helfen', *THAT* I [1971], pp. 790). None of the texts he cites is earlier than the eighth century.

71. On the balance between vv. 16 and 19 see Vincent, 'Recherches exégétiques', p. 450.

72. Zimmerli, *Old Testament Theology*, p. 146. Cf. H.W. Wolff, 'Elohistic Fragments in the Pentateuch', in Walter Brueggemann and Hans Walter Wolff, *The Vitality of Old Testament Traditions* (Atlanta: John Knox, 1975), pp. 67-82.

73. Note especially that they wait for Yahweh and trust in his name. This confident trust is based on the expectation that Yahweh will be faithful, an expectation which is itself grounded in Yahweh's creation (vv. 4-7).

74. See Richard Clifford, *Cosmic Mountain*, pp. 177-78; J.J.M. Roberts, 'ṢAPON in Job 26,7', *Biblica* 56 (1975), pp. 554-57. Cf. Fritz Stolz, *Strukturen und Figuren im Kult von Jerusalem* (BZAW, 118; Berlin: Walter de Gruyter, 1970), p. 164, and especially Martin Metzger, 'Himmlische und irdische Wohnstatt Jahwes', *UF* 2 (1970), pp. 139-58.

75. Dahood argues that the *niphal* נושע should be taken in a reflexive sense, translating 'gives himself victory' (*Psalms I*, p. 203).

76. On 'creation by the word' in Egypt and Mesopotamia see Kraus, *Psalmen*, pp. 263-64; Vincent, 'Recherches exégétiques', p. 452; Klaus Koch, 'Wort und Einheit des Schöpfergottes in Memphis und Jerusalem', *ZTK* 62 (1965), pp. 251-93.

77. Vincent, 'Recherches exégétiques', p. 449.

78. With reference to our discussion of creation in ch. 3, note that in this Psalm creation as both origination and maintenance, or creation of the El and Baal types, is in view (cf. Stolz, *Strukturen und Figuren*, p. 102, note 50).

79. Kraus, *Psalmen*, p. 264. Commenting on Isa 5.8-24; 10.1-4, Hans Wildberger says, 'That Isaiah speaks so emphatically of Yahweh's plan is tied up with his vision of Yahweh as king on his exalted throne (6.3): Yahweh's

plan is seen as analogous to the plans of earthly rulers. But it is, to be sure, an analogy which explodes the notions that comprehend temporal experience. For that reason 28.29 speaks of הפליא עצה' (*Jesaja 1–12* [BKAT, 10; Neukirchen-Vluyn: Neukirchener Verlag, 1972], p. 189).

80. Reading יחד as יחיד, 'only', or 'by himself', with the LXX. Contrast Kraus (*Psalmen*, p. 261), and Dahood (*Psalms I*, p. 202).

81. The language of v. 20b, especially the description of Yahweh as a shield, is royal language. In Ps 84.10, 12, the term מגן is most likely applied to the king. Cf. Dahood, *Psalms II*, p. 282, relying on a suggestion by Freedman.

82. Cf. John Gray, *The Reign of God*, pp. 8-9, and note 6.

83. I choose this term self-consciously. *Webster's New World Dictionary of the American Language* (second college edition; New York: World Publishing, 1972) defines humility as 'absence of pride or self-assertion' (p. 684a). It is especially pride and self-assertion that characterize אדם/אנוש, insofar as he or she lacks humility, and it is precisely humility that characterizes עני in the language of the Jerusalem cult. Cf. Donald E. Gowan, *When Man Becomes God: Humanism and Hybris in the Old Testament* (Pittsburgh: Pickwick, 1972).

84. This would be, for example, the position of von Rad, *Der Heilige Krieg*. He is followed by most others. Cf. Hans-Joachim Kraus, 'Vom Kampf des Glaubens: Eine biblisch-theologische Studie', in *Beiträge zur alttestament-lichen Theologie: W. Zimmerli zum 70. Geburtstag*, ed. by H. Donner, R. Hanhart and R. Smend (Göttingen: Vandenhoeck & Ruprecht, 1977), pp. 239-56, especially pp. 240-41.

85. This distinction was elaborated by Rudolf Smend, *Yahweh War and Tribal Confederation: Reflections upon Israel's Earliest History*, trans. by Max. G. Rogers (Nashville: Abingdon, 1970). Cf. also Gwilym H. Jones, '"Holy War" or "Yahweh War"?', *VT* 25 (1975), pp. 642-58; Hans-Martin Lutz, *Jahwe, Jerusalem und die Völker: Zur Vorgeschichte von Sach 12.1-8 und 14.1-5* (WMANT, 27; Neukirchen-Vluyn: Neukirchener Verlag, 1968), p. 181, note 1; Robert Bach, '"... Der Bogen zerbricht, Spiesse zerschlägt und Wagen mit Feuer verbrennt"', in *Probleme Biblischer Theologie: Gerhard von Rad zum 70. Geburtstag*, ed. by Hans Walter Wolff (München: Chr. Kaiser, 1971), p. 19; Friedrich Huber, *Jahwe, Juda und die anderen Völker beim Propheten Jesaja* (BZAW, 137; Berlin: de Gruyter, 1976), p. 222, note 50. The term 'Holy War' goes back at least to Schwally, who derived it not from Israelite texts but from the Islamic institution of *jihad*. Cf. Peter C. Craigie, *The Problem of War in the Old Testament* (Grand Rapids: Eerdmans, 1978), pp. 48-50; Friedrich Schwally, *Der heilige Krieg im alten Israel* (Leipzig: Theodor Weicher, 1901).

86. Cf. Jones, '"Holy War"'.

87. While Cross and Miller, for example, have made brilliant contributions to the understanding of these matters, they have not always distinguished

sufficiently between the motif of the Divine Warrior, which is pervasive in the Old Testament (as it should be, since Yahweh is pervasively understood as king), and either the practice of warfare itself or the holy war schema. On the pervasiveness of Yahweh as Divine Warrior, and hence the difficulty of assigning texts in which this term occurs to specific strata or social locations, see most recently John N. Oswalt, 'Recent Studies in Old Testament Eschatology and Apocalyptic', *JETS* 24 (1981), pp. 289-300, especially p. 297.

88. See Fritz Stolz, *'Jahwes und Israels Kriege: Kriegestheorie und Kriegeserfahrungen im Glauben des alten Israel* (ATANT, 60; Zürich: Theologischer Verlag, 1972), p. 191. To be precise, I would suggest four sources for Israel's holy war traditions: (a) the experience of warfare itself; (b) the notion of Yahweh as king and creator/defender (Exod 15; Judg 5); (c) the Jerusalem cult's liturgical tradition; (d) common ancient Near Eastern notions of warfare (cf. Weippert, '"Heiliger Krieg"'; H.W.F. Saggs, 'Assyrian Warfare in the Sargonid Period', *Iraq* 25 [1963], pp. 145-54; Martin Rose, 'Entmilitarisierung des Krieges? Erwägungen zu den Patriarchen-Erzählungen der Genesis', *BZ* 20 [1976], pp. 197-211). The Deuteronomic tradition first brought all of these together into a holy war schema. It should be noted that items (b) and (c) have internal connections and that they also have ancient Near Eastern backgrounds (for a good summary see Thomas Mann, *Divine Presence and Guidance*, pp. 123-43, 176-95).

89. Cf. von Rad, *Der Heilige Krieg*, p. 58, commenting on Isa 7. Lind would see matters quite differently, arguing that such reflection was in view already in the earliest stages of Israel's history, as in Exod 15 and Judg 5 (*Yahweh is a Warrior*). Part of the confusion can be eliminated if Exod 15 is compared with texts such as Ps 24 and others from the Jerusalem cult, rather than simply with the holy war narrative from the period of the judges.

90. G.H. Jones argues with some plausibility that 1 Sam 11 presents the practice of warfare with the highest degree of historical reliability ('"Holy War"').

91. See von Rad, *Der Heilige Krieg*, pp. 9-13, on Judg 5.23; cf. Weippert, '"Heiliger Krieg"', p. 462; Lind, *Yahweh is a Warrior*, pp. 69-73.

92. Von Rad, *Der Heilige Krieg*, p. 49.

93. Stolz, *Jahwes und Israels Kriege*, pp. 96-97, 115-22. See also Urs Köppel, *Das deuteronomistische Geschichtswerk und seine Quellen: Die Absicht der deuteronomistischen Geschichtsdarstellung aufgrund des Vergleichs zwischen Num 21,21-35 und Dtn 2,26-3,3* (Europäische Hochschulschriften, 23/122; Bern: Peter Lang, 1979), especially p. 180. Both Stolz and Weinfeld have argued that much of this theologizing took place with respect to leadership in war, bringing to the fore the military leadership of Joshua and Gideon. Weinfeld believes that this occurred as the Deuteronomists were coming to grips with the new military realities of the Josianic age and that the language used was taken from contemporary Assyrian descriptions of

warfare (Weinfeld, *Deuteronomy*, pp. 45-48; cf. von Rad, *Der Heilige Krieg*, p. 78). For a view to the contrary see Peter Weimar, 'Die Jahwekriegserzählung in Ex 14, Jos 10, Richter 4 und I Sam 7', *Biblica* 57 (1976), pp. 38-73.

94. See Labuschagne, *The Incomparability of Yahweh*; Manfred Görg, *Gott-König-Reden*.

95. Otto Bächli, *Israel und die Völker: Eine Studie zum Deuteronomium* (ATANT, 41; Zürich: Theologischer Verlag, 1962), p. 94; cf. also p. 107; Köppel, *Das Deuteronomistische Geschichtswerk*, p. 180.

96. It is important to keep in mind that we are here discussing the peculiarly Deuteronomic/Deuteronomistic interpretation of Israel's warfare, not the character of that warfare itself. For the 'idealistic and unrealistic character' of this Deuteronomic conception see Peter C. Craigie, *The Book of Deuteronomy* (NICOT; Grand Rapids: Eerdmans, 1976), pp. 270-71. For some reason he thinks that this idealistic and unrealistic character is an indication of Deuteronomy 20's antiquity (p. 271).

97. See again the comments of von Rad, *Der Heilige Krieg*, pp. 82-83. For the possibility of influence from the Jerusalem cult tradition on the concept of holy war see Steck, *Friedensvorstellungen*, pp. 18-19, note 25; H.H. Schmid, 'Heiliger Krieg und Gottesfrieden im Alten Testament', in *Altorientalische Welt in der alttestamentlichen Theologie* (Zürich: Theologischer Verlag, 1974), pp. 91-120, especially p. 96.

98. Jones, '"Holy War"', p. 654. See also the references to Stolz and Weinfeld in note 93, above, and Richard D. Nelson, 'Josiah in the Book of Joshua', *JBL* 100 (1981), pp. 531-40.

99. See above, note 96. Cf. Wildberger, *Jesaja* (BKAT, 10/13-15), p. 1186.

100. I.L. Seeligmann argues that this opposition in Isaiah to preparations for war and alliance with Assyria is grounded in the prophetic opposition to foreign gods ('Menschliches Heldentum und göttliche Hilfe: Die doppelte Kausalität im alttestamentlichen Geschichtsdenken', *TZ* 10 [1963], pp. 385-411). This is nowhere explicit in the texts.

101. Reading רכב for דרך, with LXX. For discussion see Wolff, *Hosea*, trans. by Gary Stansell (Hermeneia; Philadelphia: Fortress, 1974), p. 181. As Wolff notes, דרך can mean 'dominion' in Ugaritic. The present reading of the MT may thus have arisen as an interpretation of 'chariots'.

102. On the structure of the text cf. Wolff, *Hosea*, pp. 182-83; J.L. Mays, *Hosea. A Commentary* (OTL; Philadelphia: Westminster, 1969), pp. 148-49. For the term 'prophecy of punishment' see Gene Tucker, 'Prophetic Speech', *Interpretation* 32 (1978), pp. 31-35.

103. This motif of destruction at dawn is also used in texts associated with the Zion tradition. Cf. Ps 46.6. See Josef Schreiner, *Sion-Jerusalem Jahwes Königssitz: Theologie der Heiligen Stadt im Alten Testament* (SANT, 7; München: Kösel-Verlag, 1963), p. 224; Stolz, *Strukturen und Figuren*, p. 214. Stolz shows that the motif cannot be limited to Israelite traditions.

104. Cf. D.R. Ap-Thomas, 'All the King's Horses', in *Proclamation and Presence: Essays in Honour of G. Henton Davies*, ed. by J.I. Durham and J.R.R. Porter (Richmond: John Knox, 1970), pp. 131-51.

105. According to Weinfeld, Deut 17 stems from the anti-Solomonic polemic of the Josianic court (*Deuteronomy*, p. 169).

106. Wolff, *Hosea*, pp. 223, 226.

107. *Ibid.*, p. 233.

108. Following basically the reconstruction of Wolff, *ibid.*, p. 221; cf. *BHS*.

109. Morton Cogan, *Imperialism and Religion: Assyria, Judah and Israel in the Eighth and Seventh Centuries BCE* (SBLMS, 19; Missoula: Scholars Press, 1974); J.W. McKay, *Religion in Judah under the Assyrians* (SBT, 2/26; London: SCM, 1973).

110. Cf. Helen Schüngel-Straumann, *Gottesbild und Kultkritik vorexilischer Propheten* (SBS, 60; Stuttgart: KBW Verlag, 1972), p. 88: 'The book of Hosea is full of the sharpest polemic against Baal. Indeed, the battle against Baal is really the main theme of Hosea and runs through the whole book like a scarlet thread.' Cf. also the references in note 95, above. Jörg Jeremias argues that Hos 14.4 is late, reflecting the influence of Isaiah. He claims that Hos 13.9-11 and 10.3 are Hosea's way of expressing the problem. He does not recognize, however, the connection between trust in the king and the presence of weapons. See Jeremias, 'Zur Eschatologie des Hoseabuches', *Die Botschaft und die Boten. Festschrift für Hans Walter Wolff zum 70. Geburtstag*, ed. by Jeremias and Lothar Perlitt (Neukirchen-Vluyn: Neukirchener Verlag, 1981), pp. 217-34, especially pp. 231-32.

111. Schüngel-Straumann, *Gottesbild und Kultritik*, p. 102. Her remarks here are relative to Isaiah, but they apply equally to Hosea. Cf. W.H. Schmidt, *Zukunftsgewissheit und Gegenwartskritik: Grundzüge prophetischer Verkündigung* (BibS[N], 64; Neukirchen: Neukirchener Verlag, 1973), pp. 74-75.

112. See W.H. Schmidt, 'Kritik am Königtum', in *Probleme Biblischer Theologie*, pp. 450-51. The same thing is noted by Karl-Heinz Bernhardt, *Das Problem altorientalischer Königsideologie im alten Testament* (VTS, 8; Leiden: E.J. Brill, 1961), pp. 139-40. Both Schmidt and Bernhardt believe that Hosea rejected kingship totally. Such a conclusion depends ultimately on the interpretation of 9.15 and 10.9, and on the authenticity of 3.4-5. Similar expressions are found in Ezekiel, but they seem to rest on different theological motivations. See Bernhard Lang, *Kein Aufstand in Jerusalem: Die Politik des Propheten Ezechiel* (SSB; Stuttgart: Katholisches Bibelwerk, second edition, 1981), pp. 105-108, 182-86. For a recent argument in favor of Hosea's complete rejection of kingship see Robert Gnuse, 'Calf, Cult and King: The Unity of Hosea 8.1-13', *BZ* 26 (1982), pp. 83-92, especially p. 89.

113. This may be because Hosea is more interested in reviving traditions

of the pre-monarchic era (cf. Schmidt, 'Kritik am Königtum', p. 451). If 'Yahweh of Hosts' is, as I believe, a title originally associated with Yahweh's kingship, Hos 12.5 may conceive Yahweh as 'king', as may his designation as 'savior'.

114. Schmidt (*ibid.*, p. 456 and note 40) follows Bach and Rendtorff in seeing the unity of 'charisma' and 'leadership' during the period of the judges divided between prophet and king, respectively, during the period of the monarchy (Robert Bach, *Die Aufforderungen zur Flucht und zum Kampf im alttestamentlichen Prophetenspruch* [WMANT, 9; Neukirchen-Vluyn: Neukirchener Verlag, 1962], pp. 92-101; Rolf Rendtorff, 'Erwägungen zur Frühgeschichte des Prophetentums in Israel', *ZTK* 59 [1962], pp. 145-67, especially pp. 154-56). It was the prophets, according to Schmidt, who continued the holy war tradition of ascribing victory solely to Yahweh and thus criticized the royal tendency to arrogate this power to themselves. It may be correct to see this tendency developing in opposition to the kings of Israel and Judah, but the distinction between charismatic 'prophet' and leader in war may have already existed in the pre-monarchic period, as Ackerman has recently shown with reference to the Zakir inscription and other texts (J.S. Ackerman, 'Prophecy and Warfare in Early Israel: A Study of the Deborah-Barak Story', *BASOR* 220 [1975], pp. 5-13).

115. If, that is, Deuteronomy came to its final formulation in Jerusalem. I believe that Weinfeld has made it virtually imposible to think otherwise. Cf. also Dieter Eduard Skweres, *Die Rückverweise im Buch Deuteronomium* (An Bib, 79; Rome: Pontifical Biblical Institute, 1979), p. 219.

116. This problem is discussed in detail by Huber, *Jahwe, Juda und die anderen Völker*, pp. 200-25. See also Stolz, *Jahwes und Israels Kriege*, p. 218. That Isaiah radicalized the notion of Yahweh's exclusive prerogative is argued by almost everyone (cf. most recently, A.H.J. Gunneweg, 'Herrschaft Gottes und Herrschaft des Menschen: Eine alttestamentliche Aporie von aktueller Bedeutung', *KuD* 27 [1981], pp. 164-79), while his intention and the significance of this notion are widely disputed.

117. *Jahwes und Israel's Kriege*, p. 118.

118. The most thorough treatment of these texts is to be found in Huber, *Jahwe, Juda und die anderen Völker*. For critical discussion see Wildberger, *Jesaja* (BKAT 10) on the relevant passages; Brevard Childs, *Isaiah and the Assyrian Crises* (SBT 2/3; London: SCM, 1967); Hermann Barth, *Die Jesaja-Worte in der Josiazeit: Israel und Assur als Thema einer produktiven Neuinterpretation der Jesajaüberlieferung* (WMANT, 48; Neukirchen-Vluyn: Neukirchener Verlag, 1977).

119. Wildberger, *Jesaja* (BKAT 10/13-15), pp. 1152-54. He sees holy war language in vv. 1 and 2, but the Old Testament texts he relies on for this judgment are all later than Isaiah. He acknowledges that some of the terms are from the Jerusalem cult and are used to indicate that 'what is sought in Egypt is to be found in Jerusalem' (p. 1154).

120. Childs and Donner want to delete v. 2 as an interpolation (Childs, *Isaiah and the Assyrian Crisis*, pp. 33-34; Herbert Donner, *Israel unter den Völkern: Die Stellung der klassischen Propheten des 8. Jahrhunderts v. Chr. zur Aussenpolitik der Könige von Israel und Juda* [VTS, 11; Leiden: E.J. Brill, 1964], p. 135). But Wildberger has shown that already v. 1 modifies the form of a prophecy of punishment and v. 2 should not be deleted on this basis (*Jesaja*, pp. 1227-28). Cf. also Barth, *Die Jesaja-Worte*, pp. 79-80, with further bibliography.

121. On the historical setting of the text see Wildberger, *Jesaja*, p. 1229. He suggests that the text is set in the period just after the battle at Eltekeh. This would be just prior to the defeat of Timnah (*ANET*, p. 287a). From around 713 BC a coalition led by Ashdod had tried to draw Egypt and Judah into a revolt against Assyria, but Egypt was probably not prepared to engage in such an action until internal affairs were settled around 711/10.

122. On the verbs here see *GK* #151n, o, 2 (cf. Barth, *Die Jesaja-Worte*, p. 79, note 1).

123. See Childs, *Isaiah and the Assyrian Crisis*, p. 35; cf. William McKane, *Prophets and Wise Men* (SBT 1/44; London SCM, 1965), pp. 72-73; J. William Whedbee, *Isaiah and Wisdom* (Nashville: Abingdon, 1971), pp. 62-63.

124. Cf. Hans Walter Wolff, *Anthropology of the Old Testament*, trans. by Margaret Kohl (Philadelphia: Fortress, 1974), pp. 28-35.

125. Cf. especially McKane, *Prophets and Wise Men*. McKane follows the standard procedure of crediting Isaiah with profound, but in the final analysis irrelevant, insights into the nature of politics. See his conclusions in *ibid.*, pp. 113-30.

126. On the critical problems see Barth, *Die Jesaja-Worte*, pp. 222-25; Hans Werner Hoffmann, *Die Intention der Verkündigung Jesajas* (BZAW, 136; Berlin: Walter de Gruyter, 1974), pp. 105-19; Wildberger, *Jesaja*, pp. 92-114; Klaus Seybold, 'Die anthropologischen Beiträge aus Jesaja 2', *ZTK* 74 (1977), pp. 401-15; F.E. Deist, 'Notes on the Structure of Isa 2:2-22', *ThEv* 10 (1977), pp. 1-6; Henri Cazelles, 'Qui aurait visé, à l'origine, Isaïe II 2-5?', *VT* 30 (1980), pp. 409-20; Joseph Blenkinsopp, 'Fragments of Ancient Exegesis in an Isaian Poem (Jes 2.6-22)', *ZAW* 93 (1981), pp. 51-62; Joseph Jensen, 'Weal and Woe in Isaiah: Consistency and Continuity', *CBQ* 43 (1981), pp. 167-87, especially pp. 181-86.

127. On the problem of v. 6, which is apparently addressed to Yahweh, see Wildberger, *Jesaja*, pp. 92-93. Cazelles reads 'house of Jacob' as a vocative addressed to the refugees from the North' ('Isaïe II 2-5', p. 412). This appears very strained. If 2.1-5 are regarded as secondary additions, 2.6-22 could easily be considered the continuation of ch. 1. The address to Yahweh would be in place if this text were located in the cult, as the language suggests it might have been.

128. Cf. Wildberger, *Jesaja*, p. 99. All of what is mentioned in vv. 6b-8 is

probably meant to signify 'idol' worship, which is summed up in v. 8b: 'the work of their hands . . . what their fingers have made'. I.e., the people rely on their own measures for their security. See also below.

129.   While this is often thought to be an addition, with perhaps all of vv. 6-9, I see no reason to regard it as such (cf. Barth, *Die Jesaja-Worte*, pp. 222-23).

130.   עיני גבהות אדם שפל ושח רום אנשים (v. 11a).

131.   *Ibid.*, pp. 222-23; cf. Blenkinsopp, 'Fragments of Ancient Exegesis'. Contrast the treatment of Kevin J. Cathcart, who makes a plausible case for the unity of the poem ('Kingship and the "Day of YHWH" in Isaiah 2.6-22', *Hermathena* 125 [1978], pp. 48-59).

132.   Cf. Cazelles, 'Isaïe II 2-5', p. 411.

133.   Blenkinsopp, 'Fragments of Ancient Exegesis', pp. 53-54.

134.   Cf. also Wilhelm Rudolph on Mic 5.9-14 (*Micah* [KAT 13/3; Gütersloh: Gerd Mohn, 1975], pp. 105-106). Condemnation of illegitimate cultic practices and reliance upon them for security, which seems to lie behind Isa 2.6b, may also lie behind Isa 29.4, 5. The reference to Ariel's speaking 'from the earth' may refer to the underworld as in *CTA* 24 and text #2 from *Ugaritica V* (printed in J.C.L. Gibson, *Canaanite Myths and Legends* [Edinburgh: T. & T. Clark, second edition, 1978], pp. 137-38). The thin voice of the spirits of the dead characterizes the leadership of Ariel, which is itself a name probably chosen because of its cultic connections. See Wildberger, *Jesaja*, p. 1105. He notes the term *'r'l* in *KAI* II, p. 175, from Mesha, meaning 'an altar'. Cf. also Ronald Youngblood, 'Ariel, "City of God"', in *Essays on the Occasion of the Seventieth Anniversary of Dropsie University*, ed. by A.I. Katsch and Leon Nemoy (Philadelphia: Dropsie University, 1979), pp. 457-62. He believes 'city of God' is the meaning of the term. The divinatory practices of this cult are denounced as impotent, as they are also in 2.6b. Cf. also Isa 8.19-20 and 2 Kgs 21.6, where there seem to be references to divination in the presence of a military threat.

135.   Cf. Jensen, 'Weal and Woe in Isaiah', p. 183: ' . . . "pride" now stands for trust in power and gold and idols'. See Ps 97.7.

136.   Blenkinsopp, 'Fragments of Ancient Exegesis', pp. 53-54, 57-58.

137.   *Ibid.*, p. 57.

138.   Isa 5.15-16 is generally thought to be out of place in its present context, but it seems to me that it fits very well just where it is and need not be moved to some place after Isa 2.21 (Otto Kaiser, *Isaiah 1-12*, trans. by R.A. Wilson [OTL; Philadelphia: Westminster, 1972], pp. 32-33) or treated as redactional (R.E. Clements, *Isaiah 1-39* [NCB; Grand Rapids: Eerdmans, 1980], p. 64). It is simply part of the theological basis for the judgment against arrogance expressed in 5.8-14, 18-23. The fact that here and in 2.9, 17 אדם is used instead of 'Judah' or 'Israel' does not mean either that they are late, or that they are taken from wisdom traditions (Wildberger, *Jesaja*, pp. 103-104, 108; Jensen, 'Weal and Woe in Isaiah', p. 183). Cf. Ps 18.18; 1 Sam 2.9; Isa 31.3.

139. Note how vv. 11b and 17a, 'and Yahweh alone will be exalted in that day', provide a framework around the Day of Yahweh passage in vv. 12-17.

140. Note that Gray and Erlandsson emphasize the connection of Yahweh's Day in Amos 5 and Isaiah 2 with the condemnation of idolatry (cf. Amos 5.27). See John Gray, 'The Day of Yahweh in Cultic Experience and Eschatological Prospect', *SEÅ* 39 (1974), pp. 5-37, especially p. 23; S. Erlandsson, *The Burden of Babylon: A Study of Isaiah 13.2-14.32* (ConBOT, 4; Lund: CWK Gleerup, 1970), p. 147, and see pp. 146-53. Cf. Cathcart, 'Kingship and the "Day of YHWH"', p. 54; Gowan, *When Man Becomes God*, pp. 35-37.

141. Most recently in *The Reign of God*, pp. 141-42. Cf. also Cathcart, 'Kingship and the "Day of YHWH"', pp. 55-56, where he compares *CTA* 4.7.8-12, 29-37. Baal is here celebrating his victory over his rivals. Cathcart fails to note that in 4.4.49-50 Baal declares that *aḥdy dymlk 'l ilm*—'I alone am he who reigns over all gods'.

142. Gray, *The Reign of God*, p. 141, note 67.

143. J.J.M. Roberts, 'Zion in the Theology of the Davidic-Solomonic Empire', *Studies in the Period of David and Solomon*, ed. by Tomoo Ishida (Winona Lake: Eisenbrauns, 1982), p. 103.

144. Walther Eichrodt, *Der Heilige in Israel: Jesaja 1-12 übersetzt und erklärt* (BAT 17/1; Stuttgart: Calwer, 1960), p. 56.

145. Stolz, *Jahwes und Israels Kriege*, pp. 161, 191.

146. *Ibid.*, p. 117. Although I would agree with Klaus Seybold that there is an important anthropological thrust to this chapter, I would differ from some of his conclusions as to the character of that thrust (Seybold, 'Die anthropologischen Beiträge').

147. Cf. Barth, *Die Jesaja-Worte*, pp. 49-50, and note 3. On pp. 271-74 Barth defends the attribution of these texts to Isaiah and critiques Otto Kaiser's method in assigning them to a redactor (Kaiser, *Isaiah 13-39*). In exact agreement with Barth is C.A. Keller, 'Das quietistische Element in der Botschaft des Jesaja', *TZ* 11 (1955), pp. 85, 87. Barth does not refer to Keller. See also Childs, *Isaiah and the Assyrian Crisis*, p. 65, and also pp. 36-37; von Rad, *Old Testament Theology*, II, trans. by D.M.G. Stalker (New York: Harper & Row, 1965), pp. 160-61.

148. Cf. Barth, *Die Jesaja-Worte*, p. 50, note 194. The meaning of the term is discussed by Huber, *Jahwe, Juda und die anderen Völker*, pp. 140-47.

149. *Psalms I*, p. 148. Earlier Dahood had derived the term from ישב. Alternatively ונחת could be understood as *waw*-explicative, 'in returning, that is in rest . . . '. Cf. *WHS* #434; *GK* #154, note 1(b).

150. Wildberger, *Jesaja*, pp. 1181-85.

151. *Ibid.*, p. 1185.

152. Cf. George Betram, '"Hochmut" und verwandte Begriffe im griechischen und hebräischen Alten Testament', *WdO* 3 (1964/66), pp. 32-

43; J.J.M. Roberts, 'The Young Lions of Psalm 34.11', *Biblica* 54 (1973), pp. 265-68. Note also Bernhard Lang, *Kein Aufstand in Jerusalem*, p. 104.

153. Roberts, 'A Note on Isaiah 28.12', *HTR* 73 (1980), pp. 49-51. Roberts compares the thought of the reconstructed 28.12 to Isa 14.29-32 (p. 50).

154. *Ibid.*, p. 51.

155. Cf. Barth, *Die Jesaja-Worte*, p. 50, note 196; Wildberger, *Jesaja*, pp. 1060-61; Roberts, 'Isaiah 28.12', pp. 50-51. Wildberger refers to Deut 12.9-10; 1 Kgs 8.56. More important is the comparison with Ps 132. Cf. Wildberger, p. 1060, and, with a different point, Roberts, p. 51.

156. David L. Petersen has argued that vv. 7b-13a and 14-19 were originally juxtaposed and were separated by v. 13b, which is the work of a redactor ('Isaiah 28, A Redaction Critical Study', in *SBL Seminar Papers*, vol. II, ed. by Paul J. Achtemeier [Missoula: Scholars Press, 1979], pp. 101-22). Wildberger compares v. 15, which is very difficult, to the text from Arslan Tash and suggests that there may be a reference here to incantations intended to remove spirits (*Jesaja*, pp. 1073-74). See also W.H. Irwin, *Isaiah 28-33: Translation with Philological Notes* (BibOr, 30; Rome: Pontifical Biblical Institute, 1974), pp. 28-29.

157. Wildberger emends בָּה to בה (in him), following 1QIs[a]. He notes, however, that Isaiah sees Yahweh and Zion in especially close connection (*Jesaja*, pp. 573, 575).

158. *Die Jesaja-Worte*, p. 15. He refers to Pss 18.18; 25.16 and other texts. Rohland notes that the founding of Zion mentioned here is different and not derived from the 'historical tradition' that associates the 'election' of Zion with that of David. He assumes that the founding of Zion goes back to pre-Israelite notions ('Die Bedeutung der Erwählungstraditionen Israels', pp. 146-47).

159. Of this presumed 'utopian' aspect in Isaiah's politics, Kaiser says, ' . . . a king who bears a real responsibility for his people cannot indulge in the luxury of waiting for a besieged Jerusalem to be saved by the theophany of Yahweh in a storm and an earthquake. Nor are such ideals possible for a prophet who still lives in the midst of a people capable of an active part in shaping its own history' (*Isaiah 13-39*, p. 86). Wildberger counters: '"Utopian" politics grounded in faith is a daring venture. But there are situations in which a daring venture must be undertaken, and there are prophetic figures to whom the ἐξουσία is given to push out into such a daring venture . . . There are moments in which faith must assert itself against 'reason' and against the apparently incontestable force of a threatening reality' (*Jesaja*, pp. 676-77). Keller says that Isaiah was, among other things, 'a quietist, perhaps even a religious "Schwärmer"' ('Das quietistische Element', p. 89). I think he is using the term in a pejorative sense. Cf. also Gunneweg, 'Herrschaft Gottes und Herrschaft des Menschen', pp. 172-73.

160. Once again, note Schreiner's emphasis on the distinction between

'Judas Hauptstadt und die heilige Stadt Jahwes' (*Sion-Jerusalem*, p. 256). It is also interesting to recall that in several of the Psalms from the Jerusalem cult tradition arrogance or self-reliance was associated with mistreatment of the poor and violence. With this we may compare Isa 30.8-14, and the surrounding verses, especially 30.1-5, 15-17. On Isa 14 see Gowan, *When Man Becomes God*, pp. 45-67.

161. Barth, *Die Jesaja-Worte*, p. 51, and note 200.

162. E.g. Kaiser, *Isaiah 13-39*, p. 248; Wildberger, *Jesaja*, pp. 1065-66.

163. *Isaiah 28-33*, p. 30. On p. 168 he refers to this passage and translates the prospective suffix literally, 'Behold me who have founded . . .'. A similar construction is found in 29.14 and 38.5. Cf. *GK* #155f. Contrast Barth, *Die Jesaja-Worte*, p. 12.

164. A number of them are listed by Kaiser, *Isaiah 13-39*, p. 253; cf. Wildberger, *Jesaja*, pp. 1066, 1076-77.

165. *GK* #119i, followed by Irwin, *Isaiah 28-39*, p. 30.

166. Note the use of the verb יסד in both passages, 28.16; 14.32.

167. Dahood, *Psalms III*, p. 159.

168. Quoted in S.H. Hooke, 'The Corner-Stone of Scripture', in *The Siege Perilous: Essays in Biblical Anthropology and Kindred Subjects* (London: SCM, 1956), p. 240. LeBas's essay appeared in *PEQ* 78 (1946), pp. 103-15. On his interpretation the reference to the stone in Isa would be messianic.

169. Hooke, 'The Corner-Stone', pp. 240-41.

170. Ludwig Köhler, 'Zwei Fachwörter der Bausprache in Jes. 28.16', *TZ* 3 (1947), pp. 390-93. G.R. Driver suggests that this sort of stone may be 'identical with the Egyptian *bhn-w*, "diorite, granite" or other hard, dark-coloured stone, quarried in the Wady Hamamat and called *lapis niger* or *Thebaicus* by ancient writers', which was used in ancient monuments. He suspects that the allusion here is to the great stones of the temple (1 Kgs 5.17). Driver, '"Another Little Drink"—Isaiah 28.1-22', in *Words and Meanings: Essays Presented to David Winton Thomas*, ed. by P.R. Ackroyd and B. Lindars (Cambridge: Cambridge University Press, 1968), pp. 59-60. Irwin simply renders the term 'granite' (*Isaiah 28-33*, p. 31), while Galling goes farthest in recognizing the ambiguity by rendering the phrase '*Bochansteine*' ('Serubbabel und der Wiederaufbau des Tempels in Jerusalem', in *Verbannung und Heimkehr: Festschrift für W. Rudolph*, ed. by A. Kuschke [Tübingen: J.C.B. Mohr, 1961], p. 73).

171. Cf. Köhler, 'Zwei Fachwörter'; Galling, 'Serubbabel', p. 73, note 28; *GK* #130f., note 4.

172. Irwin, *Isaiah 28-33*, p. 31. He points to enclitic-*mem* in Hebrew and Ugaritic. Wildberger points to a similar construction in Deut 21.11 and translates 'ein Eckstein, kostbar im Hinblick auf die Grundsteinlegung' (*Jesaja*, p. 1067).

173. The second מוסד presents a problem. See Wildberger, *Jesaja*, p. 1067. It could represent simply an alternative spelling (cf. *GK* #71).

174. But cf. Dahood, *Psalms III*, p. 159.

175. See J.D.M. Derrett, '"The Stone that the Builders Rejected"', in *Studies in the New Testament*, II: *Midrash in Action and as a Literary Device* (Leiden: E.J. Brill, 1978), pp. 60-67; Galling, 'Serubbabel', pp. 72-73.

176. *A Lexicon Abridged from Liddell and Scott's Greek-English Lexicon* (Oxford: Clarendon, 1966), p. 28. Galling takes the 'Bochansteine' as a composite structure of stones at the extreme end of the wall and cites Megiddo as an example ('Serubbabel', pp. 72-73).

177. The most recent discussion is by Baruch Halpern, 'The Ritual Background of Zechariah's Temple Song', *CBQ* 40 (1978), pp. 167-90, especially pp. 170-78. See also David L. Petersen, 'Zerubbabel and Jerusalem Temple Reconstruction', *CBQ* 36 (1974), pp. 366-72; E. Lipiński, 'Recherches sur le livre de Zacharie', *VT* 20 (1970), pp. 25-55. The Near Eastern material is surveyed in R.S. Ellis, *Foundation Deposits in Ancient Mesopotamia* (New Haven: Yale University Press, 1968).

178. Barth, *Die Jesaja-Worte*, p. 12. It may be possible to consider this final phrase the inscription on the cornerstone. This is the position of Eichrodt, *Der Herr der Geschichte: Jesaja 13–23 und 28–29* (BAT 17/2; Stuttgart: Calwer, 1967), p. 151. The verb is often emended to something else. Cf. Wildberger (*Jesaja*, p. 1067) for discussion, and note the verb's use in Hab 1.8

179. Cf. Barth, *Die Jesaja-Worte*, pp. 47-54. See the discussion in Hans-Jürgen Hermisson ('Zukunftserwartung und Gegenwartskritik in der Verkündigung Jesajas', *EvT* 33 [1973], pp. 54-77) and W.H. Schmidt ('Die Einheit der Verkündigung Jesajas. Versuch einer Zusammenschau', *EvT* 37 [1977], pp. 260-72), and contrast Jensen, 'Weal and Woe in Isaiah'. It may be in some sense correct to speak, as Jensen does, of Yahweh's 'pedagogical' action in creating the proper disposition in the people of Judah, but that does not mean that Isaiah expected less than complete destruction; neither is it inconsistent to speak of a new beginning after destruction in ch. 28, or in 1.21-26. Cf. further Barth, *Die Jesaja-Worte*, pp. 50-54; von Rad, *Old Testament Theology*, II, pp. 164-67; Leonhard Rost, 'Das Problem der Weltmacht in der Prophetie', *TLZ* 90 (1965), pp. 241-50 (now in Rost, *Studien zum Alten Testament* [BWANT, 101; Stuttgart: W. Kohlhammer, 1974], pp. 76-78). The message of Isaiah is discussed in J.J.M. Roberts, 'Isaiah in Old Testament Theology', *Interpretation* 36 (1982), pp. 130-43.

180. Cf. also Isa 7.3. See the discussion of 'Shear-Yashub' in Wildberger, *Jesaja*, pp. 276-79. On the possibility of interpreting this as a remnant who will repent see Th.C. Vriezen, 'Essentials of the Theology of Isaiah', in *Israel's Prophetic Heritage: Essays in Honor of James Muilenburg*, ed. by B.W. Anderson and Walter Harrelson (New York: Harper & Row, 1962), p. 138, note 16; Siegfried Herrmann, *Die prophetischen Heilserwartungen im Alten Testament: Ursprung und Gestaltwandel* (BWANT, 85; Stuttgart: W. Kohlhammer, 1965), p. 129; Hermisson, 'Zukunftserwartung', pp. 61-63; Donner, *Israel unter den Völkern*, p. 152.

181. On האמין see Rudolf Smend, 'Zur Geschichte von האמין', in *Hebräische Wortforschung: Festschrift für W. Baumgartner* (VTS 16 [1967]), pp. 284-90; Wildberger, '"Glauben", Erwägungen zu האמין', in *ibid.*, pp. 372-86; Wildberger, '"Glauben" im Alten Testament', *ZTK* 65 (1968), pp. 219-59. According to Smend, none of the uses of the verb is earlier than Isa 7.9 (pp. 286-88).

182. See Nadav Na'aman, 'Sennacherib's "Letter to God" on his Campaign to Judah', *BASOR* 214 (1974), pp. 25-39, especially p. 33 (see note 37).

183. It is also important to caution against regarding Isaiah as simply a politician arguing for a more reaonable political option. He is really arguing for political choices based on an alternative view of reality, namely one in which Yahweh is king. Cf. Bernhard Lang, 'Prophetie, prophetische Zeichenhandlung und Politik in Israel', *TQ* 161 (1981), pp. 275-80, especially p. 276; Karl Elliger, 'Prophet und Politik', *ZAW* 53 (1935), pp. 3-22. See the extensive discussion in Walter Dietrich, *Jesaja und die Politik* (BEvT, 74; München: Chr. Kaiser, 1976), pp. 246-68.

184. See above, note 125.

185. Schreiner, *Sion-Jerusalem*, p. 256.

186. These two terms are, in the Jerusalem cult tradition, synonymous. See above, ch. 3.

187. It is theologically interesting that 'faith' is the characteristic language of the Jerusalem cult tradition and is almost entirely lacking in the Pentateuchal traditions. In those traditions a characteristic term is שמר, which appears in Isaiah of Jerusalem only in ch. 21, in an entirely different sense, and in 7.4 (*niphal*), where it is related to faith.

188. See especially Isa 29.1-8, where even the battle against Jerusalem does not eliminate Yahweh's faithfulness to Zion. On this reversal of the 'Völkerkampf' see Lutz, *Jahwe, Jerusalem und die Völker*, ch. 3, especially p. 114; Stolz, *Strukturen und Figuren*, p. 90; Duane L. Christensen, *Transformations of the War Oracle in Old Testament Prophecy* (HDR, 3; Cambridge, MA: Harvard University Press, 1975), pp. 141-42; J. Alberto Soggin, 'The Prophets on Holy War as Judgement Against Israel', in *Old Testament and Oriental Studies* (BibOr, 29; Rome: Pontifical Biblical Institute, 1975), pp. 67-71 (= *VT* 10 [1960], pp. 79-83). Millard Lind has noted examples from the Near East in which a divinity fights against his or her own city. For example Inanna forsook her temple and city and fought against them. For the text see *ANET*, p. 455. Lind, *Yahweh is a Warrior*, pp. 110-11; cf. W.G. Lambert, 'Enmeduranki and Related Matters', *JCS* 21 (1967), pp. 126-38; J.J.M. Roberts, 'Nebuchadnezzar I's Elamite Crisis in Theological Perspective', in *Essays on the Ancient Near East in Memory of Jacob Joel Finkelstein*, ed. by M. de Jong Ellis (Hamden, CN: Archon Books, 1977), pp. 183-87.

189. In addition to 14.32, cf. 10.2; 11.4; 14.30; 29.19; 32.7. Note especially 3.14-15. See Barth, *Die Jesaja-Worte*, pp. 14-15. He deletes 14.30 from 14.28-

32 on what seem to me to be dubious grounds (it does not fit the *Gattung* of a 'call to joy', issued in v. 29; the structure of vv. 28-32 is sound without v. 30; v. 30 does not fit the content of v. 29).

190. On pride as the basis for Yahweh's judgment in Isaiah see Christensen, *War Oracle*, p. 137; Gowan, *When Man Becomes God*. One must reject Christensen's contention that the 'poor' of 14.30 are 'the rural peasants as a social class in Palestine' (p. 136). G.R. Hambourg notes that Isaiah's reasons for judgment against Israel are strikingly similar to his reasons for judgment against the nations. Chief among these reasons is 'the sin of pride' ('Reasons for Judgment in the Oracles Against the Nations of the Prophet Isaiah', *VT* 31 [1981], pp. 145-59, especially p. 157).

191. John H. Hayes, 'The Tradition of Zion's Inviolability', *JBL* 82 (1963), pp. 419-26.

192. These texts are treated according to what I judge to be their logical and theo-logical relationships, not according to their chronology in the life of Isaiah or according to what might be seen as the evolution of his thought. On the latter cf. Georg Fohrer, 'Wandlungen Jesajas', in *Studien zu alttestamentlichen Texten und Themen* (1966-1972) (Berlin: de Gruyter, 1981), pp. 11-23. The essay was originally published in 1967. When Isaiah is seen as a theologian rather than as a minister of defense his message appears to be radically consistent (contra Jochen Vollmer, *Geschichtliche Rückblicke und Motive in der Prophetie des Amos, Hosea und Jesaja* [BZAW, 119; Berlin: de Gruyter, 1971], p. 193).

193. Cf. W.H. Schmidt, *Zukunftsgewissheit und Gegenwartskritik*.

194. Among the few defenders of the Isaianic authorship of these passages is Wildberger, *Jesaja*. See also Christensen, *War Oracle*, pp. 143-53; Walter Dietrich, *Jesaja und die Politik*, pp. 120-21, 134-35.

195. Clements, *Isaiah 1-39*, p. 6; cf. Barth, *Die Jesaja-Worte*, pp. 204-205.

196. Peter Höffken believes that the present form of Isaiah 7 was achieved at a later time, perhaps after 701 ('Notizen zum Textcharakter von Jesaja 7, 1-17', *TZ* 36 [1980], pp. 321-37, especially p. 336). While the present text may have been edited at that time, as is possibly indicated by v. 17, I believe that an oracle of Isaiah to Ahaz can be reconstructed. Cf. O.H. Steck, 'Rettung und Verstockung: Exegetische Bemerkungen zu Jesaja 7, 3-9', *EvT* 33 (1973), pp. 77-90. This article presupposes his earlier study of Isaiah's call, 'Bemerkungen zu Jesaja 6', *BZ* 16 (1972), pp. 188-206.

197. When Assyria's defeat is depicted in post-Isaianic texts it is in quite different language. Cf. 31.8-9; 37.33ff.; contrast 1.4-8 (see R.E. Clements, *Isaiah and the Deliverance of Jerusalem* [JSOT Supplement Series, 13; Sheffield: JSOT Press, 1980], pp. 34-36).

198. See H.-P. Müller, 'Glauben und Bleiben: Zur Denkschrift Jesajas Kapitel vi 1-viii 18', *VTS* 26 (1974), pp. 24-54, especially pp. 48-52.

199. Saebø, 'Zur Traditionsgeschichte von Jesaia 8,9-10, Klärungsversuch einer alten *crux interpretum*', *ZAW* 76 (1964), pp. 132-44 (now in *Ordene og*

Ordet: Gammeltestamentlige Studier [Oslo: Universitetsforlaget, 1979], pp. 71-83). Saebø, who took his suggestion ultimately from H. Schmidt (according to Wildberger, *Jesaja*, p. 329; cf. Barth, *Die Jesaja-Worte*, p. 178, note 4) is followed by most commentators (cf. Steck, 'Rettung und Verstockung').

200. See also Wildberger, *Jesaja*, p. 330. Both Saebø and Wildberger depend on the form-critical work of Robert Bach in identifying this text as an 'Aufforderung zum Kampf' (cf. above, note 114).

201. As Saebø himself acknowledges ('Jesaja 8, 9-10', p. 82). He insists that middle-weak roots show so much variation that one cannot insist on a geminate root in this case.

202. See Lloyd Neve, 'The Common Use of Traditions by the Author of Psalm 46 and Isaiah', *ExpTim* 86 (1975), pp. 243-46; John Day, 'Shear Jashub (Isaiah VII 3) and "the Remnant of Wrath" (Psalm LXXVI 11)', *VT* 31 (1981), pp. 76-78. Day also relates Isa 8.6, 'the gentle waters of Shiloah', to Ps 46.4-5.

203. Verse 13a is deleted as a variant of v. 12b. See Dietrich, *Jesaja und die Politik*, p. 135, note 11; Kaiser, *Isaiah 13-39*, p. 84; Barth, *Die Jesaja-Worte*, p. 181, note 16. On the form and tradition-historical questions see Childs, *Isaiah and the Assyrian Crisis*, pp. 51-53, and on the 'summary-appraisal' in v. 14, pp. 128-36. On the translation of הוֹי in 17.12a see most recently J.J.M. Roberts, 'Form, Syntax and Redaction in Isaiah 1.2-20', *Princeton Seminary Bulletin*, n.s. 3 (1982), pp. 293-306, especially pp. 296-301.

204. See the superb discussion by Victor Maag, 'Jahwäs Begegnung mit der kanaanischen Kosmologie', in *Kultur, Kulturkontakt und Religion: Gesammelte Studien zur allgemeinen und alttestamentlichen Religionsgeschichte*, ed. by H.H. Schmid and O.H. Steck (Göttingen: Vandenhoeck & Ruprecht, 1980), pp. 203-20.

205. Cf. Huber, *Jahwe, Juda und die anderen Völker*, pp. 233-40, especially p. 237.

206. Dietrich, *Jesaja und die Politik*, p. 136, note 20; Lutz, *Jahwe, Jerusalem und die Völker*, pp. 43-44. He compares this passage with 7.3-4. Contrast Vollmer, *Geschichtliche Rückblicke*, p. 102; Huber, *Jahwe, Juda und die anderen Völker*, pp. 71-82. They argue that these passages do not come from Isaiah.

207. Cf. Kaiser, *Isaiah 1-12*, pp. 115-16; Lutz, *Jahwe, Jerusalem und die Völker*, p. 150. Contrast Saebø, 'Jesaja 8,9-10', p. 80.

208. The language of 8.10, יָעַץ, עֵצָה, indicates that Isaiah himself may be responsible for the composition of these texts, rather than drawing them whole from the existing tradition. Cf. von Rad, *Old Testament Theology*, II, pp. 161-62.

209. Cf. Walter Zimmerli, 'Prophetic Proclamation and Reinterpretation', in *Tradition and Theology in the Old Testament*, ed. by Douglas A. Knight (Philadelphia: Fortress, 1977), pp. 69-100, especially p. 87.

210. For recent discussion of this text see Ernst Würthwein, 'Jesaja 7,1-9: Ein Beitrag zu dem Thema: Prophetie und Politik', in *Wort und Existenz: Studien zum Alten Testament* (Göttingen: Vandenhoeck & Ruprecht, 1970), pp. 127-43 (originally published in 1954); Klaus Seybold, *Das davidische Königtum im Zeugnis der Propheten* (FRLANT, 107; Göttingen: Vandenhoeck & Ruprecht, 1972), pp. 66-78, 100-102; O.H. Steck, 'Rettung und Verstockung'; Peter Höffken, 'Jesaja 1, 1-17'; A.H.J. Gunneweg, 'Herrschaft Gottes'; J. Vermeylen, *Du prophète Isaïe à l'apocalyptique: Isaïe, I–XXXV, Miroir d'un demi-millénaire d'expérience religieuse en Israël,* I (Paris: J. Gabalda, 1977), pp. 199-211. In my view 7.10-17 are probably to be considered separately from 7.1-9. See Peter Ackroyd, 'Isaiah I–XX: Presentation of a Prophet', *VTS* 29 (1977), p. 40. On the possible setting of 7.1-9 in the context of 6.1-9.6 see Anton Schoors, 'Isaiah, the Minister of Royal Anointment?', *OTS* 20 (1977), pp. 85-107. Cf. von Rad, *Old Testament Theology,* II, pp. 170-75.

211. See the previous note. He was partially dependent upon the earlier essay of Walter Elliger, 'Prophet und Politik', and that of Albrecht Alt, 'Das Königtum in den Reichen Israel und Juda', *VT* 1 (1951), pp. 2-16.

212. Hugo Gressmann, *Der Messias,* ed. by H. Schmidt (FRLANT, 43; Göttingen: Vandenhoeck & Ruprecht, 1929), p. 237. Gressmann characterizes this advice as 'unklug' and 'unbrauchbar' (p. 283, note 1). See above, note 159. Similar comments by Gunneweg and Keller that Isaiah was a sectarian and a 'Schwärmer' are typical.

213. See also Seybold, *Das davidische Königtum,* p. 68; Wildberger, *Jesaja,* p. 271; and most other commentaries.

214. See R. Killian, *Die Verheissung Immanuels. Jes 7,14* (SBS, 35; Stuttgart: KBW Verlag, 1968), pp. 26-27.

215. Würthwein, 'Jesaja 7,1-9', p. 143, note 1.

216. Cf. J. Lust, 'The Immanuel Figure: A Charismatic Judge-Leader', *ETL* 47 (1971), pp. 464-70; Herrmann, *Die prophetischen Heilserwartungen,* p. 131, note 21. Isa 7.13 hardly shows confidence in the permanence of the Davidic house.

217. Cf. Edzard Rohland, 'Die Bedeutung der Erwählungstraditionen', pp. 157-58.

218. *Canaanite Myth and Hebrew Epic* (Cambridge, MA: Harvard University Press, 1973), pp. 157-58.

219. Cf. Smend, 'Zur Geschichte von אמן'.

220. See above, note 109.

221. By denying that Isaiah grounded his expectation in the Davidic covenant tradition I am not suggesting that he had no connection with royal theology, however much he may have modified and even muted that tradition. What I am denying is that the tradition of a covenant with David, as articulated in 2 Sam 7, Pss 89 and 132, forms the basis of his proclamation.

222. Contra Magne Saebø, 'Formgeschichtliche Erwägungen zu Jes. 7:3-9',

ST 14 (1960), pp. 54-69 (now in *Ordene og Ordet*, pp. 55-70). Saebø is followed by most of those listed in note 210, above.

223. Wildberger, *Jesaja*, p. 282.

224. Wolff, *Hosea*, p. 63.

225. *Ibid.*, p. 139; cf. Joachim Becker, *Messianic Expectation in the Old Testament*, trans. by David E. Green (Philadelphia: Fortress, 1980), pp. 18-24.

226. See above, and cf. Frank Crüsemann, *Der Widerstand gegen das Königtum: Die antiköniglichen Texte des Alten Testamentes und der Kampf um den frühen israelitischen Staat* (WMANT, 49; Neukirchen-Vluyn: Neukirchener Verlag, 1978), especially p. 92 and note 16.

227. See the superb discussion of this issue in Wildberger, *Jesaja*, pp. 188-89, on Isa 5.12.

228. On this text see W.S. Prinsloo, 'Isaiah 14.12-15—Humiliation, Hubris, Humiliation', *ZAW* 93 (1981), pp. 432-38. The earlier literature is there cited.

229. That 14.24-27 are from Isaiah is argued by Dietrich, *Jesaja und die Politik*, pp. 120-21; Wildberger, *Jesaja*, pp. 567-68; contrast Vermeylen, *Du Prophète Isaïe à l'Apocalyptique*, pp. 261-62.

230. For the 'Jesajanität' of these verses see Wildberger, *Jesaja*, pp. 812-13. Interestingly, Yahweh is described in Isa 22.11 as the creator of history (עשׂיה . . . ויצרה). On מרחוק in v. 11 see the discussion in *ibid.*, pp. 825-26.

231. 'Rettung und Verstockung', p. 90. While Steck believes that this is the thrust of the text, he also believes that the 'intention' of Isaiah in ch. 7 was really to interpret the effect of the 'Verstockung' declared in ch. 6.

232. Both of these theological assumptions are stated in other Isaianic texts, e.g. ch. 6 and 29.1-7/8. However, I believe that the texts cited above state them most clearly.

233. Note also chs. 1-5. Keller points out that what Isaiah opposes is all the frenetic activity in Judah, be it in the social, political or the cultic sphere ('Das quietistische Element', p. 91).

234. See John Barton, 'Ethics in Isaiah of Jerusalem', *JTS* 32 (1981), pp. 1-18. Barton's conclusions about Isaiah and my own are in virtual agreement. I demur, however, from his artificial distinction between 'subordination' and 'assuming one's place in the natural order' (p. 9), as well as from his attempt to place Isaiah's ethics under the umbrella of natural law (p. 1).

235. Isaiah 7.4 is usually identified with holy war traditions (Wildberger, *Jesaja*, pp. 270-72). To the contrary see James M. Ward, *Amos and Isaiah: Prophets of the Word of God* (New York: Abingdon, 1969), pp. 188-89. Ward apparently thinks that Isaiah could not have made use of the 'legendary' holy war traditions, because the notion of holy war 'was not and could not be the basis of policy for the leaders of Israel regardless of how pious they were' (p. 189). One could imagine the response of Ahaz being expressed similarly.

236. Seybold (*Das davidische Königtum*, pp. 52, 101-102) seems completely

to misunderstand this and finds it necessary to invent a whole series of relationships between Isaiah and Israel's covenant tradition. Cf. Walther Eichrodt, 'Prophet and Covenant: Observations on the Exegesis of Isaiah', in *Proclamation and Presence*, pp. 167-88.

237. The notion also seems to occur in Amos 2.14-15 and in Mic 5.9-14 (cf. Blenkinsopp, 'Fragments of Ancient Exegesis'). The Amos text is generally regarded as a late addition to the book, while the Micah text may well stem from a circle influenced by the followers of Isaiah. Cf. A.S. van der Woude, 'Micah IV 1-5: An Instance of the Pseudo-Prophets', in *Symbolae biblicae et Mesopotamicae: Francisco Mario Theodoro de Liagre Böhl dedicatae*, ed. by M.A. Beek, A.A. Kampen, C. Nijland, J. Ryckmans (Studia Francisci Scholten memoriae dicta, 4; Leiden: E.J. Brill, 1973), pp. 396-402. These texts may thus be left out of the discussion here.

238. As Steck has pointed out, the holy war 'ban' is to be distinguished from the apparent prohibition of weapons found in our texts (*Friedensvorstellungen*, p. 24). Contrast Kraus, *Psalmen*, p. 346, on Ps 46.10.

239. See especially Crüsemann, *Widerstand gegen das Königtum*, pp. 85-94. Crüsemann too is convinced that this could not have originated with Hosea, although he is interested only in Hosea's criticism of kingship, not the notion of Yahweh's exclusive prerogative. This criticism originated, according to him, in the anti-royal movements of the tenth century BC, especially in those inspired by the examples of Absalom and Sheba.

240. We note here also, in preliminary fashion, that McCarter regards this as the argument of Samuel in 1 Sam 7-12, that the institutions of pre-monarchic Israel were in fact capable of withstanding the threat of external aggression from the Philistines. Commenting on 1 Sam 8.1-22 he says, 'the pre-monarchical institutions are presented in this material as completely adequate, indeed as ideal . . . , and the people's insistence upon change must be seen as a strange denial of this plain fact' (*I Samuel*, p. 160). Hosea presents the reverse side of this same argument.

241. See, however, von Rad, *Old Testament Theology*, II, pp. 170-75; Hermisson, 'Zukunftserwartung und Gegenwartskritik', pp. 61-63; and cf. Bernhard Duhm, *Das Buch Jesaja* (HKAT; Göttingen: Vandenhoeck & Ruprecht, fifth edition, 1969 [= fourth edition, 1922]), p. 105; Herrmann, *Die prophetischen Heilserwartungen*, p. 147.

242. See above, note 112. We would want to qualify Crüsemann's statement that in Hosea the alternative posed in such texts as 1 Sam 8.7 and 12.12 between Yahweh's sovereignty and the institution of kingship no longer appears (*Widerstand gegen das Königtum*, p. 92). It is muted in Hosea, because his principal interest is in condemning the influence of the Baal cult on Israel, but this condemnation itself is brought under the contrast of Baal and Yahweh (ch. 2), which poses a similar alternative to Yahweh and kingship, in that both of them offer at least potential options to the sovereignty of Yahweh.

243. Among the many studies of these chapters and their sources see especially Artur Weiser, *Samuel: seine geschichtliche Aufgabe und religiöse Bedeutung. Traditionsgeschichtliche Untersuchungen zu 1. Samuel 7–12* (FRLANT, 31: Göttingen: Vandenhoeck & Ruprecht, 1962); Hans Jochen Boecker, *Die Beurteilung der Anfänge des Königtums in den deuteronomistischen Abschnitten des 1. Samuelbuches* (WMANT, 31; Neukirchen-Vluyn: Neukirchener Verlag, 1969); Dennis J. McCarthy, 'The Inauguration of Monarchy in Israel: A Form-Critical Study of I Samuel 8-12', *Interpretation* 27 (1973), pp. 401-12; Bruce C. Birch, 'The Rise of the Israelite Monarchy', *ZAW* 90 (1978), pp. 1-19.

244. The older tendency to attribute anti-monarchical portions of this account to late Deuteronomistic sources is now generally rejected. Cf. Birch, *The Rise of the Israelite Monarchy*, pp. 1-7.

245. Mayes has argued, with others, that chs. 8 and 12 are Deuteronomistic formulations in their entirety. Cf. Mayes, 'The Rise of the Israelite Monarchy'; R.E. Clements, 'The Deuteronomistic Interpretation of the Founding of the Monarchy in 1 Sam VIII', *VT* 24 (1974), pp. 398-410. Crüsemann has shown, however, that 1 Sam 8.7 and 12.12 are incompatible with the Deuteronomistic *Tendenz* in the redaction of these chapters (*Widerstand gegen das Königtum*, pp. 73-75).

246. The language of 10.18-19 does not include reference to Yahweh as king, but cf. McCarter, *I Samuel*, pp. 192, 195.

247. *Ibid.*, p. 160.

248. Crüsemann puts both of these txts in the Solomonic or immediately post-Solomonic period (*Widerstand gegen das Königtum*, pp. 30, 52). He is motivated in part by his belief that the kingship of Yahweh was a notion originating in Jerusalem, not in the pre-monarchic era.

249. Benjamin Uffenheimer, 'Die biblische Vorstellung vom Königtum Gottes und deren Dynamik', in *Zukunft in der Gegenwart: Wegweisungen in Judentum und Christentum*, ed. by Clemens Thoma (Judaica et Christiana, I; Bern: Herbert Lang, 1976), pp. 17-42. Cf. the essay in the same volume by Rudolf Schmid, 'Gottesherrschaft und menschliche Institution—Die Bedeutung menschlicher Initiative im Licht von 1 Sam 8 und 12', pp. 43-56.

250. Schmidt, 'Kritik am Königtum, pp. 441-42. Schmidt follows the reconstruction of H.J. Boecker, *Die Beurteilung der Anfänge des Königtums*. Schmidt speaks of Yahweh war instead of holy war.

251. Schmidt, 'Kritik am Königtum', p. 442, note 6. He refers here to his earlier work, *Königtum Gottes in Ugarit und Israel* (BZAW, 80; Berlin: Alfred Töpelmann, second edition, 1966), pp. 80-91.

252. See above, ch. 3. On Exodus 15, in addition to the literature already cited, see Thomas Mann, *Divine Presence and Guidance*, p. 129: 'The march of Israel through the wilderness and her approach toward Canaan in part 2 of Exodus 15 is thus presented in a manner strikingly similar to the march of

the imperial king in the Assyrian texts'. This supplements the usual comparisons with Ugaritic literature.

253. See Cross, *Canaanite Myth*, pp. 99-111.

254. This does not rule out, of course, that Yahweh was already conceived as king before this. It means simply that the language now used to express his kingship was taken over from the Canaanite context.

255. See especially Otto Eissfeldt, 'El und Jahwe', in *Kleine Schriften III*, ed. by Rudolf Sellheim and Fritz Maass (Tübingen: J.C.B. Mohr, 1966), pp. 386-97, especially pp. 396-97; cf. Schmidt, *Königtum Gottes*, pp. 86-87.

256. Eissfeldt, 'Monopol-Ansprüche des Heiligtums von Silo', *Kleine Schriften IV*, pp. 8-14. Cf. Akio Tsukimoto, '"Der Mensch ist geworden wie Unsereiner"—Untersuchungen zum zeitgeschichtlichen Hintergrund von Gen. 3,22-24 und 6,1-4', *AJBI* 5 (1979), pp. 3-44, especially pp. 42-43, note 131; Albrecht Alt, 'The Formation of the Israelite State in Palestine', in *Essays on Old Testament History and Religion*, trans. by R.A. Wilson (Garden City: Anchor Books, 1968), pp. 225-309, especially pp. 251-52.

257. Martin A. Cohen, 'The Role of the Shilonite Priesthood in the United Monarchy of Ancient Israel', *HUCA* 36 (1965), pp. 59-98. Note also the connections of the Song of Hannah with Shiloh. Cf. John T. Willis, 'The Song of Hannah'.

258. On the genealogy of Abiathar see McCarter, *I Samuel*, p. 239; Tsukimoto, 'Der Mensch ist geworden wie Unsereiner', p. 31; Aelred Cody, *A History of Old Testament Priesthood* (AnBib, 35; Rome: Pontifical Biblical Institute, 1969), pp. 70-71, 82-83; A.H.J. Gunneweg, *Leviten und Priester: Hauptlinien der Traditionsbildung und Geschichte des israelitisch-judäischen Kultpersonals* (FRLANT, 89; Göttingen: Vandenhoeck & Ruprecht, 1965), pp. 104-14. Gunneweg is more skeptical than McCarter, Tsukimoto or Cody about the genealogical links of Abiathar to Shiloh. Cody shows that the Levites were indeed the custodians of the Ark (p. 70), while Tsukimoto points out that Abiathar was custodian of the Ark, was in possession of the Urim and Thummim, a prerogative of the Levites (Gunneweg, p. 73), and that he was expelled to Anathoth, a Levitical city according to Josh 21.18 (Gunneweg, pp. 64-65). See Tsukimoto, pp. 31, 42-43, note 131.

259. Cross, *Canaanite Myth*, pp. 230-32.

260. See Cross, 'The Priestly Tabernacle in the Light of Recent Research', in *Temples and High Places in Biblical Times* (Jerusalem: Hebrew Union College—Jewish Institute of Religion, 1981), pp. 169-80, especially p. 176.

261. Cohen, 'The Role of the Shilonite Priesthood', p. 90. Cf. Tomoo Ishida, *The Royal Dynasties in Ancient Israel* (BZAW, 142; Berlin: de Gruyter, 1977), pp. 90-93, 140-49. While Ishida does not accept the particular argument of Cohen, because he believes the Ark came to have special significance only after it was brought to Jerusalem, he does agree that Shiloh was a center of resistance to the monarchy in Jerusalem.

262. Cohen, 'The Role of the Shilonite Priesthood', pp. 92-93. Cf. Robert

R. Wilson, *Prophecy and Society in Ancient Israel* (Philadelphia: Fortress, 1980), pp. 302-305.

263. See Hans Walter Wolff, 'Hoseas geistige Heimat', *Gesammelte Studien zum Alten Testament* (TBü, 22; München: Chr. Kaiser, 1964), pp. 232-50; Wolff, *Hosea*.

264. Tsukimoto, '"Der Mensch ist geworden wie Unsereiner"', p. 43, note 136; O.H. Steck, 'Genesis 12.1-3 und die Urgeschichte des Jahwisten', in *Probleme Biblischer Theologie*, pp. 525-54, see especially p. 553, note 73.

265. Abiathar has been credited with the authorship of other Old Testament material as well. See Cody, *History of Israelite Priesthood*, p. 83, note 58.

266. 'Menschliches Heldentum und göttliche Hilfe'.

267. Seeligmann himself refers to the study by E.A. Speiser, 'Ancient Mesopotamia', in the volume edited by R.C. Dentan, *The Idea of History in the Ancient Near East* (New Haven: Yale University Press, 1955).

268. Daniel David Luckenbill, *Ancient Records of Assyria and Babylon*, II (Chicago; University of Chicago Press, 1927), #900. I have omitted Luckenbill's translation comments and critical notations within the text.

269. Weippert, '"Heiliger Krieg" in Israel und Assyrien'.

270. *Ibid.*, p. 483. The goddesses, according to Weippert, are Ishtar of Nineveh and Ishtar of Arbela. The full text (K 1290) is provided by S. Langdon, *Babylonian Penitential Psalms* (OECT, 6; Paris: Paul Geuthner, 1927), pp. 69-71.

271. Weippert, '"Heiliger Krieg" in Israel und Assyrien', p. 483, note 110. The 'they' referred to are the kings Sanduarri of Kundi and Abdimilkutte of Sidon. Interestingly, Esarhaddon had claimed that it was because Sanduarri and Abdimilkutte had failed to recognize *his* lordship that they were forsaken by the gods and defeated by him (*ANET*, p. 290b).

272. Weippert, '"Heiliger Krieg" in Israel und Assyrien', p. 465; *ANET*, p. 389b. One might compare this text with the Zakir inscription.

273. Stolz, *Jahwes und Israels Kriege*, p. 189. Stolz also refers to Mesopotamian texts on pp. 187-88.

274. Quoted according to *ANET*, p. 257a.

275. There is some evidence of this also from Ugarit. See *CTA* 4.7 and cf. J.J.M. Roberts, 'Zion in the Theology of the Davidic-Solomonic Empire' p. 104. Note also *RS* 24.266 V°, 9-19 in Andrée Herdner, 'Une Prière à Baal des Ugaritiains en Danger', *CRAIBL* (1973), pp. 693-97. An English translation is provided by J.C. de Moor in *IDBS*, p. 930a.

276. Luckenbill, *Ancient Records*, #906.

277. Langdon, *Babylonian Penitential Psalms*, p. 68. The underlined words indicate Langdon's reconstruction.

278. Stolz, *Jahwes und Israels Kriege*, p. 190.

279. On the text see above, ch. 3.

280. Thomas Mann, *Divine Presence and Guidance*, pp. 218-24.

281 W.H. Schmidt ('Kritik am Königtum') tries to trace a development *toward* the conception of Yahweh's 'Alleinwirksamkeit' *within* the Psalms themselves. This attempt is compromised, however, by the problematic dating of the Psalms and texts such as 1 Sam 8 and 12, as well as by Schmidt's insistence that the conception itself is preserved by prophets who derive it from the Yahweh-war tradition.

282. Simon B. Parker suggests that a similar qualification of royal prerogatives, or perhaps merely qualities, in favor of the status of El may be reflected in the *KRT* text from Ugarit. See his essay, 'The Historical Composition of KRT and the Cult of EL', *ZAW* 89 (1977), pp. 161-75.

283. See especially Seeligmann, 'Menschliches Heldentum und göttliche Hilfe', and cf. Rudolf Schmid, 'Gottesherrschaft und menschliche Institution'; A.H.J. Gunneweg, 'Herrschaft Gottes'.

284. Seeligmann is correct in commenting that for Isaiah 'true ישועה and גבורה lie in the renunciation of human political and military activity' ('Menschliches Heldentum und göttliche Hilfe', p. 409), although this assumes too narrow a definition of what is 'political'. Note also his conclusion that in Isaiah 'The exclusivity of God's help is completely determined by the contrast between God and humanity' (*ibid.*).

285. The speaker in Ps 118.5-21 is of course ambiguous. There is also some ambiguity about the speaker in Ps 44.7. Things are naturally quite different in Ps 18, which drinks more deeply of the royal wine.

286. See above, especially note 93.

287. Bach, '"... Der Bogen zerbricht und Wagen mit Feuer verbrennt"', in *Probleme Biblischer Theologie*, pp. 13-26, thinks that Mic 5.9-10 is the earliest prophetic witness to this theme (or specifically, the motif of Yahweh destroying weapons), which was ultimately derived from the tradition of Yahweh war. However, he makes this claim with no consideration of the problem of dating this text, which is usually considered an addition to Micah (cf. in summary James L. Mays, *Micah: A Commentary* [OTL; Philadelphia: Westminster, 1976], p. 124: 'The basic oracle can hardly have come from Micah'). This involves Bach in the dubious argument that Mic 5.9-10 is earlier than Ps 46.10. See further on Bach, below.

288. Victor Turner, 'Symbols and Social Experience in Religious Ritual', in *Worship and Ritual in Christianity and Other Religions* (Studia Missionalia 23 [1974]), p. 8. Yahweh's exclusive prerogative is thus a part of Zion's 'evocation field'. Cf. ch. 1, note 49.

289. Dahood proposed that עגלות be translated 'shields', on the basis of עגלה in 1QM 6.15 (*Psalms I*, p. 281). However, in *Psalms II*, p. 220, he changed his mind and agreed that 'war chariots' was the best rendering.

290. 'Flames of the bow' should be taken to mean 'flaming arrows', as in RSV. On these two texts see J.J.M. Roberts, 'Zion in the Theology of the Davidic-Solomonic Empire', p. 104. Note that in Ps. 76.10 Yahweh's action is described as justice 'for all the poor of the earth'.

291. See Bach, '" . . . Der Bogen zerbricht"', p. 16. He relies here on Lutz, *Jahwe, Jerusalem und die Völker*, pp. 163, 170. Cf. however, Stolz, *Strukturen und Figuren*, p. 156, note 35.

292. As one might expect, Yahweh's destruction of weapons is often said to derive from the holy war tradition (cf. Lutz, *Jahwe, Jerusalem und die Völker*, p. 163; Schreiner, *Sion-Jerusalem*, pp. 225-26). Schreiner does relate Ps 46.10 to Yahweh's exclusive prerogative, but he does this on the basis of Exodus 14. There is really nothing in the Yahweh war or holy war tradition from which Ps. 46.10 and 76.4 could derive, especially since these texts are connected explicitly to what Yahweh does, or has done, in Zion. That Ps 2 does not contain an instance of the *Völkerkampfmotiv* was argued above, ch.3. Mowinckel is one of the few who insist on a connection between Pss 46.10; 76.4 and the *Völkerkampf* (*Psalmenstudien II*, p. 184). Contrast Heinrich Gross, *Die Idee des ewigen und allgemeinen Weltfriedens im alten Orient und im alten Testament* (TTS, 7; Trier: Paulinus Verlag, 1956), pp. 116-17. See also Paul D. Hanson, 'Zechariah 9 and the Recapitulation of an Ancient Ritual Pattern', *JBL* 92 (1973), pp. 37-59.

293. Kraus, *Psalmen*, p. 339.

294. Dahood, *Psalms I*, p. 282.

295. *Ibid.*

296. Broadly the same sort of connections seem to be drawn in Ps 76.4ff., although problems of translation obscure the precise meaning of v. 5. See further Isa 28.12; 30.15; and note Steck, *Friedensvorstellungen*, p. 28, note 55.

297. See above, note 287.

298. See above, note 59.

299. Wolff, *Hosea*, pp. 48, 50-51.

300. Delbert Hillers, *Treaty-Curses and the Old Testament Prophets* (BibOr, 16; Rome: Pontifical Biblical Institute, 1964), p. 41. The broader Near Eastern background of the 'breaking of the bow' motif is examined by Nahum M. Waldman, 'The Breaking of the Bow', *JQR* 69 (1978), pp. 82-88.

301. *Ibid.*, p. 60. The text is I.A.38-39.

302. *Ibid.*

303. See above, note 287.

304. On the tradio-historical background see Hanson, 'Zechariah 9', and Magne Saebø, *Sacharja 9-14*, pp. 175-88. They both associate this text with holy war tradition. Benedikt Otzen, on the other hand, associates it with the New Year festival of enthronement (*Studien über Deutero-Sacharja* [Acta Theologica Danica, 6; Copenhagen: Prostant Apud Munksgaard, 1964], pp. 134-45).

305. Luckenbill, *Ancient Records*, #987. This notion of an age of peace following on the accession of the appropriate king is further developed in the 'Akkadian prophecies'. See the recent works of Rykle Borger, 'Gott Marduk

und Gott-König Sulgi als Propheten', *BO* 29 (1971), pp. 3-24; A.K. Grayson, *Babylonian Historical-Literary Texts* (Toronto Semitic Texts and Studies, 3; Toronto: University of Toronto, 1975); Hermann Hunger and Stephen A. Kaufman, 'A New Akkadian Prophecy Text', *JAOS* 95 (1975), pp. 371-75.

306. I say 'radicalized' in Isaiah, because while it is not absolutely certain that Yahweh's exclusive prerogative excludes military action on the part of the king in Pss 20, 33 and 44 (though this is commonly asserted; cf. Bach, '"... Der Bogen zerbricht"', pp. 21-22), in Isaiah this exclusion is stated with clarity. Cf. Herbert Donner, *Israel unter den Völkern*, pp. 168-73.

Notes to Chapter 5

1. Juan Luis Segundo, *Liberation of Theology*, trans. by John Drury (Maryknoll: Orbis, 1976), pp. 112-13. See also Elisabeth Schüssler Fiorenza, 'Toward a Feminist Biblical Hermeneutics; Biblical Interpretation and Liberation Theology', in *The Challenge of Liberation Theology: A First World Response*, ed. by Brian Mahan and L. Dale Richesin (Maryknoll: Orbis, 1981), pp. 91-112.

2. For one of the more enlightened studies on the relation of the Bible to ethics see James Gustafson, 'The Place of Scripture in Christian Ethics: A Methodological Approach', *Interpretation* 24 (1970), pp. 430-55. Dale Patrick speaks of 'Political Exegesis' (in *Encounter with the Text: Form and History in the Hebrew Bible*, ed. by Martin J. Buss [SBL Semeia Supplements; Philadelphia: Fortress, 1979], pp. 139-52), but it is unclear just what is and is not meant by the term.

3. See the seminal study of Gerhard von Rad, 'Das formgeschichtliche Problem des Hexateuch', in *Gesammelte Studien zum Alten Testament* (TBü, 8; München: Chr. Kaiser, third edition, 1965), pp. 9-86. (ET: 'The Form-Critical Problem of the Hexateuch', in *The Form Critical Problem of the Hexateuch and Other Essays*, trans. by E.W.T. Dicken [Edinburgh: Oliver & Boyd, 1966], pp. 1-78).

4. *Rich Christians in an Age of Hunger: A Biblical Study* (Downers Grove: Intervarsity Press, 1977), p. 61.

5. This assertion has to be qualified with reference to those who are principally concerned with the liberation of women in North America. See the themes selected for study by Phyllis Trible, *God and the Rhetoric of Sexuality* (Overtures to Biblical Theology; Philadelphia: Fortress, 1978).

6. Gustavo Guttierez, *A Theology of Liberation: History, Politics and Salvation*, trans. by Sr. Caridad Inda and John Eagleson (Maryknoll: Orbis, 1973), p. 155. On the use of the Exodus in theologies of liberation see J. Andrew Kirk, *Liberation Theology: An Evangelical View from the Third World* (New Foundations Theological Library; Atlanta: John Knox, 1979), pp. 95-103. See also Segundo, *Liberation of Theology*, pp. 110-24.

7. *Exodus: A Hermeneutics of Freedom*, trans. by Salvator Attanasio (Maryknoll: Orbis, 1981), p. 11. The emphasis is his.

8. For a critique of some aspects of the use of the Exodus by liberation theologians see John Howard Yoder, 'Exodus and Exile: The Two Faces of Liberation', *Missionalia* 2 (1974), pp. 29-41. Yoder's critique is directed to the discussion of liberation in the World Council of Churches. See also Hans-Joachim Kraus, 'Das Thema, "Exodus": Kritische Erwägungen zur Usurpation eines biblischen Begriffs', in *Biblischtheologische Aufsätze* (Neukirchen-Vluyn: Neukirchener Verlag, 1972), pp. 102-19. Kraus's remarks are directed principally against Ernst Bloch.

9. For an early example see Leonhard Rost, 'Sinaibund und Davidsbund', *TLZ* 72 (1947), pp. 129-34.

10. Mendenhall, 'The Monarchy', *Interpretation* 29 (1975), pp. 155-70.

11. Brueggemann, 'Trajectories in Old Testament Literature and the Sociology of Ancient Israel', *JBL* 98 (1979), pp. 161-85. Brueggemann utilizes this polarization in other of his works: *The Land* (Overtures to Biblical Theology; Philadelphia: Fortress, 1977); *The Prophetic Imagination* (Philadelphia: Fortress, 1978); 'The Crisis and Promise of Presence in Israel', *HBT* 1 (1979), pp. 47-86. He makes it the basis for conceptualizing Old Testament theology in 'A Convergence in Recent Old Testament Theologies', *JSOT* 18 (1980), pp. 2-18.

12. Brueggemann, 'Trajectories', p. 180.

13. *Ibid.*, p. 180. Cf. Brueggemann, 'The Epistemological Crisis of Israel's Two Histories', in *Israelite Wisdom: Theological and Literary Essays in Honor of Samuel Terrien*, ed. by John G. Gammie, Walter Brueggemann, W. Lee Humphreys and J.M. Ward (Missoula: Scholars Press, 1978), pp. 85-105, see especially p. 101, note 18.

14. Brueggemann, 'Trajectories', p. 171.

15. Brueggemann, 'Epistemological Crisis', p. 88. The emphasis is his. He goes on to say that 'the question of *prudence* and *singular reliance* focuses the epistemological issue' between the two traditions (*ibid.*). In his earlier work, *In Man We Trust: The Neglected Side of Biblical Faith* (Richmond: John Knox, 1972), Brueggemann seemed to consider a virtue what he now deems a vice. See also 'The Triumphalist Tendency in Exegetical History', *JAAR* 38 (1970), pp. 367-80. He concludes this article by suggesting that 'the major new direction in Old Testament theology which now stands at the focus of fresh investigation is study in the wisdom traditions . . . Our time calls for a form of biblical study which works at questions of faith and life-style without great stress on salvation history, an intruding God, authoritarian forms of guidance, and all that has been associated with the hypothesis regnant for the last two decades' (p. 378). See his words to the contrary quoted above.

16. Brueggemann, 'Epistemological Crisis', p. 87.

17. Brueggemann, 'Trajectories', p. 173.

18. The same could be said of the term 'justice'. A quick check of the

concordance reveals how firmly it is rooted in the Jerusalem tradition. Justice, we may even argue, presupposes a theology of creation. See H.H. Schmid, 'Schöpfung, Gerechtigkeit und Heil: "Schöpfungstheologie" als Gesamthorizont biblischer Theologie', *ZTK* 70 (1973), pp. 1-19.

19. I refer again to my remarks at the beginning of this chapter. If social location is significant for biblical interpretation then it is important that we should not fool ourselves into thinking that we, as North American Christians and theologians, are oppressed. Whatever the degree of our 'relative deprivation', it is only self-deception to think that our situation is in some sense the same as that of, say, Segundo, who is (or was) forbidden by the government to be present in any assembly of more than five persons.

20. See Schmid, 'Schöpfung, Gerechtigkeit und Heil'; Rolf Knierim, 'Cosmos and History in Israel's Theology', *HBT* 3 (1981), pp. 59-123.

21. Croatto, *Exodus*, p. 42. Croatto does not spell out what is the theological basis of this critique in Isaiah.

22. See the works cited in note 20, above, and in note 32, below.

23. If, as Brueggemann and others suggest, the ancient Near Eastern treaty background to the covenant tradition is to be followed, then this illustrates that it is the order established by a suzerain that the vassal partner in a covenant is obligated to honor and observe. Thus the decalogue could be understood as the pattern of the social order commensurate with the suzerain Yahweh and, we may suppose, commensurate with the order of his creation.

24. Clifford Geertz, 'Religion as a Cultural System', in *The Interpretation of Cultures* (New York: Basic Books, 1973), pp. 87-125, especially p. 121.

25. This does not mean, of course, that once a choice is made all policy options are clear. It means at least, however, that certain options are clearly excluded.

26. I am not arguing that the Exodus tradition has nothing to offer North American Christians, or that the Zion tradition has nothing to offer Latin American Christians. However, if the Exodus has a special relevance to the oppressed, then Zion has a special relevance to those who oppress them.

27. A serious hermeneutical treatment of the interpretation of Zion symbolism for the present would have to show clearly that the application of that symbolism cannot be made without some consideration of the church's relation to the Old Testament generally. I take it as axiomatic, however, that the theology focused by Old Testament symbolism is in some sense normative for the life of the Christian community. In what precise *sense* it is normative I here leave unspecified.

28. Daniel L. Migliore, *Called to Freedom: Liberation Theology and the Future of Christian Doctrine* (Philadelphia: Westminster, 1980), p. 72.

29. It should also be pointed out that 'king' is not the only image of God used in Zion texts. In Isa 49.15 Yahweh is a mother whose breasts nourish Zion; in Isa 54.6 Yahweh is Zion's grieving wife (although in 54.5 he is Zion's

husband); in 66.13 Yahweh is a mother comforting the children returned to her in Zion. See Trible, *God and the Rhetoric of Sexuality*, pp. 22, 51-52.

30. Karl Barth, *Church Dogmatics: A Selection*, trans. and ed. by G.W. Bromiley (New York: Harper Torchbooks, 1961), p. 154.

31. Whether, or the degree to which, natural theology is justified is a matter to be decided on systematic theological grounds which I cannot, and hence will not, debate.

32. See H.H. Schmid, *Gerechtigkeit als Weltordnung: Hintergrund und Geschichte des alttestamentlichen Gerechtigkeitsbegriffes* (BHT; Tübingen: J.C.B. Mohr, 1968); 'Altorientalische *Welt in der* alttestamentlichen *Theologie*', in *Altorientalische Welt in der alttestamentlichen Theologie*' (Zürich: Theologischer Verlag, 1974), pp. 145-64.

33. This claim, as stated, has nothing to do with the question of whether the primary form of Israel's theology was historical narration. They are, in my view, two distinct issues.

BIBLIOGRAPHY

A. *Primary sources and linguistic aids*

Aistleitner, J. *Die mythologischen und kultischen Texte aus Ras Schamra*. Budapest: Akademiai Kiado, second edition, 1964.

Brown, Francis; Driver, S.R.; and Briggs, C.A. *A Hebrew and English Lexicon of the Old Testament With an Appendix Containing the Biblical Aramaic*. London: Oxford University Press, 1907.

Biblia Hebraica. Edited by Rudolf Kittel. Stuttgart: Württembergische Bibelanstalt, third edition, 1937.

Biblia Hebraica Stuttgartensia. Edited by K. Elliger and W. Rudolph. Stuttgart: Deutsche Bibelstiftung, 1977.

Brockelmann, Carl. *Hebräische Syntax*. Neukirchen: Verlag des Erziehungsvereins, 1956.

Donner, H., and Röllig, W. *Kanaanäische und aramäische Inschriften*. 3 vols. Wiesbaden: Otto Harrassowitz, 1971.

Driver, G.R. *Canaanite Myths and Legends*. Old Testament Studies, 3. Edinburgh: T. & T. Clark, 1956.

Falkenstein, A., and von Soden, W. *Sumerische und Akkadische Hymnen und Gebete*. Die Bibliothek der alten Welt. Zürich: Artemis Verlag, 1953.

Gibson, J.C.L. *Canaanite Myths and Legends*. Edinburgh: T. & T. Clark, second edition, 1978.

Gordon, C.H. *Ugaritic Textbook*. 3 vols. Analecta Orientalia, 38. Rome: Pontifical Biblical Institute, 1965.

Grayson, A.K. *Assyrian Royal Inscriptions*. 2 vols. RANE. Wiesbaden: Otto Harrassowitz, 1972.

Herdner, Andrée. *Corpus des tablettes en cunéiformes alphabétiques découvertes à Ras Shamra-Ugarit de 1929 à 1939*. 2 vols. Paris: Imprimerie Nationale, 1963.

—'Une prière à Baal des Ugaritiains en danger', *CRAIBL* (1973), pp. 693-97.

Kautzsch, E. *Gesenius' Hebrew Grammar*. Translated and edited by A.E. Cowley. London: Oxford University Press, 1910.

Langdon, S. *Babylonian Penitential Psalms*. OECT, 6. Paris: Paul Geuthner, 1927.

Liddell, H.G., and Scott, R. *A Greek-English Lexicon*. Edited by H.S. Jones and R. McKenzie. London: Oxford University Press, ninth edition, 1940.

Luckenbill, Daniel David. *Ancient Records of Assyria and Babylon*. 2 vols. Chicago: University of Chicago Press, 1927.

Mandelkern, Solomon. *Veteris Testamenti Concordantiae Hebraicae atque Chaldaicae*. Jerusalem: Schocken, 1978.

Pritchard, James B., ed. *Ancient Near Eastern Texts Relating to the Old Testament*. Princeton: Princeton University Press, third edition, 1969.

Rahlfs, Alfred. *Septuaginta: Id est Vetus Testamentum Graece iuxta LXX Interpretes*. 2 vols. Stuttgart: Württembergische Bibelanstalt, 1935.

Scrolls from Qumran Cave I: The Great Isaiah Scroll, the Order of the Community, the Pesher to Habakkuk. From Photographs by John C. Trever. Jerusalem: The Albright Institute of Archaeological Research and the Shrine of the Book, 1974.

Williams, Ronald J. *Hebrew Syntax: An Outline.* Toronto: University of Toronto Press, second edition, 1976.

Ziegler, Joseph. *Isaias.* Septuaginta, 14. Göttingen: Vandenhoeck & Ruprecht, 1939.

B. Secondary sources

Aartun, Kjell. 'Hebräisch *'ani* and *'anaw'*, *BO* 28 (1971), pp. 125-26.

— 'Studien zum Gestez über den grossen Versöhnungstag Lev 16 mit Varianten', *ST* 34 (1980), pp. 73-109.

Ackerman, J.S. 'Prophecy and Warfare in Early Israel: A Study of the Deborah-Barak Story', *BASOR* 220 (1975), pp. 5-13.

Ackroyd, Peter R. 'Isaiah I-XII: Presentation of a Prophet', *VTS* 29 (1978), pp. 16-48.

Aharoni, Yohanan. 'Arad: Its Inscriptions and Temple', *BA* 31 (1968), pp. 2-32.

Albrektson, Bertil. *Studies in the Text and Theology of the Book of Lamentations.* STL, 21. Lund: CWK Gleerup, 1963.

Albright, W.F. *Yahweh and the Gods of Canaan: A Historical Analysis of Two Contrasting Faiths.* London: Athlone, 1968.

Alt, Albrecht. 'The Formation of the Israelite State in Palestine', *Essays on Old Testament History and Religion.* Translated by R.A. Wilson. Garden City: Anchor Books, 1968, pp. 225-309.

— 'Gedanken über das Königtum Jahwes', *Kleine Schriften zur Geschichte des Volkes Israel*, I. München: C.H. Beck, 1959, pp. 345-57.

— 'Jes. 8.23-9.6', *Kleine Schriften zur Geschichte des Volkes Israel*, II. München: C.H. Beck, 1959, pp. 206-25.

— 'Das Königtum in den Reichen Israel und Juda', *VT* 1 (1951), pp. 1-22.

— 'The Origins of Israelite Law', *Essays on Old Testament History and Religion.* Translated by R.A. Wilson. Garden City: Anchor Books, 1968., pp. 101-71.

Anderson, A.A. *The Book of Psalms.* 2 vols. NCB. London: Oliphants, 1972.

Anderson, Bernhard W. 'Exodus and Covenant in Second Isaiah and Prophetic Tradition', *Magnalia Dei: The Mighty Acts of God. G. Ernest Wright in Memoriam.* Edited by F.M. Cross, W.E. Lemke, P.D. Miller. Garden City: Doubleday, 1976, pp. 339-60.

— 'Exodus Typology in Second Isaiah', *Israel's Prophetic Heritage: Essays in Honor of James Muilenburg.* Edited by B.W. Anderson and Walter Harrelson. New York: Harper & Row, 1962, pp. 177-95.

— 'The Messiah as Son of God: Peter's Confession in Traditio-historical Perspective', *Christological Perspectives: Essays in Honor of Harvey K. McArthur.* Edited by Robert F. Berkey and Sarah Edwards. New York: Pilgrim, 1982, pp. 157-69.

— *Out of the Depths: The Psalms Speak for Us Today.* Philadelphia: Westminster, 1974.

— 'Tradition and Scripture in the Community of Faith', *JBL* 100 (1981), pp. 5-21.

Ap-Thomas, D.R. 'All the King's Horses', *Proclamation and Presence: Essays in Honour of G. Henton Davies.* Edited by J.L. Durham and J.R. Porter: Richmond: John Knox, 1970, pp. 131-51.

Bach, Robert. *Die Aufforderungen zur Flucht und zum Kampf im alttestamentlichen Prophetenspruch.* WMANT, 9. Neukirchen-Vluyn: Neukirchener Verlag, 1962.

— '". . .Der Bogen zerbricht, Spiesse zerschlägt und Wagen mit Feuer verbrennt"', *Probleme Biblischer Theologie.* Gerhard von Rad zum 70. Geburtstag. Edited by Hans Walter Wolff. München: Chr. Kaiser, 1971, pp. 13-26.

Bächli, Otto. *Israel und die Völker: Eine Studie zum Deuteronomium.* ATANT, 41. Zürich: Theologischer Verlag, 1962.

Barker, Margaret. 'The Two Figures in Zecharia', *HeyJ* 18 (1977), pp. 38-46.

Barth, Herrmann. *Die Jesaja-Worte in der Josiazeit: Israel und Assur als Thema einer produktiven Neuinterpretation der Jesajaüberlieferung*. AMANT, 48. Neukirchen-Vluyn: Neukirchener Verlag, 1977.

Barth, Karl. *Church Dogmatics: A Selection*. Translated and edited by G.W. Bromiley. New York: Harper Torchbooks, 1961.

Barton, John. 'Ethics in Isaiah of Jerusalem', *JTS* 32 (1981), pp. 1-18.

Beck, B. 'Kontextanalysen zum Verb *bṭḥ*. . .', *Bausteine Biblischer Theologie: Festschrift für G. Johannes Botterweck*. BBB, 50. Köln: Peter Hanstein, 1977, pp. 71-98.

Becker, Joachim. *Israel deutet seine Psalmen*. SBS, 18. Stuttgart: Katholisches Bibelwerk, 1967.

—*Messianic Expectation in the Old Testament*. Translated by David E. Green. Philadelphia: Fortress, 1980.

Beeston, A.F.L. 'Angels in Deuteronomy 33.2', *JTS* 2 (1951), pp. 30-31.

Begrich, Joachim. 'MABBUL, Eine exegetisch-lexikalische Studie', *Gesammelte Studien zum alten Testament*. TBü, 21. München: Chr. Kaiser, 1964, pp. 39-54.

Bernhardt, Karl-Heinz. *Das Problem der altorientalischen Königsideologie im Alten Testament*. VTS, 8. Leiden: E.J. Brill, 1961.

Bertram, Georg. '"Hochmut" und verwandte Begriffe im griechischen und hebräischen Alten Testament', *WdO* 3 (1964/66), pp. 32-43.

Beyerlin, Walter. *Die Rettung der Bedrängten in den Feindpsalmen der Einzelnen auf institutionelle Zusammenhänge untersucht*. FRLANT, 99. Göttingen: Vandenhoeck & Ruprecht, 1970.

Birch, Bruce C. *The Rise of the Israelite Monarchy: The Growth and Development of 1 Samuel 7-15*. SBLDS, 17. Missoula: Scholars Press, 1976.

Black, J.A. 'The New Year Ceremonies in Ancient Babylon: "Taking Bel by the Hand" and a Cultic Picnic', *Religion* 11 (1981), pp. 39-60.

Blenkinsopp, Joseph. 'Fragments of Ancient Exegesis in an Isaian Poem', *ZAW* 93 (1981), pp. 51-62.

—*Gibeon and Israel: The Role of Gibeon and the Gibeonites in the Political and Religious History of Israel*. SOTSMS, 2. Cambridge: Cambridge University Press, 1972.

Boecker, Hans Jochen. *Die Beurteilung der Anfänge des Königtums in den deuteronomistischen Abschnitten des 1. Samuelbuches*. WMANT, 31. Neukirchen-Vluyn: Neukirchener Verlag, 1969.

Boer, P.A.H. de. 'Einige Bemerkungen und Gedanken zum Lied 1. Samuel II 1-10', *Beiträge zur alttestamentlichen Theologie. W. Zimmerli zum 70. Geburtstag*. Edited by H. Donner, R. Hanhart and R. Smend. Göttingen: Vandenhoeck & Ruprecht, 1977, pp. 53-59.

Boling, Robert G. *Judges*. AB. Garden City: Doubleday, 1975.

Borger, Rykle. 'Gott Marduk und Gott-König Sulgi als Propheten. Zwei prophetische Texte', *BO* 29 (1971), pp. 3-24.

Botterweck, G. Johannes. '*'ebhyon*', *Theological Dictionary of the Old Testament*, I. Edited by G.J. Botterweck and H. Ringgren. Translated by John T. Willis. Grand Rapids: Eerdmans, revised edition, 1977, pp. 27-41.

Braulik, Georg. *Psalm 40 und der Gottesknecht*. Forschung zur Bibel, 18. Würzburg: Echter Verlag, 1975.

Bright, John. *Covenant and Promise: The Prophetic Understanding of the Future in Pre-Exilic Israel*. Philadelphia: Westminster, 1976.

—*Jeremiah*. AB. Garden City: Doubleday, 1965.

Brueggemann, Walter. 'A Convergence in Recent Old Testament Theologies', *JSOT* 18 (1980), pp. 2-18.

—'The Crisis and Promise of Presence in Israel', *HBT* 1 (1979), pp. 47-86.

—'The Epistemological Crisis of Israel's Two Histories', *Israelite Wisdom: Theological and Literary Essays in Honor of Samuel Terrien*. Edited by John G. Gammie, Walter Brueggemann, W. Lee Humphreys and J.M. Ward. Missoula: Scholars Press, 1978, pp. 85-105.

—*The Land*. Overtures to Biblical Theology. Philadelphia: Fortress, 1977.

—*In Man We Trust: The Neglected Side of Biblical Faith*. Richmond: John Knox, 1972.

—*The Prophetic Imagination*. Philadelphia: Fortress, 1978.

—'Trajectories in Old Testament Literature and the Sociology of Ancient Israel', *JBL* 98 (1979), pp. 161-85.

—'The Triumphalist Tendency in Exegetical History', *JAAR* 38 (1979), pp. 367-80.

Buber, Martin. *Königtum Gottes*. Heidelberg: Lambert Schneider, third edition, 1956. ET: *Kingship of God*. Translated by Richard Scheimann. New York: Harper & Row, 1967.

Buss, Martin J. 'The Psalms of Asaph and Korah', *JBL* 82 (1936), pp. 382-92.

Carroll, R.P. 'Psalm 78: Vestiges of a Tribal Polemic', *VT* 21 (1971), pp. 133-50.

Cathcart, Kevin J. 'Kingship and the "Day of YHWH" in Isaiah 2.6-22', *Hermathena* 125 (1978), pp. 48-59.

Causse, Antonin. *Du groupe éthnique à la communauté religieuse*. Paris: Librairie Felix Alcan, 1937.

Cazelles, Henri. 'Qui aurait visé, à l'origine, Isaïe II 2-5?', *VT* 30 (1980), pp. 409-20.

Childs, Brevard. *The Book of Exodus: A Critical Theological Commentary*. OTL. Philadelphia: Westminster, 1974.

—*Isaiah and the Assyrian Crisis*. SBT 2/3. London: SCM, 1967.

Christenson, Duane L. *Transformations of the War Oracle in Old Testament Prophecy*. HDR 3. Cambridge, Mass: Harvard University Press, 1975.

Clements, R.E. 'The Deuteronomistic Interpretation of the Founding of the Monarchy in 1 Sam viii', *VT* 24 (1974), pp. 398-410.

—'Deuteronomy and the Jerusalem Cult Tradition', *VT* 15 (1965), pp. 300-12.

—*God and Temple: The Presence of God in Israel's Worship*. Philadelphia: Fortress, 1965.

—*Isaiah 1-39*. NCB. London: Marshall, Morgan & Scott, 1980.

—*Isaiah and the Deliverance of Jerusalem*. JSOT Supplement Series, 13. Sheffield: JSOT Press, 1980.

—*One Hundred Years of Old Testament Interpretation*. Philadelphia: Westminster, 1976.

Clines, D.J.A. 'The Evidence for an Autumnal New Year in Pre-Exilic Israel Reconsidered', *JBL* 93 (1974), pp. 22-40.

—'New Year', *The Interpreter's Dictionary of the Bible: Supplementary Volume*. Edited by Keith Crim. Nashville: Abingdon, 1976, pp. 625-29.

Cody, Aelred. *A History of Old Testament Priesthood*. AnBib, 35. Rome: Pontifical Biblical Institute, 1969.

Cogan, Morton. *Imperialism and Religion: Assyria, Judah and Israel in the Eighth and Seventh Centuries BCE*. SBLMS, 19. Missoula: Scholars Press, 1974.

Cohen, M.A. 'The Role of the Shilonite Priesthood in the United Monarchy of Ancient Israel', *HUCA* 36 (1965), pp. 39-98.

Cohn, Robert L. 'Jerusalem: The Senses of a Center', *JAAR* 26 (1978), pp. 1-26.

—*The Shape of Sacred Space: Four Biblical Studies*. AAR Studies in Religion, 3. Chico: Scholars Press, 1981.

Conrad, Edgar W. 'Second Isaiah and the Priestly Oracle of Salvation', *ZAW* 93 (1981), pp. 234-46.

Craigie, Peter C. *The Book of Deuteronomy*. NICOT. Grand Rapids: Eerdmans, 1976.

—*The Problem of War in the Old Testament*. Grand Rapids: Eerdmans, 1978.

Croatto, J. Severino. *Exodus: A Hermeneutics of Freedom*. Translated by Salvator Attanasio. Maryknoll: Orbus, 1981.

Cross, Frank M. *Canaanite Myth and Hebrew Epic*. Cambridge, Mass.: Harvard University Press, 1973.

—'Notes on a Canaanite Psalm in the Old Testament', *BASOR* 117 (1950), pp. 19-21.

—'The Priestly Tabernacle in the Light of Recent Research', *Temples and High Places in Biblical Times*. Jerusalem: Hebrew Union College/Jewish Institute of Religion, 1981, pp. 169-80.

—'Yahweh and the God of the Patriarchs', *HTR* 55 (1962), pp. 236-56.

—and Freedman, David Noel. *Studies in Ancient Yahwistic Poetry*. SBLDS, 21. Missoula: Scholars Press, 1975.

Crüsemann, Frank. *Studien zur Formgeschichte von Hymnus und Danklied in Israel*. WMANT, 32. Neukirchen-Vluyn: Neukirchener Verlag, 1969.

—*Der Widerstand gegen das Königtum: Die antiköniglichen Texte des Alten Testaments und der Kampf um den frühen israelitischen Staat*. WMANT, 49. Neukirchen-Vluyn: Neukirchener Verlag, 1978.

Curtis, A.H.W. 'The "Subjugation of the Waters" Motif in the Psalms: Imagery or Polemic?', *JBS* 23 (1978), pp. 245-56.

Dahood, Mitchell. *Psalms I: 1-50*. AB. Garden City: Doubleday, 1966.

—*Psalms II: 51-100*. AB. Garden City: Doubleday, 1968.

—*Psalms III: 101-50*. AB. Garden City: Doubleday, 1970.

Davies, G. Henton. 'The Ark in the Psalms', *Promise and Fulfilment: Essays Presented to Professor S.H. Hooke*. Edited by F.F. Bruce. Edinburgh: T. & T. Clark, 1963, pp. 51-61.

—'Psalm 95', *ZAW* 85 (1973), pp. 183-95.

Day, John. 'Shear-Jashub (Isaiah VII 3) and "the Remnant of Wrath" (Psalm LXXVIII)', *VT* 31 (1981), pp. 76-78.

Deissler, Alfons. 'Das Israel der Psalmen als Gottesvolk der Hoffenden', *Die Zeit Jesu: Festschrift für Heinrich Schlier*. Edited by G. Bornkamm and Karl Rahner. Freiburg: Herder & Herder, 1970, pp. 15-37.

Deist, F.E. 'Notes on the Structure of Isa. 2.2-22', *ThEv* 10 (1977), pp. 1-6.

Delekat, L. 'Zum hebräischen Wörterbuch', *VT* 14 (1964), pp. 7-66.

Derrett, J.D.M. '"The Stone that the Builders Rejected"', *Studies in the New Testament*, II: *Midrash in Action and as a Literary Device*. Leiden: E.J. Brill, 1978, pp. 60-67.

Dietrich, Walter. 'Gott als König', *ZTK* 77 (1980), pp. 251-68.

—*Jesaja und die Politik*. BEvT, 74. München: Chr. Kaiser, 1976.

Donner, Herbert. *Israel unter den Völkern: Die Stellung der klassischen Propheten des 8. Jahrhunderts v. Chr. zur Aussenpolitik der Könige von Israel und Juda*. VTS, 11. Leiden: E.J. Brill, 1964.

Driver, G.R. '"Another Little Drink"—Isaiah 28.1-22', *Words and Meanings: Essays Presented to David Winton Thomas*. Edited by P.R. Ackroyd and Barnabas Lindars. Cambridge: Cambridge University Press, 1968, pp. 47-67.

Duhm, Bernhard. *Das Buch Jesaja*. HKAT. Göttingen: Vandenhoeck & Ruprecht, fifth edition, 1969.

Eaton, John H. *Festal Drama in Deutero-Isaiah*. London: SPCK, 1979.

—*Kingship and the Psalms*. SBT 2/32. London: SCM, 1976.

Eichhorn, Dieter. *Gott als Fels, Burg und Zuflucht: Eine Untersuchung zum Gebet des Mittlers in den Psalmen*. Europäische Hochschulschriften, 23/4. Bern: Herbert Lang, 1972.

Eichrodt, Walther. *Der Heilige in Israel: Jesaja 1–12 übersetzt und ausgelegt*. Die Botschaft des alten Testament, 17/1. Stuttgart: Calwer Verlag, 1960.

—'Prophet and Covenant: Observations on the Exegesis of Isaiah', *Proclamation and Presence: Essays in Honour of G. Henton Davies*. Edited by J.L. Durham and J.R. Porter. Richmond: John Knox, 1970, pp. 167-88.

Eickelpasch, Rolf. *Mythos und Sozialstruktur*. Studien zur Sozialwissenschaft, 7. Düsseldorf: Bertelsmann Universitätsverlag, 1977.

Eiler, David L. 'The Origin and History of Zion as a Theological Symbol'. Unpublished Th.D. dissertation, Princeton Theological Seminary, 1978.

Eissfeldt, Otto. 'El und Jahweh', *Kleine Schriften*, III. Edited by Rudolf Sellheim and Fritz Maass. Tübingen: J.C.B. Mohr, 1966, pp. 386-97.

—'Jahwe Zebaoth', *Kleine Schriften*, III. Edited by Rudolf Sellheim and Fritz Maass. Tübingen: J.C.B. Mohr, 1966, pp. 103-23.

—'Kultzelt und Tempel', *Kleine Schriften*, VI. Edited by Rudolf Sellheim and Fritz Maass. Tübingen: J.C.B. Mohr, 1979, pp. 1-7.

—'Die Lade Jahwes in Geschichtserzählung, Sage und Lied', *Kleine Schriften*, V. Edited by Rudolf Sellheim and Fritz Maass. Tübingen: J.C.B. Mohr, 1973, pp. 77-93.

—'Monopol-Ansprüche des Heiligtums von Silo', *Kleine Schriften*, VI. Edited by Rudolf Sellheim and Fritz Maass. Tübingen: J.C.B. Mohr, 1979, pp. 8-14.

—'Jahwes Königsprädizierung als Verklärung national-politischer Ansprüche Israels', *Kleine Schriften*, V. Edited by Rudolf Sellheim and Fritz Maass. Tübingen: J.C.B. Mohr, 1973, pp. 216-21.

—*The Old Testament: An Introduction*. Translated by P.R. Ackroyd. New York: Harper & Row, 1965.

—'Psalm 76', *Kleine Schriften*, III. Edited by Rudolf Sellheim and Fritz Maass. Tübingen: J.C.B. Mohr, 1966, pp. 448-57.

—'Silo und Jerusalem', *Kleine Schriften*, III. Edited by Rudolf Sellheim and Fritz Maass. Tübingen: J.C.B. Mohr, 1966, pp. 417-25.

—*Zeus Kasios und der Durchzug der Israeliten durchs Meer*. BRGA, 1. Halle Max Niemeyer, 1932.

Elliger, Karl. 'Prophet und Politik', *ZAW* 53 (1935), pp. 3-22

Ellis, R.S. *Foundation Deposits in Ancient Mesopotamia*. New Haven: Yale University Press, 1968.

Engnell, Ivan. *Studies in Divine Kingship in the Ancient Near East*. Uppsala: Almqvist & Wiksell, 1943.

Erlandsson, S. *The Burden of Babylon: A Study of Isaiah 13.2-14.32*. ConBOT, 4. Lund: CWK Gleerup, 1970.

Fiorenza, Elisabeth Schüssler. 'Toward a Feminist Biblical Hermeneutics: Biblical Interpretation and Liberation Theology', *The Challenge of Liberation Theology: A First World Response*. Edited by Brian Mahan and L. Dale Richesin. Maryknoll: Orbis, 1981, pp. 91-112.

Firth, Raymond. *Symbols: Public and Private*. Ithaca: Cornell University Press, 1973.

Fisher, Loren R. 'Creation at Ugarit and in the Old Testament', *VT* 15 (1965), pp. 313-24.

— 'From Chaos to Cosmos', *Encounter* 26 (1975), pp. 183-97.

— and Knutson, Brent. 'An Enthronement Ritual at Ugarit', *JNES* 28 (1967), pp. 157-67.

Fitzmyer, Joseph A. *Essays on the Semitic Background of the New Testament.* Missoula: Scholars Press, 1974.

Fohrer, Georg. *History of Israelite Religion.* Translated by David E. Green. Nashville: Abingdon, 1972.

— 'Die Ladeerzählung', *JNWSL* 1 (1971), pp. 23-31.

— 'Wandlungen Jesajas', *Studien zu alttestamentlichen Texten und Themen (1966-1972).* BZAW, 155. Berlin: Walter de Gruyter, 1981, pp. 11-23.

Fraine, Jean de. *L'Aspect religieux de la royauté Israélite.* AnBib, 3. Rome: Pontifical Biblical Institute, 1954.

— 'La Royauté de Yahvé dans les textes concernant l'arche', *VTS* 15 (1966), pp. 139-44.

Frankfort, Henri. *Kingship and the Gods: A Study of Ancient Near Eastern Religion as the Integration of Society and Nature.* Chicago: University of Chicago Press, 1948.

Freedman, David Noel. 'Divine Names and Titles in Early Hebrew Poetry', *Magnalia Dei: The Mighty Acts of God. G. Ernest Wright in Memoriam.* Edited by F.M. Cross, W.E. Lemke and P.D. Miller. Garden City: Doubleday, 1976, pp. 55-102.

— 'Early Israelite History in the Light of Early Israelite Poetry', *Unity and Diversity: Essays in the History, Literature and Religion of the Ancient Near East.* Edited by Hans Goedicke and J.J.M. Roberts. Johns Hopkins Near Eastern Studies. Baltimore: Johns Hopkins University Press, 1975, pp. 3-35.

— 'Psalm 113 and the Song of Hannah', *Eretz Isrel* 14 (1978), pp. 56*-69*.

Fretheim, T.E. 'The Cultic Use of the Ark of the Covenant in the Monarchial Period'. Unpublished Th.D. dissertation. Princeton Theological Seminary, 1967.

— 'Psalm 132: A Form-Critical Study', *JBL* 86 (1967), pp. 289-300.

Fulco, William J. *The Canaanite God Resep.* AOS. New Haven: American Oriental Society, 1976.

Galling, Kurt. 'Die Ausrufung des Namens als Rechtsakt in Israel', *TLZ* 81 (1956), pp. 65-70.

— 'Serubbabel und der Wiederaufbau des Tempels in Jerusalem', *Verbannung und Heimkehr: Beiträge zur Geschichte und Theologie Israels im 6. und 5. Jahrhundert v. Chr. Festschrift für W. Rudolph.* Edited by Arnulf Kuschke. Tübingen: J.C.B. Mohr, 1961, pp. 67-96.

Gaster, T.H. 'Angels', *Interpreter's Dictionary of the Bible*, I. Edited by George Arthur Buttrick. Nashville: Abingdon, 1962, pp. 128-34.

Geertz, Clifford. *The Interpretation of Cultures.* New York: Basic Books, 1973.

Gerleman, Gillis. 'Psalm 110', *VT* 31 (1981), pp. 1-19.

Gerstenberger, Erhard. 'Psalms', *Old Testament Form Criticism.* Edited by John H. Hayes. TUMSR, 2. San Antonio: Trinity University Press, 1974, pp. 179-223.

— '*bṭḥ* vertrauen', *Theologisches Handwörterbuch des alten Testaments*, I. Edited by E. Jenni and C. Westermann. München: Chr. Kaiser, 1971, pp. 300-305.

— '*ḥsh* sich bergen', *Theologisches Handwörterbuch des alten Testaments*, I. Edited by E. Janni and C. Westermann. München: Chr. Kaiser, 1971, pp. 621-23.

Gese, Hartmut. 'Der Davidsbund und die Zionserwählung', *Vom Sinai zum Zion: Beiträge zur biblischen Theologie.* BEvT, 64. München: Chr. Kaiser, 1974, pp. 113-29.

—*Die Religionen Altsyriens*. Die Religionen der Menschheit, 10/2. Stuttgart: W. Kohlhammer, 1970.

Ginsberg, H.L. 'Some Emendation in Psalms', *HUCA* 22 (1950), pp. 97-104.

Glock, Albert E. 'Early Israel as the Kingdom of Yahweh. The Influence of Archaeological Evidence on the Reconstruction of Religion in Early Israel', *CTM* 41 (1970), pp. 558-605.

Gnuse, Robert. 'Calf, Cult and King: The Unity of Hosea 8.1-13', *BZ* 26 (1982), pp. 83-92.

Gordis, Robert. 'Psalm 9-10—A Textual-Exegetical Study', *The Word and the Book: Studies in Biblical Language and Literature*. New York: KTAV, 1976, pp. 114-32.

Görg, Manfred. *Gott-König-Reden in Israel und Ägypten*. BWANT, 105. Stuttgart: W. Kohlhammer, 1975.

Gottwald, Norman K. *The Tribes of Yahweh: A Sociology of the Religion of Liberated Israel, 1250-1050 BCE*. Maryknoll: Orbis, 1978.

Gowan, Donald E. *When Man Becomes God: Humanism and Hybris in the Old Testament*. PTMS, 6. Pittsburgh: Pickwick, 1972.

Gray, John. *The Biblical Doctrine of the Reign of God*. Edinburgh: T. & T. Clark, 1979.

—'A Cantata of the Autumn Festival: Psalm LXVII', *JSS* 22 (1977), pp. 2-26

—'The Day of Yahweh in Cultic Experience and Eschatological Prospect', *SEÅ* 39 (1974), pp. 5-37.

—'The Hebrew Conception of the Kingship of God', *VT* 6 (1956), pp. 268-85.

—*I & II Kings: A Commentary*. OTL. Philadelphia: Westminster, 1970.

—'Sacral Kingship in Ugarit', *Ugaritica* VI (1969), pp. 289-302.

Grayson, A.K. *Babylonian Historical-Literary Texts*. Toronto Semitic Texts and Studies, 3. Toronto: University of Toronto Press, 1975.

Gressmann, Hugo. *Der Messias*. Edited by H. Schmidt. FRLANT, 43. Göttingen: Vandenhoeck & Ruprecht, 1929.

—*Der Ursprung der israelitisch-jüdischen Eschatologie*. FRLANT, 6. Göttingen: Vandenhoeck & Ruprecht, 1905.

Gross, Heinrich. *Die Idee des ewigen und allgemeinen Weltfriedens im alten Orient und im Alten Testament*. TTS, 7. Trier: Paulinus Verlag, 1956.

Gunkel, Hermann. *Genesis, übersetzt und erklärt*. HKAT, 1/1. Göttingen: Vandenhoeck & Ruprecht, fourth edition, 1917.

—and Begrich, Joachim. *Einleitung in die Psalmen: Die Gattungen der religiösen Lyrik Israels*. Göttingen: Vandenhoeck & Ruprecht, 1933.

Gunneweg, A.H.J. 'Herrschaft Gottes und Herrschaft des Menschen: Eine alttestamentliche Aporie von aktueller Bedeutung', *KuD* 27 (1981), pp. 164-79.

—*Leviten und Priester: Hauptlinien der Traditionsbildung und Geschichte des israelitisch-judäischen Kultpersonals*. FRLANT, 89. Göttingen: Vandenhoeck & Ruprecht, 1965.

—'Sinaibund und Davidsbund', *VT* 10 (1960), pp. 335-41.

Gustafson, James. 'The Place of Scripture in Christian Ethics: A Methodological Approach', *Interpretation* 24 (1970), pp. 430-55.

Gutierrez, Gustavo. *A Theology of Liberation: History, Politics and Salvation*. Translated by Sr. Craridad Inda and John Eagleson. Maryknoll: Orbis, 1973.

Gutman, Jospeh. 'The History of the Ark', *ZAW* 87 (1971), pp. 22-30.

Habel, Norman C. '"Yahweh, Maker of Heaven and Earth": A Study in Tradition Criticism', *JBL* 91 (1972), pp. 321-37.

Habets, Goswin N.M. 'Die grosse Jesaja-Apokalypse (Jes 24–27): Ein Beitrag zur

Theologie des alten Testament'. Unpublished D.Theol. dissertation. University of Bonn, 1974.

Halpern Baruch. *The Constitution of the Monarchy in Israel*. HSM, 25. Chico: Scholars Press, 1981.

—'The Ritual Background of Zechariah's Temple Song', *CBQ* 40 (1978), pp. 167-190.

Hambourg, G.R. 'Reasons for Judgment in the Oracles Against the Nations of the Prophet Isaiah', *VT* 31 (1981), pp. 145-59.

Hanson, Paul D. 'Zechariah 9 and the Recapitulation of an Ancient Historical Pattern', *JBL* 92 (1972), pp. 37-59.

Haran, Menahem. 'The Ark and the Cherubim', *IEJ* 9 (1959), pp. 30-38, 89-94.

—*Temples and Temple Service in Ancient Israel*. Oxford: Clarendon Press, 1978.

Harvey, Dorothea Ward. '"Rejoice Not, O Israel!"', *Israel's Prophetic Heritage: Essays in Honor of James Muilenburg*. Edited by B.W. Anderson and Walter Harrelson. New York: Harper & Row, 1962.

Hayes, John H. *Introduction to Old Testament Study*. Nashville: Abingdon, 1979.

—'The Tradition of Zion's Inviolability', *JBL* 82 (1963), pp. 419-26.

Held, Moshe. 'The Root ZBL/SBL in Akkadian, Ugaritic and Biblical Hebrew', *JAOS* 88 (1968), pp. 90-96.

Hermisson, Hans-Jürgen. 'Zukunftserwartung und Gegenwartskritik in der Verkündigung Jesajas', *EvT* 33 (1973), pp. 54-77.

Herrmann, Siegfried. *Die prophetischen Heilserwartungen im alten Testament*. BWANT, 85. Stuttgart: W. Kohlhammer, 1965.

Hillers, Delbert. 'The Bow of Aqhat: The Meaning of a Mythological Theme', *Orient and Occident: Essays in Honor of Cyrus Gordon*. AOAT, 22. Neukirchen-Vluyn: Neukirchener Verlag, 1973, pp. 71-80.

—*Treaty Curses and the Old Testament Prophets*. BibOr, 16. Rome: Pontifical Biblical Institute, 1964.

Höffken, Peter. 'Notizen zum Textcharakter von Jesaja 7,1-17', *TZ* 36 (1980), pp. 321-37.

Hoffman, Hans Werner. *Die Intention der Verkündigung Jesajas*. BZAW, 136. Berlin: Walter de Gruyter, 1974.

Hooke, S.H. 'The Corner-Stone of Scripture', *The Siege Perilous: Essays in Biblical Anthropology and Kindred Subjects*. London: SCM, 1946, pp. 235-49.

Huber, Friedrich. *Jahwe, Juda und die anderen Völker beim Propheten Jesaja*. BZAW, 137. Berlin: Walter de Gruyter, 1976.

Humbert, Paul. '"Laetari et exultare" dans le vocabulaire religieux de l'Ancien Testament', *RHPR* 22 (1942), pp. 185-214.

—*La 'Terou'a': Analyse d'un rite biblique*. Neuchâtel, 1946.

Hunger, Hermann, and Kaufman, Stephen A. 'A New Akkadian Prophecy Text', *JAOS* 95 (1975), pp. 371-75.

Irwin, W.H. *Isaiah 28-33: Translation with Philological Notes*. BibOr, 30. Rome: Pontifical Biblical Institute, 1974.

Ishida, Tomoo. *The Royal Dynasties in Ancient Israel*. BZAW, 142. Berlin: Walter de Gruyter, 1976.

Jacobsen, Thorkild. 'The Battle Between Marduk and Tiamat', *JAOS* 88 (1968), pp. 104-108.

Janzen, Waldemar. 'God as Warrior and Lord: A Conversation with G.E. Wright', *BASOR* 220/21 (1975/76), pp. 73-76.

Jensen, Joseph. 'Weal and Woe in Isaiah: Consistency and Continuity', *CBQ* 43 (1981), pp. 167-87.

Jepsen, Alfred. *'aman', Theological Dictionary of the Old Testament*, I. Edited by G. Johannes Botterweck and Helmer Ringgren. Translated by John T. Willis. Grand Rapids: Eerdmans, revised edition, 1977, pp. 292-323.

—*'batach', Theological Dictionary of the Old Testament*, II. Edited by G.J. Botterweck and H. Ringgren. Translated by John T. Willis. Grand Rapids: Eerdmans, revised edition, 1977, pp. 88-94.

Jeremias, C. *Die Nachtgesichte des Sacharja. Untersuchungen zu ihrer Stellung im Zusammenhang der Visionsberichte im Alten Testament und zu ihrem Bildmaterial.* FRLANT, 117. Göttingen: Vandenhoeck & Ruprecht, 1976.

Jeremias, Jörg. 'Lade und Zion: Zur Entstehung der Zionstradition', *Probleme Biblischer Theologie. Gerhard von Rad zum 70. Geburtstag.* Edited by Hans Walter Wolff. München: Chr. Kaiser, 1971, pp. 183-98.

—*Theophanie: Die Geschichte einer alttestamentlichen Gattung.* WMANT, 10. Neukirchen-Vluyn: Neukirchener Verlag, 1965.

—'Zur Eschatologie des Hoseabuches', *Die Botschaft und die Boten. Festschrift für Hans Walter Wolff zum 70. Geburtstag.* Edited by Jörg Jeremias and Lothar Perlitt. Neukirchen-Vluyn: Neukirchener Verlag, 1981.

Johnson, Aubrey. *The Cultic Prophet and Israel's Psalmody.* Cardiff: University of Wales Press, 1979.

—*The Cultic Prophet in Ancient Israel.* Cardiff: University of Wales Press, second edition, 1962.

—*Sacral Kingship in Ancient Israel.* Cardiff: University of Wales Press, second edition, 1967.

Jones, Gwilym H. '"Holy War" or "Yahweh War?"', *VT* 25 (1975), pp. 642-58.

Junker, H. 'Die Entstehungszeit des Ps 78 und des Deuteronomiums', *Biblica* 34 (1953), pp. 487-500.

—'Sancta Civitas, Jerusalem Nova. Eine formkritische und überlieferungsgeschichtliche Studie zu Jes. 2', *TTS* (1962), pp. 17-33.

Kaiser, Otto. *Isaiah 1-12: A Commentary.* OTL. Translated by R.A. Wilson. Philadelphia: Westminster, 1972.

—*Isaiah 13-39: A. Commentary.* OTL. Translated by R.A. Wilson. Philadelphia: Westminster, 1974.

Kapelrud, Arvid S. 'Creation in the Ras Shamra Texts', *ST* 34 (1980), pp. 1-11.

—*The Message of the Prophet Zephaniah: Morphology and Ideas.* Oslo: Universitetsforlaget, 1975.

—'Nochmals Jawä malak', *VT* 13 (1963), pp. 229-31.

—'The Relationship Between El and Baal in the Ras Shamra Texts', *The Bible World: Essays in Honor of Cyrus H. Gordon.* Edited by Gary Rendsburg, Ruth Adler, Milton Arfa and Nathan H. Winter. New York: KTAV, 1980, pp. 79-85.

—'Sigmund Mowinckel and Old Testament Study', *ASTI* 5 (1967), pp. 4-29.

Keck, Leander. 'The Poor Among the Saints in Jewish Christianity and Qumran', *ZNW* 47 (1966), pp. 54-78.

Kilian, Rudolf. *Die Verheissung Immanuels. Jes 7,14.* SBS, 35. Stuttgart: KBW Verlag, 1968.

Kimbrough, S.T. *Israelite Religion in Sociological Perspective: The Work of Antonin Causse.* SOR, 4. Wiesbaden: Otto Harrassowitz, 1978.

Kirk, J. Andrew. *Liberation Theology: An Evangelical View from the Third World.* New Foundations Theological Library. Atlanta: John Knox, 1979.

Kirkpatrick, A.F. *The Book of Psalms.* Cambridge Bible for Schools and Colleges. Cambridge: Cambridge University Press, 1902.

Knierim, Rolf. 'Cosmos and History in Israel's Theology', *HBT* 3 (1981), pp. 59-123.

—'Offenbarung im Alten Testament', *Probleme Biblischer Theologie. Gerhard von Rad zum 70. Geburtstag*. Edited by Hans Walter Wolff. München: Chr. Kaiser, 1971, pp. 206-35.

Knight, Douglas A. *Rediscovering the Traditions of Israel*. SBLDS, 9. Missoula: Scholars Press, revised edition, 1975.

Koch, Klaus. 'Wort und Einheit des Schöpfergottes in Memphis und Jerusalem', *ZTK* 62 (1965), pp. 251-93.

Köhler, Ludwig. 'Die Offenbarungsformel "Fürchte dich Nicht!" im Alten Testament', *STZ* 36 (1919), pp. 33-39.

—'Zwei Fachwörter der Bausprache in Jes. 28.16', *TZ* 3 (1947), pp. 390-93.

Köppel, Urs. *Das deuteronomistische Geschichtswerk und seine Quellen: Die Absicht der deuteronomistischen Geschichtsdarstellung aufgrund des Vergleichs zwischen Num 21,21-35 und Dtn 2,26-3,3*. Europäische Hochschulschriften 23/122. Bern: Peter Lang, 1979.

Kraus, Hans-Joachim. 'Vom Kampf des Glaubens: Eine biblischtheologische Studie', *Beiträge zur alttestamentlichen Theologie. W. Zimmerli zum 70. Geburtstag*. Edited by H. Donner, R. Hanhart and R. Smend. Göttingen: Vandenhoeck & Ruprecht, 1977, pp. 239-56.

—*Die Königsherrschaft Gottes im Alten Testament: Untersuchungen zu den Liedern von Jahwes Thronbesteigung*. BHT, 13. Tübingen: J.C.B. Mohr, 1951.

—*Psalmen*. BKAT 15. 2 vols. Neukirchen-Vluyn: Neukirchener Verlag, fourth edition, 1972.

—'Das Thema "Exodus": Kritische Bemerkungen zur Usurpation eines biblischen Begriffs', *Biblischtheologische Aufsätze*. Neukirchen-Vluyn: Neukirchener Verlag, 1972, pp. 102-19.

—*Theologie der Psalmen*. BKAT, 15/3. Neukirchen-Vluyn: Neukirchener Verlag, 1979.

—*Worship in Israel: A Cultic History of the Old Testament*. Translated by G. Buswell. Richmond: John Knox, 1966.

Kuntz, J. Kenneth. *The Self-Revelation of God*. Philadelphia: Westminster, 1967.

Labuschagne, C.J. *The Incomparability of Yahweh in the Old Testament*. Pretoria Oriental Series, 5. Leiden: E.J. Brill, 1966.

Lambert, W.G. 'Enmeduranki and Related Matters', *JCS* 21 (1967), pp. 126-38.

—'The Great Battle of the Mesopotamian Religious Year: The Conflict in the Akitu House (A Summary)', *Iraq* 25 (1963), pp. 189-90.

Lang, Bernhard. *Kein Aufstand in Jerusalem: Die Politik des Propheten Ezechiel*. SBB. Stuttgart: Katholisches Bibelwerk, second edition, 1981.

—'Prophetie, prophetische Zeichenhandlung und Politik in Israel', *TQ* 161 (1981), pp. 275-80.

Levenson, John D. 'The Davidic Covenant and its Modern Interpreters', *CBQ* 41 (1979), pp. 205-19.

L'Heureux, Conrad E. *Rank Among the Gods: El, Ba'al and the Repha'im*. HSM, 21. Cambridge, Mass.: Harvard University Press, 1979.

Lind, Millard. *Yahweh is a Warrior: The Theology of Warfare in Ancient Israel*. Scottdale, Penn.: Herald, 1980.

Lipiński, Edward. *Le Poème royal du Psaume LXXXIX 1-5, 20-38*. Paris: J. Gabalda, 1967.

—'Recherches sur le Livre de Zacharie', *VT* 20 (1970), pp. 25-55.

—*La Royauté de Yahwé dans la poésie et le culte de l'ancien Israël*. Brussels: Paleis der Acadamiën, 1965.

Loretz, Oswald. 'Die Analyse der ugaritischen und hebräischen Poesie mittels Stichometrie und Konsonantenzählung', *UF* 7 (1975), pp. 261-64.

—*Die Psalmen, Teil II. Beitrag der Ugarit-Texte zum Verständnis von Kolometrie und Textologie der Psalmen.* AOAT, 207/2. Neukirchen-Vluyn: Neukirchener Verlag, 1979.

Löwenclau, Ilse von. 'Der Prophet Nathan im Zwielicht von theologischer Deutung und Historie', *Werden und Wirken des Alten Testaments. Festschrift für Claus Westermann.* Edited by R. Albertz, H.-P. Müller, H.W. Wolff and W. Zimmerli. Göttingen: Vandenhoeck & Ruprecht, 1980, pp. 202-15.

Ludwig, Theodore H. 'The Traditions of Establishing the Earth in Deutero-Isaiah', *JBL* 92 (1973), pp. 345-57.

Lust, J. 'The Immanuel Figure: A Charismatic Judge-Leader', *ETL* 47 (1971), pp. 464-70.

Lutz, Hans-Martin. *Jahwe, Jerusalem und die Völker: Zur Vorgeschichte von Sach 12,1-8 und 14,1-5.* WMANT, 27. Neukirchen-Vluyn: Neukirchener Verlag, 1968.

Maag, Victor. 'Jahwäs Begegnung mit der kanaanäischen Kosmologie', *Kultur, Kulturkontakt und Religion: Gesammelte Studien zur allgemeinen und alttestamentlichen Religionsgeschichte.* Edited by H.H. Schmid and O.H. Steck. Göttingen: Vandenhoeck & Ruprecht, 1980, pp. 203-20.

—'Malkut Jhwh', *VTS* 7 (1960), pp. 129-53.

Maass, Fritz. '^{e}nosh', *Theological Dictionary of the Old Testament, I.* Edited by G. Johannes Botterweck and Helmer Ringgren. Translated by John T. Willis. Grand Rapids: Eerdmans, revised edition, 1977, pp. 345-48.

Maier, Johann. *Das altisraelitische Ladeheiligtum.* BZAW, 93. Berlin: Alfred Töpelmann, 1965.

Mann, Thomas W. *Divine Presence and Guidance in Israelite Traditions. The Typology of Exaltation.* Johns Hopkins Near Eastern Studies. Baltimore: Johns Hopkins University Press, 1977.

Martin-Achard, R. '*nh* II elend sein', *Theologisches Handwörterbuch zum Alten Testament, II.* Edited by E. Jenni and C. Westermann. München: Chr. Kaiser, 1976, pp. 341-50.

May, H.G. 'Some Cosmic Connotations of Mayim Rabbim, "Many Waters"', *JBL* 74 (1955), pp. 9-21.

Mayes, A.D.H. 'The Rise of the Israelite Monarchy', *ZAW* 90 (1978), pp. 1-19.

Mays, James L. *Hosea: A Commentary.* OTL. Philadelphia: Westminster, 1969.

—*Micah: A Commentary.* OTL. Philadelphia: Westminster, 1976.

McCarter, P. Kyle. *I Samuel.* AB. Garden City: Doubleday, 1980.

McCarthy, Dennis J. 'The Inauguration of Monarchy in Israel: A Form-Critical Study of I Samuel 8-12', *Interpretation* 27 (1973), pp. 401-12.

—*Old Testament Covenant: A Survey of Current Opinions.* Growing Points in Theology. London: Basil Blackwell, 1972.

McKane, William. *Prophets and Wise Men.* SBT 1/44. London: SCM, 1965.

McKay, J.W. *Religion in Judah under the Assyrians.* SBT 2/26. London: SCM, 1973.

Melugin, Roy F. 'The Conventional and the Creative in Isaiah's Judgment Oracles', *CBQ* 36 (1974), pp. 301-11.

Mendelsohn, I. 'Samuel's Denunciation of Kingship in the Light of the Akkadian Documents from Ugarit', *HUCA* 143 (1956), pp. 17-22.

Mendenhall, George. 'The Monarchy', *Interpretation* 29 (1975), pp. 155-70.

Mettinger, Tryggve N.D. *King and Messiah: The Civil and Sacral Legitimation of the Israelite Kings.* ConBOT 8. Lund: CWK Gleerup, 1976.

Metzger, Martin. 'Himmlische und irdische Wohnstatt Jahwes', *UF* 2 (1970), pp. 139-58.

Meyer, Eduard. *Die Israeliten und ihre Nachbarstämme*. Halle: Max Niemeyer, 1906.

Meyer, F. de. 'La Dimension sapientale du Psaume 62', *Bijdragen* 42 (1981), pp. 350-65.

Michel, Diethelm. 'Studien zu den sogenannten Thronbesteigungspsalmen', *VT* 6 (1965), pp. 40-68.

Migliore, Daniel L. *Called to Freedom: Liberation Theology and the Future of Christian Doctrine*. Philadelphia: Westminster, 1980.

Milgrom, Jacob. *Studies in Levitical Terminology, I: The Encroacher and the Levite. The Term 'Aboda*. Berkeley: University of California Press, 1970.

Millar, W.R. *Isaiah 24-27 and the Origin of Apocalyptic*. HSM, 11. Cambridge, Mass.: Harvard University Press, 1976.

Miller, Patrick D. *The Divine Warrior in Early Israel*. HSM, 5. Cambridge, Mass.: Harvard University Press, 1975.

—'El, the Creator of Earth', *BASOR* 239 (1980), pp. 43-46.

—'El the Warrior', *HTR* 60 (1967), pp. 411-31.

—and Roberts, J.J.M. *The Hand of the Lord: A Reassessment of the 'Ark Narrative' of 1 Samuel*. Johns Hopkins Near Eastern Studies. Baltimore: Johns Hopkins University Press, 1977.

Mittmann, Siegfried. 'Komposition und Redaktion von Psalm 29', *VT* 28 (1978), pp. 172-94.

Molin, George. 'Das Motiv vom Chaoskampf im alten Orient und in den Traditionen Jerusalems und Israels', *Memoria Jerusalem; Freundesgabe Franz Sauer*. Edited by J.B. Bauer and J. Marböck. Graz: Akademische Druck- und Verlagsanstalt, 1977, pp. 13-27.

Moor, Johannes de. *New Year with Canaanites and Israelites*. 2 vols. Kamper Cahiers, 21. Kampen: Uitgeversamaatschappij, 1972.

—*The Seasonal Pattern in the Ugaritic Myth of Ba'lu*. AOAT, 16. Neukirchen-Vluyn: Neukirchener Verlag, 1971.

—'Ugarit', *The Interpreter's Dictionary of the Bible: Supplementary Volume*. Edited by Keith Crim. Nashville: Abingdon, 1976, pp. 928-31.

Moran, William. 'The Hebrew Language in its Northwest Semitic Background', *The Bible and the Ancient Near East: Essays in Honor of William Foxwell Albright*. Edited by G. Ernest Wright. Garden City: Anchor Books, 1965, pp. 59-84.

Mowinckel, Sigmund. *He That Cometh*. Translated by G.W. Anderson. Nashville: Abingdon, 1956.

—*Psalmenstudien*. 6 volumes in 2. Amsterdam: P. Schippers, 1961.

—*The Psalms in Israel's Worship*. 2 vols. Translated by D.R. Ap-Thomas. Nashville: Abingdon, 1962.

Müller, Hans-Peter. 'Glauben und Bleiben: Zur Denkschrift Jesajas Kapitel vi 1-viii 18', *VTS* 26 (1974), pp. 25-54.

Murphy, Roland. 'A Consideration of the Classification "Wisdom Psalms"', *VTS* 9 (1962), pp. 156-67.

Na'aman, Nadav. 'Sennacherib's "Letter to God" on his Campaign to Judah', *BASOR* 214 (1974), pp. 25-39.

Nelson, Richard D. 'Josiah in the Book of Joshua', *JBL* 100 (1981), pp. 531-40.

Neve, Lloyd. 'The Common Use of Traditions by the Author of Psalm 46 and Isaiah', *ExpTim* 86 (1975), pp. 243-46.

Nordheim, Eckard von. 'Königtum und Tempel. Der Hintergrund des Tempelbauverbotes in 2 Samuel 7', *VT* 27 (1977), pp. 434-53.

Noth, Martin. 'God, King, and Nation in the Old Testament', *The Laws in the*

Pentateuch and Other Studies. Translated by D.R. Ap-Thomas. Philadelphia: Fortress, 1966, pp. 145-78.

—'Jerusalem und die israelitische Tradition', *Gesammelte Studien zum Alten Testament*. TBü, 11. München: Chr. Kaiser, 1960, pp. 172-87. ET: 'Jerusalem and the Israelite Tradition'. *The Laws in the Pentateuch and Other Studies*. Translated by D.R. Ap-Thomas. Philadelphia: Fortress, 1966, 132-44.

Oden, Robert. 'Ba'al Samem and 'El', *CBQ* 39 (1977), pp. 457-73.

Oswalt, John N. 'Recent Studies in Old Testament Eschatology and Apocalyptic', *JETS* 24 (1981), pp. 289-301.

Ota, Michiko. 'A Note on 2 Samuel 7', *A Light Unto My Path: Old Testament Studies in Honor Of Jacob M. Myers*. Edited by H.N. Bream, R.D. Heim and C.A. Moore. Philadelphia: Temple University Press, 1974, pp. 403-408.

Otto, Eckart. 'El und JHWH in Jerusalem: Historische und theologische Aspekte einer Religionsintegration', *VT* 30 (1980), pp. 316-29.

—*Jerusalem: Die Geschichte der heiligen Stadt von den Anfängen bis zur Kreuzfahrerzeit*. Urban Taschenbücher, 308. Stuttgart: W. Kohlhammer, 1980.

—*Das Mazzotfest in Gilgal*. BWANT, 107. Stuttgart: W. Kohlhammer, 1975.

—'Silo und Jerusalem', *TZ* 32 (1976), pp. 65-77.

Otzen, Benedikt. *Studien über Deutero-Sacharja*. Acta Theologica Danica, 6. Copenhagen: Prostant Apud Munksgaard, 1964.

Pallis, S.A. *The Babylonian Akitu Festival*. Copenhagen: A.F. Horst, 1926.

Parker, Simon B. 'The Historical Composition of KRT and the Cult of El', *ZAW* 89 (1977), pp. 161-75.

Patrick, Dale. 'Political Exegesis', *Encounter With the Text: Form and History in the Hebrew Bible*. Edited by Martin J. Buss. SBL Semeia Supplements. Philadelphia: Fortress, 1979, pp. 139-52.

Petersen, David L. 'Isaiah 28, A Redaction-Critical Study', *SBL Seminar Papers*, II. Edited by Paul J. Achtemeier. Missoula: Scholars Press, 1979, pp. 101-22.

—'Zerubbabel and Jerusalem Temple Reconstruction', *CBQ* 36 (1974), pp. 366-72.

Polk, Timothy. 'The Levites in the Davidic-Solomonic Empire', *SBTh* 9 (1979), pp. 3-22.

Pope, Marvin. *El in the Ugaritic Texts*. VTS, 2. Leiden: E.J. Brill, 1955.

—*Job*. AB. Garden City: Doubleday, third edition, 1974.

Porteous, Norman W. 'Jerusalem-Zion: The Growth of a Symbol', *Verbannung und Heimkehr: Beiträge zur Geschichte und Theologie Israels im 6. und 5. Jahrhundert v. Chr. Festschrift für W. Rudolph*. Edited by Arnulf Kuschke. Tübingen: J.C.B. Mohr, 1961, pp. 235-52.

Poulssen, Niek. *König und Tempel im Glaubenszeugnis des Alten Testaments*. SBM, 3. Stuttgart: Katholisches Bibelwerk, 1967.

Prinsloo, W.S. 'Isaiah 14.12-15—Humiliation, Hubris, Humiliation', *ZAW* 93 (1981), pp. 432-38.

Procksch, Otto. *Theologie des Alten Testaments*. Gütersloh: C. Bertelsmann, 1949.

Rabe, Virgil. 'Israelite Opposition to the Temple', *CBQ* 29 (1967), pp. 228-33.

Rad, Gerhard von. *Deuteronomy: A Commentary*. Translated by Dorothea Barton. OTL. Philadelphia: Westminster, 1966.

—'Das formgeschichtliche Problem des Hexateuch', *Gesammelte Studien zum Alten Testament*. TBü, 8. München: Chr. Kaiser, third edition, 1965, pp. 9-86. ET: *The Form Critical Problem of the Hexateuch and Other Essays*. Translated by E.W.T. Dicken. Edinburgh: Oliver & Boyd, 1966, pp. 1-78.

—*Der heilige Krieg im alten Israel*. Göttingen: Vandenhoeck & Ruprecht, third edition, 1958.

—*Old Testament Theology*. 2 vols. Translated by D.M.G. Stalker. New York: Harper & Row, 1962, 1965.
—'Die Stadt auf dem Berge', *Gesammelte Studien zum Alten Testament*. TBü, 3. München: Chr. Kaiser, third edition, 1965, pp. 214-24. ET: 'The City on the Hill', *The Form Critical Problem of the Hexateuch and Other Essays*. Translated by E.W.T. Dicken. Edinburgh: Oliver & Boyd, 1966, pp. 232-42.
—'Das theologische Problem des alttestamentlichen Schöpfungsglaubens', *Gesammelte Studien zum Alten Testament*. TBü, 8. München: Chr. Kaiser, third edition, 1965, pp. 136-47. ET: 'The Theological Problem of the Old Testament Doctrine of Creation', *The Form Critical Problem of the Hexateuch and Other Essays*. Translated by E.W.T. Dicken. Edinburgh: Oliver & Boyd, 1966, pp. 131-43.
—'Zelt und Lade', *Gesammelte Studien zum Alten Testament*. TBü, 8. München: Chr. Kaiser, third edition, 1965, pp. 119-24. ET: 'The Tent and the Ark', *The Form Critical Problem of the Hexateuch and Other Essays*. Translated by E.W.T. Dicken. Edinburgh: Oliver & Boyd, 1966, pp. 103-24.
Rappaport, Roy A. 'Liturgies and Lies', *Internationales Jahrbuch für Wissens- und Religionssoziologie: Beiträge zur Wissenssoziologie*. Edited by Günter Dux and Thomas Luckmann. Opladen: Westdeutscher Verlag, 1976.
Rendtorff, Rolf. 'Beobachtungen zur altisraelitischen Geschichtsschreibung anhand der Geschichte vom Aufstieg Davids', *Probleme Biblischer Theologie. Gerhard von Rad zum 70. Geburtstag*. Edited by Hans Walter Wolff. München: Chr. Kaiser, 1971, pp. 428-39.
—'El, Ba'al und Jahwe', *ZAW* 78 (1966), pp. 277-92.
—'Die theologische Stellung des Schöpfungsglaubens bei Deuterojesaja', *ZTK* 51 (1954), pp. 3-13.
Riding, Charles B. 'Psalm 95.1-7c as a Large Chiasm', *ZAW* 88 (1976), p. 418.
Ringgren, Helmer. *The Faith of the Psalmists*. Philadelphia: Fortress, 1963.
—*Israelite Religion*. Translated by David E. Green. Philadelphia: Fortress, 1966.
—'Zur Komposition von Jesaja 49-55', *Beiträge zur alttestamentlichen Theologie. W. Zimmerli zum 70. Geburtstag*. Edited by H. Donner, R. Hanhart and R. Smend. Göttingen: Vandenhoeck & Ruprecht, 1977, pp. 371-76.
Roberts, J.J.M. 'The Davidic Origin of the Zion Tradition', *JBL* 92 (1973), pp. 329-44.
—'Form, Syntax and Redaction in Isaiah 1,2-20', *Princeton Seminary Bulletin*, New Series 3 (1982), pp. 293-306.
—'Isaiah in Old Testament Theology', *Interpretation* 36 (1982), pp. 130-43.
—'Myth *Versus* History: Relaying the Comparative Foundations', *CBQ* 38 (1976), pp. 1-13.
—'Nebuchadnezzar I's Elamite Crisis in Theological Perspective', *Essays on the Ancient Near East in Memory of Jacob Joel Finkelstein*. Edited by M. De Jong Ellis. Hamden, Conn.: Archon Books, 1971, pp. 183-87.
—'A Note on Isaiah 28.12', *HTR* 73 (1980), pp. 49-51.
—'The Religio-Political Setting of Psalm 47', *BASOR* 220/21 (1975), pp. 129-32.
—'SAPON' in Job 26.' *Biblica* 56 (1975), pp. 554-57.
—'The Young Lions of Psalm 34.11', *Biblica* 54 (1973), pp. 265-68.
—'Zion in the Theology of the Davidic-Solomonic Empire', *Studies in the Period of David and Solomon*. Edited by Tomoo Ishida, Winona Lake: Eisenbrauns, 1982, pp. 93-108.
Robinson, Alan. 'The Zion Concept in the Psalms and Deutero-Isaiah'. Unpublished Ph.D. dissertation. University of Edinburgh, 1974.
Rohland, Edzard. 'Die Bedeutung der Erwählungstraditionen Israels für die

Eschatologie der alttestamentlichen Propheten'. Unpublished D.Theol. dissertation. University of Heidelberg, 1956.

Rose, Martin. 'Entmilitarisierung des Krieges? Erwägungen zu den Patriarchenerzählungen der Genesis', *BZ* 20 (1976), pp. 197-211.

Rosenbaum, Stanley R. 'New Evidence for Reading GE'IM in Place of GOYIM in Pss 9 and 10', *HUCA* 45 (1974), pp. 65-70.

Ross, J.P. 'Jahwe S^{e}ba'ot in Samuel and Psalms', *VT* 17 (1967), pp. 76-92.

Rost, Leonhard. 'Das Problem der Weltmacht in der Prophetie', *Studien zum Alten Testament*. BWANT, 101. Stuttgart: W. Kohlhammer, 1974, pp. 76-86.

— 'Sinaibund und Davidsbund', *TLZ* 72 (1974), pp. 129-34.

Rowley, H.H. *Worship in Ancient Israel*. London: SPCK, 1967.

Rudolph, Wilhelm. *Haggai; Sacharja 1-8; Sacharja 9-14; Maleachi*. KAT 13/4. Gütersloh: Gerd Mohn, 1976.

—*Jeremiah*. HAT, 12. Tübingen: J.C.B. Mohr, third edition, 1968.

—*Micah; Nahum; Habakkuk; Zephanja*. KAT 13/3.

Ruprecht, Konrad. *Der Tempel von Jerusalem*. BZAW, 144. Berlin: Walter de Gruyter, 1977.

Rylaarsdam, J. Coert. 'Booths, Feast of', *Interpreter's Dictionary of the Bible*, I. Edited by George Arthur Buttrick. Nashville: Abingdon, 1962, pp. 455-58.

Saebø, Magne. 'Formgeschichtliche Erwägungen zu Jes. 7.3-9', *ST* 14 (1960), pp. 54-69. Now in *Ordene og Ordet: Gammeltestamentlige Studier*. Oslo: Universitetsforlaget, 1979.

—*Sacharja 9-14: Untersuchungen von Text und Form*. WMANT, 34. Neukirchen-Vluyn: Neukirchener Verlag, 1969.

—'Zur Traditionsgeschichte von Jesaja 8,9-10: Klärungsversuch einer alten *crux interpretum*', *ZAW* 76 (1964), pp. 132-44. Now in *Ordene og Ordet: Gammeltestamentlige Studier*. Oslo: Universitetsforlaget, 1979.

Saggs, H.W.F. 'Assyrian Warfare in the Sargonid Period', *Iraq* 25 (1963), pp. 145-54.

Sarna, Nahum M. 'The Divine Title *'abhir ya'aqobh*', *Essays on the Occasion of the Seventieth Anniversary of the Dropsie University*. Edited by A.I. Katsch and Leon Nemoy. Philadelphia: Dropsie University, 1979, pp. 389-96.

Schildenberger, Johannes. 'Psalm 29, Ein Hymnus auf den machtvollen Gott zu Beginn eines neuen Jahres', *Erbe und Auftrag* 57 (1981), pp. 5-12.

Schmid, H.H. 'Altorientalische *Welt in der* alttestamentlichen *Theologie'*, *Altorientalische Welt in der alttestamentlichen Theologie*. Zürich: Theologischer Verlag, 1974.

—'Heiliger Krieg und Gottesfrieden im Alten Testament', *Altorientalische Welt in der alttestamentlichen Theologie*. Zürich: Theologischer Verlag, 1974.

—*Gerechtigkeit als Weltordnung: Hintergrund und Geschichte des alttestamentlichen Gerechtigkeitsbegriffes*. BHT, 40. Tübingen: J.C.B. Mohr, 1969.

—'Schöpfung, Gerechtigkeit und Heil: "Schöpfungstheologie" als Gesamthorizont biblischer Theologie', *ZTK* 70 (1973), pp. 1-19.

Schmid, Herbert. 'Jahwe und die Kulttraditionen von Jerusalem', *ZAW* 67 (1955), pp. 168-97.

Schmid, Rudolf. 'Gottesherrshaft und menschliche Institution—Die Bedeutung menschlicher Initiative im Licht von 1 Sam 8 und 12', *Judaica et Christiana*, I: *Zukunft in der Gegenwart: Wegweisungen in Judentum und Christentum*. Edited by Clemens Thoma. Bern: Herbert Lang, 1976, pp. 43-56.

—'Opfer mit Jubel. Die *zibhe t^{e}ru'a* von Ps 27.6', *TZ* 35 (1979), pp. 48-54.

Schmidt, Hans. *Der heilige Fels in Jerusalem: Eine archäologische und religionsgeschichtliche Studie*. Tübingen: J.C.B. Mohr, 1933.

—*Die Thronfahrt Jahves am Fest der Jahreswende im alten Israel*. Tübingen: J.C.B. Mohr, 1927.

Schmidt, K.-L. 'Jerusalem als Urbild und Abbild', *Eranos-Jahrbuch* 18 (1950), pp. 207-48.

Schmidt, W.H. *Alttestamentlicher Glaube in seiner Geschichte*. Neukirchener Studienbücher, 6. Neukirchen-Vluyn: Neukirchener Verlag, second edition, 1975.

—'Die Einheit der Verkündigung Jesajas. Versuch einer Zusammenschau', *EvT* 37 (1977), pp. 260-72.

—'Jerusalem El-Traditionen bei Jesaja', *ZRGG* 16 (1964), pp. 302-13.

—*Königtum Gottes in Ugarit und Israel*. BZAW, 80. Berlin: Alfred Töpelmann, second edition, 1966.

—'Kritik am Königtum', *Probleme Biblischer Theologie. Gerhard von Rad zum 70. Geburtstag*. Edited by Hans Walter Wolff. München: Chr. Kaiser, 1971, pp. 440-61.

—*Zukunftsgewissheit und Gegenwartskritik: Grundzüge prophetischer Verkündigung*. BibS(N), 64. Neukirchen-Vluyn: Neukirchener Verlag, 1973.

Schmitt, John J. 'The Zion Drama in the Tradition of Isaiah ben Amoz'. Unpublished Ph.D. dissertation. University of Chicago, 1977.

Schoors, Anton. 'Isaiah, the Minister of Royal Anointment?', *OTS* 20 (1977), pp. 85-107.

Schreiner, Josef. *Sion-Jerusalem: Jahwes Königssitz. Theologie der heiligen Stadt im Alten Testament*. SANT, 7. München: Kösel-Verlag, 1963.

Schüngel-Straumann, Helen. *Gottesbild und Kultkritik vorexilischer Propheten*. SBS, 60. Stuttgart: KBW Verlag, 1972.

—'Kritik am Königtum im Alten Testament', *BK* 36 (1981), pp. 194-200.

Schunk, K.-D. 'Zentralheiligtum, Grenzheiligtum und "Höhenheiligtum" in Israel', *Numen* 18 (1971), pp. 132-40.

Schwally, Friedrich. *Der heilige Krieg im alten Israel*. Leipzig: Theodor Weicher, 1901.

Seeligmann, I.L. 'Menschliches Heldentum und göttliche Hilfe: Die doppelte Kausalität im alttestamentlichen Geschichtsdenken', *TZ* 10 (1963), pp. 385-411.

Segundo, Juan Luis. *Liberation of Theology*. Translated by John Drury. Maryknoll: Orbis, 1976.

Seybold, Klaus. 'Die anthropologischen Beiträge aus Jesaja 2', *ZTK* 74 (1977), pp. 401-15.

—*Das davidische Königtum im Zeugnis der Propheten*. FRLANT, 107. Göttingen: Vandenhoeck & Ruprecht, 1972.

Shenkel, James D. 'An Interpretation of Psalm 93,5', *Biblica* 46 (1965), pp. 401-16.

Sider, Ronald. *Rich Christians in an Age of Hunger: A Biblical Study*. Downers Grove: Intervarsity Press, 1977.

Skorupski, John. *Symbol and Theory*. Cambridge: Cambridge University Press, 1976.

Skweres, Dieter Eduard. *Die Rückverweise im Buch Deuteronomium*. AnBib, 79. Rome: Pontifical Biblical Institute, 1979.

Slater, Peter. *The Dynamics of Religion: Meaning and Change in Religious Traditions*. New York: Harper & Row, 1978.

Smend, Rudolf. 'Zur Geschichte von ׳האמין׳, *Hebräische Wortforschung: Festschrift für W. Baumgartner*. VTS, 16. Leiden: E.J. Brill, 1967, pp. 284-90.

—*Yahweh War and Tribal Confederation: Reflections upon Israel's Earliest History*. Translated by Max G. Rogers. Nashville: Abingdon, 1970.

Soggin, J. Alberto. 'God the Creator in the First Chapter of Genesis', *Old Testament and Oriental Studies*. BibOr, 29. Rome: Pontifical Biblical Institute, 1975, pp. 120-29.

—'Gott als König in der biblischen Dichtung: Bemerkungen zu den יהוה מלך-Psalmen', *Proceedings of the Fifth World Congress of Jewish Studies*, I. Edited by Pinchas Peli. Jerusalem: World Union of Jewish Studies, 1969, pp. 126-33.

—*Das Königtum in Israel*. BZAW, 104. Berlin: Alfred Töpelmann, 1966.

—'Der prophetische Gedanke über den heiligen Krieg als Gericht gegen Israel', *VT* 10 (1960), pp. 79-83. ET; 'The Prophets on Holy War as Judgement against Israel', *Old Testament and Oriental Studies*. BibOr, 29. Rome: Pontifical Biblical Institute, 1975, pp. 67-71.

Speiser, E.A. 'Ancient Mesopotamia', *The Idea of History in the Ancient Near East*. Edited by Robert Dentan. New Haven: Yale University Press, 1955, pp. 37-76.

Sperber, Dan. *Rethinking Symbolism*. Translated by Alice L. Morton. Cambridge Studies and Papers in Social Anthropology. Cambridge: Cambridge University Press, 1977.

Springer, Simone. *Neuinterpretation im Alten Testament*. SBB. Stuttgart: Katholisches Bibelwerk, 1979.

Steck, Odil Hannes. 'Bemerkungen zu Jesaja 6', *BZ* 16 (1972), pp. 188-206.

—*Friedensvorstellungen im alten Jerusalem: Psalmen, Jesaja, Deuterojesaja*. TS, 111. Zürich: Theologischer Verlag, 1972.

—'Genesis 12.1-3 und die Urgeschichte des Jahwisten', *Probleme Biblischer Theologie. Gerhard von Rad zum 70. Geburtstag*. Edited by Hans Walter Wolff. München: Chr. Kaiser, 1971, pp. 525-54.

— 'Das Problem theologischer Strömungen in nachexilischer Zeit', *EvT* 28 (1966), pp. 445-58.

—'Rettung und Verstockung: Exegetische Bemerkungen zu Jesaja 7,3-9', *EvT* 33 (1973), pp. 77-90.

—'Theological Streams of Tradition', *Tradition and Theology in the Old Testament*. Edited by Douglas A. Knight. Philadelphia: Fortress, 1977, pp. 183-214.

Stoebe, Hans Joachim. *Das erste Buch Samuelis*. KAT 8/1. Gütersloh: Gerd Mohn, 1973.

Stolz, Fritz. *Jahwes und Israels Kriege: Kriegestheorie und Kriegeserfahrungen im Glauben des alten Israel*. ATANT, 60. Zürich: Theologischer Verlag, 1972.

—'js' hi. helfen', *Theologisches Handwörterbuch des Alten Testaments*, I. Edited by E. Jenni and C. Westermann. München: Chr. Kaiser, 1971, pp. 785-90.

—*Strukturen und Figuren im Kult von Jerusalem*. BZAW, 118. Berlin: Walter de Gruyter, 1969.

Stuart, Douglas. *Studies in Early Hebrew Meter*. HSM, 13. Cambridge, Mass.: Harvard University Press, 1976.

Stuhlmueller, Carroll. 'Yahweh-King and Deutero-Isaiah', *BR* 15 (1970), pp. 32-45.

Tadmor, Hayim. 'Assyria and the West: The Ninth Century and its Aftermath', *Unity and Diversity: Essays in the History, Literature and Religion of the Ancient Near East*. Edited by Hans Goedicke and J.J.M. Roberts. Johns Hopkins Near Eastern Studies. Baltimore: Johns Hopkins University Press, 1975, pp. 36-48.

Thompson, John A. *The Book of Jeremiah*. NICOT. Grand Rapids: Eerdmans, 1980.

Trible, Phyllis. *God and the Rhetoric of Sexuality*. Overtures to Biblical Theology. Philadelphia: Fortress, 1978.

Tsevat, Matitiahu. 'Yhwh Seba'ot', *The Meaning of the Book of Job and Other Biblical Studies: Essays on the Literature and Religion of the Hebrew Bible*. New York: KTAV, 1980, pp. 119-29.

Tsukimoto, Akio. '"Der Mensch ist geworden wie Unsereiner"—Untersuchungen zum zeitgeschichtlichen Hintergrund von Gen. 3,22-24 und 6,1-4', *AJBI* 5 (1979), pp. 3-44.

Tucker, Gene. 'Prophetic Speech', *Interpretation* 32 (1978), pp. 31-45.

Turner, Victor. *Dramas, Fields and Metaphors: Symbolic Action in Human Society.* Ithaca: Cornell University Press, 1974.

—*The Ritual Process: Structure and Anti-Structure.* Ithaca: Cornell Paperbacks, 1977.

—'Sacrifice as Quintessential Process: Prophylaxis or Abandonment?', *HR* 16 (1977), pp. 189-215.

—'Symbols and Social Experience in Religious Ritual', *Worship and Ritual in Christianity and Other Religions.* Studia Missionalia 23 (1974), pp. 1-21.

Uffenheimer, Benjamin. 'Die biblische Vorstellung vom Königtum Gottes und deren Dynamik', *Judaica et Christiana I: Zukunft in der Gegenwart: Wegweisungen in Judentum und Christentum.* Edited by Clemens Thoma. Bern: Herbert Lang, 1976, pp. 17-42.

Ulrichsen, Jarl H. 'JHWH MALAK: Einige sprachliche Beobachtungen', *VT* 27 (1977), pp. 361-74.

Vaux, Roland de. *Ancient Israel.* 2 vols. New York: McGraw-Hill, 1961.

—'Arche d'Alliance et Tente de Réunion', *Bible et Orient.* Paris: Les Editions du Cerf, 1967, pp. 261-76. ET: 'Ark of the Covenant and Tent of Reunion', *The Bible and the Ancient Near East.* Translated by Damian McHugh. Garden City: Doubleday, 1971, pp. 136-51.

—'Les Chérubins et l'Arche d'Alliance, les spinx gardiens et les trônes divins dans l'Ancien Orient', *Bible et Orient.* Paris: Les Editions du Cerf, 1967, pp. 231-59.

—*The Early History of Israel.* Translated by David Smith. Philadelphia: Westminster, 1978.

—'Jerusalem and the Prophets', *Interpreting the Prophetic Tradition.* Edited by H.M. Orlinsky. Cincinnati: Hebrew Union College, 1969, pp. 275-300.

Veijola, Timo. *Die ewige Dynastie: David und die Entstehung seiner Dynastie nach der deuteronomistischen Darstellung.* Annales Suomalaisen Tiedeakatemian, Annales Academiae Scientiarum Fennicae: Sarja-Ser. B, 193. Helsinki: Soumalainen Tiedeakteneia, 1975.

Vermeylen, J. *Du prophète Isaïe à l'apocalyptique: Isaïe, I–XXXV, Miroir d'un demi-millénaire d'expérience religieuse en Israël.* 2 vols. Paris: J. Gabalda, 1977.

Vincent, Jean M. 'Recherches exégétiques sur le Psaume XXXIII', *VT* 28 (1978), pp. 442-54.

—*Studien zur literarischen Eigenart und zur geistigen Heimat von Jesaja, Kap. 40–55.* BBET, 5. Frankfurt: Peter Lang, 1977.

Virolleaud, Ch. 'Les Rephaim. Fragments de poèmes de Ras Shamra', *Syria* 22 (1941), pp. 1-30.

Vollmer, Jochen. *Geschichtliche Rückblicke und Motive in der Prophetie des Amos, Hosea und Jesaja.* BZAW, 119. Berlin: Walter de Gruyter, 1971.

Volz, Paul. *Das Neujahrfest Jahwes.* Tübingen: J.C.B. Mohr, 1912.

Vriezen, Th. C. 'Essentials of the Theology of Isaiah', *Israel's Prophetic Heritage: Essays in Honor of James Muilenburg.* Edited by B.W. Anderson and Walter Harrelson. New York: Harper & Row, 1962, pp. 128-46.

Wanke, Gunther. *Die Zionstheologie der Korachiten in ihrem traditionsgeschichtlichen Zusammenhang.* BZAW, 97. Berlin: Alfred Töpelmann, 1966.

Ward, James M. *Amos and Isaiah. Prophets of the Word of God.* New York: Abingdon, 1969.

—'The Literary Form and Liturgical Background of Psalm 89', *VT* 11 (1961), pp. 320-39.

Watts, J.D.W. 'Yahve mālak Psalms', *TZ* 21 (1965), pp. 341-48.

Weimar, Peter, 'Die Jahwekriegserzählungen in Exodus 14, Josua 10, Richter 4 und 1 Samuel 7', *Biblica* 57 (1976), pp. 38-73.

Weinfeld, Moshe. 'Covenant, Davidic', *Interpreter's Dictionary of the Bible: Supplementary Volume.* Edited by Keith Crim. Nashville: Abingdon, 1976, pp. 185-92.

—*Deuteronomy and the Deuteronomic School.* Oxford: Clarendon Press, 1972.

Weinreich, Friedrich. *Der religiös-utopische Charakter der 'prophetischen Politik'.* Giessen: Alfred Töpelmann, 1932.

Weippert, Helga. 'Der Ort, den Jahwe erwählen wird, um dort seinen Namen wohnen zu lassen', *BZ* 24 (1980), pp. 76-94.

Weippert, Manfred. '"Heiliger Krieg" in Israel und Assyrien. Kritische Anmerkungen zu Gerhard von Rads Konzept des "Heiligen Kriegs im alten Israel"', *ZAW* 84 (1972), pp. 460-93.

Weiser, Artur. *Das Buch des Propheten Jeremia.* ATD. Göttingen: Vandenhoeck & Ruprecht, 1955.

—*The Psalms: A Commentary.* OTL. Translated by H. Hartwell. Philadelphia: Westminster, 1962.

—*Samuel: Seine geschichtliche Aufgabe und religiöse Bedeutung. Traditionsgeschichtliche Untersuchungen zu 1. Samuel 7-12.* FRLANT, 31. Göttingen: Vandenhoeck & Ruprecht, 1962.

Weiss, Meir. 'The Origin of the "Day of the Lord"—Reconsidered', *HUCA* 37 (1966), pp. 29-60.

Welten, Peter. 'Kulthöhe und Jahwetempel', *ZDPV* 88 (1972), pp. 19-37.

Westermann, Claus. 'Der Gebrauch von *'srj* im alten Testament', *Forschung am Alten Testament. Gesammelte Studien II.* TBü, 55. Edited by Rainer Albertz. München: Chr. Kaiser, 1974, pp. 191-95.

—*Genesis.* BKAT 1/1. Neukirchen-Vluyn: Neukirchener Verlag, 1974.

—*The Praise of God in the Psalms.* Translated by Keith R. Crim. Richmond: John Knox, 1965.

Whedbee, William. *Isaiah and Wisdom.* Nashville: Abingdon, 1971.

Whitelam, Keith W. *The Just King: Monarchical Judicial Authority in Ancient Israel.* JSOT Supplement Series, 12. Sheffield: JSOT Press, 1979.

Whybray, R.N. *The Heavenly Counsellor in Isaiah 40.13-14.* SOTSMS, 1. Cambridge: Cambridge University Press, 1971.

Widengren, Geo. 'The Gathering of the Dispersed', *SEÅ* 441-42 (1976/77), pp. 224-34.

Wildberger, Hans. '"Glauben", Erwägungen zu האמין, *Hebräische Wortforschung: Festschrift für W. Baumgartner.* VTS, 16. Leiden: E.J. Brill, 1967, pp. 372-86.

—'"Glauben" im Alten Testament', *ZTK* 65 (1968), pp. 219-59.

—'Gottesnamen und Gottesepitheta bei Jesaja', *Jahwe und sein Volk: Gesammelte Aufsätze zum Alten Testament.* TBü, 66. München: Chr. Kaiser, 1979, pp. 224-30.

—*Jesaja 1-12.* BKAT, 10/1. Neukirchen-Vluyn: Neukirchener Verlag, 1972.

—*Jesaja 13-27.* BKAT 10/2. Neukirchen-Vluyn: Neukirchener Verlag, 1978.

—'Die Völkerwallfahrt zum Zion', *VT* 7 (1957), pp. 62-81.

Willis, John T. 'Samuel Versus Eli, I. Sam. 1-7', *TZ* 35 (1979), pp. 201-12.

—'The Song of Hannah and Psalm 113', *CBQ* 35 (1973), pp. 139-54.

Wolff, Hans Walter. *Anthropology of the Old Testament.* Translated by Margaret Kohl. Philadelphia: Fortress, 1974.

—'Elohistic Fragments in the Pentateuch', Walter Brueggemann and Hans Walter
    Wolff, *The Vitality of Old Testament Traditions*. Atlanta: John Knox, 1975,
    pp. 67-82.
—*Hosea*. Hermeneia. Translated by Gary Stansell. Philadelphia: Fortress, 1974.
—'Hoseas geistige Heimat', *Gesammelte Studien zum Alten Testament*. TBü, 22.
    München: Chr. Kaiser, 1964, pp. 232-50.
Woude, A.S. van der. 'Micah IV 1-5: An Instance of the Pseudo-Prophets', *Symbolae
    Biblicae et Mesopotamicae. Francisco Mario Theodoro de Liagre Böhl dedicatae*.
    Edited by M.A. Beek, A.A. Kampan, C. Nijland and J. Ryckmans. Studia
    Francisci Scholten Memoriae Dicta, 4. Leiden: E.J. Brill, 1973, pp. 396-402.
Würthwein, Ernst. 'Jesaja 7,1-9: Ein Beitrag zu dem Thema: Prophetie und Politik',
    Wort und Existenz: Studien zum Alten Testament. Göttingen: Vandenhoeck &
    Ruprecht, 1970, pp. 127-43.
Yoder, John Howard. 'Exodus and Exile: The Two Faces of Liberation', *Missionalia* 2
    (1974), pp. 29-41.
Youngblood, Ronald. 'Ariel, "City of God"', *Essays on the Occasion of the Seventieth
    Anniversary of Dropsie University*. Edited by A.I. Katsch and Leon Nemoy.
    Philadelphia: Dropsie University, 1979, pp. 457-62.
Zimmerli, Walther. 'Alttestamentliche Traditionsgeschichte und Theologie', *Studien
    zur alttestamentlichen Theologie und Prophetie: Gesammelte Aufsätze* II. TBü,
    51. München: Chr. Kaiser, 1974, pp. 9-26.
—*Old Testament Theology in Outline*. Translated by David E. Green. Atlanta: John
    Knox, 1978.
—'Prophetic Proclamation and Reinterpretation', *Tradition and Theology in the Old
    Testament*. Edited by Douglas A. Knight. Philadelphia: Fortress, 1977, pp. 69-
    100.
Zobel, Hans-Jürgen. "*ron*', *Theological Dictionary of the Old Testament*, I. Edited by
    G.J. Botterweck and Helmer Ringgren. Translated by John T. Willis. Grand
    Rapids: Eerdmans, revised edition, 1977, pp. 263-74.

INDEXES

INDEX OF BIBLICAL CITATIONS

Genesis

1-11	135
1	157
18.2	186n164
27.26	186n164
34	208n41
49.24	41, 42

Exodus

14	233n292
14.13-14, 31	102
15	56, 89, 102, 133, 207n34, 208nn44,45, 213nn88,89, 229n252
15.2	208n43
15.6, 11-12	89
15.13	58
15.14-16	123
15.16-18	198n109
15.17-18	58
19	209n51
23.16	38
32.8	186n164
34.22	38

Leviticus

6.6, 25	142
19.30	209n51
23.24	46
23.39	38
25.8-9	38
25.9	46
26.1	186n164
26.2	209n51
29.1	46

Numbers

10.35-36	58
21.18	183n136

Deuteronomy

10.1-5	179n105

12.5ff.	61
12.7	183n145
12.9-10	220n155
14.22-29	183n145
14.23ff.	61
17	104, 107, 215n105
17.14-17	104
20	107, 214n96
20.1-3	104
21.11	221n172
32	32, 205n27
32.8	44
32.15, 18, 30	77
32.43	185n159
33	56, 90, 208n46
33.2-5	72, 189n17
33.2	90, 208n45
33.5	56, 171n33
33.28	90

Joshua

6	102
21.18	203n258

Judges

3-6	39
5	56, 101, 213 nn88,89
5.5	200n123
5.23	209n51
7.2ff.	102
8.22-23	132
9.8-15	132
9.27	38
18.7	69
18.25-27	207n34
18.27	69
18.31	40, 179n97
21.16ff.	38

1 Samuel

1-3	39

1.3	37
1.7	179n97
1.9	38, 39, 40, 179n97
1.11	37
1.21	38
1.24	179n97
2.1-10	85-86, 99, 204n22, 205 n27
2.7	86, 205n28
2.8	205n28
2.9	218n138
2.10	206n230
2.28	43
2.35	125
3.3	38, 39, 40, 43
3.15	179n97
4	37
4.4-7	36
4.4	37, 176n79
4.21-22	44, 182n135
7-12	228n240
8-12	131-36, 229 n245, 232 n281
8.1-22	228n240
8.1-7	131
8.7	135, 228 n242, 229 n245
10.17-18	131
10.18-19	229n246
10.24	183n144
11	213n90
12.12	131, 135, 228n242, 229n245
15.23	109
16	63
17.45-47	102
23.2	211n70
25.28	125

INDEX OF AUTHORS

JOURNAL FOR THE STUDY OF THE OLD TESTAMENT
Supplement Series

Titles in this series include: